The Road Gets Better From Here

A novice rides solo from the Ring of Fire to the Cradle of Civilisation

Adrian Scott

"The Road Gets Better From Here," by Adrian Scott. ISBN 9780980493405.

To my parents – for sparking the flame; to my wife and family for keeping it alive, and to everyone who I met on the road who sustained it

We travel not for trafficking alone;
By hotter winds our fiery hearts are fanned;
For lust of knowing what should not be known
We make the Golden Journey to Samarkand

Flecker

Table of Contents

Crash!

My head slammed into the hard gravel track with a sickening thud. Colourful particles whizzed about inside my head in a wonderful show, like fireworks exploding inside my skull. Then there was darkness and silence. For how long I cannot say. And then, suddenly, there was a blinding white light and pain, and then more pain, followed by fear and self-doubt. Why was I here? What was I doing? This was not the adventure I had planned.

***

One week earlier I had been sitting alone on an airplane heading for a remote corner of Asia to begin this *adventure of a lifetime*; I'd left my wife, my children, my comfortable home and my job all behind, to ride a motorbike 20,000 kms across ten countries and an entire continent. What was I thinking? Endless nights of pouring over maps, calculating and recalculating routes and itineraries, scouring obscure sources, dreaming of far off places had all ceased and I had now reached the point of my adventure that for so long had seemed so far away: the beginning.

I can't recall a distinct moment when the idea of the journey changed from just a notion into a distinct and concrete plan; it just evolved out of a life-long interest in these places and people and their history. Perhaps sailing around the South Pacific as an only child with my parents on Soviet cruise ships in the 1970's was to blame. Or perhaps it was growing up next door to a proud family of Ukrainian refugees in a working class suburb of Sydney that drove this obsession. More deeply, perhaps it was the universal empathy one must feel for a people who have suffered so much and for so long; losing 20 million stoically defending their country in a war they did not start – and that's before you count the millions of "non-persons" silently debited from the population in Stalin's paranoid purges of the 1930's and 1940's. Then there's the misery and hardships inflicted upon them by the great failed Communist experiment. And, beyond Russia, there were the incredible tales of monks, merchants and marauders that illuminates the history of the Silk Roads that piqued the interest of an impressionable and insatiably curious child – from Scheherazade's 1001 Nights to the adventures of Marco Polo and the conquests of Genghis Khan.

But the question of how to travel so far over such a variety of terrain in such remote areas always remained. The prospect of hitching didn't appeal – not for safety reasons – but more because I did not want to be always relying on the help of others for transport, and driving a car was far too complicated, especially across frontiers (and was probably impractical anyway in the bogs and swamps of northern Siberia and along the rutted mountain tracks of the Pamirs). So, logically, the motorbike selected itself as the only real option. But there was only one problem; I had never ridden a motorbike in my life nor taken any real interest in them, and my mechanical expertise did not extend beyond filling up my car with petrol each week. And then there was the paperwork required to cross an entire continent on motorcycle. But in the end, to an overly enthusiastic novice, these were just "details" that needed to be sorted. I took a crash course – literally – in motorcycle riding and worked the arcane back-channel bureaucracies of the more obscure countries on my itinerary, slowly but surely filling my passport with a colourful collection of visa stamps. And, along the way I took high tea with Honorary Consuls and was extended wonderful hospitality and generous diplomatic concessions by many Foreign Ministries.

It was only at about 3am on the morning of sailing, as I sat in my garage aggressively disassembling the critical parts of my motorcycle so they could fit into the small packing crate I had built, that I began to have second thoughts. Wheels, petrol tank, handle bars, brakes, clutch and more pieces – whose purpose was still a mystery to me – all lay strewn about the floor as I tried desperately to keep a mental tally of them all and the sequence in which they had been removed so that I might have some faint hope of successful re-assembly once I arrived in Russia.

Six weeks later I was standing in the office of the Master of the Port of Vladivostok, like an errant schoolboy reporting to the principal, explaining why he should even contemplate releasing *my* bike from bond storage so that I might ride it across *his* country. He was a big bear of a man, fifty-plus with a round fleshy careworn face and warm brown eyes. He wore a smart crisp military uniform and carried enough metal on his shoulders and shirt front to smelt into a nuclear submarine. He read my letter of introduction slowly, scrutinising each word and sentence as if there were some hidden meaning contained within them. He looked me up and down, barked questions at me, before making some hand-written corrections then stamping and signing my release, saying "Welcome to Russia. Have a great journey – but be careful, the roads are dangerous and the bears are hungry this time of year."

The next day, after some final bureaucratic hurdles, I retrieved my bike from its container, re-assembled it (slowly) and rode back to Vladivostok Airport whereupon I promptly disassembled it again for the promised flight to Magadan. But this time I had to reduce its footprint even further so that it might fit inside the hold of the small Soviet-era hulk that would carry us to Magadan. The Chief of Cargo was called, and armed with his official tape measure and plane specifications he gave my bike a thorough once over before shaking his head solemnly and saying laconically "Is too big for plane. Is not possible. Goodbye." Undeterred, I continued late into the night, reducing my motorcycle into so many small pieces that I could have posted it to myself. But I did eventually get the required approvals and three days later found myself on the tarmac at Magadan Airport, alongside the cargo crew desperately trying to retrieve all of the pieces of my motorcycle which had been packed in randomly with all of the mail and other parcels and supplies on this weekly lifeline delivery from the outside world.

I worked under a low-slung but bright midnight sun, slowly reassembling my bike and, once they had finished their work, Sasha and Kostya – two workers who had been intensely curious at this outsider and his strange cargo – drove me into the nearby town of Sokol to find petrol and oil. Petrol, or "benzin" as they called it, was easily found, but there was no oil – one of them joking to me that there was plenty of it here – trapped under the ground! Sokol was a bleak spread of anonymous apartment blocks and wooden huts all sinking slowly into the permafrost. We eventually found a half-used canister of engine oil in the garage of one of Sasha's friends who looked as if he had just awoken from winter hibernation. No one, including me, knew whether it was actually suitable for motorcycles, but they all re-assured me saying proudly that it was "Russian oil, good for anything!"

I finished loading my bike – which unfortunately had now become very top heavy and unstable – and finally got onto the road to Magadan just after 2:00am. The weather, however, quickly turned foul; it got very cold, dark and a thick fog set in, striking at me like ghouls in the night as I travelled across the low marshlands toward the sea. And then the rain came, freezing driving rain, and I was reduced to a crawl, shivering uncontrollably from the cold and concentrating hard on the road ahead as it emerged from the gloomy shadows just in front of me; it wasn't meant to be like this – was it?

Magadan appeared like a city under winter siege; its dim gas lights gave it a sickly yellow glow, everything was battened down and the rain had now turned to sleet. With only a very basic map, I quickly got hopelessly lost and ended up taking one of the many drunks, whom I had passed loitering on the streets, as pillion to direct me. We eventually landed at a hotel where the young lady on the night desk gave me some tea and bread and what remained of her dinner (which she politely claimed said no longer wanted). There was even a garage where I was able to lock up my bike.

I spent the next day and half catching up on sleep, laundry, checking out the sights of Magadan (very few), communicating with home and making final preparations to the bike for my journey. Magadan was grim, but at least there were some signs of development, the shops were full, the streets busy and the people, on the whole, seemed relatively happy. The city straddles a small hill; on one side the ramshackle wooden cottages of the old town roll down to the sea port, and on the other, facing inland, lays the modern city centre where the apartment blocks are scattered over the terrain like a sequence of giant cement dominoes. Many of the streets were lined with small fir trees, giving the place a surreal Christmas feel. I found a small produce market and stocked up for my journey. Sturdy looking Babushkas operated many of the stalls, supplementing their woefully inadequate state pensions by selling the fruit and vegetables they had somehow managed to grow in the short summer months.

On the Road

It didn't get beyond ten degrees during my stay and the sun never broke through the seemingly permanently leaden skies, and I wondered whether they actually had a summer here at all; no one swam in the bay and the locals *skied* nearby through May and June each year. Upon checkout I asked whether I could borrow some tools to complete one final – but critical – maintenance job on my bike. By the time I had got to the garage there were two men (one a young mechanic) ready to assist – or rather, actually do the job while I watched. They worked hard and quickly had the job done. The young mechanic was clearly a motorcycle enthusiast so I offered him a ride which thrilled both us for different reasons as he roared away, out of sight and then came skidding back into the garage, stopping just a few inches in front of us, transferring much of the rubber from my tyres onto the concrete floor.

I departed Magadan early in the afternoon, stopping briefly at the Mask of Sorrows, the local memorial for all the victims of political persecution who had died in the Kolyma goldfields or in the making of the infamous *Road of Bones* – the horrible, potted, graveyard track that connected this network of prison camps and mines to Magadan. Indeed, the only reason Magadan came into being was as the administrative centre for this evil operation. The monument was a modern concrete sculpture of a sombre face (think Picasso style) with smaller sadder faces attached, forming a large teardrop that rolled down the entire height of the statue. At the rear, inside the face, was a simple statue of girl kneeling and holding a flower under a man chained to a crucifix. It was very moving and I was disappointed I hadn't been able to learn more about this aspect of their history (the museum was closed on the previous day when I had attempted to visit).

I drove on and past the airport through sparse alpine forests and rolling hills with mountains on either side. It was getting warmer the farther inland I drove. There were a few small towns but soon I was in the middle of the taiga and rolling plains. The paved road ran out after about one hundred kilometres and my speed dropped immediately. The road became compacted gravel and loose stones. There was very little other traffic but when it did come you knew it - mostly large transport trucks with large clouds of dust billowing behind them. The road was wide and

5

I slowed to a crawl on the far side while they passed. I was enjoying the riding but it required intense concentration due to the inconsistent and quickly changing road surface. I was, however, feeling confident. The sun was shining, the bike was running smoothly and the scenery was pleasant. Then it happened.

Suddenly my front wheel sunk into a deep patch of soft dirt – more like sand – and I immediately lost control of the bike. My handlebars swung back and forth and buzzed in a wide arc before my eyes, triggering that sickening sensation, almost in slow motion; the voice inside my head saying "Now, there is nothing you can do, you are going to crash and this is really going to hurt". Oh bugger! But there was more to it as I felt a sharp tug at my left ankle. Jammed under my pannier, it had become the pivot; I was a human catapult and my head the payload. Oh dear. And before I knew anything else, the ground rushed up to meet me in a bone crunching collision. My head slammed into the hard gravel of the road like the atoms in a particle accelerator colliding with six feet of cement. Colourful sub-atomic particles whizzed about inside my head in a wonderful show, like sherbet fireworks exploding against the blackness of my skull. Then there was darkness. For how long I cannot say. Then, suddenly, there was a blinding white light and then pain, much pain, followed by fear and self-doubt. Slowly, fuzzy white clouds on a baby blue sky came into focus, followed by a shower of champagne-coloured shooting stars. OK, close your eyes, count to ten and start again. And slowly my senses started coming back online. I was lying flat on my back looking up at the sky – that much was clear. Gingerly, I turned my head to one side to discover that I now lay in the middle of the road! But it didn't matter – for there was no traffic (no one travelled here in summer); in fact there was no one and nothing for at least a hundred kilometres in either direction; I was completely alone with just some scrawny undernourished taiga and potentially some hungry bears for company. But I was in growing discomfort as the angry throbbing from my wrenched ankle raced up my body slammed into the pain nerve centre of my brain like a runaway express train. Oh bugger. That really hurt. Really, really, really hurt. Owwwhhhhhh! Whoa boy, steady... deep breath. And while it wasn't the white hot pain of a broken bone, it wasn't too far away from it either... and as I lay there I realised that my trip had probably just ended. Ended before it really began – the trip of a lifetime crushed on day one! This was tragic. More than tragic, but a tragedy of my own making, for how could I have been so stupid and careless?

My family and friends had been right – I had no experience, would certainly crash, probably hurt myself badly and it was foolhardy (some said insane) to go alone. What was I thinking? I thought about the evacuation insurance I had researched but decided against, thinking that surely it was against the odds that I would ever need it.

But then my super-ego kicked in, and slowly, with much effort and more flashes of intense pain triggered by my movements, I managed to roll over and sit up. And it was during this process that I discovered that as well as spearing my head into the gravel and wrenching my ankle nearly off, I had taken much of the impact on my left hip which now also decided to join in the chorus of screaming pain inside my head. It was already red raw and badly grazed with tiny pieces of gravel embedded in my side as neat souvenirs. Ouch!

As I sat and slowly composed myself I searched for any further injuries. Thankfully there were no other immediately obvious problems but already my ankle had ballooned inside my boot so that it had now become impossible to remove – probably better like that anyway I thought as it could act as a makeshift cast! And eventually, after about thirty minutes of heavy coaxing and intense pep talks to myself I was able to get to my feet and hobble slowly over to my bike (which had ended up some twenty yards further down the road). I looked down at it in much the same way as a jockey might his lame mount in the Grand National as it lay on its side with panniers (and frame) spread eagle, handle bars warped, mirrors ripped off, front faring bent and deeply scarred. Nice. We're not going anywhere today are we? But it wasn't time to put it down just yet...so with clenched teeth and pure adrenaline I got down, leaned hard into the bike and levered it up and onto its stand... before collapsing back onto the road, exhausted.

I looked around; it was eerily silent and still and suddenly I noticed that the river I had been tracking along was covered in thick crusty sheets of dirty ice. Beautiful Siberia, bleak and barren; why had I been so desperate to come here? It was god-awful.

With some trepidation I turned the ignition and tried the engine and incredibly it whirred into life! Surprised but pleased, I turned it off quickly to survey the damaged pannier frame – bent at angles which prevented riding – and set about re-working them with sheer brute force back into something close to their original shape. And the panniers themselves, while not actually punctured, had taken quite a beating and now had curious wave forms from the impact in their long sides. I stood on them (with my good foot) and jumped up and down to straighten them out. All back together, tied up with rope, they wobbled like jello but the configuration was rideable – barely. The only issue now was actually riding the bike with an immovable ankle (the one that changes gears too). But by now my ankle was numb from the pain so I mounted the bike carefully, turned it on, held the clutch tightly with my right (wrong) hand while bending over from the waist to move the clutch lever up into 2nd gear with my left hand before lurching off along the road. I could brake and use the throttle, but, apart from steering (with warped handlebars), that was the extent of my control. I would just keep riding until I found someone or ran out of petrol, whichever came first. And I didn't even think about in which direction to head, for turning back was never an option. So, injured, deeply depressed but faintly optimistic, I headed off deeper into the wilderness, another victim of the Road of Bones.

Then I began to think how lucky I had been – my helmet and safety gear had saved my life and my heavy motorcycle boots had probably prevented my leg from being completely snapped off. Slowly, and with a wry smile on my face, I began to whistle and sing... *Always Look on the Bright Side of Life...*

The next village was indeed more than one hundred kilometres away and it took another four hours of improbable (and painful) riding before I pulled in at a rather desperate looking gas depot on the edge of what looked at first glance like a derelict village. My left pannier had fallen even further from the rough riding and was now sitting so low as to make the bike virtually impossible to balance; I could have ridden no further anyway.

The young girl who sat behind the heavily barred windows of the fuel bunker looked at me like I was an alien as I dismounted from my broken bike and hobbled over towards her with my broken body. And when I opened my mouth and spoke in Russian, she nearly fell off her chair. I did the maths and ordered the amount of fuel I thought I needed (you pay before you get petrol here). I started filling but soon realised that I'd ordered about twice as much petrol as I needed. I did my best to explain this to the petrol girl and she kindly refunded the difference. I don't think this was a common practice, but assumed she had taken pity on me (or thought I was a complete moron). Slowly, I pushed my bike over to the side of the station, deciding that this was as good a place as any to eat a late lunch. I opened my back pack to discover that crashing had crushed most of the food packages I carried, including my container of sour cream which had literally exploded inside my bag. The stuff was everywhere; in my runners, on the inside of my pack, on the plastic bags inside my backpack, in my chocolate and on my sachets of peach flavoured oats and so on. But rather than waste good food I decided to lick/scratch/wipe and try and eat as much of the stuff as I could. I even scooped dollops of it out of my runners with a hunk of bread and ate it. I was hungry and got stuck into the block of cheese and meat that I had bought the previous day at the markets in Magadan. I ate so quickly that at one point I dropped my meat on the gravel and had to retrieve and clean it by picking little pebbles off. It was a sad sight and my ankle was really throbbing angrily now. It was early days – day one in fact – but I think I had reached a low point already.

I went to secure everything on my bike and discovered that with a gentle tug my left side pannier simply fell off. The frame had broken and was now in two pieces rather than one continuous piece of metal. Bugger. I did my best to explain my situation to the petrol girl who took one look at me and said to wait while she called someone to help. She directed me to a large long building about 100 metres directly behind the petrol station. I had to ride back and around and was met about half way by my escort in a sky blue Russian Ural with sidecar. He indicated I should follow him and he took me directly to the large entrance doors of what appeared to be a workshop. His name was Mischa and he had a friendly and curious disposition, tanned skin, dark brown eyes and hair and white teeth (unusual in Russia). Some of his colleagues arrived and they opened the doors to reveal two very large fire trucks – this was the fire fighting department. There are many bushfires in summer here and these men were all fire fighters (amongst other things). I met Vityim, Vassily and many others whom I cannot recall the names of. Luckily, there were no fires so I was the focus of their attention.

Vassily was the man in charge and coincidentally, just like me, he was also 37 with two children (boy and girl). He was a blonde haired blue- eyed Russian, powerfully built and, unlike me, extremely competent in many practical things. He quickly sized up the job and went to work, gathering scrap metal from the yard, cutting it with an arc welder, working it with his hands and tools, quickly fashioning a U-shaped piece of steel to brace and re-connect my pannier frame. But rather than welding it, he bolted all the pieces together, requiring the drilling of a number of holes in each of the component pieces – a task requiring great precision and much time, commodities he had in large measure. He worked deftly and alone while I spoke with the others, drank the many cups of coffee and vodka offered and ate something called "salla" - which I think is the white fat (cured) from the back of a pig. The traditional method shown to me was to take a piece of salla, a mouthful of raw onion and some cucumber and chew it all up together. I think the onion and cucumber are to compensate for either the lack of taste, or bad taste of salla – I wasn't going to try and establish which was true. It was now about 9:30pm and Vassily had been working for over 3 hours. He was almost finished and came to assemble the pieces – which all fitted perfectly together of course. I re-assembled my luggage and everything was back in order, apart from my ankle, which Vassily bandaged (over my boot) for extra support.

I asked whether I could put up my tent nearby to sleep for the night but he insisted I come with him to his home and that I join him in his banya (steam house) to clean-up and refresh after the long day we had both had. Vassily lived with his wife and children in a three room apartment and they also had a small wooden cottage cum-farmhouse where he kept chickens, grew vegetables and maintained his homemade banya. His wife and children were away in Magadan for a few days so we had the apartment to ourselves. The banya was incredibly hot and had three connected rooms, *hot*, *hotter* and *hottest*. It was made of scented pine wood and it was very invigorating. We only sat in the hottest room for a few minutes each time as the waves of heat pulsing from the hot rocks was ferocious. It was when Vassily indicated I should shield my eyes from the heat to stop the lenses from melting that I realised how dangerous this was.

We washed in the hotter room, and finished off with a few glasses of beer in the hot room. Vassily cooked a large dinner of eggs and cucumber with a side dish of caviar he had obtained on a recent fishing trip – it was excellent. We washed down three courses with glasses of vodka, the alcohol numbing the pain in my throbbing ankle. Vassily was a keen amateur film maker and he played me a number of his home movies (nature and family) and took me through *all* of his photo albums. He was a proud father and good husband, this was obvious, and I felt lucky to have met him and his friends and couldn't really express my thanks adequately for what he had done. I went to sleep as soon as I hit the divan.

Slow but Friendly Progress

I woke up with a dry mouth and dull throbbing behind my eyes and so did Vassily. He made tea and we sat and drank many cups, laden with sugar, to recharge. Vassily fried more eggs (straight from his chickens) and as we sat and ate he explained that although he had trained as a "forest scientist" at a technical institute, there was either no work, or work that was so low paid that it was not feasible to undertake, hence his job as chief fire ranger, doctor, town mechanic and general jack of all trades here. Atka, he explained, had been a much larger and prosperous town, but many of its inhabitants had since left, unable to make a living. The factories and workshops had stopped working abruptly and had been left derelict – as evidenced by the abandoned buildings and machinery I had seen the previous day. And many apartment blocks had been similarly deserted. But it wasn't an orderly shut down; there had been no demolition, or civic clean-up – the people had simply disappeared, leaving everything standing as they scurried off to find better lives in the cities. But nature was finishing the job that the people could not, as the sickly weeds and plants took over, wherever they could get a foot hold, slowly breaking down and reclaiming these structures back into the earth.

There were now only 80 people here and Vassily explained that most were involved in some way with either road maintenance (I wanted a word with them!) and emergency services. There was, however, a core community including a school and kindergarten and basic medical services. Before leaving I looked around the apartment and counted three rooms only – bedroom, kitchen and lounge – it was a small apartment for a family of four. I had in fact slept in the main bed and Vassily had slept on a makeshift bed of lounge cushions on the floor – I felt bad. His wife and children were in Magadan with his wife's mother and would return in a few days. Like most men in this situation he was keenly aware of the cleaning up and preparations required before their return and in this we shared a universal truth here about the differences between men and women.

We returned to the fire station and I said farewell to the entire crew and thanked them warmly for their generosity and help. Each shook my hand firmly and wished me safe travels, and I sincerely hoped for this too. It had not been a good first day; I had seriously injured myself, broken a critical part of my bike and come only a relatively short distance – on the flip side, I had taken a banya,

11

enjoyed first class Russian hospitality, eating caviar and drinking vodka with sincere and good men.

The road continued north from Atka across rugged plains of scratchy tundra between sparsely tree-covered mountains. We were snaking our way north, gradually climbing as we left the sea far behind. There was virtually no traffic which was a great relief as I battled with the road and my own confidence. Yesterday's fall had left me very tentative on the bike and I gripped the handle bars with all my strength – it would have taken a jackhammer and/or surgery to loosen my grip. I scanned every inch of the upcoming road looking for the safest, firmest, straightest path – there was a lot of information to process continuously and my brain was really working hard. At times I would spy little jagged rocks on the road pointing straight up and feel that the road was conspiring against me, trying to stab my tyres with these little daggers. Mind games. Periodically I'd look up to take in the ruggedly handsome scenery only to find that an immediate course correction was required to avoid a) a big hole, b) soft, loose surface, c) the edge of the road, etc. This was far more difficult than I had imagined or wanted and at the moment was no fun. What was I thinking sitting in my comfortable leather chair at my desk in my beautiful home with my wonderful family when I planned this part of the journey? That this would just be a string of Sunday rides through the Dandenongs? Ha! As Dirty Harry once said: "A man's gotta know his limitations" – perhaps I'd reached mine? The reality of my situation hit me like an overdue and unexpected tax bill; you might have had some fun before, but now this was big and serious and you'd better knuckle down, focus and get through it. My progress was slow and steady, and most importantly safe. I stopped every fifty kilometres or so to rest, but this was no real relief either because as soon as I stopped I was immediately attacked by fierce squadrons of giant mosquitoes. Within a few seconds of stopping they covered me in an insect blanket; those unable to get at the small patches of exposed flesh (hands and head) were trying (in vain I hoped) to pierce my Kevlar riding pants and riding jacket. There were even some trying to pierce my petrol tank and I suspected they might have succeeded had I given them enough time – they were voracious. I quickly adjusted my technique by leaving my riding gloves and helmet on while stopped, feeding small pieces of food through the opening in my helmet into my mouth – like a performing seal jumping to catch its dinner. Despite this, some still managed to stowaway in my helmet, revealing themselves only after I had started the bike and reached cruising speed by either biting me on the face at the perimeter of the visor, or by buzzing around in front of my eyes and nose in the small space between my face and visor. This, while trying to steer a safe course across a rough and uncertain surface, I did not need.

At about 3pm, I pulled into the gas station at Orutukan – another small village in the throes of dying, along the Road of Bones. I filled up and asked the kind-looking lady behind the grill whether there was a cafe or shop in the town, to which she smiled and pointed in the general direction of the decaying buildings of the village. I crossed a one lane wooden bridge across a small but fast flowing river and passed two men fishing (or two men who had drunk too much and were trying to get themselves organised for fishing). They both gave me an odd look as I passed. Despite the ubiquitous town blueprint (enforced by Moscow in Soviet times as the Far East was rapidly developed) and the rows of ugly crumbling apartment blocks, there was some relief here with a few pretty tree lined avenues stretching back from the centre of town to the foothills at the edge of the village. There was a modern style war memorial, metal and angular rising up twenty metres from the ground with a semi-circular wall of names and photos of those who had died in their Great Patriotic War far from here, separating the shops, militsia and repair workshops from the rows of apartment blocks. It was hot and sunny as I drove up and down the main street, greeting people as they approached me and looking for the promised shop. I don't think the concept of a cafe had ever come here with shops identified only by single dark open doorways in blank concrete walls covered with white fly mesh curtains and a small sign marked either "magazin" or "produkti".

After picking up some basic supplies I decided to sit outside the shop and take what I thought would be a quick lunch at which point an older man, whom I had met in the shop, introduced himself as Anatoly (or Anton) and insisted I come with him to have my lunch in more pleasant surroundings. I followed him to the town's repair workshops – a jumble of ramshackle wooden buildings surrounded by scrap metal and wood lying in pieces all over the yard. A mangy dog roamed and a small group of strange looking idle people milled around. This place seemed to be the focal point of the town's activities. Anton gestured for me to follow him inside, so nervously I locked and secured my bike and entered behind him. Inside was cool and dimly lit and a maze of hallways and rooms, some with old machinery lying dusty and disused in corners, off-cuts of metal and wood, unfinished (and never to be finished) jobs. It reminded me a

13

little of my grandfather's shed — it had a similar kind of smell too: tobacco, stale but slightly sweet BO, beer, oil and wood scent. Eventually we emerged into the nerve centre of this operation: the kitchen and smoko room. Four men sat at a long wooden table, two of them were deeply involved in a game of backgammon and there was a smaller side table for the kettle, tea, coffee and sugar.

They all acknowledged me and I was immediately offered a seat to finish my lunch along with a cup of hot sweet tea — perfect! The room had a slight yellow hue to it with fake wood panelling and a hard well- worn concrete floor. It was, however, surprisingly clean and tidy. There were the obligatory calendars of well endowed pin up girls, all tastefully clad (unlike some I have seen in other workplaces) in decent amounts of lingerie — nothing exposed thank you. I sat opposite Anton and demolished my lunch — it was a long time since I had eaten. Men came and went, and Anton was clearly in charge. An older lady with grey pallid heavily creased skin and small eyes who carried an expression that showed a lifetime of resignation to her lot approached Anton for some direction. She wore old faded patched clothes and a dirty floral scarf on her head. She waited with downcast eyes for instructions and I immediately felt for her — I couldn't begin to imagine a life like hers. Soon after, a young man, whom at first appeared to be drunk, came in. He had a fresh wound in his forehead that bled, dilated pupils and was unsteady on his feet, like a punch-drunk boxer. He was short and stocky, with a shaven head, little or no neck and dirty and dishevelled. The men angrily dismissed him — he was obviously mentally impaired and tolerated around the workshop — but was afforded nothing more than this. Some younger adolescent men, who had come in earlier and peppered me with questions, at least showed him some kindness.

At about 5pm Anton came back with a big shopping bag overflowing with food; in our basic conversation I had told him about some of my favourite foods in Russia and while I had eaten lunch and rested he had obviously gone and bought as many of these things as he could find — and many other things too! We walked slowly back to Anton's apartment — which he proudly pointed out had a balcony, and he insisted on carrying the heaviest of my luggage. His wife and youngest daughter were on holidays in Irkutsk until the end of July and his older daughter was away in Magadan studying so Anton was alone for the summer. His apartment was spacious but still according to the basic blueprint of kitchen, lounge and one bedroom.

I began to understand that the lounge almost always doubled as the master bedroom and there was of course the ubiquitous Persian rug hanging from the lounge room wall as a feature. I put my things down in the bedroom – normally occupied by his eight year old daughter and therefore full of dolls, stuffed animals, an aging computer game console, posters of pop stars (Russian of course). Before I could say "Perestroika", Anton had stripped down to his underwear and was encouraging me to do the same; it was hot and he was getting ready for his daily cold shower (which was a relief). I guess it was part of the Banya culture – an important social aspect of everyday life – as I had already discovered. Anton had explained to me that he was a "water engineer" – a critical job in a village where hot water fills the pipes in everyone's apartments to keep the minus fifty degrees outside temperature at bay in winter. In summer, however, having hot water was deemed less critical so it was only available between 5pm and midnight on Wednesdays. Today was Wednesday. It had just gone 5pm; Anton had taken his cold shower and had poured me a hot bath. He insisted I use his soap and shampoo and anything else that might take my fancy in the bathroom. Luxury! I soaked and almost fell asleep it was so good. At least when I emerged into the kitchen we were both fully dressed.

Anton had been busy in the kitchen. He had prepared all the ingredients fresh and started a huge pot of borscht, made tea, prepared a huge bowl of salad (tomatoes, cucumber, onions, mayonnaise, spiced with pepper), fried some freshly cut eggplant with garlic, mashed and fried potatoes. He sat me down at the small table and the plates started filling the table and it was all for me! It was only about 6pm and clearly I had a long night ahead of me so I buckled up and settled in for the ride. Being a big man, I am a decent eater, but this was beyond me – the salad alone could have serviced a large family dinner and then some. I diligently worked through each dish, but no sooner had I got to the bottom of a dish/bowl/plate/cup, etc than it was filled up again – leaving no evidence of my good work. I was breaking out in a sweat my metabolism was working so hard. I felt as if I would need a stomach enlargement to cope and all the time Anton was hovering, like a smiling assassin, encouraging me to pick up the pace. He was concerned about my lack of bulk(?) and wanted to make me "stronger" for the ride ahead.

He had even gone and found a litre of the creamiest milk he could find which I heartily devoured. And, despite my polite protestations the dishes just kept coming. Anton smoked heavily (packets a day) so ate very little. Luckily his good friend Nikolai, from the workshop, stopped by and helped me get through the feast. He also brought a big bottle of beer which helped wash things down. He had, however, also brought more food for me!

Anton was in his early fifties and Nikolai a little older, but both looked easily ten years older. Nikolai was a widower and worked as a carpenter in the workshop – he had the large, strong hands of someone who works with tools cutting and fashioning things from heavy blocks of raw material. They were both Ukrainian, but had lived here for over thirty years with their families. I couldn't quite figure out the reason for them coming here but I got the impression that it hadn't been by choice. I asked them about Putin, to whom they gave the big thumbs down in the universal sign of disapproval – wages were stagnant while the cost of living kept skyrocketing, putting everything bar the basics out of reach. Anton explained that in the past he and his family, along with most other Russians, had been able to travel extensively within Russia by air and rail and to take holidays in nice hotels in many locations. Not so now. They gave me the impression that for your average working class Russian, Putin was deeply unpopular. So I asked about Yeltsin, to which they put two fingers to the neck, under the jaw line - the Russian sign for alcohol. I asked about Gorbachev, to which they waved their index finger in a circular motion next to their heads; he was crazy. Finally I asked who was a good leader and when were times better, to which they both immediately said Brezhnev. I could not manage a deeper conversation on the topic, but there was so much more I wanted to understand – what did they think of the great abuse of power and shameless inequities rife under communism?

I finished as much as I could manage, Anton was a gracious host and put much of the food away for tomorrow and I rolled onto the divan bloated. Anton got out his collection of home videos and lifetime collection of photographs and we spent many hours watching baby films, camping trips, birthdays and other celebrations and methodically working through each picture in his entire collection. He, again, was a proud father and husband and had served time with the Soviet Army in Czechoslovakia in the early 1970's – the subject of many of his photos. It was well past midnight when we finished and I rolled into bed, drifting off to sleep quickly. Earlier in the day Anton had insisted that I stay another day to, a) give my ankle time to heal, and b) to each as much food as humanly possible to get stronger for the trip ahead.

In the morning, by the time I had fully woken up, Anton had already gone to work. I didn't need breakfast so just pottered about, writing and resting. Anton came home early for lunch at 11 o'clock and was extremely disappointed that I hadn't made a start at breakfast with so much food available – he just couldn't understand it. He quickly fried me four eggs with big slices of kolbasa sausage which was delicious. There was more salad, potato and fried eggplant to get through too. Anton returned to work and I rested for most of the day. It rained continuously and I was worried about how this might affect the road ahead – I was keen to get going again. Dinner was another big affair (for me at least) with meat in the form of big hunks of fried kolbasa sausage (eight inches in diameter by my reckoning) and we still had plenty of the side dishes – but this time they had to be finished!

After dinner Anton took me to his greenhouse which was nearby. He had built it himself and explained that due to the harsh climate here it was only operational for three months of the year, during which time it was extremely productive with almost all of the output being bottled/pickled for the "cold" months from September through May where the temperature and lack of light made growing anything next to impossible. He had cucumbers, tomatoes, radishes and herbs all growing well. We returned home through the laneways and paths behind the apartments and across the hospital courtyard. Everything was in a natural state of disorder but functional. We climbed the stairs and retired to the lounge, watched TV together (a good Russian flick) and the last time I checked on him, Anton was sitting up in his armchair, head back, mouth wide open snoring softly. I let him sleep, rolled over on the divan and did the same.

In the morning Nikolai came over to say farewell. He had brought with him a large pot of a honey-like substance. He explained that it was a plant extract for drinking to improve one's health. It was sweet and thick with a malt flavour and I drank plenty to help prepare for the day of riding ahead. It was still raining lightly and I knew it was going to be a hard day. I gave Anton a small souvenir and some things for his daughter which he appreciated. Nikolai and Anton came with me to the workshop to unlock my bike and to help pack my gear. They kindly provided a large plastic sheet to cover my bags and helped secure it. By the time we had finished most of the workshop crew plus a few more had assembled to wish me farewell. I took some photos, shook hands warmly with each of them and was off.

It turned out to be the worst day of riding so far. Although it had stopped raining briefly for my departure, it was now raining hard, it was cold and the road (dirt and gravel) was slippery. I cursed. I cursed again. This was hard work and slow going. I thought Siberia (away from the coast) was dry and hot in summer – this was more like a cold, wet winter's day. My gloves were soaked and my jacket was damp, but I was still reasonably dry. I battled with the road, the water turning the dry grey powder to soft and slippery mud. Argh. Each corner was a new adventure in bike control and personal stress management. I stopped regularly to keep warm and found placing my gloved hands on the engine block for a few seconds at a time effective. There wasn't much to see either due to the very low thick clouds and rain mist, although I did pass through the village of Debin – the major administrative centre of gold mining in the days of prisoner mining – which looked even more depressing in this weather. Progress was painfully slow – I was averaging no more than 20kph and worse still, I was passing some very large and fast flowing rivers, swollen with the recent and continuing rain. At some places these rivers were more than 50 metres across – I knew some time soon our paths would have to cross and this thought filled me with much trepidation as I hadn't actually ever attempted a river crossing since learning to ride a motorcycle.

After about three hours of riding I rounded a corner and came upon a long line trucks stopped dead in their tracks. There were men milling around so I asked what the problem was and they told me the river had washed away the road up ahead – their truck was 25th in line! The road was being fixed, however it would take some time, and maybe would not be passable until tomorrow. The thought of camping out here filled me with dread – many people had already warned me about bears and asked whether I was carrying a pistol.

The drivers were friendly and very interested in my bike. They shared their tea and food with me and I offered them what little I had but they refused. My Russian-English dictionary was invaluable as we worked through many topics. The older men in particular were very interested in Australia and what is was like to live there. When I explained the concept of long service leave they all fell about laughing – these men all worked every day of the year hauling diesel and other critical supplies up and down the Kolyma Highway (or at least the sections where it was possible to drive). They were away from home for long periods and often slept in their truck cabins. There was certainly no regulation of driving hours, although each truck usually had two or more drivers (the machines ran continuously) and speed was not an issue as it was impossible to drive more than 40kph in even the best weather on these roads.

I went up to inspect the scene and found that indeed a large piece of road and a fair amount of the supporting earth underneath had been washed away, replaced by a roaring torrent of wild white water. About five metres of road was missing and the hole was almost as deep! This was going to take some fixing. Already there was a bulldozer on the other side, a line of dump trucks with their trays full of road fill and a foreman coordinating everything. Where had they come from? This was an isolated spot and I was amazed that such a response could be organised this quickly. Slowly they began filling and bulldozing the hole, being careful not to cover the one remaining drain pipe that lay exposed at the bottom of the pit - the water still needed to get across the road, although I doubted its capacity to deal with such a volume of water flowing at the rate it was. There was a small crowd on both sides watching with interest. They explained this was common, smiled and said not to worry, this is Russia after all. Some very large and powerful Russian Kamaz trucks came and simply bypassed the problem with a small detour into the bush – very impressive, as they earned their reputation today. As the hole was filled, one inexorable law of physics came into play – the smaller the space for the flow, the faster it goes; the water was now moving at a colossal speed, making a huge din. The energy of the water soon caused another metre or so of road to wash away. It was now a game of cat and mouse: could the hole be filled quickly enough before more road washed away? We all shook our heads and returned to our respective vehicles with the first few drivers backing away from road-eating river.

After another hour or so, however, they had somehow managed to bridge the gap, including a ceremonial walk through and handshake between the previously separated parties on either side. A young boy even asked me to sign the book he was reading. The road fill was bulldozed and graded, but no sooner had this begun than another problem began, the water, its previous path now effectively blocked looked for alternate routes across the road - the water was now backing up along one side of the road and slowly starting to flow in thin sheets across the road. I was already on my bike and watched as the water, to a depth of a few centimetres enveloped first the vehicles in front, then me. My boots were keeping my feet dry but I wanted to move and get out of here very quickly before it got any deeper. They gave the all clear and I was given the honour of being the first to drive across – perhaps as a guinea pig? With much relief I made it across safely and was again on my way.

It was only twenty kilometres to the next small village, but I was riding slowly and all of the banked up traffic passed me before I had travelled very far. I always pulled off to the side of the road to make it easier and noticed that each of the drivers looked for a sign that everything was OK with me – that was nice. I crawled into the village, found the only hotel/dormitory available and collapsed into bed. I had been travelling for 10 hours and had covered little more than eighty kilometres. I hoped that it was going to get easier from here

The End of the Road?

I slept remarkably well in a short banana-shaped bed and woke early for breakfast of half-eaten kolbasa with a side order of dry bread, cheese, tomato, cucumber, nuts and chocolate. I was keen to get going and make some decent progress – I still had a long way to go and hadn't even reached the more "difficult" stretches of the road. The previous evening, a kind man called Zimma (the first whom I had stopped and asked about the location of the hotel) offered to garage my bike for the night. It was difficult to determine his age, he was like so many of the men in these towns, impregnated with the grit and grime of years of years of working in difficult and dirty conditions. His hair was greasy and his skin thick and creased, leaving just slits for eyes. His garage was opposite the hotel and guarded by a ferocious dog, whose killing range was limited only by the heavy metal chain that he was tethered to. The chain, in turn, was attached securely to a large metal stake driven into the ground. My bike was definitely safe with this creature on guard. Zimma shortened the dog's chain so I could pass (quickly) and enter the garage. It was musty and dark in the rooms little antechamber of rooms attached to the garage itself and it looked as if Zimma actually lived in these small rooms or had at least spent the night there. He was very excited to see me again and very interested in me, the bike and my journey. I felt I should have spent more time with him to at least repay him in kind – this was a tiny village where I guessed nothing much happened, but I packed the bike, talking with him as I did and was off.

The day was marginally better that the previous in that it wasn't raining, but it was overcast and the clouds were dark and heavy with rain that would certainly fall. I cursed. Leaving the village behind, I slowly climbed and crested a steep mountain pass. Along the way I rode past many mines – some derelict and some still operational – all ugly and open cut. The soil here, and all through the Kolyma region, is laced with gold; you just needed to dig and sift through enough of it to get your return. Previously undertaken by starving prisoners who worked the iron-hard frozen earth with hand tools, the work was now done using big machines and automated processing plants.

The terrain was still sparse tree covered hills, but now rising more sharply and steeply from the valleys. Bright yellow lichen covered the hills in the distance giving a false impression of brilliant sunshine. It was cruel. The road surface was better, although in places still very much loose gravel and plenty of mud. I passed only half a dozen trucks – all going the other way – in three hours of riding before reaching the next town of Susuman. I went through the petrol ritual, figuring out how much I needed, paying for it (always through a tiny grill and always to a lonely woman), figuring out how to enable the pump, then hoping like crazy I'd got my calculations right. Next, I needed to fill my own fuel tank so went looking for a shop or if I was lucky a cafe. Although Susuman was a reasonably sized town (about 15,000 people), it still had a deserted feel to it; for it was midday and there was barely a soul about, and many of the streets and buildings were in poor condition. I found the main street (always ul. Lenina) and hitched my bike to the iron work of a building so it couldn't be stolen. An old man asked where I was from and what I was doing and said I didn't need to worry about stealing here – the people here were good! I felt embarrassed, but left my bike secured all the same. I asked about a cafe and he pointed at what looked like a half collapsed shed about thirty metres away. I kept asking to make sure we were both fixed on the same building. I followed his instructions up a dirty broken ramp, through a fly screen curtain and it was as if I'd entered another world – the room was lovely and warm, solid wood panelling in honey colour, modern blue stained glass windows up high, comfortable modern solid tables, chairs and booths, a bar and even a pretty waitress. It was also deserted. When the through traffic runs in winter this place must be hive of activity I thought. I was overjoyed to have some relief from corner shop food eaten on the run, or, as good as it was, the obligation to eat whatever and everything that was put in front of me by endlessly hospitable hosts. There was even a menu! The first page was for food and the remaining pages devoted to the vast selection of alcohol available. I looked around a little harder and realised that this was the local nightclub, complete with a ceiling-mounted mirror ball and big speakers in each corner. I guess disco even made it here. After studying the long list of item on the menu an older women, obviously the waitress' mother, came over and asked whether I would like soup, meat or fish, to which I replied I'd have soup AND meat, which I think confused her. I was hungry. The soup was delicious and the meat was in the form of shashlik (although from which type of animal I could not say and did not want to think too hard about). And that was the other thing I noticed as I had been riding; there was no livestock at all, of any kind, along the route. There were no farms, only villages with hopeful vegetable patches and greenhouses. In fact, the only animals I saw along the entire route were the odd rabbit or two, some lovely wild horses (with thick coats and manes) and a few birds — it was quite desolate in terms of living beings. I did, however, notice and drive past many piles of animal droppings. Like horse manure in appearance, these were the calling cards of bears. The fresh ones (still steaming in the cold air) frightened me the most, and after passing one of these, my eyes would immediately scan the road ahead and the surrounding countryside looking for culprits. In this haze of terror, large boulders and burnt-out trees suddenly became alive in the distance and my pulse raced as I squeezed the throttle hard in escape. And what do you do when you meet a bear? Vassily (the Ranger from Atka) had told me: leave no food out or uncovered, never make eye contact, move slowly away and then get the hell outta there.

Anyway, it didn't matter what kind of meat it was, it was delicious and I devoured it. This reminded me that of all the meals I had shared with people so far where not a single scrap of food was ever left uneaten. Sure, there were times when I thought I'd reached my own personal threshold on what I could put in my mouth, but I always pressed on, gnawing through some unidentifiable piece of gristle or cartilage, just like my hosts! I guess when food is scarce you treasure each last morsel.

Lunch had re-charged me and I felt ready to tackle the harder road ahead. According to my maps, guides and research there were two possible routes to Yakutsk — my next major destination. My Russian Road Atlas showed one as a complete secondary road and the other (the continuation of the road I had been travelling on) as a "highway" (ha) — although, disturbingly, parts of the road ahead were marked as a dashed line rather than the solid red line I had been riding so far. Also, if I had been on the "highway", I didn't want to think about what a poorer quality secondary road might be like, let alone try and ride my bike alone across four hundred kilometres of it. Throughout my ride I had been asking anyone I could about the roads ahead and which to take. I should have started a tote book, there were that many competing theories and speculation on what existed and what might be possible: "the highway is only possible in winter, there are big rivers with no bridges — you'll never make it", "yes, the highway is good, and all the bridges are working". There did seem to be more consistent views on the back road though: "no one ever goes that way, it's too hard, the road is terrible, there are many rivers with no bridges and much water and mud — you'll never make". All very encouraging! I decided to work from the confirmed facts I had which were: I knew of no one who had used the highway but I did know about a handful a people (either on motorbikes or in trucks) who had indeed made the journey on the back road. I wasn't going to die wondering so I decided to have a crack.

I rode the next eighty kilometres to the turn off easily and then with some nervousness turned off the highway and onto the track. It was in reasonable condition although it had many more water-filled potholes slowing my speed dramatically as I zigzagged between them. The road and surrounding land was flat and covered in scrub and seemed to head for the gap in the mountains ahead. Some large wooden stakes in the ground – left by more considerate drivers – helpfully marked places where the road had collapsed completely, leaving large deep vehicle- sized holes. Then it all started to unravel. I quickly came to the first enormous pool of muddy water completely covering the entire road. Easily twenty feet in length, there was no way of seeing how deep or what was below its surface. And, as I looked up and along the road I could see that these went on and on for as far as I could see – although it was difficult with the late afternoon sun in my eyes to judge just how big and how far apart they were. My heart sank – this was going to be very slow and difficult. I walked the perimeter of the first pool. It was about half a metre deep and felt flat and solid underfoot. I decided to give it a go on the bike with the engine running. I took it slow but kept the revs high. I had got about two-thirds of the way across when suddenly I hit something in the water – it felt like a log and the bike was refused to get over it. I squeezed hard on the juice making the back wheel spin and sinking me deeper into the water. I planted my size 15 boot in the water, kicked around and pushed as hard as I could to try and lift the bike up and over whatever it was getting stuck on. The engine was howling, there was more mud and spray but the back wheel finally got some traction and we went up and over and out of the water. My heart was thumping – and I don't mean that figuratively, I could feel my chest cavity heaving and the blood pumping hard throughout my body. Fear had focused all of my energy on getting out but I was drained. I looked up – there was only another ten feet to the next water hazard, this one even bigger than the one I had just escaped from. I was not keen to try another ride through and it appeared from the numerous muddy tracks off to the side of the road that there may be an alternate path. I sized it up and went for it. I only got about six feet in before I had sunk too deep to make any further forward progress. More throttle simply removed more earth and mud from under my back wheel, sinking me deeper into the bog. My bike frame (which normally clears the ground by about twelve inches) was resting on the muddy ground and sinking. Oh Bugger. I cursed and cursed again. How stupid was that? What else did I expect would happen? Its simple physics – you send a 250 kilogram machine, with one wheel drive, with a 115 kilogram man on top into a wet muddy bog and there's only one possible outcome. For a brief moment I felt the victim syndrome pass over me – "Why me?" but what a stupid response. This was all my doing, I chose to come here with my bloody motorbike to try and cross the bloody Road of Bones and it was me who just drove his bike into this bog. All fingers pointed to me, so I took a deep breath, looked around, summed up the situation and let out a low visceral primal scream – that felt better. There was still plenty of daylight, the bike was working and I was feeling OK. I pushed and pushed as hard as I could but the bike wouldn't budge. The back wheel was wedged deep and tight between two solid walls of wet but firm earth. Just when I thought things couldn't get any worse I lost concentration for a second and the bike fell over, squelching in the mud as it grounded itself softly. I couldn't be bothered cursing, quickly realising that lifting a 250 kilogram bike from the horizontal from a very soft and slippery surface was nigh on impossible. I couldn't get enough traction and my arms and legs were no longer powerful enough to fight gravity. I cursed loudly. There was nothing else to do so I unpacked and detached my luggage, including my aluminium panniers and moved everything loose back to dry land. It's funny in these situations – as much as you may loathe doing it, there is only one course of action – you just need to summon the will power and strength and get on with it. Free of luggage I wrestled with the bike like a pig farmer, gradually rotating it away from the hole it had dug itself into and got it pointed back towards from where I had launched it. I righted the bike and with judicious amounts of throttle was able to walk it out over some slightly firmer ground. Now I really was exhausted; all I had now to do was re-assemble everything and figure out where to from here

I looked down the track – pools of muddy water bigger and better than the two I just been through covered the track for as far as the eye could see. I explored a little on foot and quickly discovered that all of the land surrounding the road was itself water logged – just one big bog. I was never going to get through this! The road stretched another four hundred kilometres to the West and it was impossible to say whether it would improve beyond this section or not. Trying it alone was crazy. I was literally in the middle of nowhere, alone and would have had to stop, unpack, walk the bike, re-pack and so on for each water hazard ahead – no thanks, I would be here for months. I don't mind travelling the hard road when necessary, but this was beyond the pale. So, with a heavy heart I decided the only sensible thing to do was to turn back – perhaps I was not going to be able to get through after all? All sorts of contingency plans raced through my head – how on earth would I get the bike out? Back to Magadan and onto a plane? You've got to be kidding. The thought of it made me sick.

I headed for the nearest village – Myandzha – and pulled up outside the central store where men were unpacking a supply truck. I asked whether there was a hotel. They all looked at me incredulously and laughed – *crazy foreigner*. A young, well fed and happy looking man with shaven head and bright blue eyes approached me. His name was Alexei (of course). I asked him about a hotel and he just laughed again and said "there is no hotel, and anyway, you must stay with me and my family – come, let's go". We garaged the bike nearby – at the kind offer of the store owner. Alexei said my luggage was unnecessary. He led me toward his apartment block which was one in a series of many, although only a few remained occupied. The ground was a mess of broken concrete – collapsed at odd angles from the permafrost, and large exposed hot water pipes, currently the focus of much repair activity. We climbed two flights of stairs, pushed back the heavy unlocked black vinyl-covered door and entered Alexei's apartment. He was twenty six years old and lived at home with his mother, father and much younger sister. Their apartment was neat and homely, with Alexei's mother camped on the lounge/divan, TV always on, permanently in her dressing gown. I said hello to her but I'm not sure she was so happy to see me. Alexei insisted I take a hot bath, shave and wash – did I look that bad? After about fifteen minutes or so he called me into the bathroom and proudly offered a bath tub full of hot yellow-brown murky water. He also invited me to use all of his bathroom accessories (razor, soap, shampoo etc) and I happily accepted. I could just make out the bottom of the bath as I stepped in – it was lovely and hot and I soaked and scrubbed for a good half-hour. I heard a loud conversation outside and suspected that Alexei and his mother were arguing about me. I got dressed quickly and tentatively emerged into the hallway to discover two local policemen in the kitchen asking Alexei and his mother questions. They were keen to meet me and get my details, but once they had this information they were happy to leave. I got the impression that this annoyed Alexei's mother – but Alexei just smiled and winked, giving me the thumbs up to indicate all was OK. In the kitchen Alexei had prepared a feast of borscht, tomatoes, kvass, fresh bread, kolbasa, pickled cucumbers, sardines, potato and meat stew and beer. It was all delicious and much more than I needed but I didn't want to disappoint Alexei so ate heartily. Alexei had none. Soon two of his friends arrived - Dima, a local school teacher, and Oxsana, a law student in Magadan. Dima was well-built, tall and blonde with a strong face – a classic Russian with a permanent smile and although young he already seemed resigned to the problems of every day life in Russia and took these in his stride. Oxsana was a little more detached from the conversation and I suspect keen to progress and perhaps move on and out of the Far East. Dima spoke a little English which helped enrich the conversation. We talked and drank late into the night. I proudly showed them the pictures of my family (as I had shown everyone I'd met) and they wanted to know why on earth I was here doing what I was doing. I tried my best to explain and muttered something in Russian about history, culture and people. I explained that all the people I'd met so far had been wonderful and hospitable. I'm not sure if they were surprised or not, but they did go on to warn me about bandits on the road and to be careful. Do people everywhere take the same perspective – "of course we're OK, but you'd better watch out for those people from over there"?

They were fascinated with our wildlife (kangaroos, koalas, crocodiles and sharks) and wished they could visit to see these rather exotic creatures first hand. After I explained that we had poisonous snakes and spiders I think they had second thoughts about which were more dangerous; Russian roads and forests (think big bears) or the Australian bush. They couldn't believe that most people lived in houses rather than apartments and the concept of a mortgage was foreign to them. By this time Alexei had drunk too much and was swaying on his chair looking at me with goggle eyes, smiling and shaking his head like Boppo the Clown. He insisted that when I got home I send him a picture of a crocodile and he kept repeating this request ad-nauseam until he was put to bed, with his head resting on his hand (elbow bent) and nose against the wall. He slept locked in this position – something I had never seen before; Dima explained that he always slept like this when drunk.

I slid into bed and woke with a sore head which was quickly relieved by a few large cups of tea. Alexei worked at the rather imposing power station I had seen on my way into town. It was enormous, and in a classic modern industrial style from the 1940's and 1950s – big, strong, regular lines, striking black and green colour scheme with white highlights. It emanated as well as produced power. It was situated down the valley near the edge of the town and almost everyone worked there. From my reading I knew that Stalin had established a uranium processing plant nearby and wondered whether this was related in some way.

Alexei had a TV, video and stereo in his room and spent much of his time with at least one of these devices on (and loud) while he was in his room. When he woke up he immediately put on "The Hunt for Red October". He had a library of classic macho action films. He hated his work and didn't want to go there today or any day. He reminded me a little of Alex from A Clockwork Orange, but with the evil and brutality replaced by sweetness and melancholy. He was a young man stuck in small village in a dead-end job living in one small room. He had mentioned a girlfriend and I hoped this aspect of his life brought him some pleasure and there was certainly some evidence of this as I looked at the rubbers discarded on the ledge that ran along the edge of the building under his bedroom window.

His mother ordered him off to work and he left angrily. He told me to wait until eleven o'clock when he said he would return from work so that we could retrieve my bike from the garage. I was hoping for an early start but did not want to be an ungracious guest. Alexei's mother, warming to me, had prepared a large breakfast so I set up camp in the kitchen and did my best to get through it all. Soon after, Alexei's father came home – he worked nights in some kind of maintenance job. He was a Rasputin-like character, no more than five feet tall with short dark brown hair, skin tanned and creased from a lifetime of outdoor work, and bright blue eyes that darted about constantly, hidden in little slits. He had only one tooth visible in the lower row and he had a long thick straight beard down to his chest. Even though he had worked all night he was still a bundle of nervous energy. He peppered me with questions, gave plenty of advice and was concerned about my plans to travel the Road of Bones alone. I listened intently absorbing more of his energy than his meaning, but took it in the spirit in which it was delivered. Eleven o'clock came and went and there was no sign of Alexei – apparently his foreman was not letting him leave work early so I said my thank yous and good-byes and retrieved my bike myself.

I had decided to try the other road – my map showed a way through but it wasn't clear whether this was an all year or just a winter road. Many of the roads here only emerge in winter when the ground is hard and rivers can simply be driven across. In December, road crews mark out these roads – including lane markings and signage across the rivers – Incredible! The riding was pleasant with the road in reasonable condition as I cut through some handsome landscapes here; low, mountain passes with thick taiga to the road edge followed by wide open plateaus of scrub and tundra. There was very little traffic – which concerned me; for if there was a through road, why wasn't there more (any) traffic? There was only one way to find out so I pressed on. At some point I looked down and noticed my speedometer wasn't working. I stopped and rested the bike on its stand and investigated. I followed the cable down to the front wheel, found the connector onto the axle, unscrewed it, jiggled it around and put it back together. The final tightening twist was just enough to overbalance the bike and down it came, crashing onto the sloping shoulder of the road – fully loaded. Bugger. I huffed and puffed but I just couldn't get the bike up through the extended arc required (it was already below horizontal). I was about to start unloading it when a truck came by, stopped and the driver immediately came running out, obviously thinking something more serious had happened. I re-assured him all was OK and he helped me right the bike. His name was Tolya and he was from Artic, a town further along the highway in the direction I was headed. He told me the only way through in summer was by airplane; there was a road but there were many rivers and no bridges. Another truck driver stopped and gave a slightly different account, but along the same lines. It was so hard to determine the truth – I guess here there were no absolutes – it depended.

Depressed, I rode on. There were still many kilometres to cover and it was getting late (but not dark). I crossed the regional border from state of Magadan to the Republic of Sakha – home to the various indigenous peoples of the region: the Yakuti, Evenki and many more – all here prior to Russian occupation and very much Asian in appearance – much like Eskimos or Native American Indians. There is a theory that all of these races are closely related, the Diaspora facilitated by the land bridge that once existed between Asia and North America. This place was incredibly sparsely populated with just one person for every three square kilometres (that's three times LESS densely populated than Australia).

I rode on and gradually the sun began to dip behind the low

mountains ahead. The road had deteriorated and was now covered with many loose and large stones. Riding into the sun across this stuff was hard going. Eventually, at about ten-thirty in the evening, I pulled up at the police checkpoint on the outskirts of Artic where the road ahead was blocked with a manually controlled heavy wooden gate. I stopped as the three policemen on duty emerged from their basic hut, rubbing their eyes in disbelief. They all shook their heads and gestured for me to park the bike beside the station and to come inside. This was my first taste of the Russian traffic police and I was a little nervous as all I had been told up to this point were tales of petty corruption and general laziness. The station was just a small hut with two rooms and a garage. Inside was dark and musty, but clean with an old wooden desk and chairs for processing the passing parade of drivers. This was the proxy border between the states and all trucks and traffic were stopped and inspected and records kept. Later I asked what – apart from the appropriate paperwork – were they looking for, and was told illegal gold exports and firearms. The policemen introduced themselves: Marat, Vladimir and Alexei. They reminded me a little of the three stooges. Alexei was a young trainee – tall, thin, angular and nervous. Vladimir was a career traffic cop – big, heavy, older, thick set and not in much of a rush to do anything. Both were Russian. Marat was about my age and in charge. He was Yakut; strong and muscular with dark hair, tanned skin and bright brown eyes. He took my passport and made some notes in a big official paper register; "crazy Australian giant on motorbike who doesn't know where he's going..." Marat said there was absolutely no way through on the road and that the only option was to fly to Yakutsk from the next big town along the road – Ust Nera – about one hundred and fifty kilometres away. This news struck me like a pick axe between the shoulder blades – no way through here either! Was this the end of the line? I knew others had done it – with some difficulty. Perhaps the fickle weather had conspired against me; this was July and normally the hottest and driest month, but it had rained almost every day and the rivers were up and breaking their banks. I shut my eyes, tried to think of something positive and fell asleep on the couch. I didn't want to wake up.

Caravan of Love

I drifted in and out of sleep on the couch in the front room of the police station, my dreams interrupted by the muted sounds of gunfire and death coming from the PlayStation being used by Alexsei – I think this was the closest he had come to seeing any real action and he was really enjoying it. There were a few early morning truck drivers to be processed but I didn't rise – I didn't have a destination.

I eventually crawled out of my sleeping bag and sat up on the couch and was surprised to see some new faces; Vladimir had been replaced by Vassily, an older, wiry character with a big moustache, long sad face, kind eyes and greasy straight hair. He had brought some large maps of the area I wanted to travel to and had some good news – there would be a passenger truck later in the week, travelling along the road I wanted to use. All was not lost! Vassily suggested that I could travel with this truck and its passengers and perhaps even place my bike on the truck when the going became too difficult. This was music to my ears and it didn't matter too much that it was still a few days away; at least I had a plan.

Marat explained that the trucks that ply this route are big, six-wheel drive Kamaz and therefore capable of conquering virtually any type of terrain. I had seen these machines on the roads and they were indeed big and powerful and not to be messed with. The Russians definitely took pride in these beasts – designed and produced in Russia – that helped them deal with nature's harsh conditions here.

I had breakfast with Marat sitting at a little table in the back room – with him cutting cheese, cucumber and kolbasa with one of the biggest hunting knives I had ever seen. It was enormous! He gripped the knife firmly in his right hand and pulled it sharply down through whatever was in the way with a sharp crack on the table. He was an experienced hunter. He explained that he was learning English (in Yakutsk) in order to get onto the promotion track within the Militsia. He had a wife and young daughter at home in Yakutsk and he worked one week on and one week off continuously throughout the year – except for the times when he was studying. He certainly had ambitions and I wondered what the future as an officer in the Russian Militsia held for him and whether this would fulfil his expectations. I mentioned Putin at which he and the others immediately gave their unanimous support. Strong and firm they said – projecting a confident and powerful image of Russia to the rest of the world – I could hardly disagree.

With my plans now shaping up, Marat made a few phone calls and before long, the town that last night had no hotel, now suddenly had one waiting for me – time to pack my bags and re-locate. Marat helped me and we trudged down the dusty main road and across some vacant blocks to a low, long rectangular stone bungalow with a wooden picket fence and a tree and a dog in the small front yard. The towns were different now, there were no ugly apartment blocks, replaced now with wooden cottages of all shapes and sizes – almost always unpainted, except for the decorative work around the windows and eaves, always off centre with long curved walls, slowly sinking into the soft topsoil.

We were greeted at the front door of the hotel by Natalya – a well built handsome lady in her early forties. She was curious to see who I was and what I was doing and immediately called for her daughter to come and see me too. Her name was Lisa and I told them that that was my wife's name too – we all smiled. The hotel was more of a dormitory for truck drivers (used heavily in winter but rarely in summer). It had two bedrooms with many cots, a basic kitchen, a lounge, a large open shower room and a banya – I was staying here alone so had all of this to myself! There was a TV so at least I had some entertainment (when the electricity ran) for a little relaxation.

I stocked up on food at the local store (bread, sausage, eggs and tomatoes) and settled in for the next few days. My ankle was still extremely swollen and tender so enforced rest was OK even though I knew I was falling further behind schedule. Natalya and her old mother came to visit each day so there was always some fun when this time rolled around. I did explore the village, but it was tiny and there wasn't really much to see – there was the obligatory statue of Lenin, the "Palace of Culture" and a few other community buildings and that was it. There was a phone and phone book on the kitchen table – in reality just a couple of small pages of photocopied paper stapled together with perhaps twenty listings all up. The first few pages were dedicated to the officials of the town and the essential and community services (medical, school, power, etc). The very first entry was labelled "Director" and I guessed this was akin to the Mayor. But I didn't have to call as he came to visit me during my stay just to make sure everything was OK and that I was happy in *his* town.

I also took the chance to refill my petrol tank and get some minor repair work done. The lady at the petrol station wouldn't sell me any petrol unless it was OK'd by *Andrei Antonovich* – the chief of the trucking centre – the main activity and place of employment in the town. She wrote down his name on a piece of paper and directed me to the large dark building where he and the trucks were located. I drove up, parked and poked my head inside the large building – it was five storeys high and had two wings that formed a U shape around the front courtyard. There were workers coming and going all the time. I asked one of them where I could find the famous Andrei Antonovich and his body immediately stiffened as he turned and took me quickly upstairs to the central office. There were three "office ladies" on duty and I was offered a cup of tea and shown into Andrei's office which was the size of, and decorated like, a boardroom. Andrei was a baby-faced roly-poly fellow, dressed in modern smart casual gear, definitely looking out of place here. He wore simple jewellery around his neck and had an expensive wristwatch – he was obviously doing OK. I explained my requirements and he quickly assembled a team of engineers to perform the necessary work on my bike; all at no cost! He took me to another room with large and detailed maps of the Kolyma region and pointed out all of the different sites where precious metals and stones (including diamonds) were mined. He explained that the trucks from this depot worked all of these routes all year round. He explained that he had moved to Artic two years ago for the work and because of the high wages. It was all making sense now. My repairs were completed quickly and efficiently and Andrei showed me out and wished me well on my travels. Just before I was about to pull away he said that tomorrow he and some of his friends were going on a hunting trip and that I was more than welcome to join them. He had a smile on his face and menacing glint in his eye – he was already salivating at the thought of guns, vodka and killing wild animals. I declined diplomatically, explaining that I hoped to be travelling by then. I shook his hand again and we said goodbye. This time there were no issues at the petrol station – for now I had the imprimatur of Andrei Antonovich.

I visited the police station a few times to check on my bike and to reconfirm that, yes, a *big, powerful truck* will be coming soon and that I could travel with it. "Yes – everything will be fine, don't worry". On the third morning as I was heading to the police station I noticed the Militsia jeep heading my way along the dusty main road. It pulled up quickly; Vassily stuck his head out and said there was a change in plan and that the truck would be here any minute. Argh – after two days of living in the hotel my gear was sprawled out over three rooms so I rushed back, swept everything up into my big bag and made a panic dash to the station. By the time I had arrived I was hot and soaking in sweat. No sign of the truck so I took a breather on my favourite couch in their front room. Half an hour passed. I asked Vassily what was going on and he just shrugged his shoulders. I suddenly realised that I didn't have any photos of Artic so I grabbed my camera and decided to take a quick stroll back into town to take a few snaps. Vassily said to look out for the truck and to come back immediately if I saw it. I hurried along the main road, back past the truck depot and on into town. A few trucks passed, but nothing fitting the description of what I had been told to expect. A small battered passenger truck passed with a tiny beat-up metal cabin full of Yakut women perched on the back — all smiling and waving making the jalopy look more like a gypsy wagon. Surely that couldn't be what they were referring to? I continued on taking some select photos of the town; statue of Lenin leading the people forward, the town hall, the main street etc. I wandered back along the main road and again saw the Militsia jeep heading toward me again — it was Vassily wanting to know what the hell I thought I was doing! That decrepit gypsy wagon was the "big powerful truck" that would help get me across some of the most horrible roads, bogs and swamps in all of Russia (and possibly the world); you've got to be kidding I thought. No, they certainly were not and I had better get a move on to catch up to them. Vassily was annoyed but still helpful as I quickly packed my bike and headed off down the road after them — the gypsy wagon had a twenty minute head start but Vassily reckoned I would catch them within the hour. I couldn't believe it — my only chance to get across the Road of Bones and I had let it slip through my fingers. I was going to ask why they hadn't made the truck stop and wait, but realised how arrogant this sounded and bit my tongue. I raced off down the road and soon caught up with them — they were crawling along. I rode behind them for a while and they soon stopped and we introduced ourselves. The truck was piloted by Boris, a thin wiry old Yakut man in fishing hat and moth-eaten old tracksuit, assisted by his young son Borya. There was an old disfigured cripple woman on crutches in the front cabin and ten women packed like sardines into the cabin attached to the tray of the truck. The roof was overloaded with luggage and there was only a small space between the cabin and the end of the truck — perhaps 30cm wide — already full of stuff. My faith was being sorely tested — these guys and this truck across the Road of Bones? I was more likely to ride across the Nullarbor Plain naked on my Malvern Star bicycle. The women were all nurses returning home from training

34

and examinations they had just taken in Ust Nera, the next town past Artic. With the exception of two, they were all native Yakuts. They were all shapes, sizes and ages and all very jolly given their cramped and uncomfortable travelling conditions – and that was before you added the bump and grind of the road to the mix. We travelled on together, with Boris insisting I travel ahead of him to avoid me eating dust for the next hundred kilometres or so. But he needn't have worried, as his truck hit the first of what turned out to be many mechanical issues. I watched closely as Boris and his son worked like open heart surgeons on their beloved machine. Some important-looking part of the engine had fallen off and was simply re-attached with coat-hanger wire. And that was the easy one as next the fuel pump broke and they spent the next two hours fixing it. They removed the tank, disassembled it, cleaned every piece and fashioned a replacement part from an old tetra pack of fruit juice they'd found on the side of the road. It was incredible – this father and son team knew every piece of their machine and how it worked and how to fix it. I was amazed each time the engine started – and this was not simple either, requiring much fiddling and hand priming deep inside the engine (front cabin up at forty five degrees) and finally some gentle tugging on starter cables – I don't think the truck had a key or ignition as such. The oil filter was next to go and they spent another hour rigging up a make-shift replacement. My confidence was dropping by the minute; how on earth was this machine held together by sticky tape, chewing gum and prayer, ever going to make it? We had already taken six hours to travel less than one hundred kilometres. It was getting late, the sky was dark and big blobs of rain were now falling. We pressed on across the dusty-but-slowly-turning-muddy roads. The rain came harder and in the twilight the grey road and grey sky became almost indistinguishable plus I had Boris bearing down on me like a maniac in pursuit. And, apart from these unplanned stops, these guys just drove and drove – driving in shifts until they reached home, one sleeping in the rear cabin with the nurses while the other drove. I drove on in the rain and the fading light, cursing every drop.

***

At about midnight we reached the turn off (where I had been three days earlier in my first failed attempt to head west) and stopped. Boris told me to wait saying he needed to get some equipment (from *where*, for *what* and from *whom* I could not imagine) but he said he would return in 20 minutes and that I should wait there for him. So there I was: in the middle of nowhere again, stranded, in the middle of the night, cold, being rained on, waiting for some old, crazy Eskimo and his gypsy wagon. I walked around, kicked a few rocks, cursed the weather and generally just filled in time. Incredibly, a jeep came out of the darkness from along the back road (where we were headed). The driver stopped and asked what on earth I was doing here – I couldn't muster a good answer and the driver went on to tell me that if I thought I was going to ride *that road* I was dreaming.

Boris returned as precisely he had promised and off we went – the pot holes from my previous visit were all still in exactly the same places and soon we came to the same big puddles of water covering the entire road. It was still raining, but Boris stopped the truck, came back to me and I explained there was no way I could continue through this stuff. He looked at me, scratched his head and looked away. It was now after 1am and I'm sure he didn't need the added burden of trying to rescue some crazy self-indulgent tourist from the obvious perils of solo motorcycle travel in remote Siberia. He looked at me, shrugged his shoulders as if to say, "Well, there's nothing else we can do is there?" I was doubtful about the bike fitting on the truck, let alone us being able to get it up onto the tray which was at least four feet above the ground. We had no lifting equipment – just ourselves. I quickly stripped as much gear from the bike as I could and then looked at Boris (who was a good eighteen inches shorter than me) and indicated this was the moment of truth. He may have been old, thin and wiry, but he was as strong as an ox. He reminded me of a Buddhist monk – very calm, relaxed and unfazed by any burden or problem. We managed to get the front wheel up over the lip of the tray of the truck – the bike was now almost vertical! Boris' son held the front wheel in place as we both lifted the back of the bike up with all our might. Slowly but surely it came up! This guy was incredible. He has like Yoda. Not a hint of emotion – job done, let's move on. Boris tied the bike fast to the truck – it was a snug fit, but it was in and then I slid over the bike and through the door of the cabin to join the sardines in their tin.

It was warm and sweaty in the tiny cabin – it was at no more than ten feet by six feet with a very, very low ceiling. There was a basic wooden bench seat that ran along three walls and a cast iron heater in one corner, next to the door. There were small rectangular windows up high so that it was difficult to see anything except the tree line and sky when seated. There were already *eleven* people in the cabin wedged tightly into various positions along the bench seat. Some were awake and others simply slept sitting upright, resting on their neighbours. Boris' son Borya was sleeping on the floor at the far end of the cabin, resting between the forest of sturdy legs and feet that filled the centre of the cabin floor. There was no space left for me – I was an unplanned guest. One of the women put her hand on a small tin canister – cut in half and used as a footrest, and indicated I should sit on it. There were no other options so I gave it a go. The canister was about six inches high and provided only a very small flat surface to sit on, but I managed to position myself with at least half my backside supported, with my back wedged tight against the door and the cast iron heater. I was wet, but at least I was warm, I was with other people and had a means of transport that just might get me across this huge bug-infested swamp. It was now well past 2am and I tried my best to sleep; I put my head in my arms resting along one edge of the heater, but the continual violent movements of the cabin (Boris was driving on) made it impossible to get a solid grip on anything. The terrain was incredibly rough and it felt like we were in a small boat at sea battling a fierce storm we were being tossed about so much. The only thing keeping the women asleep was the human insulation limiting any free movement. The cabin floor had already disappeared – covered in body parts – and there was no room to stretch out my long legs, so I tucked them under myself and settled in for an uncomfortable night. I've never had a deep vein thrombosis but I reckoned these were about the perfect conditions to bring it on. There was some brief relief when for some reason we stopped at 4am for a five minute comfort stop – perhaps even Yoda needed some rest. But we were soon moving again and by now it was already light outside making sleep just that little bit harder.

We were tossed and churned for another three hours until we stopped for breakfast. Incredibly, we were on a flat stretch of gravel running under a cliff face on the side of wide but gently flowing river. Not a breath of wind, overcast and warm with millions of mosquitoes swarming on this rare smorgasbord of human flesh. Boris was not only a master mechanic and power lifter, but also an expert woodsman, and in no time at all he had chopped down a few small trees, made a fire place including the apparatus to hold a very large pot of water and other devices securely in place to boil. He had also assembled two large logs for everyone to sit at and erected a long table using some pieces of wood from the roof of the cabin – incredible. In the meantime the women had seemingly from nowhere whipped up a breakfast feast – bread, fish, meat, tea, cheese, jam and hot noodles. I offered what I had into the mix but it was paltry compared to what they had. They might have been in a jalopy but they sure had plenty of food. We sat and ate happily and at the end of the meal a bottle of vodka was shared as we toasted our new found friendship.

We were soon back in the truck and off again – the road (track) got worse, it was difficult to see given the position of the windows, but obvious from the violent turns and large arcs that the cabin moved through. First the front corner would dip and dive, dragging the rest of the cabin along for the ride, then suddenly we'd bottom out with a thud and heave and creak back up and over whatever it was we were driving over. Or, just for some variety, there were the sideways rolls, where we'd start sliding off the track into the forest/cliff face/rushing stream at alarming angles and madly throw ourselves across the cabin to counteract the forces of gravity dragging the cabin over – like sailors on a racing catamaran. There were times when I was certain we were going to roll completely over. I wondered how the truck could take such a pounding and noticed that rather than being rigid, the whole structure was quite flexible; the cabin, although made of metal, consisted of many individual pieces and the room seemed to stretch and contract and skew as the various forces were applied to it. Impressive engineering or adaptation – I didn't know which but it sure was effective. We did, at least, have some warning for the worst of the "bumps" with the driver honking repeatedly on the horn to let us know to batten down the hatches, hold onto something firm and get ready for the storm ahead.

In spite of these conditions, the mood in the cabin was upbeat and all of the women were happy, some even managing a game of cards while all of this was going on about them. My Russian-English dictionary proved invaluable again and there were many questions about life in Australia which I was happy to answer. Their biggest complaint was low wages and limited spending power. They got by, but that was about it. There was no saving with all their money used to buy food and other essentials. They all worried about the lack of an adequate pension too – if you weren't saving this would indeed become a serious problem. I wondered how bad this would be (for Russia) and whether in a generation's time there would be some sort of crisis. The old seemed to have been neglected and without a family for support I couldn't imagine how you could possibly survive.

I also felt bad for how I had just assumed these people would help me – why should they? They already had a hard enough time getting home and then along comes a mad man on his motorbike expecting to be rescued – I was certainly extremely thankful for their help but couldn't help thinking I was a burden to them.

I kept checking on my bike through the small crack between the door and the cabin surely expecting to see that it had been ripped away from the truck through the unnatural forces being applied to it – but the rope work of Boris was excellent and it didn't move an inch.

We travelled on and on at a snails' pace for that was all that was possible – the terrain was that rough. I was amazed at how the little truck kept going and going. The coat hanger wire and tetra pack repairs were holding together incredibly well so far.

We stopped for tea at about 4pm at a river crossing and I checked the map – in *fourteen* hours we had come just *seventy* kilometres. Boris said the road definitely "got better" from here and that I should be able to ride the remaining two hundred kilometres or so to Tomtor, the next main town along the route. I looked him in the eye thinking, "*Better*? What do you mean? How much *better*?" He said there were no more "big" river crossings, bridges were in order and the road was good. I could only take him on his word so with some trepidation I helped unload the bike and got ready to ride. A couple of the women wanted a ride so I obliged and doubled them up and down the nearby track at which they giggled and screamed with delight.

A large Kamaz truck pulled up and parked in the river crossing near us and the contrast was stark. The Kamaz was relatively new, at least twice as tall as Boris' truck; it had six huge wheels and all-wheel drive and a big cabin with individual seats and plenty of windows. In comparison, we were the *little engine that thought it could*.

The moment had come and nervously I rode off down the track: a few potholes here and there but nothing too serious – good. Then it was like déjà vu – I came to some big muddy pools of water covering the road and they were deep. Very deep. Oh bugger. I wasn't mentally prepared for this yet. I sized it up. There seemed firmer ground at the edges so I gave it a go and made it across, but it was harrowing, balancing with my legs spread-eagle on a thin ridge of the hardened mud bank. There were a few more like this and I was able to get across. Then it happened. I was riding carefully along the thin lip of a large swimming-pool-sized hole when I lost balance the bike toppled over into and under the water. Argh! I fell in with the bike and struggled to right the bike. I removed as much baggage as I could quickly, but I still couldn't get the bike upright. There wasn't time to curse – I knew I had to get the bike out of the water urgently and just in the nick of time I heard Boris coming up behind me. As soon as they saw my predicament Borya came racing out to help me. I was profusely thankful and apologetic. I kept being a problem for them. Boris drove through the water and stopped about 30 metres ahead waiting to make sure I was OK. I wasn't. The engine would not start regardless of what I did. I tried and tried for about fifteen minutes until finally Boris drove back to where I was and began examining my bike. I immediately thought spark plug and tried my best to explain this to Boris, but there was only one problem – I didn't actually know where it was exactly. Borya took a careful look over the bike and pointed out that my fuel tap was off! I turned it on and the engine roared into life. They suggested I unpack some of my luggage onto the truck to make riding easier – we would be travelling together after all. I agreed and hoped this might include the bike itself, but I knew I had to ride.

The next twelve hours were hell; the hardest physical challenge of my life. The mud, bogs, rain and rivers kept coming and I had to deal with them all. Pushing the bike through mud was hardest, whilst crossing rivers (albeit only 1-2 feet deep) the most frightening. The rivers were stony and icy cold (some still with ice floes!). It was hard for the bike to get traction and soon my boots were just buckets of cold water. But Boris was relentless – he just kept coming and wasn't interested in stopping. I dropped the bike crossing a small road bridge – rough-hewn logs reinforcing the road – and in the wet (yes it was raining again) they were treacherous. Borya helped me again and I was thankful for their presence once again. At one point I was in so much sticky mud that my feet simply came out of my boots, while the bike remained stuck deep. Again Borya helped and we eventually got it out, but I could not have done this alone.

By now we had started climbing away from the marshes and were heading over the low mountain ranges to the west. The road improved and the going became a little easier, but it was cold, wet and windy. We eventually pulled up for our evening meal at 11pm – still light and soon there was a fire going and the meal ritual was underway again. The women, seeing how cold I was, got me a blanket as I shuddered over the fire absorbing as much heat as I could. I changed my pants and socks (they were soaking wet) and the women dried my boots by placing hot rocks from the fire inside them where they sizzled and steamed. One of them (the senior nurse) after noticing my severely swollen and bruised ankle (it was purple), massaged my cold feet, gave me the once over and put on a fresh supportive brace. What wonderful help for a complete stranger. Soon enough we were off again, the skies were dark and brooding and the rain had returned. Just around the corner was another river crossing where icy cold water filled my boots and soaked my dry socks, but there was some upside here as the cold acted as an anaesthetic to the constant throbbing pain in my ankle.

We drove on and on through the night. I was really struggling. The rain got harder and fell as sleet, cutting into my face. I was soaked again and it was cold, really cold. I was rigid on the bike, but I kept going, the blinding headlights behind driving me on. It was difficult to see and the rain made the track slippery and hard going. I cursed and cursed. I cursed Siberia, I cursed the weather (*summer –* ha!), I cursed the President of Magadan Airlines for letting me bring my stupid bike here, but most of all I cursed myself for this hair-brained idea. I tried my best but I simply couldn't go on. It's an awful feeling, but you know when you've reached breaking point. So, completely spent, I pulled up to a stop. Borya (on duty now) drove up beside me and looked me up and down as if to say "What's wrong with you? Sure it's 2am in the morning and it's cold and wet, and we've been driving for 24hours non-stop, but we need to keep going!" He must have been about sixteen years old and I don't think he had learnt the concept of empathy yet, or if he had he wasn't showing it for this was tough love. I sat there for a minute or two in the rain explaining to him (in English) that I was exhausted and couldn't go on, but it was no use – it just didn't register. I was thinking I had no more dry clothes when suddenly I realised that I still had a pair of long johns and waterproof pants – they were my last line of defence. I quickly retreated to the back of the truck, got changed and jumped back on the bike. I don't know how, but I kept riding, all night and into the early dawn. I was in a trance.

At about half past three in the morning we came to a small outpost, marked on my map as a *town*, but in reality more like a truck stop. I was running low on petrol and decided to try for some here. But it didn't look hopeful as this place looked more like a deserted military post, with hangars and unchained guard dogs roaming about. We eventually rustled up some assistance and I think out of sheer shock of seeing me and my bike and pity they gave me as much petrol as I wanted – a gift they said! The man who gave me the petrol said the road got "better" from here – there were so many things I could have said to him but I couldn't be bothered, I was so exhausted.

We rode on and on into the grey half-light of morning and eventually made it to Tomtor – our destination. I was escorted to the best (and only) dormitory-hotel in town where I took a hot shower and collapsed into bed and didn't wake up until evening.

It was a lovely hotel, warm, honey wood panelled, with a kitchen and small dining room – heaven – and I was the only guest. I was able to wash and dry my clothes and generally clean-up. My host was Lana, an older woman of mixed Russian and Yakut heritage. She was tall and thin with dark brown hair and eyes and there was a constant sadness in her expression. Her daughter, son-in-law and grand-daughter all lived here too it seemed. They were all extremely friendly and I didn't need to move an inch –everything I needed (really needed) was here. I needed to dry my boots and explained this to Lana who immediately picked up a hardcopy book from a shelf and started ripping out the pages, crumpling them up and stuffing them inside my boots! I couldn't believe it and tried to stop her, but she insisted. As much as I love books I took her lead when she handed over the book to me, but I did grimace as I tore each sheath of pages away.

***

I left after lunch the next day and had a good afternoon of riding until I hit more water and needed help again to right my bike. Unfortunately, this accident also put my satellite phone underwater – frying its circuits and destroying it – and thus cutting me off completely from the rest of the world and any chance of alerting anyone to a serious problem. I was getting tired of this and wondered what I was doing wrong apart from being a completely inexperienced rider in the wrong part of the world on an overloaded bike suffering exhaustion. But I pressed on and eventually made it to Kyubeme – marked as a major town on the map, but in reality another ghost town; the many derelict buildings the only remnants of more prosperous times. There was however a petrol station but it was closed. I banged on a few doors and eventually located the house of the owner. It was about 7pm and he wearily trudged up the road in his greasy tracksuit to the station with me where I filled up on *seventy-six* octane. He informed me cheerfully that the river – just down the road – was full and that the bridge was out. This was going to be a problem.

There were no other options so I was in for my first night of camping. The thought of camping had sounded nice in theory in my planning, but now that it was a practical reality I was not so enthusiastic. Hard work. I found a sheltered spot behind some derelict buildings and set up camp. There was plenty of scrap wood and soon I had a roaring camp fire going which I enjoyed sitting in front of until late into the night. I stared into the flames thinking many thoughts – my family, my work, my experiences so far – nothing definitive nor conclusive, just general mental meandering. I didn't think bears were going to be a problem here so I settled into bed confidently only to hear the soft hissing of air escaping from my "industrial strength" air mattress. I quickly descended the inch or so to the ground as it deflated. I couldn't be bothered fixing it but managed to sleep soundly anyway.

In the morning I needed water so went down to the river and it was indeed big, full with a very large and very broken bridge. I managed to boil some water (an achievement for me), ate some peach flavoured porridge, which until this point had just been impregnating my backpack and all its other contents with a funny smell. It wasn't so bad and I ate two helpings. As I was eating I spied a truck rumbling past that looked like it could make it across the river. I raced out toward the driver and tried to flag him down but I was too late (or he had chosen to ignore me). He came past again about half an hour later and I was able to stop him and explain what I needed. He seemed a little reluctant at first, but soon was hurrying me up to get ready. I wheeled the bike onto the back of his truck and we secured it with rope. I was instructed to ride on the back with the bike which I did. He didn't follow the road to the river but instead took another longer route eventually coming out on the shore much further downstream. He might have been a truck driver but he navigated the river bed and the rapids like an expert sailor and soon, after zigzagging our way across and somewhat downstream we climbed safely onto the other bank. The ride was bumpy and unfortunately had snapped my pannier frame again (the repair work completed earlier now completely undone). Fortunately it was still able to hold the pannier in place and after the application of much soft scrap wire I found on the ground and some tightening I was able to continue on.

The day was warm and sunny (the first one!) and I was now

riding across alpine meadows between tall granite peaks. After another water crossing I stopped, ate some bread and sour cream and lay in the sun to dry myself and watch the high clouds float across they sky. The flat lands disappeared and soon I was negotiating tight mountain passes – past fast flowing mountain streams and cascading waterfalls. All of the bridges were in place and road was deserted and in places the trees were in glades alongside the road. In some places the road became quite narrow and ran under rock ledges were water seeped out and across the road. There were massive warning signs before these places with complex pictograms warning drivers of the potential risks up ahead: falling rocks, loose surface, narrow road, water etc etc. You would have been lucky to take it all in and that's if you could take your eyes of the road for that long.

After a particularly treacherous mountain pass (think: recently fallen broken boulders on the road, no guard rail and a 100m vertical drop to a roaring white-water rapids) I came over a hill and upon a construction crew – they were digging a massive channel across the road to lay a large drain pipe under the road and there was no way through for me. Just as I was starting to make good progress! I pulled up and introduced myself. There was a construction crew of four – one for the digger, two for the bulldozers and one gopher, a young boy called Sasha. I had no water left so asked if I could have a drink to which they sized me up and led me off to their kitchen and living quarters up the hill. I was Sasha's responsibility and he quickly lit the boiler, put the water and a pot of stew on – it was time for a late lunch. Sasha made tea and I was invited into their cabin to sit and eat what they had. I was starving and couldn't believe their generosity – I could have just as easily been eating my loaf of bread, but this was heaven. I drank two large cups of tea laden with sugar – my new vice. Sasha was eighteen years young, short and lithe with a pixie face and bundle of raw energy. He explained that he worked on the roads every day except for when it rained and for when it was too cold (which was many months). He was from Yakutsk and spent weeks at a time away from home working on the *roads*. I looked around; their cabin was in fact a long shipping container fitted out with a kitchen and bunks. It was surprisingly modern and clean and certainly well stocked with food. I went back and watched the orchestra of equipment operate as they laid the pipe and bulldozed the road back into shape. It was mesmerising and much faster than I had expected. Sasha's job was to work inside the pipe (while earth and rocks were being dumped over it)

44

securing it to the ground with a pick axe and stakes and to add crossbeams for support where necessary. The pipe was only four feet in diameter, with flexible (weak) walls. It was dark inside and this was very difficult (and I suspected nervous) work.

Eventually the road was made and I was first across again, and on my way. It was getting late, dusk came and so did the rain for the last fifty kilometres or so as I rode into Khandyga – the end of the Road of Bones! From here it was a ferry ride down the Aldan and Lena rivers into Yakutsk – tomorrow I could put my feet up and watch the world go by from the comfort of a deckchair. I rode into town, pulled up at a Militsia van where the two policemen kindly escorted me to a very modern and comfortable hotel for the night. My host Alexsei was surprised to see me, but friendly and I couldn't wait to take a hot shower, eat and go to sleep – it was almost midnight.

Before going to bed I thought I should double check on the ferry service and confirm the departure time and location so I asked Alexsei... ."What ferry?? There is a small riverboat in four days, but they'll never take your bike, you need to cross the river and keep riding – it's another *four hundred* kilometres to Yakutsk on a very muddy road – good luck!" I could have strangled him – surely he was joking? I knew there was a ferry from the accounts of others but apparently no longer. I felt sick – more bloody bad roads. I had had enough and wanted to get off this sick amusement ride. But there were no exit ramps, just one way forward and I was going to have to give it a go. The descriptions in my guidebooks filled me with dread: "*...the road east from Yakutsk peters out in the marshes between the Lena and Aldan rivers - there is only a winter road to Khandyga*" Oh Bugger – this didn't sound promising

The Dirty Dozen

Alexsei scrambled around looking for details of the ferry, or "barzha" as he called it. He scanned the local newspaper, found a schedule and then called someone to confirm – yes, there was a barge across the Aldan, at 8am from the next village along the river from here, Kiskil – "just a forty minute drive away".

It was late, but I was hungry, so I dashed back to a store I had seen on the way into town and splurged on kolbasa, cheese, milk, bread, juice and chocolate – my spending spree conducted in candlelight due to an unexpected blackout. I ate quickly and fell into bed and slept a worried sleep: barges, more bad roads, and it was still raining – argh.

I was up early and away – it was overcast and raining again. I was getting sick of being wet and cold all the time on the bike and the road was awful – like driving across a riverbed; full of large, hard, oval shaped rocks, the size of your clenched fist and bigger, and very unstable. And this went on and on for the entire journey to Kiskil! What on earth were the demented road builders thinking? Let's dump the contents of a riverbed here and see who can make it through? If they don't crash, they will certainly damage their vehicles beyond recognition. I sure was glad when I got to the end of it; relieved that I would never have to ride over it again. I did, however, spy a native Yakut farmer who popped his head up out of his bunker like a gopher to watch me as I rattled by.

The "forty minute drive" took me an hour and a half before I came to a fork in the road with a sign indicating Yakutsk to the right and Kiskil to the left. I of course took the road to Yakutsk and this quickly delivered me to the edge of the Aldan River; the road just ended at the waters edge, so I assumed this was were the barge came but the place was completely deserted. Not a soul in sight. I looked at my watch – 7:55am, only five minutes to go – that's strange. I looked up and down the river – not a barge, or anything for that matter, in sight. I could see the village of Kiskil around the river bend, and a few barges moored there so decided to investigate. I re-traced my steps to the fork in the road and took the other road to Kiskil. I dodged some cows and tractors on the road, pulled up beside some old local men and asked where the barge went from – they pointed down the road so I followed their directions and came again to another place where the road simply ran into the river – no barge here and again no sight of anything coming or going. I decided to ride along the shore (in the mud) to the moored barges to try and find out what was going on. I spied a man walking the decks of one and pulled up alongside on the shoreline. There was a half sunken speed boat with its nose pointing straight up out of the water between me and the barge – not a confidence builder.

The man was descending some steps heading below deck and I yelled at him to get his attention – he was only twenty metres away and I knew he had seen me but he just kept going and went into hiding. I stayed on the river bank for half an hour waiting for him to re-emerge, but he never did. I shouted the best and most powerful expletives I could manage in English and rode off. He, however, had the last laugh as I failed to reach escape velocity and came tumbling off the bike trying to ride up the steep muddy incline to get back onto the "road". I spent the next hours in the pouring rain slowly removing all the gear, dragging the bike up the hill in zigzag fashion by sheer brute force and re-packing it. It was only ten o'clock, but I urgently needed a course in anger management or there would be a bloodbath in Kiskil. I cursed the rotten village and its godforsaken population and the rain and decided that the hotel was the only option to wait while the weather cleared and I could get a better handle on these bloody barges.

I rattled back along the road that "I was never going to ride again", secure in the knowledge that I would be riding it again soon on my return. I'm sure every stone took delight in trying to de-rail my path and I tried to zone-out and just get through it. Surprisingly, the journey back didn't seem so bad, and it would have been OK if it weren't for the driving rain. I eventually pulled up at the hotel and was greeted by the daytime minder – a big burly woman who was cleaning and doing the ironing. She was friendly and showed me back to my room which was now all neat and tidy again. I collapsed on the bed, depressed: was I ever going to get out of this place? Did it really have to be this hard? I slept and ate and watched Russian daytime TV with my new friend. An Armenian church was being constructed in the vacant lot next door and it was interesting to watch the antics of the builders. They were all Armenian and came to Khandyga for six months every year to work (for the high wages) and, given they spent so much time here, they wanted, and obviously had the means for building, their own church. We were situated on the bank of the Aldan River and at this part of its course it was well over 1km across. The sun even shone briefly before disappearing permanently behind the grey blanket of clouds that covered the sky.

***

I was warm and comfortable and well-fed, but nervous about the next stage of my journey. I tried to find out as much as I could about the phantom barges. No-one could explain what had happened, but they all re-assured me that the barge did indeed run every day, although now I was told that its departure time was 9am – I explained the fork in the road and the multitude of landing points I had seen. They confirmed the road to Kiskil was the correct path. So the next morning I got up early and rode out to Kiskil again (in the spitting rain). I followed their directions to the letter but again there was no barge. I couldn't believe it – I must have got something wrong. I waited for half an hour, well past 9am and there was still no sign of any barge or any traffic. This was like Groundhog Day. I rode into the village proper and discovered that, as you might expect, the barge actually left from the river bank just beyond the centre of town. The 9am barge had just gone – they all showed me excitedly where it was on the river sailing away from us – and if I was lucky, there might be another barge at 1pm. Oh dear. I found the local cafe – decorated in a surreal castaway motif – and settled in for a long morning tea of plov, hot tea, bread and sour cream. I sat and watched the locals come and go – a real mixture of older singles, young people and families – mostly Yakuts and, even in this remote outpost, young girls in the latest fashions (well, 90's at least). I stood up to pay and the family already at the counter gasped – a giant!

I found the barge – the captain and first mate were having a smoko on the small bridge – the only structure in addition to the long flat deck. I explained that I wanted to bring my bike across the river and he said "of course, no problem, but first we eat" – and off they went for an extended morning tea at the cafe. I cautiously rode my bike down the bank, up the steep ramp and onto the deck and parked it securely. The skies were brewing a dark storm – just what I needed today. I sat on a step, leaned back and fell asleep only to be awoken sometime later by someone gently kicking my leg and looking for the captain.

I was the only passenger as we pulled away from the shore – not an encouraging sign. There wasn't much traffic on the river either – just the odd freighter slowly sailing by. The river was calm and reflected the cavernous grey blue skies like an impressionist painting – massive reflections of light and splashes of colour – beautiful in its own way. The forest and scrub grew right to the water's edge and there were no signs of habitation as we sailed downstream. We did a three

49

point turn against the strong current to position the barge on the river bank for my exit. The captain had come down to talk with me for most of the journey and I bade him farewell, following his instructions to take the "big road to the right" just beyond the riverbank – the only option in reality.

The going was rough but the road was wide and dry. I passed a couple of kids on a Ural motorcycle with sidecar and confirmed with them that I was indeed heading for Yakutsk. I asked about the road ahead and they said it was "good". If these guys were related to the Eskimos (as most anthropologists assume), perhaps they might consider adding some shades of meaning to their vocabulary – like the Eskimos do to describe all the different types of snow they encounter. "Good" and "Better" for the roads just weren't doing it for me any more. I rode on and, of course, the rain came. I decided for once to get on the front foot and put on my wet weather pants before I got too wet – I had to press on. The surface became sandy and soft – evidence of recent road works. I was able to continue, but at a much slower pace. In two hours of riding I did not pass a single vehicle coming the other way – I should have known better. I quickly came upon a large stop sign behind which stood two of the biggest earth moving and road grading machines I've ever seen blocking the way – completely. Oh Bugger. There was no-one to be seen but there appeared to be a workers camp a few hundred metres up the road. I squeezed past the machines on foot and walked up to the camp and came upon two men around a fire having a cup of tea. I explained I was on a motorcycle and asked if I could pass and ride on. In classic Russian laconic style they mentioned "a little mud" but waved me on, insisting "anything was possible with a motorbike". In a way I respected this kind of advice – it was like "sure, if you want to have a go, knock yourself out – it's up to you". I did consider returning to Khandyga on the barge but couldn't really see the point, so I returned to the bike, kicked down the huge mounds of sand that were blocking the road and somehow, with much effort and cursing, managed to get my fully loaded bike around and past the behemoths. I was wet with sweat though – that was hard and heavy work. I drew breath, got on, started up the bike and rode on across the sandy surface. The going was fine for a few kilometres (if you count doing constant fishtails at 5 kph "fine") until I came to the mud. The road transformed here into a long river of thick dark brown sludge.

Initially it was manageable as long as I maintained momentum and steered a reasonably straight course. The mud was about twelve inches deep and very sticky. I was riding over gently rolling hills and this was the scene of much road works. I passed many large earthmoving and grading machines – most not in use, but the live ones were certainly a challenge on my driving skills as I overtook them *slowly*. Focus, don't look back, keep a straight line. The mud got deeper and thicker but I kept going – there was no turning back now. The mud looked like chocolate fudge and had the consistency of thick wet cement. There were deep squared-off ruts in the mud where the heavy vehicles had been driven; their tyres digging deep and their engine blocks cutting the mud off square like icing on a cake. There was only one option and that was to pick one of these ruts and stick to it, trying to steer a centre line to avoid hitting the walls of soft mud – easier said than done. My foot pegs were jammed back and I resorted to paddling my legs across the top of the muddy surface to try and keep balanced. This was hard work requiring dead-eye accuracy and perfect balance. I was riding the clutch hard in and out of 1st gear, but was making very slow but steady progress. I knew there were only a few kilometres of this stuff and then the road got "better". All I had to do was get through this section and I would be home. At the top of a rise, a jeep coming the other way stopped and the driver indicated I should do likewise – it was the chief of road works and he wanted to meet me. He was from Kazakhstan and his home town was on my itinerary – I instantly became his honorary son. He explained all of the "not-to-be-missed sights" around his home and then told me there was *only one more kilometre* of the mud to go! Just down this hill, round the corner and you're there. This lifted my spirits no end – I had conquered the Road of Bones and was about to get through on the winter road to Yakutsk! I rode on – the channels got deeper and the mud thicker, the bike was struggling and so was I. I was drenched with sweat from the physical effort required to keep the bike upright and moving forward. I made it to the corner. Almost there... I could see the end of the mud marked by a bridge and dry road ahead. I rode on for another few hundred metres until I reached a particularly bad patch. I had to stop – the bike had lost traction and I was worried I was bogged. I looked down at the back wheel and found it covered in thick mud, but not bogged. I clicked into gear but the wheel just didn't move – no drive. I checked again. I got down into the mud and pawed as much of it away from the drive chain and frame to give the wheel some clearance – again there was no drive, no power to the back wheel. Bugger – what had I done? Why wasn't the wheel moving? I had been OK with minor mechanical issues up until

51

now, but an engine problem *three hundred* kilometres from the next major town I did not need. I kept working at it – I was convinced something was jammed in the chain stopping it from moving. I spooned the wet mud out with my bare hands from every conceivable part of the bike. My boots and legs were covered in mud. I took off the luggage and panniers and tried again – nothing. I tried pushing in neutral and the bike moved forward including the back wheel so there was nothing jamming it – it just wouldn't engage in gear and drive forward.

I looked up and down the muddy road – no-one in sight. I knew there was a construction crew nearby, but what would I do to get out of this? The bike couldn't carry me on and Yakutsk was three hundred kilometres away. I was surrounded by bush, taiga and scrub in all directions. I walked around in the mud for a while – there wasn't much else to do. It started raining again. For some reason I was at peace with the world. Shit happens and you just need to deal with it. Eventually a large Kamaz truck came past and the driver stopped to see if I was OK. His name was "Lyo-ha" and he was a native Yakut with an impish face, small and lean and constantly smiling. He took a quick look at the bike, tried himself to get it going, but quickly reached the same conclusion as I had; I needed help to get it and me out of here. He knelt down in the mud, straightened his index finger and scratched a figure "1" followed by two zeroes and a little "m"; I was *one hundred* metres from the end of the mud! I could have cried but there was nothing I could do – some marginally better road was just around the corner, but I had a bike that wouldn't go. We carried on with sign language and many misunderstandings until we finally agreed that he would go and get a bulldozer to help lift my bike up out of the mud and into his empty truck tray. These Kamaz trucks were huge and their trays many metres in the air; there was no way we could have lifted it ourselves. He quickly returned with a man he introduced as his *father* – but I soon learned that all of the road crew treated each other like family while out here so they were all brothers and fathers and sons to each other. Lyo-ha located some strong steel rope and quickly lassoed my bike and hooked it onto one of the teeth of the bulldozer's front tub. Up went my expensive Japanese bike, hanging by a thread from mouth of a bulldozer. I felt sick. There was nothing I could do but watch and hope they were careful. The bike glided over the Kamaz's tray and landed softly. I jumped up into the tray and did my best to secure the bike with my tie-downs and rope. Lyoha insisted I ride in the cabin next to him, sandwiched between him and his younger brother who had just surfaced looking a little worse for wear. We bounced back along the road – not only was it soft and muddy but it was also rough and uneven, amplified inside the cabin by the large wheels and unforgiving suspension of the Kamaz. Lyo-ha's brother was tall and very thin with a shaved head and he held a large plastic bag in his lap which he periodically threw up into. I looked for a window for some fresh air but was too far from either side to reach for any relief. As we pressed on, slipping and sliding across the road, I hoped his older brother was in better shape – at least he was lucid. He explained that he was from a town near Yakutsk and that he also had a "home" not far from here – just a few kilometres back down the track – "didn't you see it on your way here?" he asked. I had no recollection of seeing anything vaguely resembling a house on my way through. Anyway, he was certain. I was conjuring up images of a cosy log cabin with a warm fire, bunk beds and something fresh and wholesome cooking in the kitchen.

We drove back past the construction crews and over the crest of the hill where I had met the chief of road works, down the other side, came to a large clearing in the forest and turned off. An area the size of 2-3 football fields had been cleared from the side of small hill and the sand and soil from here was being used for road fill. There were also three tiny square log huts with blue tarpaulin roofs; this was the road workers' camp and I was their guest. There were at least twenty men stationed here and a core group of about twelve including Lyo-ha who always worked together on a contract basis up and down the roads here. I was introduced to Zhenya, who was in charge of this crew and was invited into the kitchen hut. This hut was slightly larger than the other two and, in addition to a sleeping platform, which spanned the entire width of the cabin there was a long table and a large fire heating many pots in one corner. There were already many men inside, either dozing on the sleeping platform or eating at the table. I was offered a cup of tea and some sort of meat and noodle stew which I gladly ate – it was getting late and I hadn't eaten since early in the morning. The men all greeted me warmly and we settled down for a meal. I don't know if it was because we were so isolated and/or all male, but these guys sure made a lot of noise when they ate. They slurped, crunched, ruminated, snorted, swilled, spat and burped their way through the entire meal thoroughly enjoying themselves, laughing and telling stories. The noise was deafening and the sight of these misdemeanours breathtaking. If my mother-in-law was here there would be raw knuckles and blood on the floor quicker than you can say "can you pass the butter please?" I sipped my tea and, in spite of their table manners, felt entirely thankful for their help. Without them, I would still be scratching my head out in the middle of nowhere up to my armpits in mud. It was nearing the end of the week and they were heading home to Yakutsk tomorrow and said they could carry me and my bike there. Fantastic! I was worried about what exactly was wrong but I wasn't going to work it out here.

Lyo-ha indicated it was time for sleeping (it had just gone six o'clock) so I followed him to a sleeping hut. The huts were made of thick logs roughly hewn from the local forest and built square with interlocking joins at each corner. There was a small door made from scrap wood and one small window up high on one wall. There was a large cast iron heater in one corner with the majority of the space devoted to the sleeping platform which was just a simple flat panel of wooden logs about one and half feet off the ground and covered in sleeping mats and blankets and large pillows. There wasn't one bed as such, just this platform covered in sleeping materials; you just dived in, found a comfy position, covered up and went to sleep. The cabin was tiny, perhaps ten feet by eight feet and at least six men slept here. Lyo-ha was already lying in bed half asleep by the time I had got myself organised, so I crawled up and in and settled down for the night, feeling like I was *Scuppers the Sailor Dog*, except that I wasn't alone. The bedding was old and musty but it didn't matter, I was tired and it was comfortable.

The next thing I heard made my skin crawl; Lyo-ha was grinding his teeth with the most horrible noise emanating from his jawbone. It was like someone dragging their nails across a blackboard six inches from my ear. It was so loud and powerful I could feel the energy pulsing through the air. The noise was incredible – it sounded like his teeth would explode at any minute. I couldn't bare it. What do you do? I couldn't interrupt his sleep. Perhaps I could whack him over the head with a pillow and feign sleep just to get a break? I was worried for his safety too; what would happen if his teeth did explode? There was also the risk of spontaneous combustion – I'm sure I could see sparks in his mouth. Eventually I put two pillows over my ears and tried my best to hum a few songs and sing myself to sleep. A little later another two other men came in (I wondered why no-one else slept with him) and crawled into bed on either side of me, providing a little natural insulation from his grinding. I woke at one point to see one of them facing off directly toward me, with the gentle whoosh of his snoring blowing across my face. Back to sleep immediately, think manly thoughts.

We slept and slept... well, they slept and slept and I kept checking my watch. The darkest part of the night came and went. Dawn came and the sun rose but still they kept sleeping. It was well past seven o'clock in the morning – our *thirteenth* hour of sleep – and still no signs of life. Lyo-ha slept until almost 10am. I couldn't believe it; *sixteen* hours of sleep. Either he was extremely tired, on sleeping medication, or perhaps his body needed to make up for the poor quality of sleep by sleeping longer. They all seemed to do likewise and no-one was really going until nearly noon. Then there was breakfast to have. These guys worked, but they also rested and ate plenty. Out here there was no distinction between work and personal life; it was all one long experience. You ate, slept, washed, worked, etc together. There was no personal space or personal time; you were always with someone doing something. All of the men were good friends (you had to be) and I never saw any personal bitterness or fighting. The men were young and old, some already grandfathers (as they proudly told me). They were all Yakuts, solidly built and strong and all able to work and repair all of the machinery that was also part of their crew: bulldozers, tractors, dump trucks, graders. They were rough and ready and tough and reminded me a little of the Dirty Dozen. Zhenya was a compact Charles Bronson – what he lacked in stature he made up for in strength, and Lyo-ha was Telly Savalas – the wise cracking kid from the Bronx. It was a powerful mixture and you didn't want to mess with these guys. At one point they showed me their arsenal of semi-automatic rifles – for killing animals and dealing with *other* threats. They asked if I had a rifle at home to protect my family and I said that in Australia we didn't need that sort of protection – they didn't understand.

I got to understand that when they said "Yakutsk – tomorrow" they meant that at some time during the next 24 hours, whenever that might be, we will get started towards Yakutsk (vs. my implied understanding which was "OK - we'll get going first thing in the morning and be there as soon as we can").

After breakfast and washing and shaving, etc the entire camp had to be dismantled – luckily I had caught them at the end of a "contract" and today was the day to pack-up and go home. There seemed to be an endless array of tasks to do: machines to move, earth to move, latrines to demolish, camp kitchen to bulldoze back into the earth, food and supplies and equipment to pack into trucks for the next job. I had spent an hour in the morning securing my bike with all my ropes and tie downs to the tray of Zhenya's Kamaz and ended up spending the rest of the day helping to pack everything into the trucks for their journey home. No- one was in any kind of rush, but everyone was busy and knew what to do. Around lunchtime the chief of road works came by and he and Zhenya had an animated discussion about what needed to be done to clean up the camp site to an acceptable level. Everything had to be gone! We kept working and eventually by 4:30pm we were ready to go.

I was riding with Zhenya in the cabin of his Kamaz for the journey back to Yakutsk – an honoured position. I figured on maybe six to eight hours maximum for the journey – having us there sometime around midnight. We crawled out of camp at a snail's pace and I remembered that, of course, we had to negotiate several kilometres of mud before we could reach any speed. It had rained overnight and the mud was still as thick and as wet as before. Even though the road only rose and fell gently, there were a number of places where we virtually stopped, as Zhenya rode the clutch hard while the wheels of his truck spun full revolutions for only a few inches of forward movement. In some places he rocked the truck back and then forward to try and gain a little extra momentum to get up small inclines and out of divots in the road. At the same time he stroked the gear stick gently and caressed the steering wheel and whispered softly to his truck like a lover: "C'mon baby, do it for me this time...." – and it seemed to work... most of the time.

We were crawling along when suddenly there was a loud explosion behind us – like gunfire. Zhenya cursed, stopped the truck and jumped out – flat tyre! And these tyres are BIG. I thought – "oh well, there goes any hope of getting to Yakutsk today/tonight – maybe tomorrow morning worst case", but was surprised at how quickly the tyre was changed; a completely road-ready spare was immediately on hand and the other men came to help complete the changeover ASAP (one to jack the truck up and two others to help unload the spare) so that within twenty minutes the job was done and we were going again. Zhenya explained that this happens all the time. Back in the mud bath and it wasn't long – even with Zhenya's best efforts and cajoling – before we were stuck fast. As much as the wheels spun we didn't move an inch backwards or forwards. It was difficult for Zhenya but he had to accept a tow from a tractor. Unfortunately, this happened again and again and it took us four hours to clear the six kilometres of mud along this stretch of the track. We were definitely not going to get to Yakutsk today. We did, however, make *some* progress and the countryside quickly changed to low-lying farmland; bucolic – with green pastures, cows grazing and many farms surrounded by forests of birch. The land was rich and fertile and we passed many small villages most situated on small lagoons with muddy tracks leading off the highway to them. We drove on for an hour or so then stopped – we needed to let everyone, including the tractors and earth moving equipment in our convey catch up and re-group. Zhenya and I had cleared the mud first and made good progress since, but it didn't matter; our pace was set by the last and slowest machine. We waited over an hour for them to turn up during which time I was invited into the cabin of another driver's truck for a tea of canned pork (more congealed fat than pork), bread and jam. I was their guest so was offered most of it. I ate most gladly but discretely discarded my *fourth* sandwich of canned pork as there was only so much of the stuff that I could eat.

Eventually everyone caught up – we were a convoy of ten machines. We pressed on for another hour until dusk and turned off the road at a small village and pulled up at a farmhouse. It was on the shore of a small lagoon, had a neat yard with chickens, calves and ducks wandering about. It had a small farm house and another shed in the yard which served as a kitchen and dining hall – it reminded me of my nana's holiday house on the central coast of NSW, where I used to spend summer holidays. It even came complete with Ma and Pa – one doing the cooking and serving and the other smoking and talking men's business with Zhenya and the others. I couldn't believe it, I walked in to find a long table stacked high with food of all descriptions; some on tiered platters – there was fish, soup, potato and stew, cooked meat, bread, tea and sweets. This was a driver's secret. The old woman wore a colourful dress and headscarf and had smooth brown ageless skin. We ate heartily, joked about my bike and drank heavily.

I was wondering where we were going to sleep – there seemed to be other small huts nearby but after dinner but the question was resolved quickly when I was led back to Zhenya's truck where I was offered the drivers bunk to sleep – a prized position. Valerya – another member of the Dirty Dozen – slept across the front seat with his head on the driver's seat, his waist and legs on the passenger's seat and his upper torso wrapped around the gearstick; I couldn't imagine how uncomfortable this must have been but he seemed happy. Thankfully the cabin was just wide enough for me to stretch out full length and the last thing I remember was Valerya telling me about how he had served his two mandatory years in the Russian army (in the 1970s) in Mongolia and that his son was a doctor working in Yakutsk. I tried to keep the conversation going but failed miserably and drifted off to sleep on Zhenya's favourite pillow.

***

I slept late as did everyone else. There was another feast for breakfast at Nana's and there were chores to do around the village – perhaps this was a barter system of sorts; the men worked on repairing tractors, moving earth and generally cleaning up in return for food and lodging. Finally, at about 1pm we were off. We made slow but steady progress, but it was uncomfortable; I had to lean back then fold my long neck like a giraffe inside an elevator and hold that position to avoid my head piercing the roof of the cabin at each bump in the road, of which there were many. Again, like my ride the day before, these trucks were strong and reliable but they seemed to amplify every undulation in the road. I kept looking down from the cabin at the road and imagining how I might ride it and how much faster it would be – but that was pure fantasy at this point. And the weather was fine and clear – finally a good travelling day and here I was holed up in a Kamaz with a Yakut Charles Bronson. He had about as much conversation as Charles Bronson too and this suited me fine; I was "happy" to watch the countryside roll by in silence keeping my thoughts to myself. We didn't get too far before some road works delayed us further taking us down a long muddy sidetrack, followed by truck cleaning (1hr), followed by a picnic afternoon tea/late lunch (another 2hrs) complete with campfire, canned pork and noodle stew, beer and vodka and some sleeping in the sun. At this rate it would take a week to get to the Yakutsk. I tried to relax and enjoy the fantastic hospitality they continued to offer me.

We eventually packed up and drove on into the dusk. We got to about eighty kilometres from Yakutsk and pulled up for more tea and food at a roadside diner; I didn't know what is was, but driving certainly made them hungry and thirsty (and often). Again we had to wait for the slowest vehicles to catch up – this time two more hours! It turned out that this was a staging location for their machinery, so we spent the next few hours moving and parking most of the road building machines. It was close to midnight and now we were down to two trucks and twelve men; six in each cabin plus me! We drove on like this for another three hours with my face pinned to the windshield and my backside to the rear bench wedged in between two other men.

***

We arrived at the mighty Lena River in the darkest part of the night and looked for a ferry to take us across the river to Yakutsk. After a few false starts we were told that the next ferry was not until eight o'clock in the morning (it was Sunday) and that we would just have to wait. We all looked at each thinking through how we could possibly sleep in our current configuration and quickly concluded that the only option was to jump in the tray of the truck and find a suitable position to stretch out (it was covered in the blue tarpaulin from the huts so provided some shelter from the elements). It was dark, cold and windy and the cabin of the truck was warm and cosy, but reluctantly I climbed out and over into the tray paddling my way through our payload of food, bedding, furniture, drums of oil and spare parts. After some wriggling about I carved out an "S" shaped impression to curl up into. The tarpaulin was flapping in my face so I propped it up with a large Kamaz oil filter and somehow drifted off to sleep. The other men, well practised in the art, did likewise.

The ferry did come as promised and we did make it across the river to Yakutsk. There were other cars and trucks travelling too and I had a number of people come up to me and ask about where I was from and what I was doing – I was even asked to sign a number of autographs for complete strangers, which of course I did, always with my best wishes (what else can you say?). We drove through the back streets of Yakutsk to Zhenya's house. These parts of the city were semi-industrial and also had many shops and auto repair works. The roads were paved and I couldn't get over how good this felt after spending so long on rocky dirt tracks; it was good not to have to constantly worry about what holes, divots etc were coming up in the road and what evasive action to take.

Zhenya, his wife and son lived in a simple dacha on the outskirts of town, under the long bluff cliffs that run parallel, but back from the Lena, marking out the perimeter of Yakutsk. It was a wooden cottage with a high pitched roof, white lace curtains in the windows with a green flowering creeper growing up and over parts of it – it looked homely. Zhenya's wife was there to greet us and she had prepared a feast to welcome the crew home – including me. She cooked shashliks over hot coals which we ate directly and then moved inside to a table packed with much food and settled in for a long lunch. There were the customary vodka toasts including one I was called upon to make – mostly in English, expressing my sincere thanks for being rescued by them all.

Later in the afternoon it was time to examine my bike. There were virtually no motorcycles in Yakutsk (impractical for the ten months of sub-zero temperatures experienced here) and therefore no motorcycle mechanics, so Lyo-ha volunteered to examine my bike himself. We got the bike out of the truck and into Zhenya's large garage and Lyo-ha quickly discovered that my oil had run low and had gone off, now giving off a strong and unpleasant smell that quickly filled the garage. Lyo-ha drained the oil and then with much nervousness on my behalf began pulling the cover off the engine. A mechanic I was not, so I studied his every move carefully and thankfully he carefully placed each part with its associated nuts and bolts together on the floor as they came off. He quickly located the problem, and then it was the moment of truth – was it going to be a quick fix or something more serious? Sure, I had crossed the Road of Bones, but at what price?

Big Mama's House

As soon as he slid his finger across his throat and said in his best English "ghum ovah" I knew that the game was indeed over. Lyo-ha carefully pulled the lightly baked clutch discs from the engine and showed them to me. These had worn severely from my incompetent riding and were now slipping over each other giving no traction and hence no drive to the engine. A search party was formed and they went scouring the auto-markets of Yakutsk in vain for replacement parts; for these were proprietary parts and the nearest Kawasaki dealer was ten thousand kilometres away in another country – but at least we had tried. After some complicated preparations, I managed to speak with my local dealer at home; *he* could have the parts within two days but then it would be over to an international courier to get the parts to *me* in Yak-frigginkutsk. We even contacted a dealer in Hong Kong but I was not confident ordering over the phone from a third country in a second language and anyway, all the major courier companies quoted three weeks for delivery regardless of whether the parcel originated in Asia proper or in Australia – they all went via Europe. I called my wife who immediately got onto the job – another faultless performance and total encouragement at my nadir. It was now over to a chain of events and string of people outside my control and influence so I just had to sit back and wait for my package to arrive. A couple of weeks in Yakutsk were not on my agenda, hard to contemplate let alone follow through on, but I had little choice and I was with people who were looking after me impeccably. In spite of this I was deeply depressed – if only I had paid more attention and perhaps checked everything more often perhaps this could have been avoided? And I suspected that riding in and out of first and second gear (only) hard on the clutch over some of the worst roads in the world for two thousand kilometres had violated the guidelines in the front of my motorcycle handbook where it said "...*this product has been manufactured for use in a prudent manner by a qualified operator* " – I had failed on both counts. There was some contingency in my plans, but a delay of *weeks* would require some serious re-planning. Oh bugger.

***

That evening, Zhenya's son Leonid suggested we go into the city and take a look around. He was eighteen years old, had finished school two years earlier but was now completing further exams so he could (hopefully) enter college to study "business management". University students were exempt from the compulsory 2 years of military service and I wondered whether this was also a factor. Leonid, or *Lonya* as he was called, was a typical eighteen year old; he had a car (which didn't work), was shopping for a new mobile phone, had an over-clocked PC where he surfed the internet and played car racing games on pirated software with his friends, was highly fashion conscious (about both his appearance and his clothes) and had a girlfriend of sorts. We met his cousin and a common friend in town and walked the city's many large squares and the long main street (ul. Lenina). It was a warm summer night with the slowly setting sun casting long shadows and splashing a lovely golden hue over everything. Even though it was Sunday, the streets were full of people, especially the young crowd. Yakutsk was definitely a prosperous and thriving centre – powered by the region's immense mineral wealth, which consisted primarily of gold and diamonds in copious amounts. We crossed the town's central square which was full of young people and families enjoying the last hours of the weekend, children playing and young couples doing what young couples do on Sundays. We walked along the main street past the classically designed Pushkin Drama Theatre (complete with portico and columns), past many shops, institutes and the Sakha Opera and Ballet Theatre which unfortunately was closed for the summer. We ended under a massive statue of the revered father of Yakut literature Aleksey Kholokovski – it was at this point that I wish my research and knowledge was better – I knew the name but not the details. Yakutsk started as a Cossack settlement in the mid 1600s and despite of the fierce permafrost still had a few older traditional wooden buildings remaining which, although in various forms of subsidence and deterioration, provided some attractive relief from the rows and rows of ugly soulless block apartments.

We came to the end of the main street and to a boulevard running in a long arc with a canal and fountains on one side and Yakutsk University on the other – it was a break from the traditional soviet city grid blueprint and attractive. The boys then proudly took me to the cinema where they claimed that a number of films had had their world premiere – a claim I found hard to believe but we were a long way East and perhaps one of the last major cities before the International Date Line. I didn't argue and together we looked around inside – it had the look and feel of a traditional cinema from my childhood – thick deep red carpets, gilt edges, big sofa's, popcorn and candy stalls. I wanted to stay, but the boys were keen to do something a little more exciting so we took a taxi to the Yakutsk "Cosmobowl" – the fashionable hangout for all young people in Yakutsk, complete with pool hall, bar and ten neon-lit alleys decked out in space motif. We ordered pints of beer, fried fish and nuts and began to bowl – I could have been at Crown Casino or the Northcote Bowl – and just 24 hours ago I had been crawling along through remote Yakut villages while being tossed around inside the cabin of a Kamaz with a trained killer. The contrast from the street-scape was also stark – everything outside was dirty and dusty (or muddy) and functional but not attractive. Inside was clean, cool and modern. There was a fierce metal detector and an even more severe security guard for whom I had to jettison everything from my pockets (coins, a Swiss army knife, spare nuts and bolts and other bits and pieces from tinkering with my bike), as I tried to explain that no, I was not carrying a concealed weapon (or the spare parts to make one).

We went on to play two games which I handsomely won; I was a good guest, but I had to retain my pride. None of the locals had ever seen anyone use the size 15 balls (the biggest) or throw them down the lane quite as fast and as powerfully as I did. I even managed to bowl three strikes in a row earning us all a free round of beer – they enjoyed that. It was a fun night and some much-needed relief from the torture of the past few days and weeks and my worries about fixing the bike and the delay to my travels. There were a number of times where money was required (for taxi's, food, bowling, etc) where I offered to pay but was refused politely. I was their guest and this meant I shouldn't have to put my hand in my pocket for anything. This really made me feel bad; Zhenya was a truck driver, who worked his backside off all round the country in poor conditions, in extreme weather, away from his family for long periods, and here was I, a well paid overfed inexperienced traveller, rescued and now being treated to an all expenses paid rest in Yakutsk. All I could keep saying was thank you – it was very humbling.

When we got home my bed was already made – I was sleeping on a sofa outside Zhenya's bedroom and across the room from Lonya who didn't have a room as such but a corner of the middle room that he had zoned off. He had a computer at a writing desk and a small cupboard and that was it. There was also a small room between the front room and the sleeping area where there was a stove, a fridge and a large hole in the floor – the purpose of which I never determined. There was always something cooking in a large pot on the stove and the room was warm and rich with aromas.

*** *

Most of the next day was spent, confirming the part(s) required, locating them and arranging for delivery. Zhenya was extremely kind in letting me use his home telephone for a number of overseas calls – again I offered to pay, but again this was refused out of hand; I was their guest and whatever I needed to do to fix the bike was perfectly fine.

Zhenya's wife was a large woman, not tall, but well rounded and fulsome with the inescapable effects of gravity on a middle-aged body just beginning to show. She had a round and fleshy face with droopy sloe eyes, long hair usually tied up in scarf, and a large protruding bottom lip in a permanent and pointed pout. She shuffled rather than walked and was dressed either in her bright yellow dressing gown with wet hair wrapped in a towel or in her practical day clothes. She had a permanent expression that to me projected a heavy sense of ennui. She had a heavy and never-ending workload, responsible for preparing of each and every meal (no take-away dinners here), washing and cleaning, preparing and storing food for the long winter ahead and on top of that looking after her grandson five days a week. They had a twenty-two year old daughter who was married and lived in the city but who worked full-time as a secretary at the river port to help make ends meet. Zhenya and his wife didn't seem to mind but he was a terror and spoilt. I was introduced to her by name, but soon she simply became *Big Mama* to me and that's how it remained for the rest of my stay.

I'm not sure if it was planned already, but on the second day of my stay Zhenya announced that we would be taking a fishing trip up the Lena for two days. I tried my best to be excited about this. He asked me whether I liked fishing and I told him I'd never really spent much time doing it (the truth) and that I'd be keen to give it a go (a half-truth). He said we would leave in the morning and that I would need my camping gear – oh dear – I packed this stuff as a back-up only and now I was *choosing* to use it. I figured out quickly on this trip that I'm a bricks and mortar hotel man and definitely not the rugged

64

outdoor type. Regardless, I was their guest and I willingly and happily came along – if nothing else I would be seeing parts of Russia I never planned to and fishing might be fun? In my mind fishing was something old men who like to chat and drink take up – but here it was a national pastime and fish made up a large part of the Yakut diet as they were available all year round.

We headed off after lunch with "Simeon" (yes, that's how I heard it) – a friend of Zhenya's from the village of Namtse – some eighty kilometres north of Yakutsk on the mighty Lena River. Simeon was a roly-poly man with an air of sophistication I had not seen to date in any of the Yakut people I had met. He wore thick and stylish eye glasses and laughed hard and often when he spoke. He reminded me of and old sea salt, except he didn't drink a drop of alcohol. After a few stops around the city at various shops and markets for supplies (mostly meat and vodka) we headed off ON A PAVED ROAD to Namtse. It would have been an enjoyable ride except for three things: every fifty metres or so, there were large long deep sunken sections of road (from the annual thawing and re-freezing of the loose topsoil), we were driving WAY TOO FAST, and it was a small car – requiring me to hold on tight, body coiled with bent neck to avoid putting my head through the roof at each bump.

We stopped at a traditional Yakut site where, despite my better judgement, I tied a piece of coloured ribbon on a ceremonial wishing tree; at this point I was willing to take help in any form available. There was a lookout too and we surveyed the wide plateau below and ahead of us – there were thick black rain clouds coming our way and I could see the rain falling in sheets in the distance. Someone had begun picking pieces off the lookout structure to use for firewood and there were many bottles of empty vodka below us.

We drove on to Namtse, transferred all our gear into tiny motor boats and headed off up stream. I wore my thick, heavily lined motorcycle jacket to keep the freezing wind out and tried to keep my head below the line of the windscreen (which had already been replaced with a wooden board). The boat was old, rusting and of basic design with the motor started by pulling with all your might on a long cord along with some energetic manual fuel priming and other black magic over the engine. We dropped Zhenya off at some mud flats to collect worms and motored for about five kilometres upstream, against the might current, to a sandy beach and set up camp. The river was huge, dark and fast flowing with many eddies and different currents.

Simeon left us to set some nets so it was up to Big Mama and me to get a fire going (not easy in wind and rain) and put up the tents. It was a hard afternoon of work. After eventually getting a fire going and erecting all the tents, Big Mama ordered the collection of a massive cache of firewood. When I asked her why we needed so much, she said that the fishing would be best at about 3am and that we needed to keep the fire going all night. I looked at her incredulously and said "so we will be up all night fishing?" "Yes, of course!" I'm not sure if she noticed but all the good humour and blood immediately drained from my face. OK, some camping on a river and some line fishing – sure, but staying up all night in the wet and cold reeling clammy critters out of the river – you've got to be kidding. I could think of a million other things I'd rather be doing. I forced a little smile and said "OK, sounds great" and skulked off to look (slowly) for more friggin firewood.

The fire was roaring, assisted by the gale blowing along the beach and it required regular maintenance to keep it burning – a role which I was more than happy to fill; it was the only source of warmth going and I was cold. Big Mama periodically made cups of tea and we sat and talked (in a limited fashion) around the fire. It was getting late, we had been there for hours and still there was no sign of the others. Big Mama kept scouring the horizon for any sign of Zhenya and Simeon, but I could tell she was not overly concerned. It was spitting rain and the river looked treacherous in the half light of the dusk. Finally, at about 10pm we spied them rowing towards the beach; their engine had broken down and they had been rowing all the way back from the places where they had set nets and collected worms. And they weren't alone – as the profile of the boat became larger and clearer it was obvious there were now four men. They tied up and the two new men introduced themselves, the first was a big bear of a man, called Sergei. He was decked out from head to toe in army fatigues right down to his waterproof boots complete with camouflage lining. He had a large round and fleshy head, a large belly that hung over his belt, and his fingers were like pork sausages. He was big all over, well over six feet tall and had a bellowing deep voice and liked to slap you hard on the back often as he spoke. He was a very jovial character. The other man was Kostya – a native Yakut, well dressed in modern sporty casual gear, slightly built and to me, he looked more Chinese than Russian. He was very chatty. Simeon had gone off as soon as they had returned to fetch the nets which were now full of fish. He quickly came back and up to the campfire with at least a dozen fish – they were all still alive and squirming around and he and Zhenya had the unenviable job of gutting and preparing the fish for eating. Sergei put a whole fish on the hot ashes of the fire and I was offered this first and it was delicious. Of course, you cannot eat fish in Russia without vodka so out came the bottles and the drinking and toasts began. In the meantime, Big Mama had steamed a number of the bigger fish so everyone had more than enough. We all listened patiently as Kostya rambled on and on in a sincere but drawn out toast which we eventually drank to. Sergei was much more pithy and punchy, just a few well chosen words and then drink. This went on and on well into the night until the fish and all the other food was eaten. It was still cold and I lay beside the fire and drifted off to sleep on the wet sand. I just couldn't stay awake any longer (I couldn't stand or walk either I was so drunk). They took pity on me and carried me home, depositing me in my sleeping bag where I spent the rest of the night.

I slept soundly until after 9am – I poked me head out of my tent and could only see Big Mama's backside as she tended the fire. The others, I guessed, had fished through the night and were now sleeping. Big Mama had made fish stew for breakfast which was delicious. The weather was only slightly better than the previous day in that the wind had dropped, but it was still cool and overcast. The river was still. I counted eight places where they had planted fishing lines and walked the beach testing the tension on each. They all felt as if they had caught something but I didn't want to disturb their work. Big Mama ordered me onto firewood collection duties and I willingly complied for something to fill in the time. Twenty four hours in the great outdoors in this location had been enough for me – I was ready to move on. At the back of my mind of course was the frustration of being stuck in this place for many days and making absolutely no progress towards my next goal. I had to block these thoughts before they became destructive. I tried my best to enjoy the day. Highlights included watching Simeon gut and clean the fish and trawling a bend in the river for a large net that had been laid down the night before. Sergei called me to the little motorboat and signalled that I should get in and that this would be fun. Leaving shore was an exercise in delicate timing and balance given our payload included two very large men; one false move and we would be stuck fast or be flung head over heels into the brown brackish water. We made it out onto the river and motored about 1km downstream and with innate Yakut navigation skills, Simeon positioned us where he thought the net had been cast. He stopped the engines and threw the anchor overboard and indicated to Sergei to start rowing; we were dragging the anchor across the bottom of the river trying to snag the net. This went on and on for hours and I just couldn't work it out – had they lost a marker or was this just "the way they did things around here?" We went up and down and across the area of the river where the net was supposed to be and each time came up empty handed. The sun had broken through the clouds and it was hot when we stopped to row (which was often). I even pitched in with the rowing at one stage when it looked liked Sergei was heading for a cardiac arrest. He certainly appreciated the rest. I don't know how but eventually we did hook the net and it was *full* of fish. All through this exercise both Sergei and Simeon never showed any signs of anxiousness or even relief when we found the net – it was all just plain sailing and I guess normal. We headed back to the beach, cooked more fish, ate and drank well into the afternoon. Zhenya had to get back to Yakutsk for an unexpected but urgent job and Big Mama explained that this meant we would be leaving early and not camping out another night as they had previously thought. I almost kissed her fish lips I was so happy. Even the boat ride and car ride were tolerable knowing that I would be sleeping on a lumpy but soft sofa under a roof that night.

* * *

In the morning Big Mama had chores for the big guy – I was on potato digging duty. She dragged me out the back door and beyond their back fence to a small paddock full of potato "plants" – is that what you call them? I was a city kid and had never really got down and dirty with veggies so this was all new to me. All of my potatoes came from the fruit and veggie section of the local supermarket – likewise with fish from the seafood section – when I explained this to Big Mama she laughed. She gave me a large bin and a spade and marked out my plot. It was a hot sunny day, near noon and I soon worked up a sweat. I had never dug for potatoes before so very gingerly pushed the spade into the soft soil being careful not to cut into any potatoes. I quickly got the hang of it and after an hour or so had filled the bin. I felt good – I had helped out and contributed (in a very small way) to their well being. The growing season was only three months so most of these were headed for the bottle for eating in winter. I showed Big Mama my work and she gave a small grunt to indicate it was satisfactory and I was dismissed for the day and headed off into town to kill some time.

That night Big Mama had more chores – this time it was cutting the heads off the fish we had caught the day before and then cutting them in half again – for what purpose I could not be sure but I suspected they would end up in my stomach in some form over the next few days. We assumed our positions around the kitchen table like two gunslingers squaring off for a shootout, ready on the draw. The table was covered in a plastic sheet and in the middle was a large thick wooden chopping board. Out came the bucket of fish from the fridge and we were off. Big Mama grabbed the first one in her big fist, turned it over, slapped it down on the table and with one swift and sure precision cut slit the fish open from head to tail. It was like an episode of ER – there were internal organs and blood everywhere as Big Mama aggressively disembowelled the poor creature. She pulled out spinal cords, tugged on intestines, ripped out hearts and livers. She was certainly efficient but it was ugly. I took a deep breath to clear my head. Big Mama was really hitting her stride now and she was keen to show me how to amputate the heads and then cleave them clean in two. I pulled myself together, grabbed a big knife, and watched carefully as she powerfully snapped her knife twice; once to remove the head, and then lengthways, along the head, to complete the job – no nonsense and ultra-efficient. I swallowed hard, tried to block my senses and to think of something pleasant and got stuck into it. As they say, "it was a dirty job but someone had to do it". I didn't have the precision knife skills of Big Mama, but what I lacked in technique I certainly made up for in power. The fish had hard skulls and thick cartilage but I managed to get through a dozen or so before being relieved of my duties. I dashed outside into the cool evening and sucked in a long deep breath of fresh air, took a short walk, tried in vain to clean the fish smell from my clothes and hands and fell into bed tired but still reeking. Fishy dreams followed.

***

Every day, to take some stress out of the situation and to get out of their hair, I had taken to riding the local bus into the city centre. I would trudge along the dirt track past their neighbours' dachas, past the two storey wooden tenement building, past the property whose owner had burnished an oversized bust of Lenin in relief on his aluminium garage door, past the howling dog at number forty one, past the colourful pretty cottage at number twenty seven, past the freshly painted red fence, over the dirt bridge across the swamp and up onto the main road across from the local shops. I got to know every inch of that journey in detail and could walk it blindfolded. I had my routine: into town at ten o'clock, to the library to write a little, lunch at a cafe, ice cream from the lady on Prospect Lenina, walk some city blocks or an excursion, check and write emails at the Sakha Telecom office, sit on a park bench for an hour or so, catch the bus home, buy some treats for Big Mama at the shop (chocolates and biscuits her favourites) and perhaps a litre of milk which I would devour on the walk home. They all knew me on the bus, at the library, at the Sakha Telecom office and at the shop near Zhenya's home. I was a regular. It was depressing. For a little variety I started buying my daily dose of milk on the way into town and drinking it on the bus. I don't think they had ever seen a grown man drink so much milk before. In fact, most adults here did not drink milk and it was mainly for children and perhaps for odd cups of tea.

I would normally get home at around nine o'clock in the evening (still daylight) and usually Big Mama had some dinner prepared or something she heated up for me for which I was always grateful. I tried to eat enough in town so as not to need more food when I got home but whenever it was offered I of course could not decline. One evening I got home and Big Mama had buckets of wild mushrooms in the front room which she had collected that day. She had spent hours walking in the nearby forests finding the best mushrooms. They had a brown/yellow colour which in fact was a skin that needed to be peeled off before cooking or eating. Big Mama pulled out a little stool, indicated for me to sit on it NOW, gave me a sharp knife and showed me how to peel and inspect the mushrooms. I had a huge bucket to get through and we sat together watching Russian soap operas and old films well into the night. If nothing else it was therapeutic and at least I was able to help out a little more. Big Mama was very hard to read; her expression was almost always the same, droopy eyes, bottom lip pout and the shuffle so I took some advice from my guide book which suggested the thing that all women in Russia love is receiving flowers as a gift. I didn't feel confident from past experience elsewhere, but given the number of specialist flower shops (even here) and the number of times I had seen smiling couples on the street, the woman grasping a bunch of fresh flowers, I figured I had nothing to lose. The flowers were outrageously expensive but Big Mama loved them, so that was great and from that point on the tension seemed to ease a little. At least the pout receded and I got a smile, albeit a brief one.

***

One evening I came home at my usual time to find a deserted and locked dacha. There was only the family dog – a mangy mutt – to keep me company. It was still light but the dusk was coming earlier and more rapidly each day as we neared the end of summer and it was getting perceptibly colder in the evenings too. I felt sure they couldn't be too far away; they knew my hours and, in spite of being a burden to them, I knew they wouldn't leave me out in the cold for too long. Half an hour passed, then an hour, and still no sign of them. It was now after 10pm and it was getting dark. A concerned neighbour came in to check on me – I reassured him that I was perfectly fine and happy to wait outside until Big Mama and Zhenya returned. I decided to sit and wait on the back porch on some makeshift seats they had installed, but no sooner had I sat down than the dog began to nuzzle my legs, followed by some sharp tugs on my shoelaces, followed by some aggressive snaps at my feet. I got up and walked around the yard but the mutt wouldn't stop. Previously we had been on cautiously friendly terms, but now with his master gone and hunger setting in I was "in play". He was chomping on my feet as if they were plates of fillet stake. He was in a frenzy, and my state of mind had progressed now from mere *annoyance* to *outright fear* and I think he could sense it. I grabbed my bag, and lurched like Quasimodo to the back gate dragging the mutt along with me, only releasing him with a powerful drop punt as I hurdled the back fence to safety. I retreated to a small hill behind Zhenya's garage and sat down to compose myself and audit my body parts. I cursed the dog, I cursed Yakutsk and all its people and I cursed myself for getting into this situation; I was totally dependent on others and hated it. I had taken a motorcycle touring "holiday" for the freedom and independence it offered and here I was stuck outside some run-down matchstick hut on the outskirts of a negligible Siberian town, in the middle of the night, fearing for my own safety, trapped by my own incompetence - ARGH!

Big Mama and Zhenya eventually arrived at about 11:30; while working that day Zhenya had fallen from the top of his fully loaded truck to the ground smashing his ankle and couldn't walk without the assistance of others and needed crutches. All bad karma immediately vanished as I helped him into his dacha. Truck driving was his livelihood and this could have a serious impact on

71

his ability to work. I felt bad that I had cursed Zhenya and all his people; their hospitality had been faultless and continued to be so until the end of my stay.

***

In terms of excursions, I had to pace myself. The highlights included the Treasury and the Permafrost Institute. They had to open the Treasury especially for me and I was the only person on my tour and had a dedicated guide who spoke a little English making for an interesting tour. The wealth of the Sakha Republic is incredible; they produce 99% of Russia's diamonds and many tonnes of gold every year. The museum consisted of raw/natural gold and diamonds and other precious and semiprecious stones, traditional and modern jewellery using these materials, cut diamonds, gold bullion and ingots of silver and the even more valuable platinum. I had never seen gold bullion up close and it was indeed impressive – the bar on display, about 12 inches in length, 4 inches across and 2 inches in depth was worth almost half a million US dollars! The smaller ingot of platinum was even more valuable. There were so many diamonds on display I was overawed. It was only within the last fifteen years that the Sakha Republic had moved up the food chain from simply being a producer of raw diamonds (that were sent to other parts of Russia) to cutting, polishing, designing and fashioning jewellery. Some of the designs were exquisite with other precious stones added to make dazzling pieces both classic and modern in design. I wondered out loud who in Yakutsk would be buying such pieces and my guide explained most were made for competitions and bought by the Treasury for permanent display here. Only a small number of pieces were sold privately and mostly to people outside of Yakutia. In one cabinet there was a complete collection of small to large natural diamonds – the largest weighing in at a dazzling *130 carats*. I'm no expert in diamonds, but even to my blunt eye it was huge and beautiful. My guide explained that the brightest diamonds have exactly fifty seven facets, twenty three on top and thirty four underneath (I think). For some reason this produces the most sparkling effect. It was breathtaking and the visit had helped lift my spirits. I just hoped that the revenue from all of this natural wealth would be spent wisely and justly on much needed infrastructure around the republic vs. being pocketed by crooked cronies in government or greedy "businessmen".

***

My visit to the Permafrost Institute was exhilarating for other reasons. I caught the number seventeen bus from the city out into the suburbs where the Institute was located. The Institute consisted of many buildings in a campus arrangement where it seemed in the past many people had worked and lived, devoted to studying the nature and effects of this massive layer of frozen soil covering almost 50% of Russia's surface. Today it was less populated but still fulfilling its original purpose. I found the main building – with grand but crumbling facade and a big cement statue of a mammoth out front. I entered the lobby and waited until 2pm – the designated time for me to meet one of the scientists here for my tour. A young, dark, good looking and well built man introduced himself while I was waiting – he was a Peruvian scientist from Japan, studying earthquakes and construction techniques. He was coming in from a field trip to have a shower and clean-up. I hadn't bathed or showered or cleaned myself in any meaningful way for almost two weeks and almost decided to drop the tour and follow him to the showers – I was desperate but good manners dictated I follow through on my plans and persist for another few days with my powerful body odour. I hoped that in the cold my emissions would be reasonably inert and innocuous. "Dr Marc" was right on time (I didn't catch his last name). He was a short, well-preserved older man with grey hair and beard and sparkling blue eyes. He was genuinely pleased to see me and very interested in Australia, especially our climate. He was a geologist and had spent all of his life in Yakutsk at this institute (and in the field) studying permafrost. Initially I felt sad for him; it seemed such a lonely and single-focused job to devote a lifetime to, but his family was here, he was healthy and happy and seemed genuinely excited about his work. We put on warm coats and he led me downstairs and underground some fifteen metres where it got very cold very quickly. At fifteen metres underground we were in the middle of the permafrost layer in a special room devoted to its study. It was a constant minus five degrees Celsius here all year round while outside, on the surface, temperatures ranged from the high thirties (hard to believe) to minus fifty degrees. The soil here was like concrete and the ceiling and man made walls were covered in the most beautiful ice crystals – very large and with many facets and shapes all sparkling like diamonds in the artificial light. The crystals were formed from water vapour coming in from the

73

ventilation and from the water vapour people breathed out. Some of these crystals were many years old and were themselves the focus of research. The ceiling was low and I accidentally broke a few off as I bumped my head, an offence for which I was profusely sorry. Dr Marc didn't seem to mind, he was more fascinated by my height than the damage I was causing, but he did eventually ask me to stand in one corner while he explained more about the permafrost. He pointed to some frozen roots and vegetation in the soil – intact and over *ten thousand years old* and I could touch it – incredible. Permafrost was created during the last ice age and is no longer being created. It covers much of Siberia and runs from just a few metres thick in some places to over one thousand metres in others.

Understanding how this stuff worked was critical in the development of the far north east of Russia and across Siberia more generally. How to build apartment blocks that won't subside within five years, how to lay railroad tracks and build roads that will be stable and long lasting, how to grow crops etc. were all critical questions that needed to be resolved. Dr Marc pointed out that the permafrost layer helps provide stability in earthquake zones, taking some points off Richter scale impacts so keeping the permafrost intact where ever possible was critical. After about an hour underground my head was starting to hurt from the cold and all the information I was trying to absorb so we headed upstairs back to the Institute proper.

My body odour was a problem, if not for others then certainly for me. I stank and I knew it. All I had to do was sit still for a little while before the odours wafted up into my sensitive olfactory system. Pongo. Could others smell this too? There was no running water or bathroom as such at Zhenya's dacha – he did have a banya, but that took some organising and I think was more of a group event. He did have a semi-enclosed shed in the backyard with a tank of cold rain water on it connected to a little pipe with a tap – I tried my hardest but I just couldn't get undressed and under it. In the end I just resorted to splashing my face and under my arms every now and then. It was freezing. My feet were the worst so I began washing them daily and trying to keep my socks clean, but I think there were a few people glad to see the end of me, especially in the hot and stuffy Sakha Telecom internet room.

***

I also managed to squeeze in a visit to the *Park of Culture and*

74

Fun – set in a lovely pine tree forest near the centre of town with sad run-down amusements and rusty rides. Most people just strolled along the pleasant pathways, took picnics or sat and soaked up the weak sunshine in the late evening. I watched in horror as a group of young people enthusiastically strapped themselves into a forty year old mini roller coaster and had themselves flung around a short and tight course where each piece of track rattled and shook as they passed over it. They all screamed with delight and enjoyed it and, thankfully, all made it safely to the end of the ride. The other highlight of my visit was Zhenya's birthday – it was another huge feast with many of his extended family attending and cramming into the front room of his tiny dacha. I didn't know what to buy him so went for the safe option of a bottle of the best Russian vodka I could find which he certainly appreciated. It was a strange meal; people came and went, ate quickly, the TV was on and distracting people – but there were many toasts and a core group who stayed at the table to celebrate (including me). His son and daughter were there and both gave him cards and gifts. I felt intensely like I was intruding on a private family event, but I was seated especially next to Zhenya and that's where I stayed for every toast and I ate from every plate and didn't leave until the celebrations had concluded.

***

Near the end of my visit I had taken to visiting the FedEx office in Yakutsk morning and evening to check on my parcel of spare parts. The lovely Marina was always extremely helpful and courteous but spoke only Russian so our conversations were difficult and not so productive. Helga (that's what I decided to call her) on the other hand was an older and more officious woman. She was tall, solidly built with short peroxide blonde hair, tanned skin and blue eyes. She didn't seem pleased to see me on any of my visits. I could see her brain ticking away as she formed complete sentences in English before spraying them at me like a water canon against the wall. I asked many questions about my parcel "Where is it now?", "When will it arrive?" "Can we do anything to speed it up?" as you do when you are desperate. To all of these I got an impassive response in a slightly irritated tone "youh parrrcel vhill be hee-ah tomorrow. Sank yuh". This was not a conversation starter or an invitation for further discussion; the next step was out the door. Nevertheless, I always thanked them for their help and left politely, cursing them as soon as I got out the door. I was almost apoplectic when on the day of scheduled delivery I turned up and they had already written me a note in broken English "your parcel left Moscow yesterday but due to technical difficulties it cannot be located. Please come back later." My previous parcel did eventually arrive and I high-fived Marina and punched the air in excitement. This really rocked their collective psyche, but I was just so happy to get my ticket out of Yakutsk; two weeks is a *long time* in a small Siberian town.

Nervously I went to Zhenya's garage and looked at my bike and the pieces on the floor. I had never been inside an engine of any kind and this was daunting. Luckily I had exploded diagrams of the engine and my friends had sent me the relevant pages from the repair manual. There was nothing else to do but get started. Lyo-ha was off working a contract somewhere in the Siberian wilderness and I was alone. I followed all the instructions to the letter, found a home for each piece and miraculously the bike started and ran first time. I was overjoyed and so was Big Mama when I told her.

In the morning I packed up and prepared the bike. It was cold and it was raining – perfect. I had spent two weeks in Yakutsk and almost every day had been cloudless. I was the rainmaker. I gave Big Mama and Zhenya some special souvenirs from Australia and thanked them sincerely for all of their help. It was a brief farewell – we took a final photo together and I was off, into the rain and mud once again.

I didn't get more than five kilometres before I noticed that my temperature gauge was reading off the scale what was going on? I had connected everything back as it was before, sure some coolant had spilt but it still looked as if there was plenty left. WRONG. My coolant had almost been drained completely and I was running the bike with no mechanism to remove heat from the engine. I immediately stopped, found a shop and bought five bottles of pure water and filled up the radiator and limped back into town to a garage – Yakutsk had a magnetic pull on me and I couldn't escape. In a way I was relieved; it was cold and wet and leaving a day later was no drama. I found a garage, bought some coolant and filled up the radiator – problem fixed. In the course of doing this a man in a new car came into the garage needing his tyres repaired. He introduced himself and I started to explain what I had been and wanted to do – he stopped me mid-sentence and said yes, he knew all about my trip and promptly placed a *thousand* rouble note in my hand! I of course refused and gave it back to him, but he insisted and in the end placed it in my luggage on the bike. I didn't understand, but I kept the money and he drove off.

Afterwards I cruised the streets looking for a lock up for my bike for the night when all of a sudden a young driver in a modern Japanese car passed me and pulled me over to the side of the road. He jumped out and introduced himself – his name was Mischa and he was a member of the *Nord Brotherhood* – the Yakutsk equivalent of the Hells Angels. He wasn't riding due to some mechanical problems but he immediately got on his mobile phone and called the president of the club – Sasha, to come and meet me.

Within ten minutes Sasha and Sergei were with me. Sasha was a young baby faced, well built Russian. He wore full leathers, a bandana around his mouth and neck when riding, had a shaven and tanned head, a fluffy trim brown beard and big round bright blue eyes. He rode a Honda V twin chopper with leather tassels hanging from the handlebars – images of Easy Rider sprang to mind. It was Friday night and their regular club meeting. I explained what I was doing and where I was going and they listened intently nodding their heads and passing on much good advice. I was invited back to their clubhouse (which in reality was a small converted garage). We made a small convoy and rode across town. Sasha seemed to know everyone and, at each traffic light where we stopped, he chatted to the drivers in other cars. We pulled up at their garage where Igor – another member of the Brotherhood – keyed open the massive lock on the door. Inside was a small table, bench seat and the president's chair – a massive carved wooden chair in the shape of a simple throne. Werewolves and bears were emblazoned on the woodwork and these animals seemed to be the theme of the club. There were also trays and trays of worms (for fishing). Igor bred worms and his wife sold them at a shop in town – it was a very good business he said.

Sasha quickly dispatched his lieutenants to get food and drink and soon we were deep in discussions about bikes, life in Yakutsk, politics etc. It was a fun evening and we drank and ate well into the night. Sergei had disappeared earlier but returned at about 10pm with some equipment and spare parts – he had noticed that my panniers were unstable (read: almost falling off) and needed stabilizing and he had spent the last two hours scouring Yakutsk for the necessary parts – incredible. He and Sasha got to work on my bike, drilling, bolting and angle grinding in a frenzy of repair work. They quickly finished and it was indeed a good job for which I thanked them sincerely. All through the evening Sasha kept plying me with spam and bread and beer so that by the end of the night I thought I would burst – I just couldn't take any more. I suggested that it might be time for a shower and some sleep before my big ride tomorrow and Sergei immediately offered his apartment – his wife was a flight attendant and away on a trip and it would be no problem to stay with him. *Shower? Running water? Hot water?* Music to my ears – I couldn't remember when I last bathed and I sank into the bath and soaked for a long, long, long time that night.

In the morning, Sergei cooked me a full breakfast and then he and Sasha escorted me out of town and to the ferry across the Lena – some hundred kilometres away, incredibly helpful. These bikers were good fellows indeed.

As I sped away across the countryside, my two week stay in Yakutsk didn't seem so bad after all; I had been rescued from the middle of nowhere by am incredibly generous and hospitable man and his colleagues. I had been welcomed into his family and shared many things with them, I had explored a frontier town, hopefully understood the Yakut people and their culture a little better, I had seen fabulous wealth in gold and diamonds, I had seen and touched ten thousand year old life in permafrost and been granted honorary membership of the Nord Brotherhood motorcycle club. What else could I ask for?

Strange Bedfellows

We waited until the ferry was full – there was no schedule as such, the ferry just ran when it was full – no earlier, no later. Cars and mini-vans approached periodically and were directed with precision onto the ferry deck by the captain's son so that eventually, as the final vehicle – an old bus full of Russian tourists – was placed, there wasn't an inch of wasted deck space. Finally, at 12:30 we pulled away from the shore and headed downstream on the Lena. I had been talking with a local Yakut "businessman" who used the ferry often. He made some disparaging remarks about the Russian tourists. This was the first sign of any ethnic resentment I had come across; it was gentle and mostly harmless but nonetheless there it was. I guess you can't build a mighty empire across eight time zones incorporating so many different races, occupying their land with enforced collectivisation without *some* issues. He shared his sunflower seeds with me – this seemed to be a universal dietary supplement in Russia; everyone nibbled on them as a snack and I had seen many desperate Babushkas selling them on street corners in Yakutsk.

We sailed downstream past a bleak procession: first a prison, followed by the huge smoke stacks and grey block buildings of a cement factory. Everything was old and dusty and crumbling and the cement factory belched big plumes of thick heavy grey smoke into the sky. It was a scene straight from the industrial revolution. The waters of the Lena here too (like upstream on my fishing expedition) were also brown and murky, and the river was low creating the need for an extra long downstream leg to avoid bottoming out on sandbars.

There was much interest in my bike and many people stopped to inspect. I watched all of this at arms length from across the deck and didn't engage any of them in conversation – I just wasn't in the mood. My system was still clearing the huge payload of Spam I had been force fed the night before. Sergei had kindly made me a very large bowl of pilmeni with bread and jam for breakfast, so at least there was a little variety for my digestive system to process.

We pulled up on the far shore and I followed a driver of one of those ubiquitous grey Russian combi vans whom Sergei had lined up to show me the way to the "highway". This road was marked in my Russian Road Atlas (2004 ed.) as a major *motorway* running North-South linking Yakutsk (in summer – at least) with the railhead in Aldan, and further south to the main Trans-Siberian line that stretches across all of Russia. It was a dirt road of slightly better quality that what I had been riding pre-Yakutsk. It was wider and firmer but still had bad stretches of pot holes, mud and soft surface. Where the road was hard I could get into third gear and reach the blistering speed of 60kph – unheard of until now. Trucks were more frequent too, as this was the main freight route to Yakutsk (while the road was passable and the river crossable). For a few months, between September and November, the road is a mud bath and/or icy and the river is not hard enough or thick enough to travel across, so Yakutsk is only reachable by airplane – a tough and expensive place to live with almost everything imported.

The sun tried hard to break through the large billowing clouds that filled the sky – every now and then allowing me some sun drenched riding – but it was fleeting and I was amazed at how quickly the sky changed – the clouds moved quickly and soon I was riding under heavy thunderclouds. It's funny, I never really thought too hard about the weather when I planned the trip – I just assumed it would generally be fine, but now it was almost an obsession. I was looking at the sky almost continuously: was I heading into rain? Which way were the clouds moving? How fast? Etc, etc. But it wasn't the rain I needed to worry about today, it was mud. More frickin mud. I hated it. And just for some variety this stuff was lighter in colour (brown like honey) and thicker than the stuff that had brought me unstuck earlier. There were more road works here and there were big earthmoving and grading machines plus a bottleneck of KAMAZ trucks queued up waiting their turn to drive along the thin track of passable road. I joined the queue, hoping not to be driven over – these trucks were huge and here was I, on a tiny single cylinder motorcycle. The drivers heading the other way and waiting for us to pass all shook their heads when they saw me trying to negotiate the deep trenches of mud. It was another first gear and plenty of clutch job, and this disturbed me deeply as it was this kind of driving that ruined my clutch in the first place. Bugger. I cursed and cursed again with my worst filthy language – I thought I had passed all of the hard stuff. I pressed on, stopping frequently where the ground was firm to increase the gap between me and the truck in front so at least I had one less thing to worry about. In places the mud was like the stuff you find on pig farms – wet and sloppy, and it was hard to find a firm path, but I watched the wheels of the truck in front as they splayed the mud apart and tried hard to follow in their path before the receding mud returned. I was drenched in sweat and my heart was pounding – this was awful – again. So much for the "motorway"! Finally, after about ten kilometres, the torture ended and there was a long stretch of hard firm dirt track for which I was more than thankful. I rode on analysing the clouds and weather patterns

The terrain was long rolling hills of endless taiga and not a soul to be seen except for the occasional truck or car that sped past. At least I was able to keep my speed up at around 60 kph. I drove on with just my thoughts for company. The road was still wet from the recent rain and it glistened like a shiny silver ribbon up to the horizon ahead as I rode on into the afternoon sun.

It was getting late in the afternoon and I still had more than 200 kilometres to ride when I pulled up at a petrol station in a truck stop village. A kid on Ural was riding up and down the road highway doing donuts in the dust. A mini-van packed full of people came from the other direction and pulled up at the petrol station. An older lady with long dark semi-grey hair woven in long plaits down to her waist, with thick glasses and beanie jumped out and ran towards me. She reminded me of an old faded Navaho queen. She grasped my hand, shook it vigorously with both of hers and wanted to know everything about me and my journey. I was overwhelmed. She was from Neryungri – a large coal mining and railway town on my route ahead. She was fascinated with me and kept wishing me all the best for my journey and telling me what a fine thing it was to be doing. She didn't want to leave, but eventually the driver of the mini-van dragged her away, and even then she kept on at them about me. I was flattered.

Just before pulling out I noticed my left side pannier was hanging loose; the constant rattling from the road had loosened and removed both nuts from their bolts and the pannier was just hanging limp. I wondered for how long it had been like this. Luckily the frame was still intact and the pannier likewise. I flagged down the kid on the Ural, explained what I needed and within a few minutes we were at a small workshop fishing for nuts and bolts. In return he was keen for ride and I of course obliged – he was thrilled. The pannier was fixed quickly, but I had lost more time and now I was hungry too. I found a roadside cafe that had just closed (it was only 5pm) and convinced them that I was deserving of a meal.

It was another one hundred and eighty kilometres to Tommot (my goal for the day) and with at least three hours of good daylight I headed off along the dirt track. The road quickly deteriorated and was full of ruts, holes and big loose rocks – just what I needed after a big and quickly eaten and half digested meal of shish kebabs. After climbing for some time I crested a hill and was coasting down a gentle slope of straight road when I saw a huge reindeer grazing on the short grass near the side of the road. It was massive and beautiful, with a gleaming coat of dark silver grey fur and large black furry antlers. It had long powerful legs and strode with style. Its antlers were thick with many branches that gave it an extended reach. It stood well in excess of two metres tall and was truly impressive. I stopped and watched it from a distance until it got startled, bucked and galloped away. This experience filled me with pleasure; it was a beautiful creature and so much bigger than what I expected. I drove on and of course the road deteriorated further and the sky blackened with heavy rain clouds – at each turn in the road I hoped I would be heading away from it (the rain), but I always seemed to return to a course that headed directly for the heart of the storm. The soil here was clay and the road a bright burnt orange colour when then sun broke through and illuminated it. I drove on through thick taiga where at times I stole brief glimpses across the wide valleys of the thick forest climbing the hills and reaching to the horizon in all directions, pure and unbroken and silent – breathtaking. I crossed a small bridge over a river at a truck stop and suddenly the earth underfoot turned black and was thick with gravel – coal dust and loose rocks – just what I needed to end the day with. To top it off I reckoned there were more holes than actual road surface and the ride became a continuous bump and grind session with me zigzagging across the road trying to find the "least worst" path – it was more torture. This continued for another *hundred kilometres* as my speed dropped and my mental state flagged accordingly. The road only improved as we started climbing the hills close to Tommot and finally ended on a few kilometres of PAVED ROAD. It was heaven to ride on something smooth again. I thought about getting down on my hands and knees in Pope-esque fashion to kiss the asphalt but the moment passed and I was keen to get shelter for the night so rode on. I crested a hill and came to a valley, the river Aldan, and Tommot – my goal for the day. It was a huge relief; I had driven almost four hundred kilometres and it was dusk. As I approached the Militsia station the gate came down on the road and I was directed to pull over. A middle-aged fleshy-faced career cop approached and asked to see my passport which I handed over quickly. He passed off my papers to an assistant and began inspecting my bike out of curiosity – where was I from, where was I going etc. I asked about a hotel and he said "of course – just over the bridge, left and left again" – fantastic. A man in civilian clothes came onto the balcony of the Militsia station and asked whether I would like to join him and some others in a banya that night. I replied that of course I would, but the conversation didn't go any further and I was handed back my papers and waved off.

I stopped on the large bridge over the Aldan, parked my bike and hopped off to watch and photograph the sunset – it was the most beautiful combination of rich orange pink clouds against a brilliant deep blue sky with the sun just sinking below the horizon – absolutely beautiful. The bridge was huge and swayed and rocked disturbingly as traffic passed over and I was glad to get off it. I followed the directions and came to a long wooden cottage where I was greeted by Nina and Sasha, who were sitting on the front steps smoking and enjoying the evening. Nina was about five feet tall with a short pixie haircut, a permanent smile that revealed most of her teeth but squeezed her eyes shut and a raspy voice. She wore tight pants and a crocodile skin jacket and looked as if she was off to a disco. She cackled as she spoke to me. Sasha was a truck driver and more laconic. I asked for directions to the hotel and they both hoisted their thumbs over their shoulders pointing inside the ramshackle hut – this was it. It was more of a travellers' dormitory than a hotel, with a few large rooms, each with many cot style beds. Natasha, a young woman who did night duty was called and I "checked in". The cottage was cosy and had many rugs and old richly coloured carpets running down the long central hallway where the doors led off into all the rooms. I was shown to mine – it was enormous and had a sitting room complete with big armchairs and a sofa, a fridge and a lonely washbasin hanging off one wall at an odd angle. The adjoining bedroom had big old wooden wardrobes and three single beds all lined up neatly in parallel across the room from window to inner wall. There was another large Persian rug on the floor. The room was empty and all for me! I couldn't believe my luck – just what I wanted – some peace and quiet and some time alone.

I headed out and found the corner store and bought some treats for the night and next morning (beer, chocolate, milk, eggs, tomatoes, bread and an ice cream) – simple pleasures after such a long day in the saddle. I returned to my room and found the door wide open with a mother and her young son standing in MY sitting room. Irena introduced herself and her son Artyom. They were returning home to Khandyga (where I had been) and were staying here tonight. Of course the three beds and sitting room were not just for me – this was a travellers' inn and as soon as people arrived beds were allocated on an as needs basis. Irena looked about fifty but was in reality many years younger, she had short blonde hair and large sad eyes in a tired face reflecting years of difficult living. Her son was eleven and obviously close to his mother. I asked if this type of arrangement (i.e. sleeping in close quarters with complete strangers) was "normal" and Irena replied that yes, this was how travellers on long journeys needing just a night's rest were accommodated. Well, in that case, *I was OK if she was OK.* I felt like I was in an episode of Seinfeld. To further allay any fears that I might be more than just slightly harmless, I showed her the pictures of my family in my wallet and explained briefly what I was doing. She complimented me on having a fine family, smiled warmly and that was that. Her son listened intently as we spoke and as soon as we had finished they went into a huddle. I had already claimed the bed I wanted (not in the middle) and retreated to the "guests lounge" to watch a badly dubbed B-grade American science fiction action flick with the some of the other lodgers. We sat in silence and I drank my bottle of beer and ate my chocolate, laughing in unison with them at some of the more outrageously stupid scenes and dialogue. Artyom sat in the corner on the arm of a couch stealing long glances at me as I ate and watched the TV. I wondered what he was thinking.

The movie became more and more absurd so I headed back to the room. I opened the door to find a large, heavy-set man lolling about on the couch deep in conversation with Irena – I had no idea who he was, but he immediately shook my hand and welcomed me in. I could only assume he was Irena's partner and I immediately offered to move to the divan so that all three could sleep in the other room. He shook his head vigorously as if I had offended him, no, I was to stay put and they would work around me. I felt bad. I had come in, taken a bed and now I was splitting up a family and making one of them sleep on a fold out couch for the night. I was the guest in their country and felt that I should be the one making concessions, not them. The different permutations flashed through my head. Even though it was "normal", sharing a small bedroom with a mother and her son didn't sit comfortably with me. What was the protocol? Who gets ready for bed when? Do you avert your eyes when they get into their pyjamas? Who turns out the lights? What about my snoring? Etc, etc. It was a minefield of etiquette under a layer of cultural quicksand. I decided to get on the front foot and went through to the other room, kicked off my shoes, ripped off my outer clothes and slid quickly into bed and turned to face the wall. I was in for the night and wasn't going to budge – now it was over to them. I shut my eyes (the lights were still on) and tried to clear my mind and bring on sleep (please).

There was some muted conversation and much shuffling about, but shortly after, the lights were flicked off and we were all tucked in. But who was where? I rolled over silently and peaked over the sheets – the big man was next to me and Artyom was in the far bed and Irena had been exiled to the divan. I felt worse. There was nothing I could do now, so I settled onto the hard coils and drifted off to sleep dreaming of reindeer and brilliant sunsets.

In the morning they had already gone before I had fully woken up. Just for fun I read my Siberian guide book and was pleased, in a perverse way, to read that the road leading into Tommot – that section I had ridden last night – "*was the most treacherous section of the highway*". I was glad that was behind me – surely there was no way I was going to have to cover that kind of stuff again?

I went head to head with a big Yakut woman as I cooked my breakfast in the communal kitchen. She was there ahead of me and was heating up a big pot of potato and meat stew and an old woman, whom I think was the owner of the hotel, was also heating up a frypan full of sunflower seeds and periodically coming in and taking handfuls. I started preparing the ingredients I had bought the night before for an enormous omelette. I went to grab the only saucepan left when the old woman, seeing what I was trying to cook, poured her seeds into a bowl, oiled the pan and turned up the heating element for me to use. They were fascinated with what I was making and both stood and watched as I broke three eggs into a glass, whipped them up, poured them into the frypan and added cut sausage, tomatoes and cheese. It was delicious and I quickly ate the whole thing after offering them a taste which they both politely declined.

***

I spent the morning checking over my bike – it was amazing the number of factory-tightened nuts and bolts that had somehow loosened themselves in the course of riding over these rough roads. I checked each and every one and tightened many. Even the twenty seven inch nut at the top of the steering column was loose so that I could easily turn it by hand! I wasn't exactly sure of its purpose, but I suspected it was important and critical to be tight when riding – I had visions of the handlebars coming off in my hands as I

85

tried (and failed) to corner a dangerous bend As I went about my work the old lady owner was belting the living daylights out of the carpets that were hanging up in the yard for cleaning. She might have been old, but she sure packed a punch. Note to self: don't argue about the bill when checking out. One of the other guests, Zhenya, an Asian looking Russian from Ulan Ude, had emerged. I explained that I didn't have a twenty seven inch spanner at which, despite my protestations, he dragged me inside and proceeded to wake up all of the drivers staying at the hotel (it was Sunday morning) trying unsuccessfully to find a spanner. I stood nervously behind him as he banged on each door and they opened, half expecting the occupants to jump up and throttle him, but each was pleasant and explained, standing in their underwear that they in fact did not have a twenty seven inch spanner in their kit. I told him, with no knowledge whatsoever, that the nut was not important and that I would tighten it by hand and get help in the next big town. He was not happy (for my sake) but eventually let it go.

I finished preparing the bike and headed off back onto the dirt highway and towards Neryungri. The riding was slightly easier with an improved road surface and a few stretches of paved road. I made it in good time to Aldan and passed the railway head and the Disney-esque railway station. In Soviet times there had been some secret stuff going on here and even now the city was off limits to foreigners without special permission and the city named on their visa. I continued on through little villages. The countryside and environment was changing ever so slightly as I pressed deeper into civilisation proper. More cars and fewer trucks, more apartments and light industry, some farming and generally just more people more often. The taiga was still thick and covered much of the route, but there were stretches of open plains and scrublands too. By mid afternoon I was ready for a rest and some lunch and I looked for a place to pull over. I found a truck stop and pulled up. There was already a large tanker parked there with a driver having his lunch. I got off the bike and started digging around in my luggage for my loaf of bread and sausage. The driver got out of his cabin and approached. He introduced himself: his name was Tolyic and he was from Neryungri. He asked if I had any tea and I said I didn't – he immediately offered to share his with me and he raced back to his cabin and returned with hot tea, a spare mug and sugar. In addition – and unprompted – he also brought out a large container full of cooked pork chops (there must have been fifteen of them at least) and a bottle of spicy sauce. He insisted I eat as many as I could and I gladly used my loaf of bread to make pork chop and sauce sandwiches which were delicious. I asked him to pass on my compliments to his wife. I got through two large chops, but he insisted I have another so I did. I offered him some chocolate from my kitty but he refused — he seemed to get genuine pleasure from watching *me* enjoy eating *his* food and drinking *his* tea. This seemed to be a common thread in my experiences with people across Russia. He said he worked year- round driving back and forth to Yakutsk and sometimes even to Magadan. He shared my assessment of the roads between Magadan and Yakutsk as "bad". I wished I had a better vocabulary to give some better shades of meaning, but I had the essential aspects covered: mud, bog, icy rivers and broken bridges. He told me proudly that he had a grown son who was a doctor in Krasnoyarsk. When he smiled he revealed an almost complete set of gold teeth — very striking with his blonde hair and tanned skin. He was a big strong man and looked at ease with himself and the work he did. He wished me well and we both headed off in opposite directions, him to the north and me to the south.

The road continued to be solid and smooth in stretches and I made good progress until all of a sudden I heard what I though was a Harley Davidson passing me — a very loud thumping noise right behind me. I slowed and pulled over to discover that it was me making the horrible noise. I shut down the engine and panicked. What on earth could this be? It sounded like an engine problem and I was still over one hundred kilometres from Neryungri. I had no idea where to start. Out of sheer desperation and misguided faith I started the engine again, hoping the problem would just go way — no such luck, it was still thumping away with a deep throated throb jarring through the frame and into my body. Engine off immediately — time to inspect. I put the bike on its stand and started to look around. I found the problem almost immediately: the muffler had come off and had fallen about eight inches, but was somehow still within the bike frame — that was lucky. It had broken away from the engine — the constant jarring had loosened the two bolts that attach the muffler to the frame. I guess I hadn't quite checked EVERY nut and bolt that morning after all. Now I was worried that the muffler pipe had actually broken but "luckily" it was a manufactured join and the loose rear end had simply slid out of position. An hour and a half later I had repaired the muffler and was back on my way.

I started to climb some steep hills in switchback fashion and caught glimpses again of the almost endless taiga behind me. The rain was coming and I skirted a storm as I came into Chulman, the town on the highway at the exit to Neryungri. There was a Militsia post and I was, of course, flagged down and stopped. The station was manned by a single policeman – Andrei, a young fresh faced man from Neryungri. It must have been the end of a boring day, for he was genuinely excited to see me and the bike. He ushered me to a parking spot and called me inside for a cup of tea and some biscuits. It had been a long day for me too and I was happy to take a short rest and receive his hospitality. He took my passport and copied some details down in a big log book. He was nearing the end of his shift and explained that his boss and some colleagues would be here soon and that I should wait for them to arrive. Andrei was slightly built and his uniform was loose and ill fitting, adding to the image of a baby-faced cadet I had in my mind. He had a wife and young child waiting for him at home and he was keen to leave. He filled my cup twice and offered me more biscuits which I politely ate. The station was small and cosy with thick wood panelling and big solid, but basic furniture. One of the main features was the meal table – full of half eaten snacks and packets of tea, coffee and sugar. Soon, two more senior men appeared in the main office. I said hello and introduced myself. They wanted to check out my bike and I happily obliged and we took a few photos together too. Then the most senior man took me aside and tried his best to give me directions to Neryungri (it was another twenty kilometres further on), and also to make it quite clear that I was not to exceed *forty kilometres per hour* for the rest of my journey there. He repeated this a few times and so earnestly that I paid attention and promised solemnly to obey.

The road rose and fell as it made a straight line across the hills to Neryungri. I crested a hill and saw Neryungri rising out of the taiga in the distance. It was amazing – it looked as if someone had chopped the top off a large hill, scooped out a big hole and poured in cement, steel and asphalt; just add water for an instant city. Rows of neatly arranged tall apartment blocks rose up from the edge of the forest and sat astride wide open avenues. There were no dachas or any other intermediate buildings, the apartment blocks just rose straight up out of the taiga in a neat grid about ten blocks square. Neryungri had been purpose built in the 1970's to provide accommodation for the thousands of workers needed to operate the massive coal mine located nearby. I rode into the town centre trying hard to reconcile the streets with my inadequate guide book map. I eventually located Ul. Lenina and pulled up beside an apartment block to check my bearings. I was quickly approached by a man and his son and when I asked them about the hotel I was trying to find, they said they would show me, but first I needed to follow them to the "avtostoyanka" (car lockup); I had stumbled upon the owner of the only car lockup in Neryungri – perfect; I could now lock up my bike and settle in for the night. He gave me directions and I rode off to the entrance where he met me shortly afterwards. His name was Mikhail and he was from the Ukraine and had moved here to be with his wife thirty years ago. His car lockup was huge, was surrounded by a tall wire fence and had a watch tower which was manned around the clock. He cleared a special space for my bike and then offered to drive me straight to the hotel – which I gladly accepted with much thanks. It was just a few kilometres but carting my luggage there in the cold and dark did not appeal – apart from the fact that I still had not reconciled my map so had no idea where to go. I was chauffeured to the front door and Mikhail came in to make sure I was looked after. He didn't leave until all was settled and, before leaving, he gave me his contact number and said I should call him whenever I needed *anything*.

The hotel was a small lodge set in the taiga away from the town centre and I was pleased to be in such a cosy and friendly place. I was also surprised at how cold it was – we were much further south but the air here was cold and the night fresh. I took the chance to take a long catch up bath (in warm brown water again) and slept like a baby in a proper bed.

***

A plan was brewing. Because of my two week delay in Yakutsk I could no longer manage my itinerary which had included both Mongolia and China – one would have to go. Also, if I went across Mongolia I would need to get a new visa for Kazakhstan due to my delay. It was a tough call but it was western China and the Silk Roads that I really wanted to see (and had made special arrangements to visit). I was disappointed to have to cut my itinerary – I had worked through many options but it just wasn't feasible; I had simply run out of time. The new plan hinged on getting across Siberia quickly to reach the Russian/Kazakh border as soon as possible. I had a fixed date to meet my Chinese guide and needed to be on time to start my tour along the old Silk Road in Xinjiang Province in China. The train seemed like the only reasonable option, so in the morning, armed with my

Oxford Russian/English dictionary, clean clothes, shaven face and best smile, I headed to the train station to find out what was possible. My worst fear was that they would refuse point blank and I would be left in no mans' land with my plans. This would mean trying to get down through more of Siberia, across Mongolia and then Central Asia (no China) and get new visas along the way – a further hassle and uncertainty I did not want nor need.

The station was located at the edge of the city at the bottom of the hill and was a grand colourful affair with a big red neon "Neryungri" sign on top, big cement columns with a facade in pastel green and yellow with white highlights. There was a large waiting room with massively high ceilings, big long windows, potted plants and heavy wooden double doors. This was the Russia I knew. The decor inside was entirely functional with large maps of Russia showing the entire rail network (very impressive) – like a cross section showing the skeleton and arteries of a large animal. There were also timetables for the BAM and the trains that ran across the main Trans Siberian route – some even going as far as Moscow. I felt now like I was truly re-connected with modern civilisation and safe in the bosom of Mother Russia. I approached the ticket desk and the guard-dog-like attendant behind the counter where I explained my requirements and was directed to the "baggazhnik" department, back through the waiting room doors and into the administrative section of the station.

I found the door marked "baggazhnik", entered the large long room, stepped over a massive set of cargo scales and found three ladies holed up in a small internal office reading magazines and chatting. I approached and explained my problem (in detail) and asked what might be possible, suggesting that getting to Novosibirsk quickly would be ideal. They listened intently to my story about the Road of Bones and how bad it had been and how I needed to spend two weeks in Yakutsk fixing my bike etc, etc. I showed them the pictures of my family which they all cooed over. They seemed genuinely interested and sympathetic. They were all middle-aged Russian women; strong, sturdy and ample – attractive in a wholesome sort of way. After I had finished they all shook their heads and went into an extended rapid fire conversation. I felt for sure they were going to tell me that they were sorry but that it was not possible. Subsequently there were many questions for me which I tried to decipher and answer quickly. They made a number of telephone calls shouting at ever louder levels with each call. Whatever they were saying there was certainly plenty of emotion and energy involved.

Eventually, Natasha, the woman who had emerged as the driving force in the debate, popped her head out of the office and called me over. She had blonde hair in a fading frizz perm, a round plump face with sea green eyes, slightly Asian in appearance and fashionable pink glasses with sparkling stones embedded in the frame and exuded a maternal warmth which I found pleasant. She told me there would be a train on Wednesday (it was Monday) and that I should come back tomorrow at eleven o'clock precisely to purchase my tickets. I couldn't believe it; I now had firm travel plans on a reliable piece of Russian infrastructure and would, in a few days, be thousands of kilometres further west, with my motorbike, deep in the heart of Siberia, the capital in fact – Novosibirsk. I couldn't thank them enough and they knew it. I shook Natasha's hand, thanked her warmly again and re-confirmed that I would see her at eleven o'clock the next day. I felt now that one chapter of my journey was coming to a close and a new one beginning. I was secretly looking forward to the train journey, a chance to put my feet up, relax and enjoy the scenery without having to worry about the next rut, repair, storm or meal. I was disappointed not to be riding further across Russia and that I would not go to Mongolia, but I was trying to make the best of what remained of my journey and I had already spent over a month in some of the remotest areas of Russia, battling the roads and being swamped with endless hospitality – it was time to move on.

***

Neryungri was not exactly a tourist destination – its sole claim to fame was as the site of the world's largest open cut coal mine. As I walked the city blocks I could, at various points, see the huge open gashes in the earth in the distance where the taiga suddenly gave way to creamy coloured sandy soil that marked the beginning of the mines. My guide book raved about the place and insisted on a visit, but big machines and holes in the ground don't do it for me, so instead I pottered about the city, found an internet cafe, bought some minor spare parts for my bike, washed my bike, ate many kebabs and drank beer in cold outdoor cafes, ate ice creams, dosed up on fresh fruit and tried to get my notes up to date. Neryungri was a tough town, not pretty and with many of its people doing it hard. There was a smattering of small businesses (beauty salons, repair shops, electrical goods) but most of the shops were devoted to the essentials of food and clothing. There was the obligatory statue of Lenin on the main square which, in reality, was a boarded up, weed infested concrete plaza on the main street outside the central administrative buildings. I tried hard to find something pleasant about the city but failed. It was functional, but that was it. Almost everyone worked at the mine and this place was simply their living quarters. I guess thirty years, including some pretty tough times (i.e. when wages weren't paid for months) in a single-industry town with a harsh climate made it hard to move beyond the essentials of housing, heating, transport and food.

The next morning I awoke to snow falling steadily outside my window! I couldn't believe it – I had previously been cursing the daily rain, but this was absurd. I laughed hard; *snow in summer!* I was so glad that I wasn't on the road again today. I just couldn't face riding through snow on those roads – it really would have been diabolical. I silently thanked all of those young idealistic Komsomol Pioneers who so eagerly volunteered to come here from the relative sophistication of western Russia to build the railway line into this remote and inhospitable place.

I headed down to the station again and met Natasha on the stroke of eleven. She was waiting for me and escorted me straight away to the ticket office where she took charge, jumped to the head of the queue (past all of the locals) and purchased my ticket to Novosibirsk. I felt embarrassed for the others, but this was her turf and she took no prisoners. She ordered me back at 7pm with my bike, and then walked me to the cargo loading platform so I knew where to come. Very efficient she was.

***

I spent the rest of the afternoon cleaning and making minor repairs to my bike. The roads had certainly taken their toll – I had lost a couple of important nuts and bolts and needed replacements. The only option was the local Lada spare parts shop so I walked up the road from the avtostoyanka and was amazed at the cornucopia of stuff they had. I put the bolt on the counter that I wanted multiples of, and Boris (he had a name tag on) barely flinched, bent down and pulled out an exact match within a few seconds. I put a washer on the counter that I needed, and again, he didn't move an inch to either side. He just bent down, rifled about for a few seconds in a box and pulled out an exact match – incredible! I looked around to see what else they had – it was certainly re-assuring to be in a place where I could so easily get what I needed. Boris even helped tighten my dangerously loose steering column with the tool kit from the boot of his car.

I returned to the avtostoyanka to find Mikhail looking for me. He called me up to his "office" in the watchtower and we drank cups of tea and ate a packet of sweets he had especially gone and bought for me. His family was from a town near Sochi on the Black Sea, but he had moved here because his wife was a local. He ran his business in partnership with another man and they each worked alternate days – an arrangement he was happy with. He showed me his passport – he was only 8 years older than me but looked at least fifty. He was tall and thin with short brown hair and a peppery beard and smoked continuously as we spoke. His passport was still marked *CCCP* and he had taken just one visit outside of Russia many years ago – to a small city in Japan near Sakhalin. Just in case any one was wondering the visa had subsequently been stamped over in big red letters "USED". He seemed happy with his lot, although I sensed as a younger man, perhaps he had aimed for a little more out of life. He told me that it would be snowing regularly in one month and that winter would last until May. The thought of it made me cringe. After I had finished my third cup of tea and sixth cup cake Mikhail offered to lead me in his car to the train station just to make sure I got there for my appointment. When we arrived I explained it might take some time so, with a touch of disappointment, Mikhail drove off. I'm sure if I hadn't said anything he would have stayed all night doing whatever was necessary.

I drove up onto the cargo platform and found the crew loading the baggage wagon for Novosibirsk. Nikolai (or Kolya as he insisted I call him) was in charge, a big burly man with pot belly, ruddy complexion and sandy grey greasy hair. He wore a red white and blue track suit with "RUSSIA" emblazoned across the back. He immediately came to help me unpack the bike (panniers, bags and spare tyres) and we quickly got it on board into the little vestibule at the end of the wagon. It was packed tight with mail bags and blocks of wood and he re-assured me the ride was smooth and there was nothing to worry about. *A smooth ride*? What planet had he been on? I had forgotten that such a possibility existed – it had been beaten, rattled and shaken out of me over the last month.

There were no taxis so I walked the long walk back into Neryungri. As I entered the city proper a voice called out to me and I spun around to find Alexsei, my host from the hotel in Khandyga. I felt like throttling him, but contained the urge – this was the guy who had told me to catch the barge and ride to Yakutsk – "*there's only a little bit of mud on the road and you'll be fine...*" I asked what he was doing here and he told me that he "lived here too, sometimes". It was definitely a strange conversation. I began telling him where I had been and what I had been doing in the three weeks since we had last seen each other but he stopped me mid-sentence and said he already knew. I thought to myself "definitely getting weird now.. ..time to go" and I wrapped up our conversation quickly. I could sense he was keen to move on too. I walked at a clip back up the main street, periodically looking over my shoulder to see if he (or others) were following me. I found my favourite kebab cafe, ordered a double and cold bottle of dark beer and settled in for long dinner in the fresh evening.

***

I couldn't wait to get on board in the morning. I was at the station early and waltzed in, fresh as a daisy into a sarcophagus-like waiting room. It was packed solid with travellers in various states of disrepair. Many dozing, leaning on each other, bleary-eyed, tired and listless. It looked as if most had spent the night here – I couldn't work it out though; this was the *start* of the passenger train line – perhaps they had come from remote towns by bus or car and arrived in the night?

Eventually the train pulled up at the platform and it was time to board. I ran into Natasha – she had come especially to see me to make sure I got on board safely. I was escorted to my cabin by the attendant, an Asian Russian who was dressed smartly in a hounds tooth waistcoat and black skirt. I settled in and hoped that no one else would be joining me – at least for a while. I was looking forward to some quiet time just looking out the window. Suddenly someone was banging on the window. It was the attendant pointing to the car park. Mikhail had come to say goodbye too. I quickly got up and went to greet him. He shook my hand warmly and gave me a small souvenir from Neryungri – this was completely unexpected and I thanked him sincerely.

Soon I was gazing out the window from my compartment being gently rocked by the rhythmic *clickety-clack, clickety-clack* of the train as it sped south towards Tynda. The taiga stretched to the horizon in all directions – awesome and beautiful. I stretched out on my bench seat and fell asleep. This was great; my own room, but I knew it couldn't last. I wondered who would be joining me and when. It didn't take long to resolve. After taking a quick lunch of fish and salad at the Tynda railway station cafe, I returned to my cabin, pulled back the door to find a tall, solid, middle-aged woman dressed in black pants and a black woollen jumper with a bright red rose pattern. She had short dark hair worn in no particular style, an angular up-turned head that ended in an unfortunate and large pointed chin. She wore thick Mister Magoo style glasses with big circular lenses that made her eyes look very small and buried deep in her face.

There was an uncomfortable silence which neither of us was prepared to break. I don't know why but I just didn't feel like going through introductions again. As a visitor I knew it was poor form but I had done it so many times already, I just felt like a rest. Anyway, was it compulsory? If she felt the need she could initiate and I would happily engage. I did of course acknowledge her with a nod and a smile and then sat back on my bench seat and simply stared out the far window in the corridor while she stared out the near window in the cabin eating her sunflower seeds. And that's how we spent the rest of the day. Keeping out of each others' way – I had my space and she hers. We gave way to each other when necessary and I did leave the compartment regularly just in case she needed some time alone. These arrangements suited me fine and I think they suited her too; she obviously wasn't the talkative type. I did drink my daily litre of milk in front of her but got no reaction.

We stopped often and, at the junction with the main Trans Siberian line at Skovorodino, I bought an ice cream and stocked up on food for the night – rissoles, piroshki and nuts. I ate half of it before I had got back on the train. When I returned to the compartment Olga – that's what I decided to call her – had "slipped into something more comfortable"; a curious wrap around dress in stretch fabric still with the black and red rose motif. Like all of the other passengers, she had her *good clothes* for getting on and off the train and casual comfortable clothes for travelling. I, on the other hand, just had the same old uniform of jeans, T-shirt and long sleeve shirt. It was a *three day* journey and I didn't have a change of clothes either.

Next, I had to negotiate the tricky protocol around sleeping arrangements. We each had our own bunk, but when to go to sleep and what to wear in bed these were more complications than I needed. I finally broke the ice when I asked Olga very carefully, given the nuances that can arise in translation, at what time did she want to go to bed. I think she told me that she never slept or that she would be sleeping when she got home tomorrow afternoon. My translation skills were being tested here – surely she must need to sleep? Whatever she was telling me, I decided to leave the compartment for a while so she could decide to do whatever it was she wanted to do for the night and get settled. Sure enough, when I returned she was tucked in snugly, staring hard at the wall. I followed suit and fell asleep straight away in spite of the bed being a good six inches too short for me.

***

I woke up early and looked over at Olga who was still fast asleep. I tried to sleep more and dozed a little, but by nine o'clock I couldn't stay in bed any longer so got up, got dressed quietly and made my way to the restaurant car for breakfast. I had to pass through six carriages to get there – mostly open berth with bodies flung everywhere at all angles, feet hanging over the ends of beds into the passageway, people eating noodles and drinking tea at little tables, women deep in conversation, men smoking in the little vestibules at the end of each carriage. It was a human obstacle course.

I eventually made it to the restaurant car, which apart from the staff was completely devoid of people. It seemed that nowadays everyone brought their own food and the restaurant car had become more of a convenience store dispensing, beer, vodka, noodles, chips and soft drinks. To top it off, the waitress had some serious attitude and made me feel like I was severely imposing upon them by asking for some basic cooked food and a little service. I persevered, muddled through the menu and ended up with an apple pastry and hot tea – not what I wanted but it was a meal of sorts. I was half way through my meal when who should come in but Zhenya, the guy from the travellers' dormitory in Tommot. He greeted me warmly – it was still early but he already had a skinfull. He sat down opposite me, ordered a small bottle of vodka and a smaller bottle of water – this was his breakfast. He offered me a drink, but I steadfastly refused – I had to draw the line somewhere. He was still more or less lucid so we were able to have a basic conversation. He told me he was from Ulan Ude and that he was in the *shoe business* and that he worked up and down the road and rail network from Ulan Ude to Yakutsk year round. Shoes? Seemed strange but I went along with it. He talked *at me* rather than *with me* and I just nodded and said "uh huh" every now and then to keep things moving along. He didn't seem to notice and kept tossing down shots one after the other. He was only a little man, but he sure could hold his drink.

When I returned to my compartment Olga had arisen and was back in her comfortable train gear. The little shared table under the window was full of her stash of food: bread and butter, tea, condensed milk, a big jar of sugar, homemade biscuits, sunflower seeds and a big hunk of chicken – she was settled in for the day. Olga made tea often and rather than drink it straight from a cup, she liked to pour her tea into a large glass, add milk and copious amount of sugar and then sit and sip it slowly from a spoon – at least she didn't slurp. In the afternoon, she asked where I was from and what I was doing. She listened carefully to what I said and then gave a big sigh and a "tut tut" to indicate (I think) that it was perhaps a risky adventure from her perspective. I asked her what she did; she was an accountant at a major hospital in Chita, where she lived. I knew the answer before I asked, but I asked anyway: did she have a family? She looked out the window and without changing her expression said "Ya adno" or in English, "I am alone". Even the sound of it was cold and solitary. She had two sisters and a mother who each lived in different cities along the rail line. I felt for her and wished her well when she left the train that afternoon. She insisted on leaving all of her food behind for me. I'm not sure if she had packed too much or had been saving it for me, but there was a full chicken breast, a bag of homemade biscuits, half a loaf of bread, tomatoes, cucumbers, sugar and salt – all of which I ate before my journey ended. At various meal times, during our short time together, when I would be eating a serve of instant noodles from those horrible polystyrene bowls with the little sachets of instant vegetables and meat, Olga would look across, frown, "tut tut" and comment on how little and/or poorly I ate. Olga said she was returning to her apartment and, being alone, that she wouldn't be needing all of this food. I felt a little guilty eating her stash, but it was very good, especially the chicken breast.

I always got off, even at the smallest stations and shortest stops, just to stretch my legs and look around. It was fascinating to see the different types of stations, other travellers, people waiting for friends and relatives to arrive, farewells. At some of the longer stops I always made a point of visiting Nikolai in the baggage wagon. He and his small crew were always happy to see me and we managed to string together a few short conversations along the way. Towards the end of my time on the train he became a kind of godfather to me, taking and correctly proudly answering questions from others about me, my bike and my journey. That was nice.

After Olga had departed I hoped for some guest-relief, but after doing the obligatory platform walk at Chita I returned to my compartment to find a man sitting opposite me now. He was hot and sweaty, dressed in jeans and a singlet. He smelt of stale BO, beer and cigarettes and had greasy pock marked skin and a generally unhealthy look. He was more forthcoming than Olga so we introduced ourselves and left it at that. He phoned his family (everyone had mobile phones) and spoke nicely to his son and wife so he was redeemed. He then immediately lay down and fell fast asleep, snoring happily as the train sped into the evening across the rolling hills, farmland, villages and taiga.

The countryside had now changed markedly since our big right hand turn at the junction with the main Trans-Siberian trunk line. We were now in what I would call *prairie lands* – wide open tracts of land between low hills, with much of it under cultivation in small personal plots, numerous farms and even some bred livestock. There were many more villages here too, much closer together than in the remote regions of Siberia where I had been earlier. The taiga lapped at the tracks in some parts and receded in others to beyond the horizon, but it was still thick and lush, although now there were more birch and fewer fir trees. The late afternoon sun streamed golden through taiga as we headed west and deeper into the centre of Russia. I was happy just to sit and watch these pretty scenes as they rolled past my window. My companion snored rhythmically along with the soft clickety-clack pulse of the train.

Eventually I carted myself off to the restaurant to do battle with the waitress to try and get a half-decent evening meal. At least I knew I would be dining alone. Her attitude had improved only marginally but it was still a case of her asking me what I wanted, then she telling me that I could have borscht or nothing. I chose borscht and upped the ante by ordering bread – outrageous. She was young and new to the job, but she had the Russian customer service thing nailed. I was almost finished when two half-drunk men wandered in to the carriage and joined me – Sergei and Andrei, road-workers returning home from a contract further east. Sergei was much older and had thick greasy skin with deep creases and just slits for eyes and mouth with deep smoking lines around it. Andrei was my age and born in the same month – a cause, unfortunately, for a round of vodka. I asked whether they had families to which both replied yes; Sergei was already a grandfather and Andrei's wife was heavily pregnant with their first child but he was too drunk to remember when it was due. Three big cans of beer later, we were shooed from the restaurant – it was almost midnight and well past closing time. We loitered in the vestibule so they could both smoke and then when I suggested it might be time for me to get some sleep they insisted I come back to their open compartment to continue the celebrations. After fumbling through a couple of open compartments, stepping on feet, fingering loose heads and other body parts, turning on lights etc we arrived at their bunks. I was introduced briefly to their travelling friends but made my exit promptly – I think they were too drunk to get upset and I was happy to retire hurt to my cabin which by this time had been vacated. I was sleeping alone! Fantastic! I went to bed knowing I would wake up with a sore head but I was happy. Lights out and dreamtime.

I thought I was having a nightmare based on the Russian language tapes I had studied endlessly to prepare for my journey – "Hello, my name is Ira, what is your name? Hello, my name is Ira, what is your name?" kept pounding through my head relentlessly until I woke to find a strange woman standing in my compartment saying "Hello, my name is Ira, what is your name?" I almost swore. It was two frickin thirty in the morning and Ira, who had just got on, wanted to introduce herself to the big guy curled up on the lower bunk – you've got to be kidding. I went into autopilot and played my story for her to which she listened intently in the half light. I then fell back onto my pillow and shut my eyes, but she wanted to talk some more, I tried my best to answer one or two questions, but that was my limit, any more would have to wait until the morning. Her phone rang at various times throughout the night and she took short calls in hushed voice. Surely this was outside the bounds of regular train etiquette? I wanted to pull her up, but I was too tired and simply drifted back off to sleep.

Finally, at about nine o'clock, I got up, got dressed quickly and snuck out before she could nab me. She was still fast asleep. I made the now familiar trek to the restaurant car and ate my breakfast of pilmeni and tea in silence. It was good and I watched the countryside roll by. There is something peaceful and relaxing about dining on a train; no pressure to finish in a hurry, plenty of stimuli outside to keep your mind occupied, long cups of tea mulling things over – very pleasant indeed.

There were three staff in the restaurant car, the waitress, someone book-keeping and the chef – a huge woman who I suspected made up for the lack of patrons by eating almost all that she cooked. It was also their breakfast time and after serving me they all sat together in the next booth with a big burly and animated man. After a while he introduced himself – he was Sergei, and in his own words "*the chief of the train*". He was dressed casually in three-quarter length shorts, sandals and singlet (it was hot) but I took him at his word and certainly when other workers from the train came in to be fed they paid him the respect owed a boss.

He was extremely friendly and invited me to his table. He immediately called for the drink – this time a very cold apple-flavoured spirit. Perhaps vodka – I couldn't be sure. It was very, very cold and very, very sweet and was accompanied by a lemon and sugar chaser – eaten whole, including the rind. A not unpleasant combination, although at ten o'clock in the morning, I was struggling to reconcile this with my *no drinks before evening* policy. We all drank equal portions, even the chef, waitress and book-keeper. They all introduced themselves: the waitress was Alyona and she was from Tynda, the book-keeper was her aunt (think child bride), Lena, and the chef was Lyuba (of course), from Neryungri. Sergei was also from Neryungri. They were a happy bunch. Lena explained that she had got Alyona a job on the train as there was no work in Tynda and this, in fact, was her first trip – she was in training. I didn't bother pointing out that it looked like the restaurant business on the train was in decline – at least she was occupied and busy at times selling beer and noodles. I considered giving her some customer service feedback, but I didn't want to crush her so early in her career – she still had thousands of customers to annoy. Lena went on to explain that Sergei couldn't keep his hands off Alyona and had been chasing her all around the train for the last three days. I looked at Sergei and he smiled mischievously. He reminded me of Sid James in all those terrible Carry On films. I couldn't tell whether she was exaggerating, or whether he was just playing, but all the same I felt sorry for her. We finished the bottle and then out came the *real* food. Lyuba had prepared beautiful stuffed peppers with vegetables and rice in a tasty sauce. This stuff definitely was NOT on the menu and was Sergei's favourite dish. Out also came another small bottle of vodka, this time just for Sergei and me. It only amounted to three shots each (does that sound like an alcoholic in denial?) but I was at my limit. All I could remember was the advice from my guidebook: eat plenty of fat before drinking and eat something after each drink. I ordered seconds and was feeling a bit like the stuffed peppers myself but I persevered and saw the session through. Sergei had work to do and I returned a little groggy (but happy) to my cabin for some rest.

***

My final travelling companions were a family of three from Barnaul who joined the train in Krasnoyarsk. They interrupted my afternoon nap and busted me using one pillow over my quota when they entered the compartment. I surreptitiously threw it back onto the pile of bedding on the top bunk when they were all looking out the window. I tidied up the table – which by this time I had completely taken over, and I tried to spend as much time outside of the cabin as possible – it was now more than *three days* since I had bathed or changed clothes and I was feeling like Pongo the Pirate again. They were a young family, mother, father and their five year old son. He was a polite but excited kid and was bouncing off the walls playing games, singing and shooting imaginary villains with imaginary guns. He also liked to ask me long questions in a loud voice – it was amusing and I tried my best to answer but I think his parents were a little embarrassed.

Again, at bed time, I gave them plenty of space and time to prepare and I didn't enter the compartment until I was sure they were tucked in and heading towards sleep. She slept on the bottom bunk with her arms around her son and the father was on the top bunk. It sure felt strange getting out of my jeans and shirt and sliding into my bunk bed with them all so close but I zoned out, rolled over to face the wall, curled up into the S shape required to fit inside the dimensions of the bed and dropped off to sleep. I did roll over a few times in the night and it was very strange to see through bleary eyes in the half light a young woman just eighteen inches away from me – either facing me or the back of her head. Each time I immediately rolled back over and tried to blank my mind – it was hard work.

Morning came and this time I didn't even have to order at the restaurant – they were waiting for me and had a special meal prepared. It was delicious and entirely satisfying. I complimented the chef and thanked them for the improved service. We got talking and I tested their views on Russia's political leadership. They all felt Putin was a very good leader, strong and an effective statesman. Lena ran through the roll call of recent and not so recent leaders; Yeltsin, Gorbachev, Andropov, and Chernyenko – she used an adjective I didn't recognise to describe them all, and I asked her

101

to repeat it so I could look it up in my dictionary: SHAMEFUL. Lena then produced a thick wad of family photos (she was Alyona's mother's sister). There were candid family shots, picnics, baby photos – we studied each one carefully and Lena explained who the key members of their families were. She proudly pointed out her husband in many photos. She seemed happy and the photos definitely showed some happy times in a close extended family. I felt glad for them both and hoped there was a future on the railways for them.

I counted down the last one hundred kilometres from the corridor from the signposts by the side of the tracks as we approached Novosibirsk. I was glad to be nearing the end of the train journey. It had been eventful and memorable, but the short holiday was over and it was time to try and piece back together the rest of my intended journey. I had certainly caught up many days by crossing central Russia on the train – I had covered a few thousand kilometres in just *three and a half days*.

***

As soon as we arrived in Novosibirsk, I found Nikolai and the baggage wagon and we quickly got my bike and all of the related bits and pieces onto the platform. I looked around inside the wagon to make sure nothing was left behind. I saw Nikolai's tiny room, just a little bench and a cot in a small room at the end of the wagon with a small window on one wall. This was where he had spent the last three and a half days – loading and unloading cargo at major stations, day and night. It was a tough job and I felt for him – at least he had friends to travel with and talk to.

There was stuff everywhere; tyres, panniers, bags, toolkit, helmet, jacket, nuts and bolts – all spewed out onto the platform in a hurry, for the train had to vacate its position to let others come and go. This was a busy station in a large city with many train services both long distance and urban. People came and went too, inspecting my work but not bothering me. It was hot and sunny – over thirty degrees – and I quickly worked up a sweat putting all the pieces back together AGAIN. I sure was sick of doing this job. Within an hour, however, I had it all back together and was riding down the busy platform dodging commuters and travellers. I crossed the tracks with some tractors and cargo moving equipment and was suddenly on the streets of Novosibirsk, solo and dangerous – all I had to do now was ride down through Barnaul, to Semipalatinsk, across the steppes of northeast Kazakhstan to a remote and seldom used border crossing with China in the next eight days

Family Feud in Kazakhstan

It felt as if I had been spat out of a time machine, so stark was the contrast between where I had come from and where I was now. I had spent over a month in the far north east corner of Russia in remote parts of Siberia. I had lived on a diet of bread, tea, sausage and tinned food. I had lived with locals and shared in their difficult conditions, stayed in the occasional "hotel", bathed in muddy tap water, ridden through mud, bog, swamp and rivers, drunk too much vodka, shared feasts of the best local food with generous hosts, eaten freshly cooked fish straight from rivers, slept in police stations, Kamaz cabins, workers' camps, apartments and camped in derelict ghost towns. Now I was riding along the wide open boulevards of central Novosibirsk in the hot summer sun. There were sidewalk cafes, restaurants, fancy shops, neoclassical buildings, modern sky scrapers and people who had some time and money to devote to things beyond just the bare essentials. The "New York Pizza Bar" and a large Levi Strauss store complete with matching cafe and denim menus helped reinforce this impression. There was not a Kamaz in sight and the roads were filled with new Japanese and European cars. There were young people everywhere, couples strolling, groups of young men in the latest fashions huddled on street corners and women devoted to their appearance on parade in the late afternoon sun.

I found the old Intourist Hotel which had received a make-over (including the room rates). It was big and impersonal but I had a room on the top floor with a comfy bed and after three days and nights on the train I was happy to be resting in private. I washed and showered, then headed out into the city, found an outdoor beer garden restaurant and settled in for a wonderful meal of humus, Turkish bread, tabouli and spicy kebabs washed down by a few cold beers. It was a new taste sensation and I savoured each mouthful. The other patrons consisted of either groups of over-dressed and anxious young women (it was Saturday night) or well heeled and well dressed couples, usually with one or both people chatting (or shouting) into their mobile phones. I was next to a gangster type, complete with big chains and ostentatious jewellery, open-necked shirt and adoring but bored and restless moll. After barking orders down his phone in a loud voice he would turn to her and tell her how beautiful she was and all was good again. I kept my head down and focused on the food just in case a volley of gun fire was in the offing.

***

It was a hot night and I slept with the big porthole window in my room wide open which, in the morning, just before dawn, began letting in the loud sounds of construction coming from a massive half completed- church across the road. The workers looked like they were from Armenia or Georgia and they were working hard, even at 5:30am on a Sunday. If they were Christians, I'm not sure how they reconciled working on a Sunday – perhaps they were getting conscience money? This was just one of many "new" churches I had seen being built across Russia on my journey – I wondered what was driving this rush back to Orthodoxy? It seemed, here at least, incongruous with all the trappings of the material world I had seen being enjoyed by most young people.

I spent the morning writing notes and preparing for the next leg of my journey. I was keen to cover some miles on the bike – it had been over a week since I had ridden and although I was now thousands of kilometres from Neryungri (emotionally and physically), I wanted to return to the intended mode of transport for my journey. Before leaving I found a fast food restaurant, ate a horrible burger, chips and corn cob but found the most delicious chocolate thick shake. It's always the same in those places – the glossy pictures of the perfectly formed bun, juicy beef patty and salad convince you that, yes, you would be prepared to eat this and might possibly enjoy it, then out comes the reality: a deflated and soggy bun with a thin greasy grey slither of meat with a scrape of sauce and some dead transparent lettuce leaves. But it didn't matter, the chocolate thick shake was sublime – I closed my eyes and was transported to another level of physical pleasure as I slowly sucked the thick cold sludge. I ordered another and then another in a rash of gluttony and I left feeling like a new man.

***

It was a long hot ride to Barnaul across rolling hills and wide tracts of farm land. There didn't seem to be a piece of open land that wasn't cultivated. There were many small villages along the way and we seemed to chase the Ob River as it made its way southwards. It was a Sunday afternoon, in excess of thirty five degrees and very windy. The roads were busy and many cars came up close behind me and sped past at well over 100 kph. It was such a change from riding in remote Siberia and I really had to concentrate hard on, a) keeping the bike at the right angle to the wind, and b) keeping an eye on the rear view mirrors for fast approaching cars, some of whom seemed to pass within inches of my left side.

We also passed through stretches of thick tall and cool forest which provided some relief from the heat. The road was very good and I was able to make decent progress covering the two hundred and fifty kilometres in only a few hours. I arrived at the outskirts of Barnaul after 6pm but it was still dazzlingly hot. I stopped just after a toll booth to check the directions for entering the city and in just a few seconds my side stand had sunk deep into the soft bitumen and my boots were sticking to it as well. I crossed the Ob and rode past sandy beaches where people were still sunning themselves and swimming in the late afternoon sun. There were boats, diving pontoons, children splashing about in the shallows and families enjoying picnics – I felt like jumping straight in to cool off but decided it was more important to locate a hotel and get settled first.

I found a hotel recommended by my guide book, which was small, centrally located, looked cosy and clean, but the woman at reception steadfastly refused to accept me, claiming that I needed to be "registered" and that they "didn't do that here". I couldn't believe it – I was hot and tired and didn't want to get back on the bike and ride somewhere else. I pleaded with her, I promised to be an excellent guest, I showed her my money, I put my head in my hands on the counter and sobbed, I sat on the floor in protest – these regulations were just so silly – but all to no avail. I lost the battle and retreated to the main street and found the equally pleasant, more stylish and much larger Hotel Altai where they accepted me with open arms and never mentioned the "R" word. It seemed over staffed with three older women on duty, but each seemed to have role to play: one for the money, one for the key and one for the linen – all important jobs. They were extremely friendly and the hotel had a kitsch old world charm with high ceilings, balconies, a large central staircase, colourful carpets and Persian rugs on the walls in the rooms. The "key lady" took me to the room they had allocated but took one look at the size of the bed and then the size of me, did the maths quickly in her head and shut the door before I could get a foot in. She kindly found a larger room with a double bed (at no extra cost) for which I thanked her. I got settled and then strolled along the wide tree-lined avenue that was the main street. There was a central pedestrian walkway with trees, grass and seats, dividing the street into two and providing even more shade and the streets here were lined with pretty five storey classical buildings in different shades of pastel pink and green – altogether very pleasant. Although much smaller than Novosibirsk, Barnaul was still cosmopolitan and sophisticated with a similar feel on the streets. The impressive University buildings fronted the main street and there were a number of large squares and parks as I walked the long main street. Dinner was cheap and nasty but it didn't matter, I had completed day one of the rest of my trip without incident – a major achievement.

* * *

I spent the next day completing a number of maintenance jobs on the bike (changed over to bitumen tyres, changed the oil and coolant) and walking further along the long main street to the museums and art galleries. It was hot so I joined the locals in drinking *kvass* in large plastic cups from big canisters by the side of the road – it was surprisingly refreshing and I drank many cups. I also indulged in many ice creams helping to keep the street vendors busy.

* * *

The morning of my departure broke cold and wet and windy. I was in two minds whether to press on or wait, but I was keen to get across the border and into Kazakhstan and to keep making progress towards my Chinese deadline. I filled up with petrol and headed out along the highway towards the border. The wind was icy and the rain, although not heavy, was annoying and I was slowly getting soaked all over. I got so cold that I started shuddering and had to stop and change into my long johns, zip up top and add the winter lining back into my jacket. I watched the trucks and cars zoom by with their occupants warm and dry inside and wished – just for a second – that I might join them for some relief. The day was bright enough and visibility was good, it was just the cold, wet and wind I had to deal with, so I jumped back on and headed out onto the road again. It was just going to be one of those days where you needed to zone out and keep riding.

It was a long day in the saddle and the scenery wasn't particularly rewarding, just flat farmland and open plains. The occasional field of sunflowers lifted my spirits but there wasn't much else. The entire sky was covered in clouds and again I seemed to be chasing the darkest corner as I headed south. I stopped briefly for lunch (a loaf of bread, a stick of sausage from which the life had been almost entirely sucked out of, and some nuts). A carload of young men pulled up with loud music blaring and I thought it could be trouble, but they just wanted to check out my bike and me. They were fascinated and wished me well on my travels. The rain did eventually clear as I got closer to the border, but the wind picked up further and I was buffeted by high winds for the rest of the day – slowing my speed dramatically and impacting my mental health. The environment around me became much harsher and desert- like with sand and rocky soil surrounding the road, few trees and very, very flat.

After interrupting some local boys from their mid-afternoon dreams in their hotted up Ladas in a local village and seeking directions, I crossed the last piece of Russia on my trip, an uninspiring piece of road works, before hitting the border controls. There was a queue and I lined up dutifully behind a family of Kazakhs in their overloaded station wagon. The rain had returned so I put my helmet back on and just sat on my bike waiting for the queue to clear. I was eventually processed at the rudimentary Russian post (two guys behind a high counter) and then headed across no-mans' land to the Kazakh border controls which were much more impressive and modern in comparison. It was here that I met "Inoorrrr" (roll the Rs please!) – a feisty young Kazakh border policewoman. This was my first real introduction to Kazakh physiognomy and it was fascinating. She had high cheekbones, a flat elongated oval shaped face with eyes in the shape of flattened teardrops – accentuated by heavy mascara and eyeliner and a soft punk hairstyle. There wasn't much you could do with basic military green, but she had certainly pushed the limits with a smart tight-fitting short skirt, her shirt worn fashionably in blouse form and black patent leather boots with shiny silver studs. She examined my papers carefully then proceeded to haul me all over the compound completing other immigration processes mostly related to my bike. She walked faster than I could (which is a feat in itself) and barked directions at me in a thick Russian accent; "Ahdreean Dooglasss come zis vay!" The only time she got stuck was when it began raining; she absolutely could not get her hair or patent leather shoes wet. I wondered silently what her role would be in the event of a border skirmish with the Russians. We walked over to my bike and it was sprayed with some type of disinfectant or anti-bacterial agent. We were right in the middle of a bird flu zone so I guessed this was some type of containment measure, but no-one mentioned this – it was just a "water spray" to clean my bike. We then proceeded to the massive customs inspection shed for vehicles. There were five men lolling about and Inoorrrr obviously had all of them under the thumb. She marched in, swinging her hips, slapped my papers and passport on the table and handed me over. They looked at my big steel panniers and asked whether I was carrying any narcotics, I said "No" and that was it, no inspection, just on your way please. I asked about hotels in Semipalatinsk and they provided some good advice so at least something good came of it.

The rain had stopped and the sun was nearly crossing the horizon as I rode through the open gate to Kazakhstan and past the long queue of people in their vehicles waiting to cross into Russia – they all stared as I rode past agog. I was soon alone on the road and riding through flat scrub. There was the occasional small village or farmhouse but not much else. It was getting dark quickly and I still had ninety kilometres to cover to get to Semipalatinsk, but there was no way I was going to pull up prior to reaching the city, so I pressed on into the night. The road was rough in places with plenty of surprise potholes jumping out of the dark at the last minute so I wasn't riding too fast and I knew it would be at least another hour and a half before I was finished. In addition, my headlight was badly misaligned, so rather than illuminate the road immediately ahead of me, it shone up and hit the eyes of the drivers of all the oncoming traffic – which nearly all of them let me know via their horns and powerful, blinding high beam lights. I hated riding at night – especially the transition from dusk to night –and the road was busy, which meant I was focused on keeping a steady line and watching everything else very, very carefully.

By 9:30pm, however, I had made it to the outskirts of Semipalatinsk. It wasn't particularly well lit and there were absolutely no signs and when the road came to a fork I had to stop and ask for directions. I pulled up at a petrol station in the middle of an unofficial taxi rank. Out of the darkness came faces and bodies of all shapes and sizes. This was the place where the Russians had exploded over *four hundred and fifty* nuclear bombs – right up until the late 1980s – and it looked to me as if most of the guys here were a few chromosomes short of a full deck. It was like I had landed on the Island of Dr. Moreau. One man in particular was very peculiar – he had short hair on the top of his head, but big side burns and long curly hair from both the sides and back of his head down to his chest and I don't know how he ate without puncturing his lips – so badly arranged were his teeth. But he, like all of them, was extremely friendly and curious about me and my bike. It was as if an alien had landed and they were trying to make sense of it – that's the impression I got anyway. Another man, dressed in a shell suit and looking the most normal, approached me. He was drunk and insisted I stay with him and his family – an offer I politely declined, but after asking about hotels three of four times it was clear I wasn't going anywhere. We talked about where I had come from and where I was going and they all inspected my bike in detail and were impressed. Some teenagers on motorcycles pulled up and also joined in. We took some photos and as I was getting ready to leave an older man, who had been quiet most of the time, came forward, touched my arm and insisted I stay with him and his wife. He introduced himself as Mikhail but immediately said I should call him Mischa. He had a kind face, wore a hearing aid and was so sincere in his invitation that I thought if it had to be anyone, at least he looked somewhat normal, so I followed him home along the dark dirt laneways to his small dacha where we I was greeted very warmly by his wife Lyuba. She was a big woman with short peroxide blonde hair with an equally big warm smile full of gold fillings. Unfortunately the drunk man in the shell suit (he called himself "Beck") was still with us. Lyuba immediately warmed up a delicious pot of stew on the stove in the front room of their tiny dacha and we sat around the small kitchen table and ate bread, tea and stew and, at Beck's insistence, drank a few vodka toasts. I was exhausted and very hungry after riding more than four hundred and fifty kilometres in one day and the last thing I wanted was a high octane chaser with my food, but it seemed the polite thing to do, and I took my cue from Mischa who sat quietly listening to Beck ramble on and on. He was in some sort of construction business that involved trade with China and he insisted that tomorrow I take a guided tour of the city in a chauffeur driven company car then meet the president of the company at a grand factory opening. Nothing ever came of this and Mischa and Lyuba just shook their heads in quiet embarrassment and apologised later – Beck was a Kazakh and the drink had got the better of him.

We walked Beck home and by the time we returned Lyuba had prepared the divan in the living room into a lovely bed. I thanked them again, wished them a good night and fell asleep immediately. I slept and slept, but not for as long as Mischa. Finally at ten o'clock, I had to get up, so I tiptoed across the lounge room and tried to make a B-line for the back door, but being a big guy in a small wooden house my every move came complete with loud squeaks and squeals waking Mischa immediately; he and Lyuba had slept on the floor in a make-shift bed of cushions and blankets. I knew to expect this but still felt bad. Lyuba had a cleaning job in the city so had left early but Mischa was struggling to shake off the cobwebs of deep sleep. He caught me out of the corner of his eye and immediately jumped to his feet. He was dressed only in his boxer shorts but this didn't seem to bother him. He apologised (for what I'm not sure), got dressed quickly and prepared breakfast. I was amazed how quickly we had become so intimate; less than twelve hours ago I was a complete stranger to these people, now we were walking around in our underwear talking to each other about what I would like for breakfast.

The highlight of breakfast for me, apart from actually having it, was the large jug of fresh cold cows' milk; Lyuba's mother lived in a small village not far away and had milked the cows herself. It was wonderful and I drank four cups in quick succession. This made Mischa very happy so I didn't feel too bad about drinking so much. Mischa took me outside to see their massive vegetable garden. It had so many types of fruit and vegetables that I quickly lost count as Mischa reeled them off – there were potatoes, tomatoes, cabbage, zucchinis, peppers, apples, apricots, strawberries, raspberries, more berries, carrots, beans, and many herbs. Lyuba – who loved flowers – had planted many varieties of wild flowers down the middle of the garden and they were in full bloom. It was a sea of colour and the air was sweetly perfumed. The only downside for me was the two ferocious guard dogs – one at the rear, and one at the entrance to the property. They were restrained on solid chains, but it didn't matter, as soon as I came anywhere near them they bared their big fangs, started salivating heavily and making noises as if they hadn't been fed for a week and couldn't wait to chomp on my rather big thigh bones. I'm sure they could smell the fear too.

Mischa began to tell me about himself; he was from Belarus and the oldest in a family of six children. His father had died when he was 13 and he was immediately forced out of school and into work to help support his family. He rolled up his sleeves and shyly showed me the faded simplistic tattoos covering his forearms – he said he had been silly as a young man and still had these to remind him of his foolishness. He had his name tattooed across one set of knuckles and the year of his birth across the other. He also explained

112

that as a young man he had been a street fighter then a boxer – he certainly had the face of a boxer with his large green eyes sunken below the bruised and permanently raised cartilage of his brow, nose and eye sockets. He had completed his two years of compulsory military service in Moscow (a plum posting). He never completed his formal education and had since worked primarily as a policeman, a driver of trucks and cars, also spending time as a driving teacher both in the classroom and in cars with learner drivers. He was currently driving taxis part-time and also worked three nights a week as a security guard at the office of the National Lottery of Kazakhstan. Mischa had large hands with thick stubby fingers and strong forearms and he explained that whenever there was any hint of trouble in his taxi (like someone coming at him with a knife) his fell back onto his boxing days and delivered a few choice blows to anyone who threatened him. He was a gentle soul but well armed and not afraid to use force when needed. I understood.

We drove into the city to meet Lyuba as she was finishing her work. She cleaned offices in the building where Mischa worked. We met some of the small business owners working there including a real-estate agent whose business I was fascinated with. Yes, private real-estate was well established and there was certainly a market, but who could afford it and where did the money come from? Difficult questions to which I never got a full answer.

We then met Bolyat, a short, portly and proud Kazakh man who owned the building (aka the Landlord). There was also a driving school here, the Lottery Office and a large bar and restaurant on the ground floor. It was he who employed both Lyuba and Mischa in their respective jobs here. Bolyat was about five foot tall, had a large Buddha belly and a ruddy complexion with a full fleshy face and a tiny moustache with a good head of thick black hair swept straight back off his face. He was certainly impressed when he saw me and complimented me on being so big and tall which was nice and must have been hard for a small man. He introduced his wife, Olya; she was short and solidly built, reminding me of a Soviet shot putter or hammer thrower. Olya had short spiky hair tinted with just the slightest shade of powder blue to compliment her big pale blue eyes. They were certainly a formidable couple. They lived in rooms on the top floor of their building and had a large dining-roomcum-kitchen in one to which we were directed presently; it was time for my second breakfast of course. Out came the bread, tea, jam, honey, eggs, eggplant, tomatoes, potatoes, mutton stew, biscuits, sweets, as I was sentenced to three courses of hard labour.

I'm a big guy with a reasonable appetite, but this was beyond me (again). I had just finished breakfast number one and there was some room left downstairs, but not this much. I ate slowly and tried to get through as much as I could. As soon as I had finished a plate it was re-filled and Olya sat next to me heaping dollops of sour cream onto big hunks of bread topped with jam. I thought at one point she was going to say, open up the tunnel here comes the train, but instead she just kept handing these bricks to me. As she was preparing the third one I boldly said to her, "I hope that's not for me", to which she just smiled and handed another to me – they seemed convinced that I was malnourished and needed to be bigger and stronger (or fatter and heavier) for the next leg of my journey. Lyuba stopped by briefly on her way home but politely declined any food and refused to sit and join us. I sensed a little tension between her and Olya and realised it must be difficult for her and Mischa as they both were employed by Olya's husband. I eventually convinced them that I was fully satiated and could not physically fit one more ounce of anything inside me. I was finding it hard to breathe as it was, and needed to stand up and loosen my belt for some relief.

* * *

I was keen to visit the Abay museum celebrating the life and works of Kazakhstan's own Shakespeare and Mischa kindly drove me to the building where the museum was located. Unfortunately, it was closed for renovations, but undeterred, Mischa, broke through the boarded up entrance, found a sleeping female security guard and insisted that as a foreign guest deeply interested in Kazakh people, history and culture, it would be treason not to show me through. After some heated exchanges, all was settled and we were escorted through the museum by the security guard who kept a close eye on both of us. She was an odd looking creature too. Could have been Chinese for all I knew. She was dangerously thin and wore long baggy pants with a military style tunic top and a small neat fitting non-peaked hat (like French soldiers wear). All in shades of military grey/blue. She had a sharply defined *single* black eyebrow, bright red lipstick and high heel patent leather shoes. I was going to ask if she and Inoorrrr had been classmates in military school. In addition to statues and selected works of Abay, there were Kazakh works of art (traditional, modern and abstract), traditional clothing and furniture, a full size yurt and a small section on Kazakh history. What struck me most profoundly was the "newness" of most items and the limited range. As nomads, there was little or no written history or collected works until the mid to late nineteenth century. There was certainly an oral tradition with big long spoken or sung poems but nothing written down. Abay had been the first and even then part of his collections were Russian classics translated.

After the museum we walked through the large central (Lenin) park where Mischa told me how he had come as a young man with his girlfriends. It was overgrown but still functional with shady seats, ice cream and soft drink stalls, kiddies instant photos and shashlik vendors. I mentioned I was in need of a haircut so Mischa carefully selected a "beauty salon" along one of the quiet city streets. Semipalatinsk was centred on a tight grid of streets and didn't follow the typical Soviet style largesse in city design – it seemed more like a community neighbourhood. Sure, there were large open squares with statues and government buildings, but somehow the city had evolved away from these places into much more intimate places.

The woman who cut my hair was more *engineer* than *artist* so carefully did she measure and clip. I tried to explain at the start that I just wanted "a trim" even holding my thumb and index finger about an inch apart to indicate how far she should go, but it didn't seem to matter – she had her own plan and I was coming along for the ride. I lost count of the number of circuits she did around my head – starting with large clumps of hair and then gradually reducing the scope of each brush and cut until finally it seemed she was trimming individual hairs. Toward the final stages she agonised over each cut, scouring my head like a sniffer dog looking for the slightest recalcitrant strand and trimming it aggressively. I'm only middle-aged but I felt decidedly aged when she trimmed my ear hair. In the end I decided she was an obsessive compulsive and it was best not to interrupt nor complain. And, after one hour (during which time Mischa waited patiently for me on a couch at the back of the shop) when she told me the cost was the equivalent of *one dollar fifty*, I felt there was nothing I could say but thank you and goodbye. Judging from the young men on the street I had the "Semi Style" which was clean cut if nothing else – it could have been a lot worse.

It was after 2pm but we had a lunch date with Lyuba and returned home for another big meal – this time chicken stew and the usual fare. There had been an outbreak of bird flu in northern Kazakhstan and this did play on my mind ever so slightly as I chomped into a fat, greasy and fleshy thigh bone. The chicken came complete with more of its internal bits than I am used to but I managed to steer a safe course avoiding too much psychological trauma. It was delicious and I was slightly relieved when Lyuba told me the chicken had come straight from her mother's village.

After lunch we returned to Bolyat's where we met the rest of his family. He had three sons and one daughter ranging in ages from twenty four to sixteen; Ruslan, Rafael, Christina and Danya. Christina lived and worked in Germany and was home for a two week visit. I couldn't quiet figure out this arrangement but she had been there for five years already so it must have been agreeable. I met Bolyat's brother and his mother who was frail but feisty, keeping her son and grandchildren in line with a deep throaty cackle and walking stick which she waved about.

As his special guest, Bolyat had prepared the traditional Kazakh dish of "bishbarmak" for me. It consisted of thin sheets of pasta soaked in mutton fat with many tough pieces of meat to chew on for good measure. I found it really hard going but was polite and managed to get through two big bowls of the stuff – it just lacked any real flavour and after a while, chewing on fatty mutton got the better of me and I needed to punctuate the greasy blandness with mouthfuls of bread and sweet tea. I could feel the stomach cramps coming on.

Bolyat was very interested in Australia, how we lived and in particular what we ate. As a Kazakh he was keen on horse meat and when I explained to him that he would probably be locked up for killing and then eating a horse he was taken aback – what sort of country were we? He wanted to eat crocodiles and kangaroos too. Not deterred, he kept repeating at me, like a parrot: "Melbin, let's go!" which was amusing, but tiring after the fifteenth time he had said it. I just laughed and said sure, let's go!

After letting the sludge settle at the bottom of my stomach like wet cement, Olya dragged me into the room next door, which was bare, apart from a small desk, an electronic keyboard and two chairs. It was concert time and I was the captive audience. Olya unfurled her song book and fiddled with the dials and buttons on top of the complicated computerised keyboard to line up backing percussion and electronic orchestral support. She then began playing and singing traditional Russian folk songs for me. The music was just simple notes and key progressions but she did have a good voice, so I sat back with a far away look in my eyes, gently swaying to the music and making appreciative cooing noises every now and then. Olya was really getting into the folk groove, so I encouraged her to play a few more songs which she did happily. Again, I had felt we were getting very close very quickly which I found hard to adjust to.

After the impromptu concert, Bolyat's sons invited me to the basement of their building where in the midst of a construction zone they had billiards and table tennis set up. It was Australia vs. Kazakhstan, head to head, no holds barred, over three gruelling hours of competition and I am happy to report that the visitors had a close away win. The billiards were in the Russian format with over-sized balls and under-sized pockets so that only the most precise of shots were successful. Ruslan was the man about town and played aggressively, while Rafael was sleepy and docile and Danya was just the energetic baby. Bolyat was obviously very wealthy owning an entire building and I wondered how the three sons got on with each other and divided the spoils – it had all the ingredients for a modern day Russian family saga.

Olya kindly offered me a room in the basement (Danya's) to sleep in for the night which I gladly accepted (not understanding the terrible breach of etiquette I was making). Close to midnight cues and paddles were downed and I was locked up inside the basement for the night. It was a huge space; dark and cavernous with only one entrance out onto the *street*, hence the need to be locked in. It did feel a little creepy, crawling over sand and bricks and then back through the big billiards and table tennis room and getting into bed in a room with no windows and no outside light at all. I was buried deep inside a massive concrete bunker and the only thing that was going to wake me was another Soviet nuclear test. They gave me a key and explained that under no circumstances was I to open the door. I fell fast asleep and didn't stir until 9:30 the next morning awoken by Mischa's loud and relentless banging on the outside door. He had worked through the night at his security post upstairs. He had only slept a little but he was still bright eyed and bushy tailed.

The morning was spent rather aimlessly playing more billiards waiting for the afternoon when Bolyat had promised to take Mischa and me to his dacha on the outskirts of town on the Irtyush River. I could tell Mischa was not entirely happy with these arrangements but he said nothing and smiled happily throughout. After lunch Bolyat drove us out of the city towards the river and his dacha. First we stopped for some supplies where I made the vaguest of enquiries about the smoked fish hanging up on a road side stall. We left with two big fish and four bottles of beer – it was a

Russian tradition to chew on dried fish while drinking beer so Mischa encouraged the purchase.

First stop was Olya's father's dacha. He was a big barrel-chested former wrestler still in good shape in his late seventies and tending a very large garden-cum-orchard that backed onto the river Irtyush. He proudly showed us all of his fruits and vegetables including the many varieties of apples he grew. He also made large sheets of dried apple paste – some of which he ripped off and gave to me as a gift along with many other fruits such as plums and cherries. The sheets of apple paste were chewy and delicious and I folded it carefully (like a thick plastic tablecloth) and packed it in my bag. He also grew wildflowers and they were in full bloom adding to the colours and fragrances. The afternoon sun was shining brightly and it was an idyllic setting. For a moment I was envious but then contemplated the work involved and the living conditions. Olya explained that her father had built the dacha himself and he proudly took us on a tour – it had three tiny rooms; a kitchen, a living room and a bedroom upstairs (very steep stairs). There were also two balconies which looked out over the front and back yards respectively. Gennady (Olya's father) lived here with his son, daughter-in-law and their two young children. How they all managed to squeeze into the tiny dacha I do not know.

Contrary to my expectations we didn't stay long and were soon driving deeper into dacha territory. Bolyat and Olya's dacha also backed onto the river and was another simple affair – even smaller than her father's but neat, simple, compact and colourful. It had a small kitchen and an upstairs attic room in the pitch of the roof, full of beds with open windows at either end where the summer breeze would flow through – just large enough for three people. It also had a large garden full of fruit trees and vegetables with much shade and pretty bricked pathways. There was an outdoor area with a table setting where we sat and enjoyed our dried fish and beer followed by a special dish of pilmeni that Bolyat prepared especially. After our meal we walked down to the river, took our shoes and socks off and paddled in the shallow water which was very refreshing, especially for my plates of meat that had spent most of the previous six weeks trapped inside my motorcycle boots.

***

After returning to Bolyat's, Olya called me into the room where she had previously sung and played for me. Christina was there and to my horror Olya was dressed in a *belly dancing costume*. It was like I Dream of Jeannie meets Roseanne. I was hoping she would pull her elbows up, arms crossed and say "Yes Master Nelson" so I could ask her to disappear, but it didn't happen so I just smiled and tried to look everywhere but at her. It wasn't that she was a bad dancer – I just wasn't ready for this up close and personal experience. The music rattled on and so did she. Running out of places to look, I foolishly asked her daughter whether she danced too – thankfully she said no (not yet). The performance finally ended and I couldn't manage a "Bravo", but I did applaud sincerely; she certainly had plenty of self confidence which I admired.

We didn't linger and after Olya's show, Mischa and I drove home into a raging storm; Lyuba was furious and bitterly upset and angry with Bolyat and Olya for "stealing" her guest away. I had unwittingly stepped into a long running feud between the couples. I had broken ranks by sleeping with the enemy and partaking in their meals and hospitality. I was the pawn in this ongoing battle and I felt terrible; why didn't I realise earlier? Lyuba had been preparing meals and beds expecting us to return but instead we were playing billiards, sunning ourselves in the countryside and taking private audiences with the cavorting Mata Hari. Lyuba bemoaned the low wages they were both paid and made disparaging remarks about both Olya and Bolyat in a torrent of hard core Russian cursing which I (luckily) didn't fully understand. Mischa did his best to calm her down and to apologize – he walked a fine line in this regard and I admired his sensitivity, level headedness and balance. After about fifteen minutes peace had been restored and it was safe to walk the streets. Lyuba had prepared a large and delicious evening meal and I felt relieved that I hadn't eaten so much during the day so I could eat heartily now and try to make amends.

That night as we sat in their lounge room watching TV, Lyuba noticed my still swollen and painful ankle, so I told them how I had crashed on the very first day one of my trip. They were most concerned (like parents with their own child) and insisted that I visit the hospital the very next day to have it examined. I told them I thought it was unnecessary, but they said they couldn't relax – after I had gone – without knowing whether everything was OK or not. I reluctantly agreed – what did I have to lose?

The next morning I had a list of mundane chores to complete (like posting now unwanted books home and fixing my rear view mirror which had cracked). Mischa was also keen that we get to the hospital, so we set out early (i.e. just before noon) and stopped first at the finest optical lens shop in all of Semipalatinsk to get a replacement mirror. The shop was full of people being tested and choosing frames; little girls with their hair in buns with their concerned mothers, older sophisticated Russian women shopping together and encouraging each other to be more daring in their appearance, and middle-aged men looking sheepish. They were all out of clear glass so in order to get the job done quickly we settled for blue-tinted smoky glass – still fully functional and adding a little variety for those long hours on the road ahead. The post office was a bureaucratic minefield with many forms and declarations to complete but we eventually got through it all. Then it was off to the hospital

I don't know why but I was a little nervous about seeing a doctor. I knew they would do an x-ray and I played out the possibilities in my head; the worst of course being you must stop riding now. But I had been hobbling around for weeks on it, so felt sure the news couldn't possibly be that bad. In we went – it was an old three storey brick building with long dark narrow corridors and old worn brown linoleum on the floors with long hard wooden benches for the unlucky patients along one wall outside the examination rooms. Thankfully there wasn't much of a crowd so I was seen quickly by the doctor and a crew of nurses. He took one look at my ankle got out his biro and drew a cross on the point of my ankle (at which I flinched) and immediately ordered an x-ray. Mischa was extremely anxious and peppered the doctor with many questions. He was a tall, thin and weary looking young man who looked over-worked but competent and he had a friendly manner. I was in a queue for the eponymous but rather sinisterly named "Roentgen Kabinet". After I had arrived there was a string of old ladies and young men with ankle and wrist injuries – Mischa had obviously brought me to a specialist department for broken or injured bones. I was soon called into the room and asked to lay flat on the elevated table. Mischa came along too and helped as the nurse positioned my massively heavy legs for the best angle shot. The room was dark and the equipment was old and when the nurse gave me a sheet of lead, about the size of school exercise book, covered in vinyl and motioned that I put it between my private parts and the huge x-ray gun, and then left the room telling me not to move, I did start to sweat a little and was thankful that I had already sired two beautiful children. It was ironic; if I didn't get irradiated by all those stray neutrons from all of those nuclear tests then this would certainly do the trick I thought. The machine came on with a crack and then a loud buzz and it seemed like I was alone in that room for minutes but soon enough the nurse came back in, re-positioned me for a final snap then it was all over.

I was quickly seen by the same doctor who confirmed that I did indeed have a *fractured ankle*. Apart from the strapping which I and others along the way had done, there was nothing else that could have been done at the time nor could be done now (although pushing a two hundred and fifty kilogram motorcycle solo through bogs, swamps and icy rivers did not help my recovery). He said I was fine to ride *now*, but that I should have it checked when I returned home. Mischa touched his heart with his open palm and said how relieved and happy he was for me. He almost had a tear in his eye and I was moved by his level of concern and attention. I was not asked to pay and when I asked Mischa he said it was not necessary, but I did wonder. Then I reflected that most of the predictions of my family and close friends were spot on; "*you will fall off and hurt your ankle seriously*", and "*you will need an arc welder in your tool kit*" – all of which occurred on day one!

***

We had a happy final evening meal together with Lyuba, who was equally relieved that I had received a relatively clean bill of health. I slept soundly and prepared myself mentally for another two big days of riding; I needed to cover about eight hundred kilometres to get to the Kazakh/Chinese by Sunday evening.

In the morning I awoke to find Mischa meticulously cleaning every inch of my bike with a small rag and a bucket of water. He worked from top to bottom and around both sides for at least an hour, scouring and scrubbing and washing until the bike looked almost brand new. I tried to help, but he wouldn't have a bar of it – insisting that I was his guest and this was a gift from him to me. I ate a huge breakfast of kolbasa, eggs, bread, jam, sour cream etc, etc, and was completely full by the time we headed into town to say goodbye to Bolyat and Olya (sans Lyuba of course). Then the torture of breakfast #2 began. I couldn't believe it, it was an even larger fare than I had just consumed. I didn't know how I was going to manage it, so I just ate very, very, very slowly, chewing each mouthful as much as I could before trying to force it down. I felt they were at risk of breaching the UN charter for the protection of human rights. It took me a full two hours to get through just a fraction of what they had laid out. Luckily they weren't too offended and packed the balance in big plastic bags as add on luggage for my trip. There was half a loaf of bread, honey, nuts, biscuits, potatoes, tomatoes, eggs and more. This would be lunch and snack food for the next few days.

I waddled down the stairs and flopped onto my bike, said my goodbyes quickly and rode off, following Mischa who had promised to show me the way out of town. But we weren't heading out of town at all. We soon pulled up at a large Russian Orthodox cathedral along the river bank near the centre of town. Mischa motioned that I follow him inside, so I entered the solemn space of the church vestibule facing the wall of icons common to all these churches. The priest was chanting prayers in deep monotones, seeing other people and trying to deal with their issues and requests. Mischa interrupted and politely dragged the priest over to meet me. He explained what I was doing and pulled out of his pocket four tiny golden crosses which he had purchased earlier. Mischa then gave these to the priest who blessed them and then carefully and earnestly hung one around my neck, singing softly in prayer as he did so. He then handed the other three crosses to me for safe keeping (one for each member of my family). Mischa definitely had a tear in his eye now and I was touched yet again by the depth of his feelings and his efforts to support and help me. We composed ourselves (well Mischa did anyway) and I followed him in his car to the very edge of the town at the start of what looked like a barren and rocky desert. He stopped and got out, we gave each other a big hug, observed a minute's silence (a Russian tradition?) and then I was off across what turned out to be a barren and rocky desert; this was the beginning of the Steppes.

***

It was hot and windy and the scenery didn't really improve much but I was glad to be on the move again and making reasonable progress towards my next goal. I rode all day, passing through a few small villages and the occasional town. They were all pretty desolate places, some with no vegetation at all; just grids of ugly block houses in the dust. It reminded me of some of the Mongolian towns I had seen on an earlier trip across the edge of the Gobi which in turn reminded me of the classic footage of the American nuclear testing in the desert when a mushroom cloud sweeps across a desolate row of houses before blooming up and out. As unforgivable as it was it was clear to see why the Russians had chosen this place for their nuclear testing. It probably looked the same after as it did before the explosions.

In the late afternoon the steppes slowly transitioned to gentle undulating rocky plains and at about six o'clock I rode into the small town of Oyaguz – my goal for the day. I pulled off the main road and started to look for somewhere to stay, or at least someone to ask about where to stay when all of a sudden a late model black Mercedes Benz drove past me quickly and stopped dead in front of me. The driver jumped out and came running toward me with his hand outstretched and a smile on his face. He was a short, compact man, middle-aged and dressed sloppily in track suit, T-shirt and thongs. He had blood-shot eyes, greasy unkempt hair and talked with a slight slur. I told him what I was doing and what I was looking for and he said he was very interested in motorbikes and my journey and that I should follow him home. He introduced himself and pronounced his traditional Kazakh name which was just a string of consonants consisting of B's, K's, M's and S's. I strung a few together, muttered them quickly and that seemed to work, so from then on he was simply "BKMS" in my mind. Our first stop was to meet his parents and his grandmother – who was still alive and who he introduced as being one hundred and three years old. She certainly looked older than anyone living I had ever seen. She had cataracts in both eyes, barely shuffled along and was bone thin. I introduced myself but I'm not sure whether it registered as she just kept shuffling along. I also met his father – only eighty years old – who he explained had suffered terribly in the Great Patriotic War and was senile. He still participated in our conversation, but speaking bad Russian with a senile old man was a challenge.

BKMS's wife was here too and he introduced me. She was a lot younger than him and had a toddler in tow who she was trying to feed. Somehow she also managed to produce a big plate of hot and spicy dumplings which I ate ferociously – this was the first tasty food I had enjoyed for a long time and I wondered where it fitted in the narrow spectrum of Kazakh cuisine that I had seen to date. BKMS's brother in law was there too and he produced a small bottle of vodka which the four of us managed to finish quickly. I followed BKMS home in his Mercedes and we came to his house – a two storey semi-detatched with a high fence, big garage and backyard – surprisingly modern in such a remote and small town. He had two older boys – one eleven and one fifteen. It was a male dominated household and I got the impression BKMS was someone you did not argue with. The boys had a new computer so I showed them all of my photos to date which fascinated them. We retired to the garage which doubled as a makeshift dining room where BKMS's brother in law and I sat and talked and examined my maps and reviewed my plans. His best advice was along the lines of "avoid Kyrgyzstan and Tajikistan at all costs; they're all savages who will kidnap you and slit your throat" reinforced by a short and grainy video one of the boys had on his mobile phone of gruesome acts perpetrated by terrorists. If they were trying to make me feel nervous they were certainly succeeding. China, "no worries" they said, but Kyrgyzstan and Tajikistan forget it. I asked where BKMS was and he said "business" – it was 10pm on a Saturday night and I didn't want to know what type of business he was in. Suddenly at about 10:30 a car pulled up and BKMS came through the door with about six other men. They were a motley crew, apart from one man who sat next to me and spoke at length about Russian, Kazakh and Chinese history. He was well dressed, sophisticated, spoke well and was very polite to me. They all drank a round of vodka shots, slapped each other on the back and then were gone, vanishing back into the night in their late model European sports car. I didn't want to know who they were or where they were going or what they did. I headed for a makeshift bed on the downstairs lounge that BKMS's wife had prepared and fell fast asleep dreaming of Tony Soprano.

***

I had another hearty breakfast and was on the road early, but my enjoyment was marred when I was busted in a tricky speed trap (cornering into a small town) by the Kazakh police doing seventy five in a sixty zone. Straight to the front passenger seat of the local squad car, documents please and twenty dollars thank you – no questions asked. I was speeding, but it was a two horse town and no chance of hitting anything apart from the tumbleweed. As I pulled away I noticed a long string of other offenders lining up beside the police car.

The next police stop was more helpful, providing critical directions to ensure I was headed in the right direction. The countryside was still rocky and barren, but we were following a river course and there was the occasional oasis town with thick tall trees, grass and farms providing some relief from the monotony. I pulled up at the edge of one of these towns and hid under a tree eating my lunch by the bank

124

of a small river.

When I got going again it seemed as if the road was alive and moving under me; I looked closer and little creatures seemed to be moving, running from left to right across the road. Was I hallucinating? No, these were in fact huge packs of caterpillars making their way across the road. Were they part of the silk cycle I wondered, looking for mulberry leaves and/or places to start spinning their cocoons? Anyway, whatever they were doing it was Russian roulette crossing the road – there wasn't much traffic, but what there was certainly made a mess of them.

I was getting excited as I passed the second last town before the Kazakh/Chinese border – Marakanchi. I was only fifty kilometres from my goal for the day and it was still relatively early – I might even have some daylight hours to enjoy when I got there. Then I hit a massive section of road works. Argh! Detours, big earthmoving trucks, soft sandy tracks, mud – this was not the lazy Sunday afternoon ride I had been hoping for. At one point I had to stop and ask the next car that eventually came along whether in fact I was on the right road, so bad was its condition. I rode on and eventually made it to the very small border town of Bakhti, which, in reality, was just a tiny farm village. The first woman I stopped and asked about a place to stay just shook her head and said there was nowhere. I rode on and found the Militsia post – a huge four storey barracks accommodating all of the border police. I asked to speak to their commander (I must have been feeling bold) and after about fifteen minutes he emerged from the oddly out of place apartment block across the road (again, all for border police and officials). He introduced himself as Constantine – he was a classic square-jawed Russian with chiselled features and possessed of a powerful build. He was dressed casually but the chain of command was still in place and men saluted as he passed. He looked at my bike, then at me and then asked for my passport. He slowly examined every page and asked me many questions. He asked me to follow him inside the walled compound where we sat around a gazebo under the shade of the many trees and vines that grew here. It was cool and peaceful here and I was enjoying the rest, but not the inquisition. Two of his second in command officers came down and we went through the same procedure. One in particular kept thumbing through each page of my passport repeatedly asking me from where had I come? Where was I going? What was the purpose of my trip? When did I leave home? Where did I go after that? And then where? He wanted a blow by blow itinerary, and when we got to the end he started it all over again, shaking his head in disbelief. I remained calm and answered all of their questions, all the time looking at Constantine who was looking at me like someone trying to make sense of a piece of abstract modern art; head bent to one side, mouth slightly open, slightly furrowed brow, vacant expression. I think he was having trouble piecing it all together so I tried as hard as I could to help him. To date I had been squeaky clean with my papers but somehow I had overlooked the requirement to register with the police within *five days* of entering Kazakhstan (this was day five) – and to top it off, there was a three day public holiday starting tomorrow and the border would be closed until at least Wednesday! Oh Bugger. I was supposed to be meeting my Chinese guide at eight o'clock tomorrow morning. Things weren't hanging together and I was starting to get worried. I had reconfirmed my Chinese arrangements a number of times and was sure they were set. And I had gone out of my way to get here on time. But the border police were starting to talk about me riding back to where I had come from so I could register and then returning on Wednesday to cross the border when it opened officially.

Constantine was thinking deeply and asked me to be patient – what else could I ask for? We went through the passport again and my journey two more times. I provided as much detail as I could. Then they excused themselves for a private conference. I sat and waited quietly under the shade in the gazebo admiring their pretty garden. After about an hour they returned and said they would waive the registration requirements and that the border would be open for precisely *one hour* tomorrow morning at 8am for a government delegation (three people) and I could join them in crossing the border. Unbelievable; incredibly helpful when they could have simply said, go away, get registered and come back on Wednesday. I thanked them profusely and then Constantine assigned one of his men to escort me to a home stay – or more accurately – a farm house with an old barn full of beds where travellers could stay.

The farmhouse was just around the corner and empty so I had my choice of fifteen rotten beds in three rooms. At least it had a roof and carpet on the floor and they served me a delicious evening meal. They also, unfortunately, had a very effective and ferocious guard dog who, as I was taking an evening stroll after dinner, tried savaging my leg. Luckily I was still wearing my motorcycle boots so he got a mouthful of steel, but it was not a pleasant experience (for either of us). It did, however, curtail any night time trips to the outside toilet which I found inconvenient and

126

uncomfortable.

I didn't sleep well, worrying about being late for the border. I needn't have bothered. I got to the Kazakh gate (before the border) at 7:50am sharp, but the border guards steadfastly refused to let me through. I explained that I had spoken to their commander and that he had told me to come here at 8am and the gate would be open. The young soldier looked at me stony faced, clutching his semi-automatic rifle and told me the border was closed until Wednesday, go away and come back then. There was no more conversation. I turned around and headed straight back to the barracks to find Constantine. This time he was dressed in full uniform, with many stars on his shoulders, shiny black shoes, and a big round peaked cap that sat high on his head. He told me not to worry and to follow him as he drove through the gate. This of course was successful, so that by 8:30am I was standing alone in the bright modern border checkpoint building. I was completely alone in the hall and there were three big counters through which I needed to be processed: passport control, customs and quarantine. The whole place was white-tiled and there were brand new baggage x-ray machines waiting to be turned on. To add to the surreal feel of the place, we were plum in the middle of fields of wheat; a sea of burnt yellow out each window, framed by snow capped mountains in the distance. Suddenly a woman in a white coat popped her head up from behind the quarantine counter. She had a number of phials and syringes and was self injecting something into her arm. She smiled and waved to me, but I didn't want to get any closer. She called me over and I was about to say "if you think you're sticking anything into me you're dreaming lady" when she indicated all she wanted to do was take my temperature. I stuck the thermometer under my arm as instructed and thankfully produced a very normal healthy temperature. Another officer popped into the passport control booth and after coming and going about five times he finally processed my passport. He then jumped into the customs booth next door and helped me fill out the required forms. All of this had taken well over one hour.

Then at about ten o'clock a car full of Chinese officials came tearing across the border, pulling up sharply in front of me and my bike under the enormous covered driveway of the Kazakh border post. I explained that my arrangements were to meet my guide early in the morning at the Chinese border post and when I asked whether my guide was waiting for me they all shook their heads in the negative, confounded. It was very odd to hear Russian coming from Chinese

127

faces. They all looked at my bike and said there was no record or arrangements for my trip. I gave them all the details and papers I had which only amounted to a lonely phone number in Kashgar. They took this and said they needed to return to China and that they would come back in precisely one hour. I was left scratching my head. This was the one aspect of my trip that had been pre-arranged (or so I thought) in the utmost detail. Government approval had been sought and obtained, my itinerary had been checked and OK'd, my guide and driver selected. Everything, as far as I knew was set, and now I was being told they knew nothing, there was no guide and they were going away to make a few phone calls

Dejected, I collapsed into a plastic chair and ate some dried apricots, sunflower seeds and a sheet of dried apple paste. It was a long hour. Finally the car returned with the same officials. The man in charge stepped out and handed back the papers I had given him, plus my Chinese number plate and drivers license! There was a guide and driver and they were waiting for me – I was free to leave Kazakhstan and enter China.

Chinese Walls

China was different in many ways: I had a guide and driver (read: *minders*), I had a fixed schedule and itinerary and I did not speak the language *at all*. But for me, this was where my journey joined the old Silk Roads and where I would get my first glimpse of contemporary life in the old trading cities of Hotan, Yarkand and Kashgar before plunging into the remote Pamirs.

***

I tentatively rode across the no-mans' land between the two border posts. It was just past 2pm, but the sun was still high in a cloudless sky and it was hot. Immediately upon hitting Chinese territory the road widened and was smooth and I came to an area the size of a football field with just a solitary – but large and imposing – guard tower. It had large searchlights and an open deck where the sun glistened menacingly off the soldiers' guns. They had been brought to attention by my entrance and one of them was motioning aggressively for me to stop exactly where I was which of course I did immediately.

Ahead of me was the car that had shuttled the Chinese delegation back and forth to the Kazakh border post earlier in the day. Standing beside an open door was the senior officer in charge of the Chinese border post. He was short and stout, immaculately dressed in military green with splashes of red, had well groomed dark hair brushed back framing a fleshy face. He looked, to quote a well-known former Australian Foreign Minister like "a four puppies a day man". He held up his hand in the universally understood stop sign and then motioned for me to get off my bike – it was his turn. This wasn't a request; it was a polite, but firm order. I tried to tell him that the bike was very, very, heavy and it helped if your feet actually reached the ground when you were seated on it (his didn't) – but he wasn't listening, he wanted to make it GO NOW! So, I held the bike steady and gave him a crash course on the basic controls. He paid attention for about three seconds – just enough time for me to show him where the start button was, and then he was gone. He wobbled and jerked as he pulled away and then sped up through the gears. He was far too small for the bike, but as long as it was moving forward and he didn't make any sudden moves, momentum would look after the rest. I couldn't look, so turned away and tried to make small talk with his comrades who had emerged from the car to watch their boss. My guide was here too – I hadn't noticed him in the excitement and I was introduced to him now. His name, incredibly, was *Omar*. He was Uighur (the local indigenous people before and after Chinese capture and ongoing control of Xinjiang) and looked more like a Mexican in my crude analysis. He had dark straight greasy hair, a triangular face, with big high rounded cheekbones, dark eyes and a string of hairs on his top lip that I think he had been cultivating since adolescence (which wasn't that long ago in my reckoning). He was immediately pleasant and helpful and spoke near-perfect English which took some adjusting to. I had not spoken a single word of English in almost *two months* and, apart from my writing, had not used the language. It was a strange sensation and initially I was aware of a slight delay between thinking and speaking and my speech at first was simple and slow, almost child-like. Mexican or Uighur, Omar must have wondered how I had managed to ride a motorbike here and whether I needed the special bus and a care-giver, not just a guide and driver to get across China. We walked together as we drove along the runway-sized road towards the buildings that made up the border control post proper. In the distance we could see the chief riding large figure eight's and circling the buildings happily on my bike – he was really having fun and I was happy for him. We stopped under the large canopy of the vehicle inspection area and watched as the chief approached, wobbled to a halt, lent the bike over to get off and, failing to arrest the bike's slow arc, falling off and softly crashing my bike into the hard concrete. As he lay spread-eagle on the ground, I quickly hit the kill switch and before I knew it he had bounced back up like one of those inflatable clowns, red-faced and eager to help right the bike. Unfortunately for him, most of his staff had seen his unconventional parking manoeuvre and this, I'm sure, was a substantial loss of face for him. The bike was fine and I tried to re-inflate his ego by saying I had done the same thing many times myself due to the *massive* weight of the fully loaded bike –but I don't think it helped.

We were directed towards the customs and passport control building which was huge and cavernous and completely empty bar the bored staff. There was no-one coming from Kazakhstan today (or tomorrow for that matter) except me, and there was no-one leaving China, so I was the highlight of their day. The place was typical Chinese official decor, polished stone floor, potted palms, lots of dark wood panelling with red and gold inlays; 1950's retro. First

130

stop was form filling and baggage inspection. They wanted the *entire* contents of my bags opened on the floor in front of them – I might have been the only traveller that day, but they weren't going to simply let me waltz into China without the once over, no, these guys were going to have some fun. I emptied first one bag, then another; there were rolls of toilet paper, fruit, nuts, a large sheet of apple paste (from Gennady's orchard), my "other" set of clothes (very dirty), toilet bag, beanie, video cassettes, travel guides, cameras and my tiny personal computer – all spread out over the floor with me on hands and knees passing them items they wanted to look at. They took most interest in my Polaroid camera and my computer, but after examining each closely for a few minutes they handed both back to me and said I could pack my bags. We went through the same procedure outside with my top box and panniers. By the time I got to my portable stove and bottle of chain oil they had seen enough and said stop, enough already. I even confessed to having a satellite phone (which was broken – really) and a GPS receiver (which was working) but they didn't seem interested anymore – I think I had worn them down with my honesty and openness, plus I had a minder, so there was little chance of any counter revolutionary activities taking place during my stay in China.

I jumped on my bike and followed Omar along the road leading from the border post into China proper where we met our driver who had been patiently waiting in his car – an old Toyota Land Cruiser 4WD. He was introduced simply as "Mr. Fan", no first name just Mr. Fan – so that's how I addressed him from that point on. To my eyes he had an immediately inscrutable face and reminded me of one of the entombed warriors from Xian, with a flat up-turned oval face with slits for eyes and mouth and thin straight hair growing in perfect symmetry outwards from the crown of his head. He did not speak a word of English so Omar was always our intermediary, but I immediately liked him as he looked me in the eye, shook my hand firmly and seemed only to say what was necessary and nothing more. He took my newly minted Chinese number plate and dug around for some scrap wire and then attached it firmly over my Victorian number plate. We took a picture under the shade of a tall row of poplar trees with me proudly standing next to my now Chinese registered bike. I also had a Chinese drivers' licence but that was kept under lock and key along with the myriad of other papers needed for a foreigner to (officially) ride their motorcycle in China. We had lingered here too long and a border guard who had been watching us silently suddenly broke out of his frozen pose and ordered us to move on quickly. It was already mid-afternoon, but still hot in the sun and any ideas of riding somewhere today were quickly quashed – we would head to Ta Cheng, just a few kilometres down the road and stay the night. Music to my ears – I was ready for a hotel, hot running water, a good Chinese meal and some rest.

***

The difference between Kazakhstan and China was immediate and substantial. The road was new, smooth and a pleasure to ride, there were trees, manicured grass and pretty flowers down the dividing strip and along the side of the road, street signs, lights and orderly roundabouts. Even the streets off the main road were paved and lit although most provided access to basic mud adobe houses and farms. We drove on, something more fundamental was different too, this place was BUSY, everyone was out doing something, all of the available land was being farmed and there was nothing left idle or derelict – if it was it was quickly re-used or converted into something useful. Maybe this was the great cultural divide between European Asia and Asia proper? The blood was thinner and pumping faster and it was a race to the top here versus the more sluggish and relaxed pace and laconic approach to life in Kazakhstan and Russia. Whatever it was, the change in intensity and public energy was palpable.

The city of Ta Cheng itself was also very different from where I had come; big wide open boulevards, flowers and grass down the middle, low-rise but orderly modern buildings along the streets, even a pretty city park with fountains, shady trees and lawns. In retrospect perhaps not a beauty, but so different from the parched earth and dusty, "organic" towns I had been through. I needed money so we headed to the bank, which at four o'clock on a Monday afternoon was full of locals with fistfuls of Yuan waiting patiently to be served. Omar insisted I jump to the head of the queue and be served immediately, which, to my surprise, didn't disturb anyone – if anything I think they appreciated the show for it wasn't everyday that a giant foreigner dressed menacingly in biker gear marches into the bank looking for quick money. It was all smiles as I was cashed up and ready for business with China.

I returned to my bike to find Mr. Fan intently studying the pool of blue coolant slowly leaking from my engine. He shook his head, muttered something in Chinese which Omar translated simply as "Mr. Fan thinks there is a problem and he will fix it". It was as if I were dreaming – for so long I had been solely responsible for checking and fixing everything and now I had an experienced mechanic along for the ride. The hotel was just around the corner so while I "freshened up" Mr. Fan got to work, fixing the problem by the time I had returned. I think quietly Mr. Fan was pleased he could help – and this certainly made a change from carting wealthy tourists around in his 4WD.

***

Even the hotels here were different. Although Ta Cheng was a relatively small provincial town, the hotel was massive, with manicured lawns and a sculpture garden with a small forest in the incredibly large area between the street and the hotel entrance. There were night lights which made a very pretty scene after dark. Omar asked what I wanted for dinner and I couldn't contain my excitement – I hadn't really dined in a proper restaurant as such and my diet had been limited by what I could scramble to find each day, so to have the pleasure of going to a place where you could sit in comfort, choose from a menu and relax was wonderful (in the anticipation at least). Omar pointed out the hotel's restaurant with outdoor dining and I was sold. We sat under Chinese lanterns at a table under a crop of pine trees in the mild evening. It was just the three of us and Omar took charge of the ordering and before I knew it we each had a large plate of hot noodles with stir fried meat and vegetables in a spicy sauce. I ordered a cold beer and let the explosion of flavours and spices wash over my tastebuds like a king tide over barren rocks. It was absolutely delicious and Omar was pleased as this wasn't Chinese food; it was a popular Uighur dish that according to him "all real men eat". Mr. Fan prefaced his meal by eating cloves of raw garlic, a ritual he would repeat at every meal we had together for the next two weeks. Omar said it made sitting next to him in the car difficult – but it was a Chinese practice to ensure good health so he understood.

Omar rolled out a detailed map of Xinjiang Province which had pictures of famous and beautiful scenic locations for tourists plus a little descriptive text. I looked at each scene hopefully and asked Omar whether we would be going there – "No, that's not near our route" he said each time, or "That's close, but we don't have time to go there". He told me that Xinjiang has many beautiful mountain ranges, lakes and pastureland (where most of the scenes on the map were from) and the rest is desert. And where were we going I asked?

"The desert"; we were headed along the southern Silk Road, across and around the enormous Taklimakan Desert. At this scale our journey (just in China) looked epic, and even though I had already ridden several thousand kilometres, this leg alone was going to be a few thousand more. It's funny, when I planned this trip I really had no comprehension of what riding a thousand kilometres would be like – distances between cities and across countries were just added up and averaged out in a mathematical exercise to spread the journey out over time. I had no real appreciation of the effort involved or the reality of relentless riding.

Dinner finished, we took a walk around the few blocks that made up the city centre. Omar – who was in my opinion already immaculately groomed – was looking for a haircut and Mr. Fan wanted a shave. We quickly found a unisex beauty salon staffed by two women, both Han Chinese, one of whom had cherry orange coloured hair in pig tails with a short denim skirt and a sailor hat. Omar ordered up the slightest of trims and spent the next fifteen minutes continuously checking the results of each snip making sure every hair was just where he wanted it, while Mr. Fan almost fell asleep as the other woman smoothed his face with a cut throat razor. I sat in the third chair and watched with great interest although at critical points of the shave I had to turn away so great was my fear of seeing blood spilt (which of course it wasn't).

Omar gave me a taste of what was to come by insisting we have an early breakfast (6:30am) so that we could be on the road before eight o'clock. Daybreak was early here, so it seemed logical to make the most of the day and, arriving at our destination well ahead of dark, suited me. My first Chinese breakfast was another shock for my taste buds and digestive system: milky, milky tea, peanuts, pickled vegetables, bean curd in spicy sauce, a bland almost tasteless soup and a very hard boiled egg – all eaten with chopsticks.

My bike was also in for a treat: quality petrol served by eager uniformed attendants at a real service station – no more guessing how much you needed and passing small notes through tiny holes to faceless people behind thick iron bars. This was modern, fast and friendly. The previous night over dinner I had relayed briefly some of my experiences (read: trauma) on the Road of Bones to Omar who proudly told me that all of the roads on our trip were newly laid and excellent so it was with some horror that I found myself twenty metres from the petrol station on a rough dirt track heading for a river crossing. The road here was so new in fact that they were still making it. It wasn't deep water, nor was it running fast, but it was over large slippery river rocks and not straightforward. I crossed nervously and was relieved to ride up and out of the ditch onto smooth fresh hard bitumen.

We rode out past many farms and fields of crops in rich fertile country and the road was lined with trees which made for pleasant riding. We were headed for low mountains which I could see in the distance and on our way we passed through a series of smaller towns and villages all bustling with activity and traffic. The roads were the only connection here with the rest of China so everything was based around road (truck) transport and most of the town's activity was centred on these main roads. There were truck repair shops, food stalls and trading shops with people scurrying around like ants trying to make a living. Soon enough though we were climbing the low hills and quickly the landscape changed from rich fertile farmlands to rocky, barren and windswept high plains bounded by grey brown hills on one side and the tail of the Tien Shan on the other. The wind had picked up and I was being buffeted around, reducing my speed dramatically. We stopped after a hundred kilometres for a quick rest and were approached by a young boy herding scrawny goats – he didn't say a word, he just stood and stared at me and my bike. I said "hello" but it didn't register and he ran away.

The road was excellent and there was little traffic but fighting the wind was hard work – the gusts came from side on and caught the flat, smooth profile of the bike like a sail and pushed me to the centre of the road. I had to lean into the wind and maintain a slight angle to upright to keep going straight. I was still waiting for the day when I could relax just a little and let my mind wander and contemplate the deeper questions of life, but it wasn't going to be today. We rode on into the late morning. The road had long straight sections and long easy curves just to keep it interesting, but apart from that and a few stray camels and goatherds, this place was barren – no vegetation, no animals, no people, nothing. Suddenly we passed through a low rocky canyon on a long lazy right hand turn and came down a hill to a small town hiding in a sunken basin on the otherwise empty plateau. Judging by the big factories, smokestacks and the huge piles of rocks and trucks, I guessed it was a town purpose built for the supply of materials for construction works. It was very odd, just a big main street with low rise buildings along each side – no trees, no parks, no grass, no other roads and no obvious water supply. There was an electricity sub-station and that was about all of any infrastructure that I could see. I rounded a final curve and entered the main street and changed down a gear to reduce speed but as I did, a horrible sound of crunching and grinding metal accompanied by severe vibrations came from underneath me. Oh Bugger. I squeezed the clutch hard but it wouldn't budge. I was in neutral but the noise and vibrations continued so I quickly hit the kill switch, stopped and put my head in my hands – what now? I pulled myself together and started the engine again, in the irrational hope that the problem would simply go away and be better now – it wasn't of course, and the same horrible crunching and grinding of metal noise came from the engine. Oh dear. I looked forlornly for Mr. Fan in the distance. He quite rightly thought I would manage to ride down the main street unaided so had driven well ahead of me. I could just see him in the distance, realising I was in trouble, stopping and doing a big U-turn and driving towards me.

By now I was the centre of attention on my big red and previously very noisy motorcycle. School was just out and I was surrounded by a swarm of schoolchildren all saying "Hello mister" to me incessantly. I felt so bad – more embarrassed than anything else; here I was in all my fancy gear, riding jacket, boots, helmet, ear plugs, sunglasses and I was sitting on broken machine with little or no idea what was wrong or how to fix it, being passed by locals on bicycles and donkeys. I started pushing with my head down over the bike watching the edge of the road. Omar came running towards me from the car asking what was wrong. I explained with as much technical detail as I could provide (i.e. "it makes bad noises when I start it and it won't go"). He relayed this insightful information back to Mr. Fan who knew someone in town and suggested we take the bike there to start investigating. Mr. Fan drove off and I was left to push with Omar walking beside me shooing away the schoolchildren who refused to leave us alone. It was hot and pushing a 250kg bike up a long sloping rise was hard work. Mr. Fan had driven off into the distance and we had lost sight of him. I was at my nadir – another problem, but this one seemed much more serious than the last. At least then the engine started, but now I couldn't even do that. I think I was passing into a clinical depression. I didn't want to talk to Omar and I certainly didn't want to push my frikkin bike anywhere. But Omar was the eternal optimist, re-assuring me that he would personally do whatever it took to fix the problem so that we could continue our journey. I had to admire the kid's attitude. My head was pounding from the exertion and all I could muster was half-hearted "uh huh"s. My grand Silk Road tour of China wasn't off to a great start; I had registered exactly *one hundred and thirty one* kilometres – only a few thousand short of what was necessary. We kept walking – me pushing in sweaty silence conducting a severe mental flagellation and Omar, keeping up the optimistic up-beat rhetoric. It was a long main street and I reckoned we walked at least a kilometre of it before eventually finding Mr. Fan outside a restaurant with a wide strip of pavement in front; this was his friend's place! There was no mechanic or garage in sight, just a bit of shade and some space to work. Mr. Fan was eager to re-assert his mechanical prowess so I stood aside as he stepped up with his toolkit and started to loosen the engine cover. He worked quickly with deft hands and had soon removed the engine oil, coolant and all of the engine bolts, placing the removed parts carefully to one side on the pavement on a towel. He worked in silence and alone but the engine cover just wouldn't come off – the long rod that runs vertical and turns on its long axis to push and pull the clutch plates was jammed in position, stuck to the plates preventing the cover from releasing. He tapped, pulled, pushed, inserted screwdrivers from many angles but it simply would not come off. It would move a few millimetres back and forth but no more. Undeterred, Mr. Fan persisted until finally after a couple of good thumps with my rubber mallet (I knew it would come in handy for something) the engine cover came off, and as it did, little pieces of broken metal fell from the open clutch and rained onto the pavement. Mr. Fan looked up at me slowly from his prostrated position and there was no need for words – his expression said it all; it was bad, very, very bad and wasn't going to be fixed quickly or simply here on the side of the road in a remote village. The thick vertical rod was bent and now useless, and some of the smaller bolts holding the plate in position had come free and shattered – the result of my poor repair work in Yakutsk (more self flagellation later). In addition, some of the raised bolt holes in the cover plate had snapped off. It was a real mess and I immediately went deeper into my depression – this was it, I'd tried my best, but this was as far as I was going to get I thought. My mind immediately raced onto evacuation plans – how to get a bike from the dead centre of Asia (for that's where we were geographically) to the nearest port and then home? I felt there was no way the bike could be fixed quickly enough, and re-working all my plans yet again would not be so simple with the domino effect of expired visas meaning I would need to re-apply for all of them again on the road, plus the waiting time etc. It was all too hard to even contemplate. Argh. But before I had time to reach for the Stanley knife to commit an act of self-harm, Omar and Mr. Fan suggested we retire to the restaurant for a good Chinese meal and consider our options. I could think of nothing better.

The other thing that really annoyed me was the fact that yet again I was an unexpected and unnecessary burden and problem for these guys. I was here on a tour, if I were them, the most basic expectation would include turning up with a functional bike and knowing how to maintain and fix it – but not me; day one and Kapow – time for another rescue.

In spite of the hard evidence to the contrary, Omar remained up-beat, suggesting that all we needed to do was "get it to a good mechanic who could fix it then we would be on our way again". He, like me, was not a mechanic, nor had he ever ridden a bike or driven or owned a car, so I took what he said with a grain of salt. It sounded so simple, yet I couldn't fathom how anyone, let alone a Chinese mechanic in a far flung corner of China, used to fixing locally produced bikes with little more than lawn mower engines could repair my bike. I ate peanuts with my chopsticks and something very spicy which I could not identify. A pot of green tea later, things were starting to look a little better. I had dug out of my bag the engine diagrams (used previously in Yakutsk) and also found the address and phone number of the Kawasaki dealer in Hong Kong – thousands of kilometres away, but at least technically *in China*, and the closest to us. A plan was emerging; we would transport the bike to Urumchi to the best motorcycle mechanic we could find, assess it there and decide whether to get spare parts and take it from there. Like my entire journey so far, there was no time or any point in stopping here so we continued on. I had that feeling like I had in Siberia when things were bad – "OK, I've had enough of this ride, can I get off now?" But of course that was not an option – Mr. Fan was sure my bike would fit in the back of his 4WD, but looking at the space I was not so confident. He insisted it would fit, and after much heavy lifting, grunting, manoeuvring, wheel twisting, shouting and a final angry kick, it was in and the back doors closed. My bike lay like an injured animal on the blankets in the back of Mr. Fan's car and I looked at it with some pity – for here it was again, broken and being transported somewhere to (hopefully) be fixed. The back seat was down flat and being the guest I rode in the cramped but functional front seat next to the inscrutable Mr. Fan. Omar, on the other hand, was dispatched to the rear where he was hunched over, squatting, wedged into the small space behind my seat not occupied by the bike. Omar didn't complain, and anytime I asked how he was he said he was comfortable! We had a long drive ahead of us – Urumchi was over four hundred kilometres away. We drove virtually non-stop, passing through more lifeless rocky mountain ranges before emerging on flat scrub and dry open plains that stretched all the way to Urumchi. I asked Omar if this was *desert* and he replied no, this wasn't *desert*; he would tell me when we reached the desert. This puzzled me, for these places were absolutely barren – perhaps we had different definitions of what constituted a desert?

***

We passed through new cities created recently to cater for the nascent and booming oil and gas industry. Everything was new – big wide roads, roundabouts, strips of not too ugly apartments, grass and flowers fed with precious water, even a golf course – it was very odd and incongruous to see all of this built upon the extremely arid land, and normally not sustainable, but here man had conquered nature by sheer brute force, money and willpower.

We drove on through fields of oil wells for as far as they eye could see, red and black mechanical donkeys – a sea of perpetual motion each rising and plunging into the ground to their own rhythm sucking the precious oil up and away for processing. The scale of these operations was just awesome – twenty four by seven, 365 days a year. The towns further distant from the oil wells weren't so pretty, just long low strips of truck stops along each side of the road; practical and functional but very, very ugly.

To help relieve his boredom (not mine) and perhaps take his mind off his physical discomfort, Omar started singing his favourite pop songs. His collection seemed to consist entirely of The Best of Lionel Ritchie and The Eagles Greatest Hits, and he was truly awful. I'm tone deaf but he still sounded really, really bad. He got stuck on the words for Hotel California and kept asking me to help but, alas, I could not. It was excruciating. Failing to close out the verses, he would then switch to a Lionel Ritchie love ballad; I couldn't decide which was worse. He said he sang these songs to his girlfriend in quiet, romantic moments and I felt very sorry for her. Mr. Fan rolled his eyes and smoked with a far away look in his eyes. I tried to stop the drone with some conversation and discovered that Omar was twenty six, had a serious girlfriend that he intended to marry and he wanted to start his own tourist business. Regardless of his singing abilities, I had to admire his energy and confidence. He knew what he wanted and was going for it. He asked what kind of music I liked which was a tough question that I couldn't adequately answer except by saying most types: rock and roll, folk, pop and jazz. I tried to explain the music of Billy Bragg, The Go Betweens, Bob Dylan, The Church etc but he just glazed over.

We eventually came to a freeway as evening fell and we sped the last few hundred kilometres, finally arriving in Urumchi after 10pm. It was a big bustling city of freeways, tall buildings, pulsing neon, People's parks and busy night markets. We were meeting Omar's boss – the head of the agency where he worked and he was nervous. I'm not sure if this situation was good or bad for him, but it certainly wasn't on my planned itinerary. Omar's boss would be taking us to a motorcycle repair shop that she had found since we called at lunchtime. I was introduced to her, but somehow I came to think of her as Madam Fang – she was fifty plus and extremely well preserved with white, almost flawless skin and hair pulled back from her face in a neat jet-black bun. She was dressed smartly in a modern jacket and pants with a colourful scarf and she carried an umbrella. She wore simple but elegant jade and pearl jewellery and struck me as both strong and wise. Madame Fang hailed a taxi and we followed her across town in our own. We drove along big wide city streets still busy at 11pm with traffic and people out eating and shopping. I saw many large motorcycle shops on the main streets, lifting my spirits immensely; sure they weren't name brands but the principles of operation were the same, and where there are bikes there are mechanics that can repair them. Then I remembered the extent of the damage and was not so confident. To my distress we turned off the main street and drove down dark narrow alleyways, seemingly lost until, after some round about driving, we came to a hole in the wall shopfront with a picture of a motorcycle above and a bare light bulb dangling from the ceiling illuminating a tiny concrete cell. This was the place where my bike would be fixed?? The shop was no more than 10 feet square and standing out front was a tiny thin wiry Chinese man in old track suit pants and T-shirt, unshaven with spiky black hair chain smoking. He could have been anywhere between forty and seventy. I was introduced to Mr. Shu – *master mechanic*. It took a leap of faith to believe that this guy was going to fix my bike; he didn't even come up to my shoulder and I think the bike was taller than him when we got it out from the back of Mr. Fan's 4WD and stood it upright next to him. But Madame Fang seemed quietly confident and smiled throughout as Mr.

Fan unrolled the towel where he had carefully wrapped all of the loose pieces from my clutch earlier in the day. Mr. Shu examined each piece carefully and showed us an old Kawasaki sports bike he had in his shop, partly in pieces already. I think he was suggesting that perhaps we could salvage some parts from it to put into my bike. This was not my idea of a sound repair, but I remained silent, leaving the mechanical decisions to him. It was late, almost midnight, but Mr. Shu's wife and his young assistant were there too; they had waited all night for us to arrive. We left, found a hotel and I fell into bed doubting that I would be able to continue or finish my journey as planned.

We returned late the next morning to find my bike out on the pavement with a cloth rag covering the open clutch and bits and pieces of metal and tools spread out over the pavement. An umbrella had been erected to provide some shade while they worked, and Madam Fang was in residence, watching carefully over proceedings. I did not know how long she had been there but she looked immaculate (in a new outfit), not a hair out of place and translucent skin with not a single bead of perspiration in sight. She had her own umbrella to provide relief from the intense midday sun and watched impassively as the grease monkeys went about their work. We found Mr. Shu inside, crouched on his haunches, carefully re-assembling the broken pieces of my clutch plate cover, drilling out the broken and locked-in-place bolts and re-tapping the threads in each of the shafts. It was painstaking work, had little chance of being successful in my estimation, and I couldn't believe he was even attempting it, but he persisted and told us confidently that he would have it fixed later that day! He then went on to show us a replacement long bolt (for the one that was bent and stuck in my engine cover) that had been fashioned earlier that day from a piece of scrap metal. It was an exact replica of the broken part but in shiny new metal – it was incredible and I couldn't get over the level of ingenuity here. I still doubted whether it would all work and unkindly reminded Mr. Shu that I still had over ten thousand kilometres to ride to get to Istanbul and I needed any sort of repair work to hold up for at least that much riding. I'm not sure if he was offended or not, but he shook his head violently from side to side and let fly with a torrent of Chinese invective that Omar simply translated as "Mr. Shu says don't worry, it will be alright for you".

We left Mr. Shu to his work and had lunch – more noodles, meat and vegetables – where Omar asked me more about my trip, where I had been and where I was going. He explained that as a Uighur, he was not able to get a Chinese passport and unable to leave the province of Xinjiang – that was the extent of his world. I pressed him a little further for an explanation but anything vaguely resembling a political discussion was absolutely off limits and he shut down the conversation immediately, apologising that he was not able to talk about these things. He told me that he had his own apartment here in Urumchi – that was progress – and that the quality of life for him, despite some of the restrictions, was not so bad, and always improving as the economy was booming. He was planning to open his own business, so at least the entrepreneurial spirit was (intelligently) not being stifled by the Chinese authorities. He was a proud Uighur and made a number of oblique references to the annexation of their territories by the Han Chinese to let me understand what he thought of this. I listened carefully and sympathetically but let it rest at that.

We visited what Omar called the "bazaar" which, in reality, turned out to be a modern tourist mall selling antiques, rugs and Mao memorabilia, rather than an authentic bazaar. In retrospect, however, I realised that this part of China was developing rapidly and had moved on from being a remote and unsophisticated outpost to a modern bustling city of two million people. I found a stall selling Uighur ice cream and enjoyed slowly eating a large and delicious bucket of it as we wandered about further.

We returned to the hotel where there was a message to return to the garage; Mr. Shu was finished and my bike was ready! As we pulled up at his tiny shop, there was already a crowd gathered around my bike, eagerly awaiting the return of its owner for the first test ride. Mr. Shu was there, just peering over handlebars, smiling and looking satisfied. I squeezed the clutch and, although tight and looking a little worse for wear with a big weld blob on top, it seemed to work fine. I turned on the engine, put it into gear and rode up and down the little back street much to the delight of the crowd of young boys and men. I changed up and down gear a few times and again everything seemed good. I was still very tentative and cautious and gentle but the bike was moving under its own power which meant the show could continue – incredible. I couldn't believe Mr. Shu had been able to put it all back together, plus fashion replacement parts to make it work, but he had and I was very grateful. Omar suggested we should bargain over the price with him, but in the end I paid Mr. Shu what he asked – his help more valuable than I think he knew.

***

The next morning we headed for Turpan, an old Silk Road oasis town just two hundred kilometres from Urumchi. There was some fine touring along silky smooth newly made roads that cut through low rocky mountain passes and in the distance, on my right were the spectacular snow-covered peaks at the tail end of the Tien Shan range, as it petered out into the desert here. I was enjoying this day.

We passed through a massive wind farm with hundreds of huge modern wind turbines laid out in a big grid on either side of the road. It even had a *tourist viewing platform* with a designated photo spot, so proud where the Chinese of what they had been able to achieve here in generating power. After clearing the mountains, we emerged into a Martian landscape; dusty red rocky plains for as far as they eye could see in all directions, split in two by a dead straight section of road that melted into the horizon. Absolutely no life whatsoever, and the heat here was intense, in excess of forty degrees. The road just went on and on straight and flat, and we rode like this for over an hour. I couldn't stop worrying about whether I was sitting on a time bomb and for how long Mr. Shu's handiwork would last, but the bike just kept going. At a short rest stop I asked Omar again whether this was *the desert*, but again he said no.

Finally, Turpan emerged from the heat haze and the monotony of our journey was broken by some curved road, trees and low buildings. Turpan is one of the lowest points in Asia at almost two hundred metres below sea level. It has a very small but fertile valley – well watered – where grapes (famous in China at least) are grown. We rode out under huge grape covered trellises to the valley and found a hotel. There were open water channels here by the side of the road and in addition to the grapes there were avenues of tall poplar trees providing shade and some cool relief from the intense heat. It was a pretty scene with farms and villages built up to the road with children playing in the shade and people going about their business. The level of development here was basic with most houses and buildings in mud adobe and the extent of shops running to butcher, baker and basic repairs only.

We ate at an outdoor restaurant under huge grape covered trellises where the owner would simply stand on a chair and pick ripe bunches of delicious grapes from above and place them on the table for us. It was noodles, meat and vegetables again – we had this ritual where Omar would ask me what I wanted, I'd ask him what they had and then we'd always order noodles, meat and vegetables, or *Lagman*, the traditional Uighur dish. And I always passed the ubiquitous bowl of raw garlic straight to Mr. Fan which he silently appreciated.

***

In the afternoon we visited the ruins of the ancient city of Gaocheng which is still incredibly well preserved, even after being overrun and cleared of its inhabitants by the raging Mongols more than seven hundred years ago. It was late in the afternoon but still very hot as we walked the dusty streets from the outer walls to the inner city. It was once a huge city and visited by merchants on their way to and from the West along the old Silk Roads. The city was almost deserted as we passed the city gates, guard houses and the homes of traders. Most of the city had been built up in mud and wood in adobe fashion and while the wood had deteriorated and disappeared most of the mud structures were still distinct and discernable. I asked Omar how this was possible after so long and he said simply "it never rains here". The sun was nearing the horizon in the west, illuminating the city walls and other taller exposed areas in a warm golden light against the deep blue of the sky, adding to the richness of the experience for me at least. Omar said he had been here more than a hundred times and suddenly I felt for him; the regular tours that he did most of the time were between Urumchi and Turpan, visiting the same old places and generating the same tourist patter that he didn't need to bother with for me. This job was a stepping stone, but it must have got boring for him and I was glad my tour was something a little different (he had never been to Kashgar for instance, which was where our tour would end). I noticed what looked like ploughed furrows in the sand and asked what they were and Omar said that during the Cultural Revolution the city had been given over to local farmers to grow crops wherever they could find good soil. For some reason they did not go on to destroy the city and today the site is protected and preserved with the help of UNESCO.

We also visited one of the many "Thousand Buddha" caves nearby in a deep ravine painted deep red and gold by a fiery setting sun. There were many of these caves around Xinjiang as Buddhism was the dominant religion prior to the arrival of Islam. Unfortunately however, most of the beautiful frescoes on the walls had been defiled (faces scratched away) as they contravened Islam's prohibition of depicting humans and animals in decorations and, even after that, most of what was left had been secretly stolen away in the early years of the 20th century by European *visitors*.

* * *

That night we ate outside under the stars in the warm evening and, for a change (based on block voting by Mr. Fan and myself), we had delicious meat dumplings, made fresh in front of us by a local family and served on a big plate in a high mound steaming hot, washed down by cold beer. We walked home along the quiet road under the light of a full moon with the gentle *splish-splash* of flowing water in the background and for the first time on the trip I felt content.

Another early breakfast and we were away. First stop was a water museum where this ingenious system for obtaining and irrigating this dry land was on show. Many hundreds of years ago, the locals had figured out how – by digging networks of deep wells into the mountain sides – they could capture and corral underground water to sustain life in the parched valleys and plains. It was a massive system and incredible to think it had all been done in an era well before any sophisticated machines or even tools were available. Omar was justifiably proud and I was impressed too. We then travelled a little further on to visit the ruins of another ancient city – this time a military fortress built on what was once a high river bank providing protection to cities and towns further downstream. It was only ten o'clock by the time we arrived, but the sun was already searing and I sweated a litre of water just walking up the ramparts of the entrance. I took a quick look around, admired the pretty local girls dressed in "authentic" costumes for tourist pictures and cut short our tour – I felt guilty, but I had seen enough and wanted to get going.

We drove across dusty pot-holed back roads to re-join the highway, had a quick lunch then climbed up and over a steep rocky mountain range, slowed by the many large trucks now on the roads. We descended into a narrow fertile valley and spent the rest of the day on side roads, negotiating road works and fighting local traffic and carefully watching the rear ends of trucks and buses trying hard to avoid a traffic incident. It was not pleasant riding and the day ended with us riding into a dust storm as we crossed another small mountain range. We travelled in single file behind a long row of big trucks that pumped diesel fumes straight into my helmet for the last hour or so as we headed down and into Korla – the Houston of Xinjiang. I asked Omar again whether we had travelled through any desert today and again the answer was a resounding "NO". For all of his foibles this guy was hard core when it came to his deserts.

Korla was the biggest of the new cities and had sprung up just in the last ten years on the back of the oil and petrochemical booty under the ground here. It felt like I was on the set of Blade Runner; a vast city of huge modern neon covered skyscrapers rising out of the thick and seemingly permanent dust clouds of the desert. There were gas fires in the distance adding to the effect. There were big wide streets, trees and more manicured lawn adding to the surreal nature of the place. There were new apartment buildings, schools, kindergartens, supermarkets and malls – all supporting the workforce needed to operate the machinery and process the by-products of oil and gas exploration.

This was only an overnight stay, but I had noticed a hard metallic scratching noise coming from my clutch when I changed gears, so I told Mr. Fan, who immediately called Mr. Shu and went on to suggest that we open the engine and take a look *just to be sure*. Mr. Fan was so concerned for my wellbeing that he went on to imitate – to the best of his ability – the harsh scratching noise to Mr. Shu over the telephone; it certainly livened things up in the lobby of the hotel where we were staying. The mere thought of opening the bike up again gave me the shivers and as they say, if it ain't broke but reluctantly I agreed. So, in the morning, on the footpath in front of our hotel, Mr. Fan set up shop where he carefully drained my oil and coolant and pulled the engine cover off (again) to take a look. He wasn't happy with some of Mr. Fan's work – I now had multi-coloured clutch springs and odd bolts – but he couldn't find anything materially wrong, so he tapped and tightened a few things and restored everything ready for riding. We also took a look at the clutch plate Mr. Shu had re-assembled from pieces; I had expected to see big welding blobs and bracing pieces of metal, but there was nothing of the sort; the whole piece looked like new with no evidence of any of the breaks. It was like the repairs sometimes you see of fine porcelain plates – you can just make out the cracks if you look very, very, carefully at it long enough. Even Mr. Fan shook his head in disbelief or something worse – I didn't know – which didn't help build on my already shaky confidence in the repair work. I wished we hadn't looked – now I had something more to worry about as I rode.

We were now heading along the southern, and less travelled of the old Silk Roads to Kashgar, and would be travelling around and across the Taklimakan Desert proper from here on. We spent the next six days following a rough routine: up at dawn for breakfast, riding maybe two hundred kilometres before lunch, stopping at a small village or town for – wait for it – noodles, meat and vegetables, then riding the balance of the distance in the afternoon, arriving at our destination sometime in the late afternoon, Omar finding a hotel and negotiating the best price, a quick rest, then a walk around the city/town before dinner at a local restaurant. Some nights we would cap off the day with a game of pool, usually played outside on the pavement under the stars in open-air saloons with rows of tables where young men relaxed after a hard days work.

Most of these days were very, very, hot and I remember arriving and riding the main streets with a high pitched squealing noise coming from my bike. It took a while to work out, but one day I found the problem: my petrol was boiling, bubbling away in the tank with the gas pressure building up and slowly escaping through the valve in the tank lid.

The terrain we covered was all *desert* in my book, but surprisingly varied from day to day, even hour to hour sometimes. We passed through rough treeless scrub, absolutely barren rocky plains and endless sand dunes that drifted onto the road. One morning we started with high winds and ended up battling a fierce sand storm for hours; visibility was only a few metres and the sand ripped across the road in thick streams, like a white water river driven hard by the howling wind. I could taste and feel the grit in my mouth as the grains of sand came up through the gaps my helmet. I lost sight of Mr. Fan's car almost immediately, and traffic coming from the other direction would jump out of the sandy fog without warning. It was awful, but we persisted (there was no protection or anywhere to stop anyway). When it had passed we stopped to recover – we were right in the middle of a sea of sand dunes for as far as the eye could see in all directions. Each dune was at least twenty or thirty metres high and rippled by the wind and otherwise untouched except for our footprints. We ran across a few dunes and climbed to the top of one for a panorama. There was absolutely nothing but sand EVERYWHERE. Just sand and blue sky from horizon to horizon. The only thing to distinguish elements of the landscape was the light and shade as the sunlight hit the undulations in the sand, but that was it – it was awesome and beautiful. I asked Omar whether this was a desert, and Crocodile Dundee like, he said yes, "Now this is a desert".

Other days were fine touring along perfectly made roads across starkly beautiful desert landscapes. I could cruise at 100 kph and let my mind wander. In those times I found myself watching a movie show in my mind's eye of my life to date; childhood, adolescence, working life, and of course, my family. It was in Technicolor and stereo and so vivid and sometimes the sessions would last for hours; it was fascinating as of course I was the subject. I'm not sure how the critics would have scored it, but in retrospect it wasn't a bad show and I wondered where the story would go from here. I was amazed at some of the detail locked away inside my head that these hours of passive driving had released.

***

One of my favourite times of day was riding into oasis towns in the late afternoon, down the long avenues of tall poplar trees. The cool shade and the green symmetry around the road were very pleasing to the eye after spending the day in the harsh untamed desert environment. Sometimes the trees would join at their apex, proving a continuous green canopy and forming a natural portico entrance to the towns. There were usually irrigation channels along both sides of the road providing life for the gardens and small fields of crops being tended by villagers.

All of these towns – Ruocheng, Cherchen, Keryia, Niya and Hotan – were solidly Uighur and it was interesting to see the influence and practice of Islam in these places. There were many mosques, men in long robes and skull caps and a few women covered from head to toe in burqas. Most women, however, chose the long colourful velveteen dresses in either deep red or blue and head scarves. A few of the more flamboyant souls wore long dresses decorated with sequins and similar material – like evening dresses.

It was difficult to tell, but there seemed to be no restrictions on the basic practices of Islamic life. We did of course see many police and soldiers along the way – all of whom were Han Chinese – to keep an eye on things. There had been protests here in the past demonstrating against the treatment of "locals" by the Chinese, but relations seemed cordial for the moment.

Another thing that struck me was the very basic and sometimes primitive living conditions of the vast majority of people. All of the housing outside the town centres was mud brick with a single shared water supply flowing in open channels and very few connections to mains electricity. Donkeys and carts were the dominant mode of transport and nearly every household or small community seemed to have livestock and a small plot of crops to sustain them. Life here was tough and it seemed just above subsistence level for most people. Of course, life in the big towns and cities was different, with apartments and small business dominating, but nevertheless the apartments were very small and basic and probably full with at least two or sometimes three generations living under the same roof and the businesses were simple and narrowly focused on just the essentials.

Unfortunately, in one of these towns I foolishly ate some yoghurt mixed with shaved ice from a street vendor. I love my dairy products and couldn't resist trying what was a delicious and refreshing dessert one night but it only took about six hours to develop full blown diarrhoea which lasted for days. I think Omar (and probably others) are still talking about my "funny walk" down the main street, across the courtyard of our hotel and up the stairs to my room one night when I got an urgent attack after an ill-considered dinner (think John Cleese, butt-clenched, goose stepping accompanied by soft moaning). Omar was truly concerned for my health from this point onwards, but I think he found it hard to accept that it was "something I ate" as this was a slight on Uighur food and his people.

***

In Hotan (about two thirds of the way along the southern Silk Road) we visited traditional carpet and silk factories. These were by no means grand affairs, just simple, small operations employing many people and using original techniques. At the carpet factory I watched on with much interest as women of all ages sat in rows and deftly threaded, tied and cut different coloured wools to complete their sections of fabulously complex and colourful rugs. They worked independently but in unison, and happily chatted with each other, laughing and smiling as they went about their work. There were about twenty rugs being worked on in the open plan factory, some being worked on by teams of women and some by individuals, some worked from patterns but most worked from memory alone. The factory was light and airy and I asked Omar to ask the ladies how many hours a day they worked and whether they

149

took holidays. He asked and translated their answers for me: they worked on average between eight and ten hours a day, every day of the week. They "agreed" up front on a production schedule with "management", and could take days off if they came in ahead of schedule – I didn't ask what happened if they were late. They also had regular breaks during the day and could negotiate days off in advance if necessary. They all seemed happy with their work and they worked at a fair, but not furious pace and it certainly wasn't a sweat shop.

At the silk factory I watched on as a woman who looked as old as Methuselah sat crossed legged on a high elevated stone platform pulling and winding threads from a vat of boiling cocoons. She sat entirely still except for her forearms – even her expression was unchanging, and I'm not sure whether she even blinked. She was economic in the extreme, focused entirely upon producing the fat skeins of silk thread, which were being fed from about *twenty* cocoons, so fine is the stuff. The owner explained that once the raw silk was obtained it was then tied off in sections and dyed in different colours so that when woven the famous Atlas pattern emerged. In an open plan shed next door I watched as a young man, already proficient, pressed his feet on the various pedals in rhythmic patterns lifting and dropping pieces of a loom while throwing a bobble from hand to hand as if he was catching ball. He didn't even look and was able to carry on a conversation with us without stopping. I felt sorry for him as this would be his lot for the rest of his days but he seemed genuinely happy with what he was doing so I could only hope the joy lasted.

***

We drove into Kashgar almost two weeks after starting our journey in China. We had crossed the long southern Silk Road and I felt a small sense of accomplishment in having successfully reached this point. Kashgar was at the crossroads of the numerous Silk Roads in the past and was also approximately half way (by distance) of my journey. But any notions I had of a romantic outpost with echoes of its rich past were quickly quashed by the blaring intensity and unquenchable thirst of the Chinese economic machine. This was a modern, fast-paced commercial centre with all the trappings and growing pains that come with being a rapidly growing city in China catering to an emerging middle class.

There were two highlights for me in Kashgar – one was finding a western style cafe that served the most delicious banana smoothies and the second was visiting the large and very old (but still functioning) mosque in the centre of the city which I found to be an oasis of tranquillity in an otherwise chaotic place. It had a beautiful sunken rose garden and quiet ponds outside the prayer hall where I sat for a long while just meditating in my own way.

I did walk the streets of the old town and saw artisans belting out copper plates, butchers working a side of lamb in the open air, cobblers, rows and rows of old Singer sewing machines being repaired and old men sitting around watching it all. Afterwards I retreated to the People's Park, where I found a park bench, laid down and fell asleep for hours – I was just so tired from all of my travelling. I walked past the enormous statue of Mao in central Kashgar on the way back to my hotel and wondered what he was still doing here? China had moved on so fast and so far from his days and his ideas. He was no longer relevant and I wondered whether the official party line of him being "70% right" would be revisited or whether it really mattered to people any more. My guide book urged a visit to the bazaar and animal markets but I took one look at the junk at the markets and drove on (in a taxi) and after walking about in animal droppings for fifteen minutes or so, I made a quick exit back to my hotel. Squalor – I was over.

***

That evening Omar, Mr. Fan and I had a farewell dinner at the restaurant opposite our hotel. Unfortunately, I think Omar had really got to like me so he was cut up about leaving which was nice. He said I was a "very good man" – a compliment I accepted graciously. I told him he had done a good job and that I had enjoyed an interesting journey and appreciated all of his help. I shook hands with Mr. Fan and told him in English that he had been a fine driver and a good travelling companion. He smiled, nodded a lot and said something brief but sincere in Chinese.

I had a new guide for the final leg of my journey in China who insisted we start very early for the border to make the morning session for processing, so I was under strict instructions to be ready at 5am sharp for our departure. I am not an early riser but even I knew this was well before sunrise – surely this was extreme? Was there something about the roads he wasn't telling me? No, he just said it was best to be at the border at the opening time to be processed quickly. I'd rather be late than tired but I didn't push it.

I set my alarm for 4:45am and as always when you do this I had a disturbed night's sleep, dreaming about being late and waking every hour or so to check the time. I did get some quality sleep in before waking myself naturally at 4:44am just in time to turn off my alarm. I got dressed quickly and stumbled down to the lobby to meet my guide and driver and then to the hotel car park to load my bags and warm the engine (it was a cold night). The warm up was good but as soon as I clicked the bike into gear the engine stopped. I tried a few times with the same result. This had happened before but previously with persistence the problem resolved itself – but not this morning. I pushed the bike out onto the street and tried a few more times without success. It was pitch black and the roads were empty which seemed to intensify the focus on me getting the bike started quickly. Even several vigorous pushes from my guide and driver couldn't get me going. I put my head in my hands again, skipped the emotional outbursts, and jumped straight to thinking bad black thoughts about what I wanted to do with my bike. I parked the bike, kicked it, and sat in the gutter for a while taking deep breaths and regaining my composure and watching dawn break over Kashgar. Slowly the city was coming to life – there were people on bicycles and scooters whizzing past, farmers with donkey carts delivering produce to the markets and kids off to school early.

As usual the show had to go on and there was no time for self-pity or deeper contemplation – our driver knew a repair shop, the only problem was that it was three kilometres away, across the city. There was only one option – to start pushing. I was fully geared up with boots and heavy riding jacket and although the night had been cold, the sun had risen well above the horizon now and it was getting hot. One kilometre I could have managed but three was a challenge – both mentally and physically. The most direct route was slightly uphill most of the way and along the main streets of the city. I pushed up to stoplights, turned at busy intersections manually, overtook and then was overtaken by city busses and every other man and his dog (literally) in the bike lane. I WAS NOT HAPPY. The sweat was pouring off me and dripping steadily onto the road. It was like taking a sauna. Eventually we made it to another hole in the wall bike repair shop and I collapsed in a heap on the pavement. I had not eaten yet and my head was pounding. I looked up and was introduced to the team of grease monkeys who would be working on my bike today. None of them looked like they'd hit puberty yet and the leader reminded me of the kids you see working the checkouts at Safeways or Woolworths – nice smile and keen but pretty scrawny and wet behind the ears. I had no idea where to start except to suggest it may be related to the automatic kill circuit connected to the side stand – perhaps this had malfunctioned? They went to work like a swarm of vultures devouring an animal left to die in the desert and soon all that was left of my bike was a skeleton frame – they had taken everything removable off to examine the wiring. I can't adequately describe how disturbing this was for me. There were at least six of them and each had removed different pieces and it was hard to see what system they were using to keep track of all the pieces and the bolts. How on earth would they re-assemble it all correctly? I tried to tidy up a little and keep things organised but I was outnumbered so retreated to the back seat of our car to eat a bread roll – my breakfast. My bike has a moderate level of circuitry but I had no diagrams and these guys just kept going, checking circuit by circuit trying to isolate the problem. It took about an hour but eventually they stopped and started putting things back together which I took as a signal that all was better. I tried to help put everything back together properly but when they had finished one of the kids was still holding a few largish bolts which he handed over to me quickly. I scanned the bike quickly but couldn't spot any obvious holes. Oh dear – just another thing to worry about as I'm looking for the brakes down a long mountain pass over the Pamirs. The checkout kid started my bike it and put it in gear successfully and took it for a few laps around the block before delivering it back to me. I was relieved that the problem was apparently resolved but none the wiser for what had caused the problem nor how it had been fixed, but I happily paid the fifteen dollars asking price for the repair.

We rode out of Kashgar at 10:30am with a revised plan; we would try to make the afternoon session at the border. We started climbing immediately and, of course, the weather turned cold – bitterly cold, and it started raining, which quickly became sleet. At a quick rest stop I changed into all of the warm gear I had but I still couldn't stop the shudders in my legs from the biting and persistent cold. To top it off we came to a big water crossing where recent rains had flooded and washed away part of the road. It wasn't deep but already a car and a truck were already stuck fast in the loose river bed of smooth rocks. Sensibly we stopped and examined the options both upstream and downstream. A few 4WDs were making it across on a diagonal line starting about fifty metres upstream and ending on the far side where the road recommenced. Our driver suggested we go for it and I followed him across cursing all the way. I hated water crossings and feared losing balance and getting a wet engine, but I made it across and we continued climbing to the border. The border crossing was a bleak collection of ugly buildings on a rocky hillside whipped by icy winds, keeping the huge queue of trucks and their occupants cold and miserable. I was processed clinically (no smiles here) and, after handing back all of my temporary Chinese driving papers and number plate, I was ushered through the final checkpoint and on to another no-man's land looking hopefully for some friendlier comrades in Kyrgyzstan. I don't know whether it was the language barrier, or perhaps something deeper and cultural, but I just hadn't been able to connect with the people here like I had in Russia and Kazakhstan. Travelling the old Silk Road here had been fascinating, but a very different experience to actually living with the people.

On the Roof of the World

I immediately felt at home; I was stopped by a group of truck drivers waiting patiently to be processed on the Kyrgyz side of the border. They greeted me warmly, we spoke for a few minutes and I, of course, asked about the roads and the weather further west, where I was heading. They laughed and said it had snowed today in Sary Tash and that the roads were muddy and that driving would certainly be "difficult". It was less than 100 kilometres, but nevertheless this was not the news I wanted to hear. And, just to sow the seeds of doubt in my mind one of them told me there were two roads – one "good" and the other, of course, "bad". They wished me well and I drove away towards the Kyrgyz border post thinking dark thoughts about riding in more mud and getting lost. It was cold, but the clouds were breaking in the west, revealing fragments of a brilliant blue sky and allowing just a few scattered rays of the sunshine through.

I rode into the compound and was greeted warmly and invited inside to meet the commanding officer. The buildings were basic, concrete slabs, just one level with a maze of rooms inside. Everything was whitewashed and the decor Spartan but clean and cosy. This was like old times, and all at once I felt the warm blanket of hospitality wrap itself around me again.

Crossing the border also introduced significant changes in the physiognomy of the people; the changes from China predictable, but there were noticeable differences from the Kazakhs too - the people here had longer, squarer, more structured faces, fleshy but handsome with brown (not always dark) hair, olive skin and lighter coloured eyes - predominately brown, but sometimes green and even blue, producing an exotic effect. These people weren't Asian - I was clearly back in the far- flung lands captured and occupied by the Rus.

There was even a woman officer here - she had pale lightly freckled skin, dark eyes, and she wore her dark auburn hair in a fashionable bob. She was feeling the cold, even inside, and wore an oversize military- issue green parker over her tall thin frame and smart uniform. She moved easily amongst the other officers, laughed and joked and seemed at ease in what must have been a difficult environment for her. Clearly, she held a senior rank and, after hovering for a few minutes, interrupted to assist the junior officer who was struggling to complete all of the arcane paperwork

155

required for me to officially enter Kyrgyzstan. There was not a computer in sight, nor any other form of modern technology, just a large old dusty paper register with hand-drawn columns in ink to track the movement of people, machines and cargo, based upon the judgement and inclination of the officers stationed here.

I was struggling to complete my declarations; they were printed in tiny Cyrillic typeset on flimsy translucent paper, yellow with age with impossibly small spaces to provide the details asked for (amounts of all foreign currencies carried, intended itinerary in Kyrgyzstan, etc). I handed back my perforated, ink stained, but completed forms and, without reference to anything I had actually written on them, my passport was stamped and I was directed to the customs area for a final "inspection" (i.e. a warm handshake and friendly conversation) before being waved off and ushered quickly through a large gate in the wooden framed wire fence that separated the border post from Kyrgyzstan proper. There was another young soldier here whose sole duty appeared to be the opening and closing of this gate. He was armed, shivering and cheerless, but as I approached it became clear that his main purpose was to hold back the heavy tide of trucks and their impatient drivers swelling on the other side from surging through into the small compound. With this new information I now understood why he was waving me on so urgently and why he felt it necessary to berate me emphatically as I rode past him all too casually.

I rode down the long alleyway of parked trucks and it was a bleak scene; the scruffy drivers either slept fitfully in their cabins or huddled in small groups stamping the ground with their feet to keep warm. The ground here was hard clay compacted by the endless stream of heavy traffic and the recent rain had made it soap-slippery. The alleyway opened out onto a wide expanse, sloping gently as it ran away from an exit roadway in the top corner. There were many more trucks and drivers up here, scattered around the perimeter breaking camp.

The ground here was pickled with the flotsam and jetsam from the tired trucks and their drivers - there were shards of metal, broken springs, tyres, nuts and bolts, discarded food packets, broken glass and crushed plastic bottles all baked into the surface, all conspiring to puncture one or both of my tyres.

I rode through the grim village that straddled the road; whitewashed block houses with pitched roofs scattered over the hillside where kids played in the dust and mongrel dogs wandered about scavenging hopefully. The kids saw me and

156

immediately started yelling, cheering, waving and chasing me. It was nice to see their smiles and excitement, and the first time I had experienced such a reception.

I rode on across a small concrete bridge, and started climbing. The countryside here was steep rolling, hills and mountains, barren apart from feeble tussocks of dry grass so that at a distance it all looked felt- covered, so smooth and regular was their colour and texture. The road cut sharply into the earth and twisted and turned and rose and fell sharply as it battled forward. As the border post and village receded, bobbing into the distance behind the hills in my rear view mirror, the road quickly deteriorated into an endless sea of large, deep ruts and car-sized craters, with plenty of gravel and larger rocks for good measure. The sun was still above the horizon but it was getting lower and was at times blocked by the thick blanket of heavy clouds that whizzed across the sky driven by the high winds. I was worried about snow - it was cold and these clouds looked like they could dump at any minute. The road, however, remained dry and rideable, albeit at a very slow pace with constant zigzagging required to avoid the biggest of the ruts and craters and areas of loose surface. This was the first patch of difficult road since leaving Siberia on the train more than three weeks ago. Rather than putting it all into perspective, it just got me down, but I pressed ahead knowing that it would take me a few more hours at this pace to cover the relatively short distance to Sary Tash, so I settled into the saddle and eventually found some peace in the rhythm of the slow, gentle undulations.

After some initial steep mountainside riding the terrain flattened out and I was riding through wide expanses of dry rolling pastureland. I passed the occasional yurt, always set well back from the road with puffs of blue smoke rising from their skinny makeshift chimneys and usually, close by, a solitary rider on horseback rounding up a few scrawny animals. I waved as I passed, and each, in turn, eyed me carefully and impassively from their slits of eyes in faces cut by the wind under their distinctive pointed felt hats. Some even acknowledged me with a slow cautious wave delivered from hands placed low over their saddles clutching reins.

I came to a long gently sloping hillside and rode down onto to a wide plateau bounded breathtakingly on one side by an unnaturally straight and regular series of gigantic snow-capped and jagged mountain peaks. The late afternoon sunlight, streaming in low and golden from the west, cast the exposed rock faces a rich dark brown and brought them into sharp relief against a canvas of pure white snow. The sky above and beyond the mountains had cleared and was a deep iridescent blue. The scale of the mountains was immense and awesome - stretching from the far eastern end of the plateau, continuing past me and into the distance, converging to a point at the horizon in the far west, like a dead straight rail line. The mountains exhausted my field of vision and I stood open jawed for a long time just taking it all in. It was all at once breathtaking, formidable and foreboding. Suddenly I felt good again and all the bumps and grinds from this afternoon and from even further back in Siberia melted away; this was stunning and wonderful. And there was no gentle transition here, rather the mountains just rose up all at once from the dead flat plateau and broke like a long and perfectly formed tsunami. And it wasn't just one wave, the mountains continued on deep behind the initial monster breaker in a frothy sea of white peaks to the far horizon. From this perspective the mountains looked impenetrable – a daunting natural barrier – and suddenly I felt very, very small. I had a small crisis of confidence as I contemplated my plan, while doubts about my bike niggled away at me: I was going to ride alone on my little motorbike into and over these giants?? It was more than *one thousand* kilometres to Dushanbe – mostly along mountain-goat tracks with only a few tiny settlements along the way. I worried about breaking down and then food, fuel, camping, altitude sickness, sun burn, snow, etc. The risks seemed much greater in reality than on paper in planning, but I quickly arrested this downward spiral by recalling the emphatic declarations of mechanical soundness made by Mr Shu in Urumchi when he had miraculously fixed my bike. He had re-assured me absolutely that I would get to "Istanbul and beyond" without any problems, so I started up again and headed off toward Sary Tash.

***

Long cold shadows now stretched across the road and land ahead of me as the sun fell behind the low mountains on my right. The wind picked up again, blowing me sideways off the road and down a steep, rocky embankment as I approached a raised bridge. Finally, near dusk, I arrived at a checkpoint just a few kilometres from Sary Tash. There was a heavy wooden swing gate across the road and a small guard hut on the elevated ground beside the road. A solitary teenage soldier dressed in a threadbare olive green flannel uniform and hat stood by the gate with a battered semi automatic rifle slung across his back. His cheeks were flushed crimson and his lips had turned blue from the icy winds that whipped along the valley floor. His expression seemed frozen solid by the cold too, but he managed to unlock his joints sufficiently to step forward to indicate where I should stop. I turned off my engine and rolled up to where he stood and removed my helmet, our faces now only a few inches apart (him standing, me sitting). He didn't say a word but tilted his head to one side, his mouth opened ever so slightly, his eyes narrowed even further and his brow furrowed. I sensed he was deeply troubled by my presence but before he could say anything, a burly cherub-faced senior officer sauntered down from the guard hut to join us. He was tall and powerfully built, slightly portly with thick curly dark- brown hair poking out from under his tight fitting military cap. He wore a dark green, snug-fitting modern (and obviously warmer) uniform, complete with sidearm and holster. He reached out with a big fleshy hand and shook my hand in a vice-like grip as he greeted me. We spoke briefly, but it was the bike that he was really interested in. His eyes lit up as I dismounted and immediately he began pawing at my bike. He had the usual array of questions about my bike - how big was the engine? What capacity was the fuel tank? What sort of petrol did it take? How many litres for 100kms? Electric starter only?? What repairs had been required so far? I was feeling good as I answered each question confidently but my credibility took a nosedive when he asked me his most important question - "How much power did it produce?" I fumbled about and muttered something about "many strong horses" but that didn't satisfy him and, before I knew it, he had jumped on, started the bike and was revving it hard, determined to find out the answer for himself. Like all other riders before, I cautioned about the weight and the risks of over-balancing, but he wasn't listening - he was salivating, nostrils flared, teeth gritted with a steely manic look in his eyes. Strangely, he asked about the gears and I explained it was one down and four up and how the clutch needed to work in concert with gear changing (this seemed like a new concept to him), but before I had time to explain any of the other controls, he had put the bike into gear and it was lurching forward. He bounced away and raced up though the gears to speeds I had never imagined possible on this terrain. He skidded sideways a few times before we lost sight of him over the rise in the road, leaving a long cloud of dust in his wake and a distant high pitched whining as he opened up the engine fully. Was this the last time I would see my bike in one piece? How badly would he crash and what sort of medical treatment would he require? To what extent would I be held responsible? I waited until the sound of the bike faded away, swallowed by the wind. I waited a lot longer in the icy wind making small talk with my new adolescent soldier friend, but there was no sign of him or my bike and I had begun shivering uncontrollably, so I trudged wearily up the small hill to the guard's hut for some shelter and warmth. The hut was just a single room with a cast iron stove in one corner, two old bunk beds, a small wooden table and a filing cabinet. An older, unshaven man dressed shabbily in civilian clothes sat at the table behind a pile of papers and food scraps. A single wind-up military telephone sat on the thick windowsill. The man introduced himself simply as "Alex" and invited me to sit on the small flimsy wooden chair opposite him at the table. He wore a faded blue tracksuit, had a thick patch of silver grey tousled hair and a heavy growth of peppery whiskers across a dark and creased face. His eyes were heavy with sleep and he reeked of alcohol. The room, apart from these basic furnishings, was bare and had a decidedly Mediterranean feel to it with a clean smooth stone floor, whitewashed walls and bright blue painted finishes on the wooden window frame and door. The room was warm and cosy but my reception was not. Alex, affected by the booze, alternately played good-cop then bad-cop with me; he greeted me warmly and showed genuine amazement and admiration for what I had done and still planned to do, then almost immediately he churlishly asked me to empty the contents of my small red backpack onto the table for him to inspect. Long ago I had decided to carry all of my most important and precious items in this backpack to keep them safe, so he had inadvertently hit pay dirt. Out came my cameras, my paper notebook, my money belt (yes, I never wore it), toilet paper and my stash of half-eaten food. He immediately asked for my customs papers to double-check that it matched what I had declared only hours earlier at the border. I had never bothered to hide or separate any of my money so this was all I had and I silently kicked myself for being so foolish. He made me count every note and, although there were some minor discrepancies, it tallied pretty closely with what I had declared. He watched me like a hawk until I had finished then said rather belligerently that I needed to pay a "service fee" of ten US dollars! I asked what the fee was for, but his brain was too addled to form any coherent answer. I considered my options: I was alone, without my bike and luggage with one frozen, but armed and able-bodied soldier and a schizophrenic drunk – I paid. He opened the little exercise book where he had been recording my

160

details and pushed it across the table to me - I tried to hand him the money directly but he refused to touch it, angrily pointing at the book - "Put the money in there!" he hissed at me. I complied and he quickly shut the book and pushed it to one side. Almost at that same instant the officer who had been riding my bike burst through the door like a kid whose footy team had just won the grand final - he was gushing with excitement and clapping his hands wildly and whacking me on the back saying how much he had enjoyed thrashing the life out of my bike. I was relieved to have some company, and all at once the sombre mood lifted, replaced by a party atmosphere. He introduced himself as Ivan, telling me proudly that he was the commanding officer of this post. We continued our conversation from earlier and went on to discover that our birth dates were *identical*, a fact that seemed to fill him with delight. He loved bikes, had owned many and just wanted to ride fast. He was effusive in his thanks and insisted I stay longer and join him and his sozzled colleague in some "healthy" drinking. He reached for the top drawer of the filing cabinet and produced an unopened bottle of vodka, some small china bowls, a cucumber, a knife and a jar of salt. They offered me a hunk of stale bread from under an old newspaper on the table and I took my vodka with them, toasting health and friendship. The vodka warmed me instantly and the salted cucumber was light and refreshing. I was still had a delicate stomach from my foolish street side eating in China and it groaned softly with the introduction of the toxic mixture. We drank three rounds before Ivan reached for a large battered heavy duty plastic petrol canister sitting in a corner of the room. What on earth was he going to do with petrol? Visions of him riding Evel Knievel style through a ring of fire on my bike flashed briefly through my head. He asked whether I had ever tasted horses' milk, and before I could unravel this combination in my mind, he had drawn a big breath, filling his chest and, in muscleman pose, began expounding on the virtues of the stuff - "Good for your health" and "To make you stronger for the road" he said as he pounded his chest. These endorsements had a familiar ring to them and I knew I was going to struggle to avoid drinking the stuff, so I told him truthfully that no, I had never actually drunk horses' milk before. He unscrewed the cap from the petrol canister and filled my china bowl to the brim with the thin white liquid, accompanied by about half a dozen little brown soft square pieces, floating on top like croutons. It had a sharp odour and two words immediately flashed brightly in my mind like neon warning signs on a freeway on a stormy night: "homogenisation" and "pasteurisation". Fearing I could not introduce these complex topics easily into our conversation and not wanting to offend him - this stuff was the national drink after all - I picked up my bowl and drank it all in one long dangerous slurp. It tasted like fizzy, slightly soured milk, and the aftertaste was not unpleasant. Unfortunately my reaction must have pleased him and he poured me another big bowl of the stuff. I took a deep breath and swallowed it like the first. This really made Ivan very happy and he went on to say some wonderful and hopeful things about me, my journey and his wishes for goodwill amongst all men, as we drank a final vodka toast.

Our celebrations were interrupted by a truck heading out of town and all three of them (the young soldier had joined us too) suddenly rushed out to conduct the inspection, leaving me alone in the cosy room with a slightly fuzzy head. I warmed my hands at the stove and noticed that the young soldier had left his rifle on the top bunk bed. I debated picking it up and taking it to him, but couldn't bring myself to touch it and waited patiently for them to return.

When Ivan came back I asked about accommodation in the town and he told me not to worry and that he would ride back into town and arrange everything. I was in no position to argue and didn't fancy being a pillion passenger with him, so thanked him gratefully and watched nervously as he headed out into the darkness and roared off into town again on my bike.

I sat a while longer with Alex, who was now my best friend, and we talked excitedly about my plans for crossing the Pamirs. He insisted that while I would certainly be safe in Kyrgyzstan, Tajikistan was a dark and dangerous place, infested with bandits, murderers and savages. It was hard to make sense of his drunken babbling but I think he was suggesting that we might travel together or that I should have a police escort at least. In fact, goddamn it, he was going to organize it right now! He reached for the old telephone and wound the crank handle vigorously - it had no dials and was hardwired to the other end - somewhere. He waited a long time and despite his crude cursing and protestations there was no answer. He drank some more before trying again, and then two more times again until, exasperated, he gave up.

I could hear Ivan returning on my bike so I excused myself and walked briskly down to the gate to meet him. He was followed by an old man driving an ancient pock marked orange Lada. Ivan introduced the old man as his commanding officer - by my reckoning that made him the local chief of police. He was very tall and thin and uncoiled himself slowly as he got out from his small car. He wore no uniform but stood proud and wise, immediately commanding the respect of his junior officers. He had a long rectangular face with a square jaw and sunken cheeks covered in a soft white stubble, mottled skin - slackened and craggy with age, shaved temples and a shock of short spiky white hair growing straight up and pale blue wet eyes. He stood almost as tall as me and shuffled over to shake my hand before I followed him along the dark road into town.

The town was much closer than I had imagined, emerging as a tight collection of twinkling lights nestled in the foothills of the mountains as we crested a rise in the road. The night sky was clear and inky blue/black, the wind had dropped and the air was crisp as we rode past the simple block houses of the village, each with a warm yellow light glowing in their windows. My pleasant evening ride was suddenly interrupted by a pack of mongrel dogs who were only interested in savaging me and/or my bike. I hit the throttle and sped up dangerously, almost careering into my guide's car from behind at a T-junction where he had stopped to wait for me.

He led me over the final fifty metres, across the main north-south road (this was the Pamir Highway!), down a small embankment and then up a steep rocky driveway to a long low house perched on the hillside overlooking the village. It even had a garage that he offered to me for my bike, leaving his precious Lada out in the cold.

Inside I met his daughter Maree, who operated a very basic home stay here when required. Maree had a young baby son and lived here with her parents. She was tall and strong, with thick short dark brown hair, a round, tanned and lightly freckled face and bright green eyes. She had a cheeky girl-next-door smile, greeted me warmly and showed me immediately to my room - the only traditional bedroom in the house. A blast of hot air hit me as I entered the room, like opening an oven door. The room was small and decorated simply with tell-tale traces of its previous (female) teenage occupant. There were three rickety steel sprung cots laid head to toe in a U shape around three walls, leaving just a small narrow space in the middle for access. In the corner near the door sat a homemade electric coil element heater. It looked like someone had taken a couple of coat hangers, wrapped them around some old cement bricks then pumped it full of as much electricity as it could handle before melting. I followed a makeshift cord across the floor and up into the wall, where it was hardwired into the mains, near the light switch, in two thick exposed knots of wire. I took a mental note to be careful when switching on the lights. The element glowed an angry bright orange and an old steel canister, cut in half and polished, was positioned behind it, radiating heat back into the room. The walls were thick stone and mortar with only one tiny window set high in the far wall to help ensure that most of the generated heat was retained inside.

I dumped my bags and riding jacket, unpacked a few essentials, and poured over my new map; I had now ridden off the edge of my map of China, and it was with some satisfaction that I retired it to the bottom of my case and brought out my shiny new map of Central Asia and began looking at where I had come from today and where I was heading to now. It was a long way to Iran (where this new map ended) and I still had to cross one of the highest and longest mountain ranges in the world and more big and remote deserts, but at least I had made it here, and had been able to stick to my self-imposed schedule, in spite of mechanical issues, since resuming riding in Novosibirsk three weeks ago.

Maree knocked on my door and showed me to a small room opposite where I enjoyed a wonderful meal of stuffed peppers, potatoes, meat, sweet peach flavoured tea and bread. Tired but fully satiated, I headed straight for bed, but as I lay there in the absolute still and quiet of the night I suddenly noticed how hard and deep I was breathing - I was at 3,300 metres now (11,000 feet), the air was thin and I was struggling to get enough oxygen into my lungs. I could feel my chest heaving softly even though I was at complete rest. I eventually drifted off, but slept fitfully, waking every so often gagging for air. I had taken drugs to help acclimatise quickly but even these couldn't eliminate the symptoms entirely - I had climbed over 2000 metres from Kashgar in one day's riding and would shortly climb another 2000 metres to reach the highest point along the Pamir Highway - but that was in Tajikistan and I still had to have breakfast, prepare my bike, ride up into the mountains and cross the border.

I packed up and came out onto the enclosed veranda where everyone else in the family seemed to have camped for the night, sleeping together on colourful cotton mats spread out across the floor. Old Russian cartoons played on a small TV set, entertaining Maree's son. Maree herself was busy cooking my breakfast on a tiny portable electric stove on the floor. I washed my face quickly then stepped outside to check the weather. The morning had dawned clear and cold over the little village and I looked out over a spectacular scene; down over whitewashed houses, out across the long wide valley to the majestic wall of sleeping giants, silhouetted against the bright morning sun streaming in from the east. The sky was a brilliant blue and cloudless. The sun's rays warmed my face and immediately lifted my spirits, wiping away my doubts from the previous day.

I returned inside for a hearty breakfast of eggs, bread and tea before retrieving my bike from the garage. Maree's father shadowed me, keen to help. I needed at least fifteen litres more petrol in my tank to reach the next major settlement and, unlike China, there were no shiny new gas stations here with bowsers of different types of petrol to choose from, nor were there pretty young gas girls in nice uniforms ready to fill 'er up – in fact there were no gas stations here at all; petrol was bought and sold strictly off market in private transactions. Understanding my requirements, Maree's father opened the trunk of his battered Lada, rummaged around quickly finding an old piece of thick rubber tube and a ten litre petrol canister. He removed the cover from the car's fuel tank, shoved the tube in and then bent over and began sucking hard until the petrol began flowing. He took a mouthful of petrol and spat it out immediately in a sharp reflex reaction before sliding his left wrist and forearm heavily across his mouth, wiping away and soaking up the excess fuel. Unfortunately for him, and me, and before he had time to straighten up, the flow became a trickle then stopped altogether. Not to be discouraged, he repeated the process, and again there was a short burst of fuel, then a trickle, then nothing. More fuel ended up in his mouth this time than in the canister. He gagged and coughed violently, spraying fuel and phlegm in a thick mist before doubling over and heaving as if winded. At this point I began to worry about the old man's health - surely he would have to stop now? I told him that it really was OK and that I had enough petrol. But he had made a commitment and like a proud punch-drunk prize fighter at the end of a fourteen round beating he stumbled back to his feet groggily, wiped his mouth again and gave one last massive suck on the pipe to drain his near-empty tank. This time he got a much better siphon and extracted five more litres before the flow stopped for a final time, his car tank drained. And as he poured the petrol into my tank I got a whiff of his pungent petrochemical breath – I knew he smoked and I hoped - for his sake - that he wasn't going to light up any time soon.

I now began my routine checking of the bike. I had pushed my bike to the only level ground I could find in front of the house and began pouring over it. Maree and her mother sat on the front steps in the bright sunshine as her little boy played happily nearby, curious about me and the bike. What had begun as a quick eyeball of the oil level (after destroying my clutch) had now become almost a full inspection of the bike each morning. Oil, chain tension, chain oil, critical nuts and bolts, panniers, wheels, brakes etc. To the untrained eye it must have looked as if I really knew what I was doing. I chatted happily with Maree and her mother, then, after about fifteen minutes, I tried to start it. It groaned a few times making a sound like a barking seal then went quiet. I pushed the starter again, same result. Embarrassed, I explained to my audience that, of course, it must be "cold" (despite having been in the garage all night). I tried again, same result. Now I was getting nervous. I was about to begin 1000 kilometres of tough solo riding across one of the largest and more remote mountain ranges in the world, and my bike wouldn't start. Was it a sign of some more serious problem? My mind raced and in a blaze of blind and irrational determination I pumped the starter button and throttle continuously until eventually the bike coughed and spluttered into life. Like a caveman with his precious fire stick, I coddled the bike for another five minutes keeping the revs up determined not to let the engine stop running.

I said farewell to Maree and her family, rode down to the paved main road and turned onto the Pamir Highway. I found a store, stopped and bought a bottle of yellow fizz and a big bag of assorted dry biscuits (sold by weight) - my stomach problems had returned with a vengeance that morning so this would be my only food for the day.

***

I headed out of town and came almost immediately to another checkpoint, with the ubiquitous wooden gate over the road, but this time a solitary scruffy solider bunkered down inside a huge half-buried and fortified concrete pipe. He came out, half dressed, wiping the sleep from his eyes, checked my papers cursorily, lifted the gate and waved me on.

The road here was paved but pock marked with huge holes, more ruts and loose gravel as it headed straight for the wall of mountains to the south. I stopped again to take in the incredible panorama of mountains that stretched from one end of the valley to the other. I knew there were giants in here over 7000 metres high and I was excited to finally be at this long anticipated part of my journey. Everything seemed clearer and sharper to me now. I don't know if it was the altitude or sun or perhaps the extra heavy dose of acclimatisation drugs I had taken that morning, but I certainly felt a heightened sense of reality. I could feel the road beneath me, every rock and pebble, every undulation, every twist and turn, I could smell and almost taste the dry mountain air - all of my senses were tingling.

Soon I came to a young man on horseback herding a small group of bony cows across the road between dry pastures. He rode right up to me and looked me in the eye before greeting me warmly and asking me playfully if I'd like to swap positions with him. I politely declined his offer and rode on into the shadows of the mountains. From this distance it seemed impossible that the road could possibly breach this fortress, but as I rode deeper into the steep foothills and came level with the first ramparts, a narrow winding path along a razor thin valley floor emerged on my right.

I forded a small, rocky, river crossing where the road and bridge had recently washed away. Then the road immediately began twisting and turning and climbing as it started to penetrate the mountains. There was no traffic, and after riding for another thirty minutes in the cold shadows I came to the final Kyrgyz checkpoint. The gate was manned by another frozen teenage soldier - I doubted whether the sun actually shone at all in these deep valleys, so high were the surrounding mountains. He called me to a stop and then directed me to dismount and follow him to the nearby barracks and compound where his commanding officer and the other soldiers were lolling about on a small parade ground. There were at least twenty soldiers here - all doing nothing in particular. I felt sorry for them stationed up here alone in the shadowy cold. They asked whether I had passed any cars or trucks today - it was already mid-morning and I was the first person they had seen and perhaps the last - trade between Kyrgyzstan and Tajikistan had virtually dried up in the last few years and as a result the road here had become very, very quiet. They were just filling in time. I tried to imagine how awful winter must be here.

They were extremely curious about me and my trip and we spent fifteen minutes talking before I bade them farewell. Although they had flicked through my passport and checked my other papers I wasn't officially stamped out of Kyrgyzstan and I wondered, as I rode off, whether this would pose any problems later for me. The road climbed steadily before coming to a final tiny hamlet. A mother and her children waved excitedly at me from their terraced yard high above the road. The greetings here were certainly warmer and more spontaneous than I had experienced to date in other countries. The road then ran straight into a mountain side and I began an extended series of short but sharp and steep switchbacks on dry soft dirt, climbing 1000 metres very quickly. I never got beyond 1st gear and rode very, very slowly, almost tipping over on some of the tight hairpin bends. I waited nervously for any signs of altitude sickness but remained clear headed and was able to enjoy the spectacular vista of the ring of snow-capped peaks that I was rising to meet. Eventually I reached a pass at over 4000 metres (incredibly it was signposted), the road levelled out but it had become chopped up and rocky making riding difficult. The road continued snaking up between the mountains. The earth here was a deep rich red-brown, with big loose boulders and crushed rocks from recent landslides scattered randomly over the track. The landslide debris became worse the higher I rode, eventually covering and obscuring the road completely. There was, however, a fresh track discernable through the fallen boulders and across the rocks and mud, but a highway it certainly was not. Irrationally, I worried whether I was still on the right road - surely there could not possibly be another road up here, but nevertheless I asked a passing farmer who had appeared suddenly with his flock of sheep whether this was in fact the Pamir Highway and the way to Murgab. After recovering from the initial shock of seeing me, he re-assured me that this was the only way (despite the path ahead deteriorating further into a rocky morass).

I slowed to walking pace as I navigated carefully around boulders and dipped through big muddy rock-filled pools. The bike stopped a few times as I rode the clutch before dropping it in a roller-coaster section of the track. This was like the worst parts of the Road of Bones – except it lasted only a few kilometres and not hundreds of them. All of the old symptoms from that type of riding had, however, returned: my pulse raced, I was quickly drenched in sweat and my brain had started pumping strange and powerful chemicals into my body. I had made the mistake again of assuming that a big red line on a map labelled "Highway" would somehow translate in reality, into a well maintained paved road.

I cleared the last stretch of landslide debris, stopped, bent over and folded my hands on the handlebars and rested my throbbing head. I was breathing hard now and now that I had stopped I suddenly noticed the severe pins and needles sensation in my hands and feet, making them almost numb. Surely it couldn't be that cold? Then I remembered - these were the side effects I had been warned of from taking the acclimatisation drugs, although the cold was contributing too. I had climbed 1000 metres in less than an hour and the temperature had dropped sharply. My cheap combination clock and thermometer had broken on day one (even before I crashed) so I had no idea how cold it was. I had almost reached the snow line and my heavy breath was coming out in a thick mist. I gingerly dismounted and stumbled onto what felt like stubs at the end of my legs and began limbering up like a nervous Olympic 100m finalist. I was hopping and jumping and ringing my hands for at least ten minutes before I started to feel anything. I placed my hands on the engine block for a final burst of warmth to help kick start my circulation before riding the final short uphill section of the track to a kitsch totem pole and cement statue of a ram on the crest of the pass that marked the border with Tajikistan. And that was it - there were no barriers, no gates, no soldiers, no barbed wire and no-body, just a badly weathered and rusted sign saying "Welcome to Tajikistan" in Russian.

I rode gently downhill on an easier track for a few kilometres before coming to the surprisingly large Tajik border post - remarkably they had managed to carve out an area larger than a front patio for an assortment of rough buildings and an inspection post. I was greeted by a young soldier who showed me into a long silver cigar-shaped caravan. Inside was like a gypsy wagon, with heavy wooden frame and furniture, threadbare carpets, curtains and colourful bedding strewn about on two rows of bunk beds pitched three high behind a central bulkhead. There were modest girlie posters on the wall and a large, half-dressed, greasy Tajik soldier sat at the table. He stood to greet me before asking for my passport and other papers. I sat on a bed opposite him as he slowly fingered my documents. He was neither friendly nor unfriendly and sat impassively in silence as he examined each of the pages in my passport carefully. I began to worry that this might get difficult - I was in a remote location and my progress, in reality, was completely at the discretion of these bored soldiers. Finally, he looked up, smiled, and began asking about my trip and commending me for taking such a journey. He told me solemnly that he collected foreign bank notes and coins, which I at first I thought was simply a euphemism for extracting small bribes from travellers. However, when I emptied the contents of my money belt onto the table he bypassed all of my precious US dollars (all eight hundred of them), my residual Chinese Yuan, Kazakh Tenge and Russian Roubles, and went straight to the relatively uncommon and unusual Mongolian Togrogs which I had never used and had kept well preserved in a small zip-lock plastic bag. His eyes lit up as he removed and studied each note intently. He was genuinely interested in and excited by these notes and I told him he could have whatever he liked (their total value being something less than ten US dollars). Notwithstanding this, they were incredibly valuable to him and I suspected there hadn't been too many Mongolian travellers come this way since Genghis Khan and his murdering hordes 800 years earlier. He took only a few notes before returning the balance to me, thanking me sincerely and asking me politely to pack up quickly and follow him outside. He then led me to a larger wooden hut deeper inside the compound with a slightly more formal office where I needed to complete my customs declarations. We were joined here by another man - resplendent in his new Russian national track suit of bright blue with red and white trim, and a young shy soldier. A large stove fashioned from a petrol drum stood in one corner warming the room and providing heat for endless pots of tea. There was a much larger wooden desk here with papers spread about messily. The two older men sat opposite me as we completed my customs papers and they examined my bike registration and carnet, but my visit quickly became an extended social event with bread, tea and plov coming in short order. Unexpectedly, this was going to be my lunch. I produced my large fold out map of Central Asia which they both studied with great interest as we discussed my favourite topic: the road ahead. The first solider I had met was quite definitive, telling me "From here there is eight kilometres of bad road, then some good road, then, before you reach the highest mountain pass there will be twenty kilometres more of bad roads, the road will not be paved". He was from Dushanbe and had driven these roads many, many times so I had no reason to doubt him. They gave me plenty of advice on my route and the towns along the way. We then got on to talking about travelling alone when the other man made some crude hand gestures asked me pointedly: "don't you ever want for a woman?" I explained that I was happily married to a wonderful wife and that she was the only one for me. He shook his head in disbelief and perhaps a touch of scorn and then proudly told me he had three wives who "serviced" him well and often. I congratulated him but conceded that one wife was more than a handful for me. He laughed and we ate and drank some more before I took my leave of them.

It was midday now, and although the sun was high in a cloudless sky, it was still cold; my hands and feet were still tingling uncomfortably and I had only come about 60 kilometres since starting this morning - a long way short of what was required. At this rate I would not get to Murgab until well after dark and riding in the dark, on this road, alone and cold, at high altitude, was a scenario I did not want to even begin to contemplate. My friends were exactly right though; immediately after leaving the border post the road deteriorated with a rough loose rocky icing over a hard and tightly corrugated base - running across the road like bulldozer tracks. It didn't matter what speed I tried or what line I took it was still a bone jarring ride. In the end I found some relief riding slowly along the shoulder of the road until that became too soft and slippery. Thankfully, there were more paved sections, although the most useful stretches (i.e. those with bridges crossing rivers) had been washed away, demanding difficult off-road fordings.

The landscape changed and the road now cut across a wide gently pitched valley floor; this was still above 4000 metres but it wasn't switchback mountain climbing anymore. A long, unbroken and austere looking barbed wire fence tracked parallel to the road here, emphatically marking the border with China.

I climbed a long hill and came to another frikkin checkpoint - this was getting ridiculous and tiresome - what illegal activities could I (or anyone) have possibly undertaken in the few kilometres of barren and exposed earth between here and the border? There was no-one and nothing here. There was no gate at this checkpoint and as I approached there was no sign of anyone on guard. I debated whether I should stop or just ride through and take my chances, but in the end, visions of me becoming target practice for bored, half-drunk and trigger-happy Tajik soldiers flashed through my mind, so I stopped, parked the bike and wandered into the stone hut by the side of the road. I entered a large bare room that was dark, silent and empty bar three pairs of slippers next to a closed wooden door in the far wall. I felt slightly nervous as I strode across the room, drawn towards the door which I felt compelled to open. I knocked sharply then opened the door slowly, simultaneously declaring my presence and friendly intentions. Inside the room sat three bored and half-drunk soldiers languidly taking a long lunch. They looked up in surprise and then quickly invited me to join them. The room had two double bunk beds along opposite walls and an old wooden table under a large window that looked out over the road ahead. The men sat on the bottom bunks and invited me to share in their lunch of bread, plov and melon. This would be my second lunch for today but they didn't know this - and I had been well trained in over-eating from my time in Russia and Kazakhstan - so I sat down and ate happily with them.

I sat opposite the commanding officer. He was young and had a big round shiny face, wore a wide and permanent grin and had a thin crop of light-brown hair that grew back off his forehead and temples. He was sloe-eyed, and looked decidedly Turkic to me. He wore dark green military fatigues and a regulation blue and white striped Russian military singlet. His colleague, whom I sat next to, was older and more hardened. His face was gnarled and swarthy with a thick cover of silvery stubble across his jaw and throat. He had a classic Slavic profile and was lean and muscular. The other man was visiting from a nearby post and sat reclined on the bed, resting his head against the wall. He was handsome but happily drunk and only rarely contributed to our conversation.

Based on the large number of empty vodka bottles under the table (which I had kicked when sitting down) and their happy lethargy, I guessed they had been drinking slowly all morning. Nevertheless, despite their drunken stupor, we carried on a surprisingly friendly and coherent conversation punctuated by small vodka toasts. I had tried at first to dissuade them from filling my glass for these toasts, but relented when I saw how much my participation meant to them. They told me that they saw perhaps two or three vehicles a day, even less in winter, and that they drank to relieve the intense boredom. They were stationed here two weeks at a time and spent the balance of their time in Murgab or Khorog, farther along the Pamir Highway.

To counteract the effects of the alcohol I ate big heaped spoonfuls of sweet plov straight from the large metal cooking bowl that stood in the middle of the table. The bread was stale and crusty but the yellow fleshy melon was deliciously sweet. The man sitting next to me complained of severe and persistent headaches - he had never appeared completely at ease - and I did wonder how drinking copious amounts of alcohol at high altitude under intense UV radiation might affect someone (including me), but I felt sorry for him and immediately dispensed a handful of aspros and painkillers from my medical kit. He was overjoyed and took a good dose immediately.

The day was starting to get away from me so I thanked them for their wonderful hospitality, wished them well and continued on my way. The road remained adequately paved as it wound down through a gentle mountain pass above a wide plateau where suddenly the magnificent Lake Kara-Kul came into view. It was enormous and glimmered under the intense sunshine, but its deep blue colour was unmistakable set against the lifeless dead earth brown of the lakeshore and surrounding plains. I kept watching the lake from different vantage points as I rode down and across the high plateau until I finally reached the grim and dusty village of Karakul on the lakeshore. A frenzied and most probably rabid dog sprinted out to greet me and tried unsuccessfully to bite me then my tyres before I sped away and through the town. Like the lake, the town was inert, silent and lifeless. I didn't see a soul until I came to another checkpoint on the outskirts of town where two teenage soldiers gave me the once over before letting me pass. They eyed my bike enviously and had many questions about it which I answered, perhaps too hastily, but I was keen to keep moving; I was still only half way to Murgab.

The road hugged the base of the mountains where they intersected with the high plateau. Majestic snow capped peaks began to close in around me as I climbed higher leaving the brilliant blue lake behind in the distance. I passed a family living in a single small stone hut and I waved to them as they came running to the road to greet me. How did they live here? What did they do? There were no crops – the soil and climate conspiring to defeat any attempt at agriculture here and they had only a few scrawny animals. No running water and no electricity. I wanted to stop and find out more but I still hadn't reached the high mountain pass I needed to cross and I was nervous about getting stuck out here alone for the night so I pressed on. As predicted, the road deteriorated here, the paved surface giving way to loose gravel and tight corrugations just as it had before, but this time it was going to be a much longer off-road ride, including climbing up to the Ak-Baital (White Horse) pass at almost 5000 metres.

I shuddered along slowly on gently sloping ground until the road suddenly lunged into a mountainside and heaved itself up at a sharp incline. The road deteriorated even further as it climbed, with watery run offs carving deep ruts into the surface. In places the soft edges of the track had fallen away and down the mountainside. There were neither guardrails nor warning signs and at some places the road simply went missing. I continued climbing - it was getting colder all the time and I had now risen well above the snow line. I was now on the shoulders of some of the giants I had admired earlier in the day and the snow lay deep and untouched right up to, and in some places across, the gravel track. The track widened a little here and I stopped to take it all in.

As soon as I shut off the engine I was overwhelmed by the immense silence and simple stark beauty of the mountains. The sky seemed a deeper blue up here and it was incredibly still and peaceful - a moment frozen in time for me. I had to pinch myself – for here I was, a rank outsider and amateur who had achieved this part of his unlikely plan – to be alone in the middle of the one of the highest and most remote mountain ranges in the world independently – it was wonderful and I felt special. I thought about my family and wondered where they were and what they were doing at this moment. I imagined a perspective from space looking down at me here, and them, at home. It was a strange sensation and all at once I felt utterly alone but totally connected. I thought about how far I had come, all the wonderful people I had met and all of the help I had received so far: Vassily, Anton and the Caravan of Love along the Road of Bones, Big Mama and Zhenya in Yakutsk, the train crew across Russia, Mischa, Lyuba and Bolya in Semipalatinsk, Mr Shu in Urumchi, the boys in Kashgar and many others. It was already a long list and my journey had indeed been rich in experience for me.

***

It may have been premature, and I may have been affected by any combination of altitude, sun, drugs and/or alcohol, but for the first time in my journey I felt genuinely confident about finishing. Previously I had stolen thoughts of the day when I might ride triumphantly across the Bosporus into Istanbul, but these had always been extinguished quickly by the enormous distance still to travel and by the more immediate issues I always seemed to be facing. But perhaps there was a more straightforward explanation; I was now precisely half way to Istanbul and, neatly, this was the highest point on my journey - I had been climbing ever since leaving the shores of the Sea of Okhotsk in Magadan on a cold and wet summer's day in July, it was now the middle of September, the weather across Central Asia would certainly be dry and warm and it was all downhill to the Mediterranean from here.

I was breathing hard and I soon became aware of the heaving of my chest and the rasping noise I was making sucking air into my lungs. I took a final slow 360-degree look at the panorama before re-mounting and riding the last one hundred metres to the crest of the pass. I knew I would never come here again and it was with a touch of sadness that I began the long steep descent to the valley floor below. Just below the top of the pass snow and ice had melted onto the road making a short but nevertheless tricky and messy bog, which quickly got my blood pumping again, and re-focused all my senses on safe riding.

Soon the dirt track was replaced by good paved road which twisted and turned gently as it snaked along the narrow valley floor, still hemmed in by towering giants on three sides. I passed a small hamlet and two horsemen herding sheep - they looked more like cattle rustlers or bandits to me with thick black woollen balaclavas over their faces to protect them from the cold cutting wind and the intense UV. I waved nervously half expecting one or both of them to spin a pair of six shooters on each hand and say "stick 'em up comrade", but they simply waved back and I think I even noticed a friendly smile under their balaclavas.

The road meandered on in long sweeping curves over dried out river beds and across tough dry pastureland. The late afternoon sun was streaming down the valley from behind me, casting a golden hue on everything; it was fine touring and I was happy. I rode on and the valley soon opened out onto a wide plateau bounded by large dry mountains on either side. The township of Murgab emerged from the rocks and dust in foothills at the end of the valley as a series of long low off white stone buildings scattered across the slopes. I rode into town and eventually found the KGB office (the police are still known ominously as the KGB here). I don't know why, but after being "greeted" by some serious guys in big hats I was shown to a bare room at the back of the station where an attractive older woman in a floral dress and cardigan came to meet me. She sat down at the large wooden desk and invited me to do the same. She took my passport and papers and examined them very closely, asking many questions as she did - primarily concerning the purpose of my visit. It was like having my homework checked by a maternal grade school teacher, and for a moment I wondered whether this was part of some elaborate psychological test, but she smiled warmly and stamped my papers - registering me as an official visitor here. She then showed me out of the station and back onto the main street. By this time a big crowd of policemen and curious locals had gathered around my bike. I asked about accommodation and was escorted by a crowd of enthusiastic men, boys and children through back streets, down narrow alleyways, back across the highway and up a steep hillside to a house and yurt perched high above the town. With the exception of a few blades of grass and some struggling plants outside the KGB offices, the town was ugly and barren, there were no trees, no grass, no flowers - nothing grew here except the shadows across the sun baked concrete-hard earth. The main street was paved and straight but the rest of the town made no effort to comply, with ramshackle rows of houses radiating outwards haphazardly from here. The houses were simple whitewashed mortar and stone or mud adobes, clean no doubt but with a thin film of fine dirt covering everything including the occupants, giving a muted soft brown filter to all the colours. The air was dry and cool and I noticed my lips had cracked badly from the sun and wind.

I walked and rode alternately, trying to keep slow pace with my friendly escorts. I had picked up some passengers too - two young boys had jumped silently onto my panniers where they rode side-saddle, beaming from ear to ear until I discovered them and, perhaps unkindly, shooed them away. They were so undernourished and thin as to be almost weightless to me; I hadn't noticed them getting on and certainly felt no difference when they leapt off.

I was the Pied Piper again and my coterie grew as we wended our way along the streets. Unfortunately it now also included a very drunk teenager who insisted on riding my bike - to the point where I had to deter him physically. He was harmless but annoying, and the others were embarrassed by his behaviour, eventually dragging him away and back down the hill towards the town.

From my position now, atop the hillside, I looked out over the town and beyond. The town was an eyesore, but it sat at the end of a long valley against a backdrop of huge snow capped peaks running away to the south and west. This was mountain climbing territory and for a moment I was sorry I couldn't linger here for a few days and perhaps take a gentle trek.

I was introduced to my hosts, a fine Pamiri family; a handsome doe- eyed mother with tanned skin and raven hair, a proud, tough and weathered father, two teenage sons and a young daughter. The young girl was already six but small and frail - not much bigger than my own threeyear-old daughter. I felt sure I would be heading for the yurt, but was relieved instead when the woman took me inside the house. I was shown to a large room decorated like Ali Baba's cave with soft colourful cotton sleeping mats and pillows on the floor and traditional rugs with softly rounded geometric motifs covering the walls. It was dense and dark and rich in colour -

providing wonderful relief from the harsh environment outside. There was a small desk and chair in one corner but no other hard furniture as such so I sat down on the cotton mats, rolled over, stretched out and fell asleep, overcome by tiredness - it was 6pm.

***

I had to be woken for dinner where I laboured under a heavy load of noodles and vegetables served steaming hot from enormous cooking pots carried to my table from the yurt kitchen. I sat on large soft cushions on the floor and contorted my body to slide my long legs clumsily under the very low table - it was comfortable as long as I didn't have to move. I had honourably finished the soup but foolishly eaten too many pieces of bread and sipped too many cups of sweet tea. Now I was trapped, pinned under the table by a full stomach and unable to refuse the generous helpings of main course now being proudly served up to me by my hosts. Fortunately I was left to eat alone and was able to extricate myself in private from under the table to do a few quick laps of the room to try and settle the food in the pit of my stomach before resuming. My hosts checked on me regularly and I even took a second helping to not offend them. Food was precious here and although I had severely overeaten, I felt it was unconscionable to waste it, so I ate it all. Bloated and eye-popingly full, I rolled off to bed and slept like a baby on the floor under the warm cotton filled blankets.

***

I woke to another brilliantly bright clear day. It was still early and the town was waking slowly, but already the sun shone down intensely on the buildings and their inhabitants, like the focused and scorching light from a magnifying glass annoying an ant colony. My bike had been outside all night in the cold and was still sitting in the cold shadows cast by the large outhouse that I had visited frequently during the night. I needed petrol and marched down the hillside into the township proper with one of the teenage boys from the family in search of it. We walked across the hard dusty ground until we came to a high thick mud wall with the word "benzin" painted on it in big Cyrillic letters. We followed the wall around and knocked on the front door. A dirty and dishevelled man, still in his pyjamas, and halfway through his breakfast came out and took us through a large locked side gate and into his tiny back yard compound. He pulled out a large ring of keys and unlocked a heavily fortified garden shed. Inside was dark, but as my eyes began to adjust I could make out many large glass bottles and jars, each filled with semi- opaque liquids in various dirty shades of yellow, green, brown and amber - this was his vault of precious petrol, and we ordered up fifteen litres. Discussions about fuel quality or octane ratings were pointless - this was the only source of fuel for hundreds of kilometres in either direction and he knew it. He grabbed a funnel and measured out three serves each of five litres from different bottles into our canister in a cocktail of coarse benzine. I wondered how my bike would fire on this mixture but there were no other options so we paid up (at one US dollar a litre!) and carted the canister back up the steep hill. Despite my protests and attempts to help him, the teenage son insisted on carrying the very heavy canister. Doubled over with one hand up over his shoulder and the other pushing up from behind he lugged the heavy cargo slowly up the steep hill like a sturdy pack mule. The surface was loose and uncertain and just climbing the steep hill, unencumbered, had winded me seriously – I was embarrassed.

I packed and carried out my ritual checking of the bike. The two teenage boys had joined me now – they were intensely curious and I tried my best to explain the big ticket items to them. I ended up taking Polaroid portraits of each of them sitting proudly on my bike and gave these as souvenirs – they were delighted and ran off to show their parents. Their little sister, who had been watching all of this shyly from the front steps, came over and I did the same for her. She squealed with delight when I picked her up and sat her on my bike. She was dwarfed by the bike but posed like a natural – confident and smiling. Suddenly her parents appeared dressed in their best clothes with their teenage sons trailing behind – it was time for a family portrait. They posed proudly together on the front steps of their home in the bright sunshine while I took a final portrait of them all. I handed the blank picture to the father and they all huddled around and watched with great fascination as it developed slowly before their eyes. I'm not sure if they'd ever had photos of themselves – such was their joy in having these images to keep. Once developed, the mother immediately took the photos inside and pinned them up in a prominent position on the wall in the main room of the house. The father shook my hand vigorously and thanked me profusely for these precious gifts and it felt good to be able to leave them with something so valuable. I returned to my bike and prepared to leave, but ominously had to repeat yesterday's belligerent starting technique turn over the engine. It took even longer this time and suddenly I felt the black clouds of doubt loom up large over me again. I'd made it through yesterday without incident, but what if I got stuck today? It was over 300 kilometres to the next town with nothing in between but high desert plateau. In a more rational burst of thought I did suspect the lack of oxygen up here and dirty fuel could be a problem.

I waved goodbye and rode off cautiously down the steep gravel track, back onto the road and through the town, crossed a dry river bed on a crumbling concrete bridge and had almost reached fourth gear before spying another checkpoint near the end of the short narrow valley I had just entered. The gate and guard hut stood in the long shadows cast by the morning sun, still behind the tall mountains. I rode up and, at the direction of the young soldier on duty, nervously switched my engine off - the bike hadn't warmed up fully and I was worried about being able to start it again. An older man dressed in faded flannelette shirt and threadbare tracksuit pants came out and called me in to the warm hut. We sat and talked, ate bread and had a few cups of sweet tea. I had come about one kilometre since leaving my hosts and had just eaten a big breakfast but the hospitality was impossible to refuse and I did feel for these men, stationed in these tiny huts, seeing only a handful of filthy truck drivers each day. I asked why there were so many checkpoints and what they were guarding against - "narcotica e zolota" (drugs and gold) he replied quickly in Russian before spitting lazily on the stone floor. Drugs I knew about, the Pamir Highway being one of the main transport route for heroin out of Afghanistan and onwards to the streets of Europe, but gold?? On a pound for pound basis both were certainly lucrative cargos for anyone brave enough to attempt smuggling them. He told me there were large unmined deposits of alluvial gold in the mountains nearby where rogue prospectors would set up camp for a few weeks and then make a run for it. His descriptions sounded like the Wild West to me and he stroked his AK47 gently as he reminisced about recent "intercepts". Another man walked in and announced he had just slaughtered a sheep and that it would a great honour if I would join them in cooking and eating it. I thanked them both for their hospitality but explained that I had just eaten a big breakfast, had filled up here on bread and tea and still had a long way to travel today – Khorog was more than three hundred kilometres further along the highway.

I rode off into the shadowy foothills at the end of the valley and then climbed up and over a short sharp rocky red earth canyon before arriving at the edge of the high Pamir plateau, known to early Persians as the "roof of the world." There was a final frikkin checkpoint here, this one much larger than the previous and manned by about twenty soldiers. The officer in charge came running out to meet me. He looked like a coach from the Russian Olympic team with national track suit, white T-Shirt, new runners and sports cap. He was trim, tanned, bright-eyed, freshly shaven and silvery haired and looked in the peak of condition. We spoke briefly about my trip and where I was from. I was surprised to find that a) he knew precisely where Magadan was, and even more surprisingly b) he knew without prompting that Canberra was the capital of Australia and not Sydney or Melbourne.

Feeling very small, I rode out onto the giant open expanse of the high plateau. The landscape here was even more barren than what I had travelled across the previous day - the earth was bone dry and coloured from a slim palette of lifeless light browns. The only relief coming from the white snow caps on the dead mountains that ring fenced the plateau. The sunlight up here was intense and the glare powerful - full of the light reflected back up from the ground. I rode on and on across the desolate terrain; my solitude interrupted momentarily by a group of local men camped in yurts near the side of the road. They were sitting taking a smoko around a campfire. They jumped up and waved excitedly and called me over as I rode past. I noticed an old motorbike leaning up against a makeshift wooden fence and debated whether I should join them - but, still nervous about making it across this inert but hostile section I decided to press on. Then, almost immediately, I wished I had stopped. Was I being too selfish with my time? Was I running to my schedule at the expense of a richer experience? Surely this was true. Very few travellers come this way, and as a guest I almost felt obliged to reach out and connect with them. I pressed on as the road hugged the mountain side before launching itself again out into the middle of the lifeless and rocky plateau. I rode on in long straight sections of road cutting across this natural crucible, feeling very exposed and lonely. But, incredibly, people did live here. Approaching the end of the enormous plateau I saw in the distance a ragtag collection of small off-white blocks — looking like the dried teeth of a half-buried animal jawbone pushing up through the sand. Riding closer, this resolved into a bleak and desolate scene; low rectangular block houses on parched gravel, just a skeleton of a village with no personality, and nothing - apart from these buildings - to distinguish itself from the rocky, lifeless plain it sat on.

There were no kids playing, no mothers washing, no old men sitting around talking - the whole place was eerily silent and still. The only living creatures I saw were a few mangy mongrel dogs resting in the precious shade and thankfully, even they seemed rooted to the ground, too tired to chase anything, including me.

I followed the large S bend of road beyond the settlement and began climbing up and out of the long valley. I looked back down on the desperate village - that must have been Alichur - marked on my map as a significant *town* on the highway. That meant I was now more than half way to Khorog, so I decided to take a break. I stopped at the side of the road on a wide curve high above the plateau on a steep hillside and ate some of my biscuits and drank some of my lemon fizz. But as soon as I did I knew it was a mistake – it was if someone had initiated my own internal gastro launch sequence – my stomach was full of liquid propellant and it had just been ignited. I figured I had about ten seconds to find a suitable launch pad. Its funny how, even in times of great distress like this, where time is critical, you stop and consider things like "now, where can I go to do this in private?" I could not have been more alone, but I couldn't bear the thought of soiling the Pamir Highway so I scrambled down the steep and rocky hillside, loosening my pants as I ran, quickly locating a large flat stone upon which I perched and mercifully relieved myself. My backside hung out over the long valley like a piece of giant artillery and I sat squatting like a fat cane toad in the sun, waiting patiently for this horrible episode to end. Suddenly I heard the crunching of gravel and the heavy grinding of gears above me - I looked up and realised immediately that I was positioned in clear line of sight to the road as a big Kamaz full of road workers passed by, the men in the back smiling and waving to me as the driver honked hard on his horn. I couldn't move quickly, but did manage a small salute.

Drained emotionally and physically I wearily climbed back up the hill to my bike and washed down the last of my gastro stoppers with my lemon fizz. Feeling somewhat lighter, light-headed and weaker, I resumed my journey. Beyond the hills the road flattened out again onto a causeway across softer earth and then the road deteriorated again with giant rounded, craters where the road surface had simply subsided vertically. Twenty kilometres of unpaved and badly rutted road followed, including some treacherous downhill mountain sections until finally I reached the small village of Jelandy.

From Jelandy the mountains closed in around me again, and

even though it was still early afternoon I rode along in cold shadows below massive rock walls rising almost vertically beside me. At times I thought I had entered dead-end box canyons, so sheer did the mountains rise ahead of me and seemingly across the road. I had entered the Gunt River valley and the road was much improved now as it began tracking the turbid dull turquoise waters as they raced downhill towards Khorog and the Afghan border. The road descended rapidly, following the river as it cut deep into the mountains and the air quickly became warmer and just a little moist. In places here the mountains had pulled back from the river course and slender fingers of fertile earth permitted a basic self-sufficient existence. I rode past primitive farms with stone huts and fences. Trees, grass and flowers were now suddenly abundant. Small herds of healthy looking livestock were grazing in lush but skinny paddocks and tiny plots of odd-shaped land supported base crops. After riding across the endless sandy deserts of Xinjiang and then the arid desolate high Pamirs I felt like I had arrived in a land of milk and honey.

The sun shone golden on these pretty rustic scenes as I followed the gently winding road along and down the river valley. I passed boys on donkeys, school children walking home, farmers, shepherds, giggling girlfriends walking hand in hand, grandmothers and grandchildren, and many others, all of whom - without exception - smiled and waved as I passed.

I stopped at a long lazy bend in the river, parked and sat under the shade of a big round boulder by the water's edge and ate what remained of my biscuits and fizz, happy in the knowledge that I had made it safely down from the high Pamirs, back into civilisation of sorts and that I would probably make it into Khorog before dark. After about half an hour or so I felt surprisingly rejuvenated and, even better, my stomach hadn't exploded so I headed off.

Unfortunately, the dogs here were healthier too and much more ferocious than I had encountered previously. I don't know if it was the colour of my bike, the particular sound of its engine, or the clothes I wore, or perhaps even my smell, but as I entered each village the mongrel mutts would run directly at me, head on, fangs bared and barking insanely trying to take pieces out of me and the bike. I could only speed up wildly, blast them with my horn and tearaway dangerously down these otherwise peaceful country lanes to avoid being savaged.

***

I passed through many more villages on the road to Khorog, and when I wasn't in a village I was passing a farmstead. Progress was slow but picturesque.

Eventually I came to a checkpoint just outside Khorog. It had been a long time since the last checkpoint (a few hours ago) and this one was substantial with a big heavy gate across the road and a large guard house nestled deep under an enormous shady tree beside the road. I slowly came to a stop under the nose of an anxious young soldier. I dismounted, pulled out all of my papers in anticipation and followed him inside. I couldn't put my finger on any one thing in particular, but as soon as I entered the room I began to feel very uneasy. There were four men inside the bright bare room - three sat around an old table eating messily from a huge mound of plov, and the fourth, a uniformed officer (including big brimmed hat), stood aloof by the window that overlooked the gate and the road. It was not a jovial group and I was not welcomed as I had been at previous checkpoints. I sensed some suspicion of me here and even a hint of malevolent opportunism as the officer by the window turned, narrowed his eyes and looked me up and down. I tried to present my papers and passport but he wasn't interested and brushed them aside, instead asking me pointedly whether I carried any narcotics or precious metals and/or stones. I answered honestly and forthrightly that I did not. He then casually rolled up his sleeve and asked whether I wanted to buy his watch. He was deadly serious and insisted we could "do business" but I politely declined, showing him my own (cheap) digital watch which he then proceeded to try and barter from me. The three men at the table had continued to eat and watched this unfunny farce with detached amusement until suddenly the other uniformed officer, sitting at the far end of the table, lunged forward and, in one long dramatic sweeping movement, withdrew his semi-automatic pistol from the holster on his waist and offered it to me saying urgently: "you take this please!" The gun was right under my nose and he urged me again to take it. Apart from me, no one seemed particularly concerned with his wildly dangerous suggestion. I put up my hands opened palmed and recoiled slightly in a reflex response. I pursed my lips, shook my head vigorously and said as calmly as I could fake it "no thank you". I got the impression he was baiting me to use the gun against one or all of them. These guys were seriously unhinged and I suspected they were high on a cocktail of alcohol and narcotics

183

themselves. Before I had recovered from this unwanted psychological abuse the officer at the window came closer and whispered to me in his hot vodka breath "do you want to buy some rubies?" Bewildered and disturbed by this latest advance and the others that had come before it I started moving slowly towards the door explaining that it had been a long day of riding and I was very tired and that I wanted to get to Khorog and find somewhere to stay the night. They offered me food and a bed for the night here but, after considering this scenario for a nanosecond, I thanked them for their "hospitality" and excused myself. It was a surreal experience and I wanted urgently to leave and ride away without looking back at these crazies, which is exactly what I did.

A Tale of Two Sisters

Beyond the gate the road cut into the sharply steeper mountainside and I rode on through a half-exposed concrete rib cage of a tunnel, dodging landslide debris that had recently fallen between the gaps in the roof and onto the road. Ignoring the driving hazards, this was by far the most impressive piece of road engineering I had seen since leaving China. I emerged into a steep and lush river valley, where the mountains had pulled away far enough for a large town to take root in terrace fashion up both hillsides. Beyond these terraces, sheer rock faces soared almost vertical above the town, reaching high into the sky. Looking up here, I saw more rocks and mountains than sky above me.

I came to a park where old men sat talking and dozing in the late afternoon sun. The road then ran parallel to a large open channel where the powerful river waters had been tamed temporarily for irrigation, power, drinking and sanitation. Low-rise buildings came into view and I stopped and asked a gangster type (gold jewellery, dark glasses and fancy car) for directions - perhaps "do you know where the KGB Office is?" did not translate too well, or perhaps it was a touchy subject for him - anyway he just laughed and told me to keep riding. At least there were no dogs here.

Kids played happily on the quiet road and one young boy, perhaps ten years old, beaming from ear to ear upon seeing me, decided he wanted to race. He rode a decrepit Soviet-era pushbike, probably a hand-me-down that his father might have ridden proudly to work at the local tractor factory a long time ago in better days here. I was cruising slowly and he quickly came up level with me, stood tall on his rickety pedals and looked over at me with a cheeky grin, eyes wide with excitement urging me to speed up. He was just a bony underfed kid with a crooked crew cut, but he pinned back his ears, wound himself up and launched his bike with a ferocious burst of energy, his matchstick legs whirring madly in a blur as he pedalled for all he was worth. I was still debating whether to take him on when I saw the big white 4WD turning at speed onto the road in front of him. The boy rode with his head craned back so that he could savour his victory and so didn't notice the car - the driver saw him and swerved away instinctively, I waved frantically at the boy and, looking around, seeing the big white tank almost upon him, he dived under the beefy bull bars, and then my view was obscured in a white blur as the car came between us. All I heard were his screams, the crunching of metal and the violent screech of the big car as it skidded to a stop.

An icy cold flush washed through my body and I went numb with fear for the boy's safety. I pulled up sharply, turned around and rushed back to him. I immediately felt guilty too - not for initiating the race, for I had not, but just for simply being here - if I wasn't here this certainly would not have happened.

A small crowd had gathered around the boy, including the driver of the car who was now ashen. I pushed through the crowd fearing the worst and was astounded and wonderfully relieved to find the boy sitting upright brushing the gravel off his trousers and arms. He was shaken but barely scratched and his antique bike, still functional but freshly scarred, leant up against the old stone wall that marked the corner from where the car had emerged. Somehow he had dodged the car completely, skidded on the gravel and crashed skilfully with the bike clearly taking the brunt of the impact - it could have been so much worse. Not sure what to do but still feeling somewhat responsible, I just waited and watched anxiously as he recovered. The crowd, sensing everything was fine, had dispersed, the driver had gone, and before I knew it so had the boy.

***

I soon found the KGB Office - the biggest, meanest, most austere and well guarded building on the main street - where I was interrogated by a young, aggressive, Cuban-heeled officer. All of my papers were in order but I wondered whether perhaps twisted reports of my street racing had already been relayed to him. Regardless, it was late and there was yet another office where I had to report in the morning to complete my registration. After solemnly promising to do this, I was released on my recognizance.

It had been an unsettling afternoon and it was getting late, but I still needed to find somewhere to sleep. Recommended by my guide book, I sought help from the local MSDSP office - the omnipresent Mountain Societies Development Support Programme; the primary development agency of the Aga Khan Development Network, firmly embedded and very active in this part of Tajikistan due to the Aga Khan's role as spiritual leader of the Nizari sect within the Ismaili branch of Islam - and the sect to which most Pamiris belonged. I had ridden past many of their small but immensely worthwhile projects earlier today – addressing the most critical needs of the poorest people here covering health, education, agriculture and energy. After the disintegration of the Soviet Union, with its network of highly specialised, but highly dependent and ultimately vulnerable SSRs, and the end of central planning and subsidies, the economy here had quickly collapsed. Worse still, a murderous clan- based civil war then raged violently for many years killing tens of thousands and making internal refugees of at least half a million more. The blunt logic of Soviet Republic making had already created a Tajik Diaspora across the region and only the iron-grip of Moscow had kept the lid on pre-existing inter-clan rivalries and nascent Islamic fundamentalism; now it was a free for all: Leninabaders, Kulyabis, Pamiris and Garmis – from the four corners of Tajikistan — fought each other in an internecine struggle that pulverized any remaining bedrock of social and/or economic order. If Tajikistan were a patient it would have been in intensive care on life support and they would have been asking the next of kin for permission to pull out the tubes - but the parents had vanished without a trace, un-contactable, and so it lived on, and, very slowly the diseased organs and limbs began healing – sometimes painfully and rarely perfectly. Slowly the heart began pumping harder and more firmly, and the whole began to re-emerge, different, watchful and more wary, but still intact. An uneasy and fragile peace took hold across the country and people began to piece their fractured lives back together, but still there were relapses; regional (and violent) skirmishes, private beatings, discrimination, intimidation and lingering resentment continued.

And, if all of that were not enough, nature had also dealt Tajikistan a cruel hand with almost all of the country's surface area covered in roughhewn mountains with half of that land more than 3000 metres above sea level, making any widespread agriculture or industrialization virtually impossible. And, once cut off from the central nervous system of the Soviet Union, Tajikistan had sunk like a rock and now ranks amongst the poorest nations of the world, limping along on international aid and direct injections of money, expertise and food into the Pamir region from the Aga Khan himself.

I found a very helpful man at the MSDSP Office who directed me to their home stay cum hotel located behind a high gated wall at the end of a long dusty street running down towards the river. I rode down the pleasant tree-lined street past single storey simple whitewashed houses, shop fronts and garages. I pulled up next to the abandoned guard house that sat beside the entrance and pushed open the unlocked light blue metal gate and walked into the compound. I had stepped into a garden oasis; there were large beds of red roses and other pretty flowers, lush lawns, a small wooden gazebo and shade trees surrounding a large bungalow. This was where aid workers and MSDSP visitors stayed, and was, allegedly, the only place in Khorog that had hot running water. It also had beds, a proper toilet and served "good" meals – luxury. I had been travelling for three hard days and couldn't remember my last wash. The accommodation was expensive but I felt I had earned it. Unfortunately, it was also completely full, so disheartened, I loitered – the residents seemed to consist entirely of well dressed, impeccably groomed, nice smelling, laptop-toting aid workers, some of whom I had seen earlier on the main street where they had caught my eye – incongruous against the dusty backdrop of Tajik street life. They were returning home from a hard day at the office and two of them passed me now, heading inside – they were chatting excitedly about how much they were looking forward to a "hot shower followed by a nice dinner". The staff at the hotel then rallied around to help me and I sat in the small gazebo as they kindly phoned family and friends to help find a place for me to stay. They quickly located a family willing to help and I was told to wait for my chaperone to arrive. I returned to my bike and watched the street life unfold around me as dusk fell; little children had gathered around my bike, like bees to honey, touching every dial, button and control, young men idled about proudly in their hotted-up cars, mothers and daughters bought food and supplies for dinner, old women chatted all-knowingly to each other, and young boys, dirty and dusty, happily played simple games on the street and in and around the trees.

My hostess was a strikingly handsome Pamiri woman with high cheekbones, pale skin, green eyes and dark brown shoulder length hair. She wore a pale green tunic style dress over light flaxen pants. Her daughter, I guessed, was about five years old, wide-eyed and slightly startled upon seeing me. I followed them both back along the main street and then down an alleyway, past a courtyard restaurant, over an open drain and back towards the river. We came to a pedestrian suspension bridge, turned left along a busy footpath and soon reached an ugly crumbling Soviet-era five storey concrete apartment block. Paint peeled from it like paper bark and it was surrounded by thick unkempt vegetation, weeds, wild flowers and shade trees. A few cars and one big old Kamaz truck were parked out front on wide irregular concrete slabs. I squeezed past, chained up my bike, unpacked and hauled myself and my bags up five flights of stairs to the top floor apartment. I was exhausted by the time I had reached the top and removing my boots was a real effort, but I had finally arrived. I was shown to a Spartan but clean bedroom with a large double bed, wardrobe and huge broken down TV in it. The apartment was large with at least two other bedrooms, a kitchen, bathroom and toilet – and it needed to be; I couldn't tell precisely how many people or families lived here, but when I emerged from my bedroom there was a crowd milling about in the small vestibule near the entrance. One of the men I recognized from earlier in the day at the MSDSP office – I acknowledged him and then the others. There was also another attractive woman here, dressed more traditionally in a long dark red velveteen dress with minimal decoration. She was taller and classically beautiful. There was also another child here, a boy of perhaps three years. I was struggling to match couples, parents and children. Men came and went and each seemed to have some relationship to the women and children. A CB radio deck sat on a small table and squawked intermittently. Suddenly, a large middle-aged man dressed in T-shirt, track pants and runners bounded out of the lounge room shouting urgent instructions into his radio handset. He was clearly in charge of some sort of essential service or perhaps civil defence. He kissed his wife – my chaperone – and his two children goodbye, thus solving a few of the relationship equations running through my head, and then rushed out, down the steps and into the night.

One of the other men that had remained behind insisted that I lock up my bike more securely at the MSDSP Office - they had a large fortified garage - so I followed him back across town and then returned quickly for dinner. By the time I returned all of the men had gone, leaving just the two women, the two children and me at home. The two women were preparing food in the kitchen, talking and laughing all the time as they worked. They came out to greet me and explained that they were sisters. They had set up a small portable table next to my bed and ushered me back into the bedroom to sit and have dinner. A huge mound of buckwheat groats (kasha) was lowered into position in front of me and I began methodically working through it, excited by the exceptional blandness of it. My stomach had still not settled (since China) and I hoped this heavy sludge might set like concrete in the bottom of my stomach. Sweet tea and crusty bread came too and I ate and drank happily until I could eat no more.

Just as I was finishing the two sisters came in and sat down on the floor opposite me, leaning against the wall. The "other" sister, I learnt quickly, was a little older, unmarried and worked in Khorog as a school teacher. She lived alone, but stayed here often with her sister. She spoke some basic English, but I found it hard to break the habit of forming my thoughts and speaking in butchered Russian. They sat casually, next to each other in identical positions, legs folded, knees up under their chins with arms wrapped around tight. The children came in too and lay down quietly, bone tired, on the thinly carpeted floor. They wanted to know everything about me, my family and life in Australia. We sat for a long time as I did my best to fully answer their questions. They sat and listened intently and there was a gentle sadness and resignation about them that I found compelling.

It was incomprehensible to them that I could be away from my home, my wife and my children for so long, let alone be by myself for all that time too – for them that was pure torture. They were educated and, astonishingly, knew precisely where Magadan was, as well as all the other cities and towns that I reeled off along the way where I had been in Russia, Kazakhstan, China, Kyrgyzstan and, of course, their own Tajikistan. They looked at me like I was an alien, but an alien they respected and at least partially understood. I explained that this was a journey I had always wanted to undertake - my dream, and that I had a wonderfully supportive wife who saw this as her gift to me rather than any sort of burden. They both shook their heads in disbelief.

Of particular interest to them was how we lived – in big houses with lawns and backyards and swimming pools. We drove our children short distances to schools and childcare centres in big cars and ate big healthy meals every day. We had well paid jobs and leisure time. It was fantasyland for them. Suddenly, just as I was explaining that, of course, everyone had running hot water and electricity in their houses, the lights in the apartment went out and we were left sitting in the dark. The lights went out in every other apartment too, and in all the restaurants and cafes, in the small cinema I had seen earlier that day, and in all the shops and in every other building too – the whole town had gone dark and powerless - a very regular occurrence based on the rapid and instinctive response of the young mother who got up, walked to the kitchen in complete darkness and returned quickly with three lighted candles which she placed on top of the big broken TV. The children didn't stir – they had fallen fast asleep on the floor just in front of me. So we continued, by candlelight - I could just make out their faces in the flickering light as I began to feel acutely embarrassed by the relative luxury and excesses of my life.

I asked them about their own family – they had another sister who had left recently hoping to find better prospects in Moscow. This was a big step and I knew, from reading the accounts of others in similar situations, how difficult and potentially dangerous this could be - poor young single women from rural towns were easy prey in the big cities of European Russia. They told me how difficult it had been for their sister to leave home, and most heart wrenching of all, to leave their mother.

I asked whether either of them had travelled. No, never, nowhere. They had never left this steep river valley and never ventured beyond the outskirts of their hometown. They had never seen the beautiful Gunt River Valley, and had never been to Jelandy, Alichur or Murgab. Surely they had been to Dushanbe? No, never, too far, too costly they told me. Incredibly, I had seen more of Tajikistan in three days than either of them had seen in their lifetimes – and I would soon be in Dushanbe too. To me this was incomprehensible, but they seemed to accept it as normal.

Boldly, and perhaps impertinently, I asked the older sister why she hadn't been married yet. It was very unusual for someone as old as her – she was at least twenty five – not to be married. She hesitated and looked at her sister before answering coyly that she was waiting for the right man to come along. She then went on nervously to explain that, actually, she was looking for more opportunities - beyond Khorog - to improve herself and find a better life, like her sister. I could tell this was the source of some contention - perhaps even jealousy - between them, but the older sister told me knowingly how it would be next to impossible for another daughter to leave home (and their mother).

Suddenly I had a terrible thought. What would happen if the husband, and perhaps some of the other men, had returned at this point to find us talking intimately by candlelight in the bedroom? Would they do me in, Raskalnikov fashion? I listened carefully for footsteps and noises from the stairwell but nervously continued.

They told me more about their lives – it was a bleak picture of food shortages, widespread unemployment, impossibly low wages when there was work, long cold dark winters, daily blackouts, poor water quality and frequent sickness. It was an inventory of misery and I sensed their hopelessness. I felt hopeless too. I was deeply touched by what they had told me but didn't have anything adequate to offer in response so I just said "I understand and I am sorry". They gently picked up the two children, who had remained asleep throughout, and carried them off to bed. I snuffed out the candles and went to bed feeling melancholy but thinking how fortunate I was too.

***

I rose early the next morning to fulfil my promise to the KGB officer from the day before and acted out the thinly veiled revenue raising charade called "registration". I located the Ministry of Interior offices – another imposing building with a large walled garden and grounds (far from prying eyes) – and banged on the big blue steel gate, interrupting morning callisthenics and volleyball. The men here, without exception, looked happy, healthy and well fed and they looked upon me, I think, with some suspicion. I was shown to a small office and questioned by a senior officer in civilian clothes. A large box of freshly minted bright blue Tajik passports sat on his desk and people banged on the outside window clamouring to be seen. He thumbed through my passport and papers and then scribbled something quickly on a small piece of flimsy scrap paper, handed it to me and told me to take it, along with my passport, to the bank and then come back and see him. He too was well- fed and seemed to be focused entirely on deal-making with the men who came and went as we spoke rather than genuine administration - I had already decided he was no good.

I showed the piece of paper to the lady behind the counter in the surprisingly modern offices of National Bank of Tajikistan who laughed and then called over the bank manager who also laughed. If there was a joke I wasn't getting it. They directed me back down the road (from where I had just come) to the "other bank" that was masquerading as a construction site, hidden under scaffolding and planks. I entered via a dusty entry gantry, opened a creaky wooden door and found myself in a small old fashioned, wood panelled, circa 1900's bank. The operation was entirely paper-based, with chits for everything, one abacus, a paper ledger and, holding pride of place, a typewriter. There was a small barred teller window and counter set into the far inside wall for handling cash. The vault was visible through this small window too. The whole place was decidedly old school and I wouldn't have been at all surprised if a Tajik Butch Cassidy and Sundance Kid had ridden up on their yaks, gotten us all to lie on the floor while they carried big bags of money out.

I handed my note to the old babushka behind the counter who gave me back a huge three part deposit form which I completed, copying the barely legible account number from the scrap of paper I have been given earlier, before approaching the even older babushka handling the money transactions behind the grill. She was old and frail with thick leathery skin and almost toothless save for two lonely crooked gold headstones in the front of her mouth. She snatched the paper away from me and took my cash, counting and inspecting each note closely before banking it into "consolidated revenue". It was a reasonable amount of money too, and I didn't feel good about it - I had no idea what I was being charged for, where the money was going and for what purpose it would be used. A small sense of resentment began building inside me - I would have felt much better about it if a soldier had simply taken the money directly from me and stuck it in his pocket. I took the receipt and returned to the Ministry of Interior offices where my passport was stamped thus completing my registration.

The whole crazy procedure had taken almost two hours, it was getting hot, I hadn't eaten anything yet (I still couldn't keep anything onboard for more than a few hours) and my head was starting to pound. I found a street stall vendor and asked for a bottle of Coke. The old woman picked up a bottle that had been standing in the sun all morning and handed it to me. Warm to the touch I handed it back to her immediately and asked for a cold one instead. She smiled, took the bottle over to the open drain by the side of the street, tied a string around the neck, secured the free end under a loose rock and then let it bobble around in the icy water. "No, no, no, no, no" I said rudely. It might have been safe, but the water was murky and laden with soggy refuse - I was desperately trying to re-establish peace and harmony in my gut and couldn't bring myself to put that bottle to my lips knowing where it had been. My body was a temple after all, and it had taken far too much abuse already. Feeling guilty, I ended up buying a big bottle of warm gassy water instead.

I returned to the apartment and ate a big breakfast of fried eggs, packed, took my last sachet of gastro tablets, paid and carted my bags across town to the MSDSP lockup and prepared my bike for travel.

***

Before leaving town I visited the local history museum and was escorted around by two young school children and the ancient babushkacum-curator who excitedly explained each of the exhibits in detail to me. I listened to the rhythmic lilt of her voice as we walked along, picking out the odd word or two but no more, she was happy to have an attentive visitor so I didn't interrupt her. We saw traditional Tajik costumes, brightly coloured hand woven rugs, ancient farming equipment (mostly still in use today), a sombre war memorial, sad black and white mug shots of local inductees into the Soviet Academy of Sciences (mostly geologists, with men and women in equal proportions), photos of past presidential visits opening bridges, factories and power stations, fauna and rock samples, and a small collection of stuffed wildlife - with eagles and ibex dominating in dramatic poses on papier-mâché mountain sides. A small section devoted to Stalin and Lenin had been relegated to a dusty corner of a dark hallway which my guide didn't even bother with. The final room had a massive collection of the various flags of Tajikistan as they had evolved over time, from the beginning of the Soviet Union (when Tajikistan wasn't even a full Republic) until the present day - the sheer number of flags hinting at the sometimes turbulent history of this place with the progressive replacement of Soviet red, the reduction and eventual removal of the iconic golden hammer and sickle (replaced by a red, white and green tricolour with golden crown and stars), mirroring the decline and eventual disappearance of their former masters and the stormy birth of an independent Tajikistan. Today, perhaps not so remarkably, and with a nod to their Persian ancestry, it resembles very closely the flag of Iran. It is said that the red represents Tajik independence and the land, white represents purity (and the cotton industry) and the green represents agriculture. The crown and stars, more conceptually and perhaps idealistically, "symbolize sovereignty, the union of workers and unity of social classes."

Back out on the street I admired the young people and enjoyed the relaxed feel of the place, induced I suspected, by the progressive and pragmatic Ismaili version of Islam practiced here by the majority of people. It is described as a breakaway branch of Islam - they still subscribe to the five pillars of Islam, but there are no mosques, no clerics and no weekly holy day and elders lead community affairs via inclusive town hall like meetings.

Thankfully the women here were not required to wear the repressive burqa, and relations between men and women seemed quite liberal. Khorog had grown on me; sure, it had a few rough edges, but it was a pretty town – it even had a university and botanical gardens. I could have easily stayed a few days more but I wanted to get to Dushanbe – that was my next goal. I knew if I could make it

194

there "on time" I would be back on top of my journey, having wrestled the most difficult parts to the ground. I found an internet café, wrote home briefly then retrieved my bike and rode out of town, filling up at a hand-pumped petrol bowser before hitting the T-junction where the Gunt River flows into the Pyanj River, whose course then defines the Tajik-Afghan border.

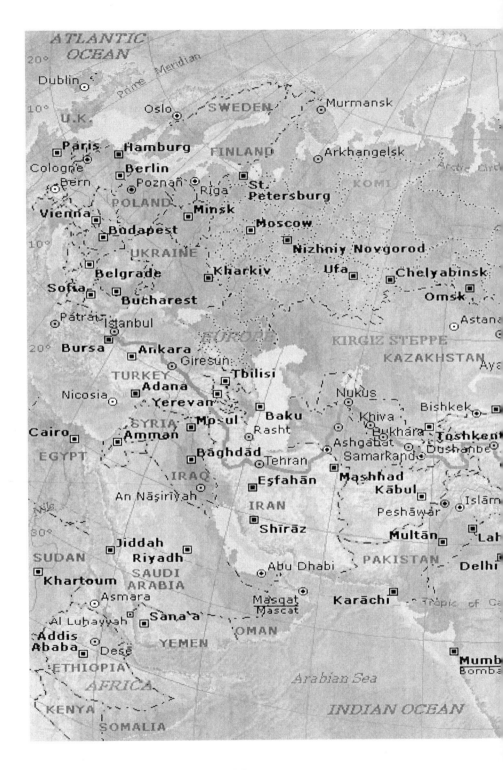

Bogged! Heading deep into the Kolyma Region, Siberia

The Rangers of Atka, Road of Bones

Breakfast with the Caravan of Love, Road of Bones

Kamaz rescue, near Yaktusk. Careful with my bike!

Sascha and Sergei, Nord Brotherhood, Yakutsk

Big Mama and fish, Lena River, north of Yakutsk

Siberian sunset, Aldan River, Tommot

Lena, Alyona and the Cook, Trans-Siberian Railway

Mischa, who looked after me like a son in Kazakhstan

The inscrutable Mr. Shu, mechanical genius

Taklimakan Desert, Xinjiang Autonomous Region, China

Atlas Silk being woven on loom, Hotan, China

The Rood of the World, Pamir Plateau, Tajikistan

The Registan, Samarkand, Uzbekistan

The Author, Karakum Desert, Turkmenistan

Land Mines and Landslides

I rode past some big construction sites on the outskirts of town where, incongruously, a new luxury hotel was being completed alongside a new school and dormitory. And, in a further sign of development I came to long stretch of road where a new high voltage electricity supply was being installed, carried by thick cables on tall metal towers. There was a tower beside the road and one much farther up the steep hillside. The cables were attached to both towers, but they were slack and snaked across the road ahead of me as workmen slowly tightened them. Luckily, I had seen the cables from far enough away to stop safely, but the driver of the bus that I had just passed had not, and he slammed on his brakes just in time to avoid, a) me, and b), the danger ahead. The cables slapped on the road as the workmen pulled them taut until, upon seeing me, they suddenly stopped and let the cables lay slack across the road. The bus driver impatiently thumped hard on his horn to try and get me to ride across, and the workmen too were urging me forward, but I was frozen with fear. I tried hard to remember my schoolboy physics and first principles of electricity; rubber was a good insulator – right? Did I need to have my feet on the ground too? Argh. I stood my ground, indicating I would ride *under* but not *over* the cables, and I waited until eventually they were high enough above the road for me ride ahead. I offered the bus driver right-of-way but he didn't budge. Nervously, I sped across the invisible danger zone and rode away relieved. You could throw bad roads, mud, water, rain and snow at me, but I drew the line at electrocution.

Beyond Khorog I found myself riding through more picturesque hamlets and villages for most of the afternoon as the river course widened and the land available for cultivation became more abundant and workable. It was a rich and fertile land and, despite the badly broken road, it was pleasant, albeit slow touring. I rode through cool glades of trees, past rustic farmhouses with stone walls enclosing shady lawns where family-owned goats, donkeys and cows grazed silently, past orchards of apple and apricot trees and small fields of crops. In a few places, where there was enough flat open space, homemade football pitches had been sketched out, and where there wasn't dusty volleyball courts sprang up. Unfortunately there were also more ferocious dogs in residence so it was with some apprehension and nervousness that I approached each village and farmhouse.

By the late afternoon though, the mountains had closed in again and I was riding deep down inside tight canyons on a twisting dirt track teetering precariously at times just above the roaring Pyanj River. The road had deteriorated now to a pulverised mess of gravel, rocks and fine grey powder. Recent landslides frequently spilled out onto the track too, making progress difficult and slow. In places the rock walls went beyond vertical and hung out over the river and road had been blasted out of the rock face creating gigantic and extended granite eaves which I rode under very nervously, accompanied by the frighteningly loud reverb from my exhaust. What held them up? My, that's a big crack isn't it? What was that creaking noise? Would the noise of a motorbike engine (not heard here often) vibrate the rock ceiling loose? I held my breath instinctively as I rode carefully under particularly large blocks of granite.

I slowed down to a crawl at the frequent blind corners, listening cautiously and then peering around before proceeding - the track, in places, only just wide enough for a single vehicle. Fortunately there was very little traffic, and when the odd truck did approach from the other direction, I would rush to find an alcove in the rock face where I would stop, pin myself to the wall, and wait for the noise and dust clouds to pass.

It was hard to believe that the adjacent rock wall, across the river and sometimes just twenty metres away was Afghanistan. It looked so close sometimes that I felt I could almost reach out and run my hand along the smooth rock face as I rode along. In other places, where the gradient and surface allowed, I spied narrow walking tracks coming from over the crest of a mountain and down to the waters edge. Further along, and still on the opposite bank, where the mountains receded a little further, primitive villages hugged the gentle fertile slopes, held captive by the tall rugged rocky rough-hewn mountains on one side and the vertical cliffs above the raging river on the other. There were no roads, no machinery, no electricity, just squat mud huts with thatched roofs, some bony oxen working a plough, chickens, donkeys and a few cows. It was mediaeval.

The sun had slipped behind the tall mountains now and I rode on in the cool shade, up and over a small gentle mountain pass then down onto a small river delta. Another frikkin checkpoint. The road ended at three- way intersection. I rode up and stopped outside the small whitewashed hut and introduced myself to the three men who were sitting outside. The oldest of the men wore traditional Muslim robes and the white topi haj skull cap – marking him as a man who had completed the pilgrimage to Mecca. He was silver haired and wizened and he acknowledged me with a small hand gesture and nod of his head. The other two were officers, both, incredibly, dressed smartly in full official police uniform. The senior officer came up to the bike to greet me. He was short, thick set, with greasy grey hair, dark tanned creased skin and beady black eyes. He prodded and probed my luggage then asked me the usual inventory of questions before calling me into his "office". Again, this hut had a Mediterranean feel about it with a bare smooth stone floor, whitewashed walls and bright blue woodwork. It was bright inside - there were only two rooms and the officer had a large old wooden table set in front of a big window that looked out over the intersection - this was his patch and he was the master. The table was covered in old newspapers and a big ledger into which he carefully copied all of my particulars. As he completed this obviously tiresome recordkeeping he began reminiscing about all the motorbikes he had owned and ridden through the years. As a young man he had owned Ural and Ish bikes and he recalled fondly better days when he would ride with his wife around his home town, and then how he would often ride at breakneck speed (alone) along this very same road to Dushanbe. It was now well past 5pm and I asked him about the road ahead and how far he thought I might get before nightfall – he said that if he were riding my bike he could get to Dushanbe tonight in less than three hours, but that it would take me at least twice as long. The only comfort I drew from this outrageous claim was that surely the road must get better from here. He escorted me outside and back to my bike. The old Muslim man rose slowly from his seat, shuffled over and presented me with a big stale loaf of bread. I tore a hunk off and chewed it, almost ripping the enamel off my teeth. It was a kind gesture and I thanked him sincerely and quickly packed the rock into my backpack, digging even deeper grooves into my shoulders. I promised the old man solemnly that I would eat it later.

I looked left and then right at the cross road confirming with them that the left fork headed to Qalaikhum, the next big town on the way to Dushanbe. I pushed off and headed out around a big sweeping right hand curve cut through low dry hills that took me back high above the river. Just over the first rise and out of sight of the checkpoint, the track suddenly became soft fine powder and then sand. The low dry hills were so dry that they were in fact sand dunes and I was surrounded by them now. The track had dissolved into the sand, leaving no distinct course for me to follow. I cursed.

My back wheel fishtailed violently underneath me and I fought hard to regain control. I lost traction and speed, got bogged deep and then fell over. I cursed again. My chain and cogs were coated in tiny gritty granules like fresh sandpaper. The bike, with me on top was far too heavy to continue riding safely on the soft sand so I walked with the bike the last fifty metres or so off the dunes and back onto the track.

I rode out high above the river; the track, carved into the mountainside, narrowed, and became hard and rutted, dusted in a thin film of fine grey powder and sprinkled generously with loose gravel. I had to concentrate hard to steer a steady line, but when I did look up I was astounded to see a huge eagle gliding silently just a few metres above my head. It must have measured six feet from wing tip to wing tip. A thick beige stripe ran from one wingtip to the other in a shallow v-shape and then bled into its chocolate brown fuselage. It was majestic and I stopped to watch the beautiful creature glide effortlessly away, swept along by invisible eddies of wind.

***

I rode along through more poor, dusty, dog-infested hamlets in semidarkness before unwittingly committing myself to a long uninhabited stretch of difficult road. Unperturbed, I rode on, but darkness came quickly, accelerated by the rapidly increasing height and narrowing of the steep river canyon. My light barely illuminated the road ahead and I slowed to a crawl to negotiate the goat track safely. There were no guard rails, no warning signs, nothing but the thundering roar of the river coming from the inky blackness just beyond my narrow field of vision. Just as I was beginning to worry about how I might possibly spend the night out here, I came to a large water crossing where a mountain stream ran dark and fast across the track, cascading over some small boulders at the edge of the track and crashing into the river below. I slowed, cursed, and pulled up in front of it. I took a closer look – the stream was about two feet deep with an uneven bed of large loose rocks and the water was finger-numbingly cold. It was certainly rideable, but my waterproof boots now leaked badly and I knew for sure I would have cold wet feet for the rest of the night. I cursed again. Just as I prepared to ride across a dirty face emerged out of the darkness to greet me. He was a small slight man with charcoal coloured skin, jet black hair, but with strikingly white teeth and eyeballs – he looked like he'd just come up from a hard 12 hour shift in a coal mine. He had a long narrow face, no chin and a large long pointed nose, and, unfortunately, gazing up at me now he looked like an excited rat chasing an illusive block of cheese. I immediately responded to his warm welcome and soon a small crowd of road workers had gathered around me. They were a motley crew; they were unshaven and grimy, had worn the same clothes for months, were bone tired, suffering from poor oral hygiene and reeked of BO - just like me in other words, and I immediately felt at home. The only obvious difference between us was our stature – my arrival must have increased the average height and weight by about fifty percent, for they were all undernourished all stood between five and five and a half feet tall. I was a giant and they all craned their necks as they greeted me. They were adamant that I should not go any further in the darkness, and I did little to resist, overcome with tiredness and relieved that I could stop somewhere safely for the night.

There was a large dilapidated caravan (their sleeping quarters) wedged tightly under the far rock face beside the track. They helped secure my bike safely off the track and out of sight and then eagerly invited me up to their living quarters, high above the track, accessible only via a steep, almost vertical, two storey staircase of giant steps cut into the rock face.

It was like a boys own adventure camp with a small covered turret lookout over the road, a small open air kitchen (i.e. ancient cast iron stove and two pots) and a long trestle table with two equally long but skinny bench seats. The kitchen and eating area was set out neatly on a large flat stone platform, protected by a thick canopy of branches and leaves from the massive old trees growing around the perimeter. A wide, fast flowing mountain stream gurgled past in a series of shallow rapids, just beyond the dinner table, before crashing onto the road below.

I ate two big bowls of thick delicious meat and potato stew with fresh bread and sweet tea with the other men. I never tired of these conversations where I explained what I was doing, why I was doing it and all of the other ancillary topics that spawned from them and tonight was no exception. A puzzled "Why?" was always the first question. Unlike almost everyone I met on my journey, I could, a) afford to travel, and b) probably travel anywhere I wanted and do anything I wanted - within reason. They knew this and the fact that I had chosen to come here and be with them now was astounding, and I sensed their pride as hosts by their unconditional willingness to share as much as they could of themselves and their culture with me and I felt privileged to be able to receive and experience it so directly. I reflected that like so many of my best experiences so far it was unplanned and spontaneous.

After dinner we climbed back down the giant staircase and they cleared some space in a corner of their caravan, under a large open window, for me to sleep in. I went to get my sleeping bag - determined to get some use out of it before the end of my trip - but they had already re-arranged the sea of soft communal bedding spread across the floor to provide me with a very comfortable place to sleep. I went outside and walked back along the track alone, above the river, to find a place to relieve myself and was struck speechless by a swollen perfectly full moon rising slowly above the tall craggy peaks at the end of the long canyon. It was simply awesome and I stood watching it in silence, mesmerised, as it cleared the peaks and shone down along the narrow canyon, like a powerful searchlight, casting the myriad of rock faces into sharp detailed relief. The previously dark and hostile river now glistened excitedly in dappled moonlight. The air was still, nothing stirred - even the river seemed peaceful now, as if under some irresistible lunar spell. It was a special moment in my journey, uplifting and sadly, but necessarily, ephemeral.

It was a mild night and I slept soundly, wedged snugly between the wall of the caravan and a warm, slightly musty, body lying next to me. None of them snored, but a soft asynchronous chorus of whistles drifted across the room as each of their tired bodies drew breath and exhaled gently. I looked out the window at the small patch of star-lit sky visible between the mountain peaks and thought to myself that, at this moment, there was no other place I would rather be. It was a nice feeling and I drifted off too, warm and secure.

I woke at dawn and joined my comrades for a breakfast of grey milky tea served in giant bowls with thick nan bread, butter and sugar. A large block of butter was passed from one man to the next, each hacking off a big chunk with his spoon and sliding it messily into his tea where it quickly melted and floated, like a golden oil spill in big round greasy blobs. Most of them tore their bread into pieces and either dunked or dropped it in, and then ate the sodden pieces. It was salty and slightly sour to taste and a big packet of sugar was passed around to sweeten it up to taste.

What struck me, now, in the daylight, was the diversity of this group; there were high-cheek-boned Pamiris, blue-eyed and fair Russians, swarthy Kulyabis and the once prosperous, but highly resented Garmis, remarkably now all living and working happily together in close quarters, where not so long ago they were would have been at each others' throats. It was encouraging and hopeful.

Just as we were finishing breakfast a battered old lorry came surging through the stream below, stopped, and the driver and his passenger came up to join us - the first man up looked like a small-time rural mafia boss and the other a classic fool straight from the pages of Russian literature. The mafia boss was an old, short, rounded Turkic man with skin tanned and wrinkled deeply from spending a lifetime outdoors. He had short white spiky hair and wore a white lace skullcap and an ill- fitting oversize cashmere overcoat, which his dumb attendant removed when called to do so. The fool was tall and thin with greasy grey hair and scraggly beard over a mottled complexion. He had large, sad blue eyes, sunken cheeks and he wore a cheap blue shell suit over a dirty white shirt, done up at the collar. His eyes bulged from his head and he did everything in a wide-eyed animated, overdrawn fashion. There were backslaps, hugs and three part cheek kisses all round as the mafia boss greeted the crew one by one. The fool stood by and seemed to be providing a running commentary on events to no one in particular. I was introduced and the man hugged me too, but we didn't kiss. We sat and drank tea together and shared another loaf of the round nan bread. They didn't stay long and we left together, but went in opposite directions. I thanked my hosts for their wonderful hospitality, took some souvenir Polaroid photos for them and then rode off into the early morning.

***

The road continued to track the Pyanj River in steep canyons and through mountain goat villages, right up until it opened out onto the main street of Qalaikhum. Massive old trees lined the street and grew together overhead providing a continuous thick green canopy all the way to the police station where I was flagged down by a surprised traffic cop and escorted into the interrogation rooms. They weren't friendly and had many questions for me and thoroughly scrutinised my passport and travel permit before asking about my intended route to Dushanbe (this was where the road forked). They insisted I go via Kulyob, farther to the west and south, as the roads were mostly paved and they reckoned the riding easier. I could see this town clearly on my map, and showed them, but the route looked like it just petered out into tangled mess of twisted back roads with uncountable river crossings. I asked about the other, older, original road and they all shook their heads telling me it was much harder, steeper, and mostly unpaved (this was the big red line on my map). They were so adamant in their advice, and so emphatically was it delivered, that after wiping their spittle off my face, I felt sure that it was an order and not just a suggestion, so it was with some nervousness that I rode off down the main road, pausing thoughtfully at the T-junction, in clear sight of the police station and turned right, following the old original road to Dushanbe. I waited for the sounds of sirens, engines, shouting, or worse still, a hail of bullets to rain down on me, but all I had to content with was another frikkin checkpoint and a mangy hungry half-crazed mongrel dog that leapt out of the dark shadows of the guard house at me. Beyond the checkpoint I rode uphill along the floor of a narrow valley where a small turquoise stream flowed, meandering gently around big boulders and splashing over smaller rocks. It was surprisingly warm in the autumn morning sun, which shone done here on pretty patches of grass and wildflowers along the banks of the stream. The cool, still pools of turquoise water looked altogether inviting and I was tempted to stop, strip off and splash about cleaning myself. I even had loneliness-inspired visions of doing all of this under the supervision of a sultry siren, perhaps frolicking naked on the grass afterwards, but I had never been comfortable bathing in public so passed over the opportunity and rode on.

The pleasant riding and day dreaming ended abruptly – just like the road itself – disappearing into a dead-end of sheer rock face. A dusty, rutted, dirt track took off steeply to the right and I spent the next two hours relentlessly climbing in switchback fashion. I lost count of the hairpin corners and got dizzy as the switchbacks shortened with each rise as I climbed to the top. Along each length of track I would sneak a quick look at the scene below, just a little higher each time, slowly building up to a birds' eye perspective. Eventually I rounded the final corner that cut across the peak of the mountain and found myself on the shore of an endless sea of dry brown peaks. It was as if someone had drawn up the land, like a stiff paper tablecloth, crumpled it savagely and spread it out again. I was above 3000 metres again and it had gotten cold again quickly, but there was no snow here nor anywhere on the mountains ahead of me that I could see. It wasn't going to be a fast ride to Dushanbe – it was almost noon and I had just spent the last few hours effectively moving only about 100 metres forward. If you had been tracing my path with a pencil on a map you would have worn through the paper and left a deep, thick deposit of lead in your furniture.

The road now gently snaked its way along the dry mountain sides, but its surface had deteriorated further into deep hard ruts, loose gravel and powder filled corners. I used first and second gear exclusively and averaged no more than ten kilometres per hour. It was painful, but to travel any faster would have been suicide, as evidenced by the crumpled and burnt out wrecks of trucks I spied frequently at the bottom of mountain sides. I rounded a bend that afforded another spectacular view of the mountains ahead and decided to take a short rest in an unusually wide stretch of road. I was about to get off my bike when I looked up to see what looked like a combi van parked in the distance. Two men in white suits were waving at me, calling me down. Who were they and what were they doing? I had already turned off my engine so I rolled silently down the gentle sloping track toward them.

The two men greeted me warmly. They both wore matching one piece white zip-up jump suits and looked like they belonged deep inside a nuclear reactor handling fissile material. The younger of the two men was twenty-something, with bouffant dark curly hair and had a youthful, rock'n roll exuberance. I searched in vain for his ipod, which would have completed "the look". His compadre was older, middle aged, grizzled and laconic.

They explained that they were clearing landmines and worked for a Swiss NGO sponsored by the UNDP. Their little van was overflowing with electronic equipment and they pointed down the steep hillside where the rest of their crew worked in what looked like a large forensic crime scene - with small squares and narrow connecting corridors staked out in red and white plastic tape. They were all dressed in the same white uniforms and most sat on their haunches as they sifted and sieved the dry soil in painstaking backbreaking work. They told me that the land here was riddled with unexploded land mines – all laid during the civil war. They warned me in the gravest terms not to leave the road for any reason, unless, of course, I wanted to be blown to pieces. They also pointed to a half-demolished stone hut on top of a neighbouring hillside and described how they had seen an over zealous Russian soldier, who refused to follow their warnings, blown to Kingdom Come. It was a sombre end to our conversation and I thanked them wholeheartedly for their warnings – I had not been aware of this issue and without this knowledge I could have easily wandered off the track for a final, fatal comfort stop.

***

I rode on as the track wound its way first down then up, hauling itself circuitously around the steep mountains. I passed through a tiny hamlet, which, perhaps subconsciously prompted, had a decidedly Swiss chalet look and feel about it; the houses were prettier here with high pitched rooves and decorative woodwork around windows, doors, gables and eaves. Dairy cows struggled bravely on tiny plots of brown grass and small plots of dry crops were tended by optimistic farmers. Beyond the hamlet the road took a hairpin bend to the left, over a small stream and suddenly became soft pink sand. I battled forward but was almost run off the road by three very old and very large trucks, travelling in convoy, carrying aid. I think the first driver saw me, but, obscured by the thick red dust clouds of his wake, the others certainly did not. Shaken, I pressed on and rode under a huge natural rock archway, over the stream again and emerged into a wide flat-bed valley where the stream became a river, agriculture became more widespread and villages were small but frequent. The road, however, did not improve and became worse still, as its loose surface broke up with mountain run offs eating away at the surface leaving a wet rocky rutted residue behind. I still hadn't got beyond second gear all day and began to wonder whether I would reach Dushanbe by nightfall. This was agony and my backside was stinging from the long bone-jarring ride. A quick check of my map showed that I wasn't even half way there. I foolishly accelerated past an ancient unroadworthy bus carting dowdy locals and tired school children only to be stopped dead in my tracks a few kilometres later at another checkpoint. I stopped behind a large lorry belching diesel fumes into my helmet and was eventually processed by a disinterested policeman. I asked about the road ahead and he pointed at the ground dismissively and simply said, in the classic Russian laconic way, "vot tak", or "and so it is, like this, more of the same!" Great!

I rode over more rocky spillways and on, past farms, larger villages and along high river banks, sometimes passing towns only accessible by rickety suspension bridges suitable only for their underweight (read: malnourished) inhabitants. I climbed back up into steep jagged mountains again and took my lunch alone on a large boulder under the shade of a tree. It was hot and the shade provided a relief from the intense sun. I drank my bottle of hot fizz and more tea biscuits for that was the extent of food I had been able

216

to gather earlier in the morning.

I rode on and came to a large rusting abandoned tank at the side of the road – a relic, I suspected, from the Russian invasion and war with Afghanistan. Just beyond the tank I came to a large checkpoint, with parade ground, barracks and barbed wire fence. Two sleepy soldiers came out to meet me and explained that the road ahead was impassable with the road and bridge washed away. There was, however, a "temporary" road that crossed the river downstream (no bridge though) and rejoined the highway again. They took one look at me, and then my bike, and said "nyet problema" and waved me on down the sidetrack toward the rapids below. My heart sunk like a lead weight and I broke out in a cold sweat - I had a pathological fear of water crossings and this one looked particularly nasty. The water ran deep, fast and white over big rocks, collecting briefly in a large pool before crashing over a high waterfall down onto more rocks metres below. I cursed and cursed again. I looked up at the checkpoint and raised and shook my fist in anger, cursing them (who else could I blame?) and was sure I could see the two dopey soldiers pointing, slapping their thighs and laughing hard at me.

With a heavy sense of dread I rode up slowly and parked at the stony riverbank. It was a good twenty yards across with no discernable break in the strong current. I tried to remember the advice I had been given that said head for the roughest water because it is usually most shallow, but the whole river was full of rough water and none of it looked particularly shallow.

There was no point lingering here so I found what I thought looked like a good launching spot and tentatively pushed my front wheel into the water - engine running of course. The tip of the wheel was wet, more throttle, less brake and more of the wheel went in, now half underwater and still no sign of the river bed. Oh shit. There was no turning back now for it was impossible to arrest the forward movement as momentum and gravity conspired against me and pulled the bike along and the front wheel deeper into the water. I was now on a forty-five degree downwards trajectory heading straight for the foaming water; it was like I was trapped on a roller coaster that I had foolishly agreed, but never really meant, to ride. Argh. Stop – I want to get off! The front wheel went deeper into the water and I slid forward on the seat desperately trying to find the riverbed with my outstretched legs and feet. My boots were now completely full of icy water and heavy to lift. I could now feel the full force of the water against the wheel and it was strong. What would happen when the whole bike was in the water? I began to topple over - this is it, I'm going under I thought - but somehow I was able to get a foothold and drive the bike forward and stabilise it. Now I really felt the full force of the water as it built up against the bike frame and panniers urging compliance. The back wheel skidded on the slippery rocks and I slipped sideways before lurching forward unsteadily again. My left leg was locked straight and was my only brace against falling over. I went deeper, panicked and hit the throttle hard, stalling the bike. Oh crap, no power. I looked nervously at the waterfall, which I had been slowly edging towards since leaving the shore, pulled across by the current, like an airplane flying a seemingly straight course into strong side winds. I jumped off and planted both feet into the riverbed, leant over and pushed, and with a huge rush of adrenalin, moved the bike a few feet forward and slightly higher, before reaching for the starter and (luckily) igniting the engine for the final push up and onto the far shore. I turned the bike off and leant it against the nearby rock wall and collapsed exhausted on the riverbank. I lay there for fifteen minutes recovering. My pants were soaked and my boots and socks waterlogged. I drained my boots but they were so sodden I wore my sneakers instead; I might as well have worn thongs, such was the protection they afforded. I rode up and out of the tiny river canyon and back onto the highway.

***

I rode on through more difficult and tight mountain tracks until reaching Komsomolobad, where the road improved dramatically (i.e. flat and some patches of asphalt) and the landscape opened out onto a long wide flat river valley. It was hot down here and where the road was tarred it was sticky and soft under the wheels of my bike.

I stopped at a small village, in the late afternoon, and the two small boys running a food and drink stall must have misunderstood my polite request for a cool drink as, "can I have the hottest, foulest, worst imitation coke drink you have, oh, and while you're at it, can you shake it up as hard as you can before you give it to me so that when I open the bottle it sprays all over me in a warm brown shower and then dries sweet and sticky all over my clothes and bike?" The old white-haired one-eyed village Imam, who had seen all of this from his vantage point under a nearby shady tree, came over and consoled me and then wiped me down with a wet rag, before severely scolding the boys. The old man was curious about my journey and after I had explained it all to him he shook my hand for a long time, looked me in the eye – with his one good eye – placed his other hand on my shoulder and said warmly "Peace be upon you, and the mercy of Allah and His blessing". He wished me well again and I rode off through the town feeling a little better. It made me think again (it had been a recurring thought) about the corrupt stereotypes we have of Muslim people and the vast generalisations we make to categorise them all as hate-filled terrorists. It made me think about all the warnings I had received from people earlier in my trip who felt sure I would be taken hostage and have my throat slit by the savages here. I laughed then quickly felt depressed for their ignorance, and ours, and what it has lead to and what it might lead to in the future.

***

I rode on down the wide river valley toward a setting sun, around soft winding cliff-top dirt tracks and then finally down and out onto a plateau of low rolling hills and rich farm land with much improved roads. I scattered flocks of sheep being herded slowly home by tired shepherds and rode on past vast cotton and wheat fields and orchards. I rode directly into the huge blazing orange fireball of the setting sun and had to shield my eyes dangerously with my left hand while steering and maintaining the throttle with the other – I was tired and getting lazy and should have stopped. The road widened into a vast expanse of wide smooth and unmarked fresh bitumen and I sped up excitedly for the last hundred kilometres or so into Dushanbe in the crimson dusk that had now settled over the countryside. Just as I started to enjoy the smooth, easy riding, I was flagged down by two pot-bellied policemen, who came running out from under a tree waving a radar gun at me. I had no idea what the speed limit was, but knew I had been riding too fast and had resigned myself to being fined, but once they realised I was from Australia the conversation quickly turned to kangaroos, Kostya Tsu and crocodiles and, after I had told them that I had come all the way from Magadan - which of course they knew of - I was beyond reproach and immediately elevated to the pantheon of Tajik folklore. I shook their hands and they both slapped me hard on the back before I rode off into the dusk.

It was warm, humid and night had fallen by the time I rode into Dushanbe. I had been riding for more than twelve hours, my back ached and my backside throbbed angrily – this had been the toughest day of riding since the Road of Bones and I was glad it was nearly over. I rode down wide tree-lined boulevards illuminated in a soft dim yellow electric light, past enormous parks and Soviet-style apartment blocks, flower shops and little corner stores. I came to my first traffic light since leaving China and pulled up to a stop in traffic – a strange sensation and such a contrast after riding for so long alone in remote and barely civilised areas. There were trams, trolleybuses, cars, motorbikes, department stores, markets, cafes, tea-houses and restaurants. It was a Friday night and the city was alive. People strolled leisurely. I rode past a beautiful white marble opera house standing majestic behind an illuminated fountain that shot silvery water in a high parabola against the black velvet of the night sky. I rode past pretty pastel coloured neo-classical buildings rich with white decorative icing. I was back in civilisation again and it felt different, but good. It had been a gruelling five days of travel, intense in rich experience for me, since leaving Kashgar. China seemed a world away now and I had been glad to be back on my own again on the open road free of any restraints. I had crossed the Pamirs independently, and the starkly beautiful but lifeless high plateaus, endless snow-capped giant mountains and iridescent blue skies had been etched into my mind's eye forever. I had tasted Tajik hospitality first hand and become a little more confident on my bike and felt my health was now improving. I was excited about the remainder of my journey through the ancient Silk Road towns of Uzbekistan, but now it was time to a rest awhile and I rode wearily off into the night looking for somewhere to stay.

A Night at the Opera

I squinted in the sparse streetlight as I struggled to make out the address and directions I had scrawled in my notepad a few weeks earlier. The page was dog-eared, water stained and grimy with fingerprints. Finally, failing to locate any of the imagined or real street names or landmarks on my wholly inadequate guidebook city map, I asked a teenager lurking in the shadows nearby for directions - he knew the place immediately: "follow Rudaki, past the big Tea House, go left at the Presidential Palace, ride past the Bazaar and then take the second left just beyond the carpet factory " Great, that really cleared things up, I thought. My head was swimming as I tried to keep up with this deluge of directions - translating as quickly as I could manage, while still listening to his lengthy and rapid-fire instructions. I repeated back to the boy what I thought he had told me, but like a long Chinese whisper it had been so seriously corrupted that it had almost entirely lost its original meaning. He laughed and came closer - I had accurately recalled the sequence of landmarks but failed terribly with the *actual* directions. We tried again with slightly better results, and, not wanting to embarrass myself any further, I rode off repeating the sequence of landmarks and instructions aloud inside my helmet like a mantra, in the vague hope they might help me hone in on my destination: "Tea House, Palace, left, Bazaar, Carpet Factory, second left... Tea House, Palace

The road was lined with tall lush trees that formed a thick dark canopy over the dimly lit streets. Grass and flowers grew in a verdant narrow parkway that divided the road. It was a languid night and people strolled slowly or sat on benches speaking softly to each other. I rode on past large striking floodlit Neo-classical government buildings and past the huge gushing fountains and large decorative pools of water in the foreground of the gated, guarded and fenced-off compound.

Dushanbe was an attractive city with a relaxed mood - at night at least, and the prettiest I had visited in my entire trip so far, but just as I began to hook into the vibe I noticed that the streets were crawling with sly policemen fattening their meagre paycheques by stopping drivers at random and holding them to ransom for imaginary traffic infringements, decided on a whim. They were universally despised and each driver threw up their hands in angry exasperation upon being stopped. I felt for the drivers - there was no escape, no pleading their case, no courts to deal with disputes, no recourse, they simply had to hand over what was demanded; no receipts, no records, move along please. Hard-earned and precious cash was resentfully and angrily slapped into greasy palms in these illicit transactions. I watched more closely and noticed that police rarely targeted the drivers of the numerous late model European cars or luxury 4WDs cruising the streets, and when they did it was always to greet them not to fine them - it was the hard working, cash-carrying taxi drivers and poor private citizens that were their prey.

I stopped at what looked at first glance to be a large white marble palace. Tall slender white columns stretched from the foundations to a flat squared-off roof, spanning two massive open storeys and the whole facade glowed in a brilliant phosphorescent white, illuminated spectacularly against the black night sky. The interior ceiling was a large grid of colourful, intricate geometric mosaics. At each end of the building the walls facing the street were covered in a giant hexagonal mosaic in hues of golden brown and sea blue. A grand wide staircase rose up from the centre of the ground floor and fanned out to the left and right, linking the busy floors. Each floor was crammed full of animated groups of men crowded around tightly packed tables eating, drinking and smoking. Women dressed in the wonderfully colourful "Atlas" silk dresses whizzed around frantically providing thankless service in a blur of yellow, brown, black, white, green, red and blue. On its far side the building looked out over a large open courtyard where water cascaded gently from a small illuminated fountain into quiet pools. Smoke wafted up into the night sky and the almost-full moon provided additional atmosphere and I could hear a soft drum beat and the jangling, urgent sounds of traditional Tajik music - it was an exotic scene.

Suddenly a tide of men rose and came rushing out onto the street. It looked like the break up of a Mafia convention; dark swarthy men in shell suits and white shirts - buttoned up but with no tie - bustled past me. Drivers in fancy black cars appeared from nowhere to pick up the wealthier men. Others continued their camaraderie out onto the sidewalk and street. Casting aside my prejudices and narrow stereotypes it could just as well have been the weekly meeting of the Dushanbe Rotary Club – how would I know? A big burly man came up and asked me aggressively what I wanted. I was sitting on my stationary motorbike, which at this point began to feel like a very good security blanket, with my helmet and gloves off, fumbling forlornly with my map. I explained what I was looking for again, and he repeated the same directions I had received earlier. He asked where I was from and from where had I had ridden and when I answered "I am from Australia and have ridden from Magadan", he seemed amused and amazed in equal measure. He shook my hand, wished me well and I rode away.

I stopped three more times as I rode beyond the scope of my directions, disoriented in the dimly lit streets as unfamiliar landmarks whizzed past in a shadowy blur. What exactly does a Tajik Presidential Palace and Bazaar look like anyway? I was helped in turn by a husband and wife taking a leisurely evening stroll, a mother and her young son shopping at the Bazaar (just a roundabout with a few street stalls and bare light bulbs), and finally, by a man out walking alone along a dark backstreet with his dog until finally I found the place.

I banged on the heavy steel gate set securely in the thick, tall concrete wall until finally someone came and let me in. I had been expected and was greeted warmly by Anatoly, who manned the night desk. He was tall and slim, with short thick dark wiry hair, fair skin, a broad flat rectangular face and small pale blue eyes. He was young, barely beyond adolescence, but still not yet a man. There was an open, uncomplicated naivety in his expression and he carried himself with an unusual lightness, seemingly untroubled or unaffected by life to date. He opened his mouth to smile widely, revealing a wonderful gap-toothed Terry Thomas-like grin. He wore track suit pants, a sweater and slippers and carried a thick paperback under his arm which he had been reading and I liked him instantly.

He opened a larger heavier gate further along in the compound wall and wearily I pushed my heavy bike over the grate and into the large tree-lined courtyard. I stopped and leaned the bike on its side-stand, finally bringing a very long and tough day of riding to an end - I was exhausted. I had been travelling for more than fourteen hours and now I hobbled, bow-legged around the courtyard like a saddle-sore j ackeroo. Mercilessly assisted by gravity, the circulation quickly returned to my compressed and aching backside and it throbbed angrily as if I had been branded with a giant red-hot horseshoe with its sizzling apex on my butt and its searing prongs running down the back of my thighs. I let out a mournful sigh of relief as the pain dissipated to an acceptable level.

Bemused, Anatoly did his best to absorb the scene in front of him without laughing too hard. His offer to help with my luggage, which normally I would have refused out of hand, was accepted gladly - I was bone tired and it felt like all of my strength had been sapped by today's riding.

I looked around - it was a substantial concrete bungalow with a pitched tiled roof and a shady inner courtyard surrounded by a grove of apple trees, heavy with fruit, and the whole property was surrounded, like a fortress, by a thick high stone wall.

Anatoly explained that he was a student at the University in Dushanbe and that he did this job to help make ends meet and to practice his English. He sailed serenely across the courtyard like a Buddhist novice - the warmth of his smile and his eagerness to help me were altogether overwhelming. He showed me to my room, buried deep inside the house. There was a sitting room and three bedrooms for guests and a modern bathroom with laundry facilities. I had to pinch myself - I hadn't seen, let alone sat on, or used a proper toilet for more than a month and I wanted to get down on my knees right there and then and hug the clean gleaming soft white ceramic curves; barring my horseshoe rash, this would certainly be a wonderful relief from the roadside nature stops and dirty flyblown holes in the ground I had become accustomed to. There was even a *clean* bath with shower and curtain. A washer and tumble dryer sat wondrously in another corner. There was a basin with hot and cold running water and a large mirror on the wall. I tested the taps – they both worked, a first!

Anatoly unlocked my room, handed me the key and left. I entered the room and was immediately overwhelmed by both its cleanliness and its contents: it had a *real* bed (a sprung mattress, proper bed linen a soft fluffy white doona and plush pillow) which I threw myself upon immediately, burying my head in the soft white pillow, closing my eyes and hauling my weary body up onto the large mattress. This bed was different - my body didn't immediately take on the shape of an over ripe banana and I couldn't feel the hard floor through it and I could already feel the pain and tiredness draining away, like toxins drawn out through my skin by silent osmosis. An intense feeling of well being and relief washed through my body and I momentarily felt like I had achieved a higher state. My brain was pumping out pleasure chemicals in large doses – it was wonderful and I didn't want to move. There were no windows in my room but the centre of the ceiling had been cut away to the roof in an irregular four sided empty space to make a large skylight and I could see the massive almost-full moon again as it slowly crossed my narrow field of vision. It was only twenty four hours ago that I had looked up at the same but slightly fuller moon from the banks of the Pyanj River, deep inside a steep mountain canyon along a remote stretch of the Pamir Highway with a rag-tag collection of dirty road workers - it was an odd, slightly jarring and disorientating sensation. I didn't have any roots and the relentless travel and movement was catching up with me. I was ready for a rest here, at least for a few days.

I felt like a kid in a candy store and couldn't decide which treat to take next: bathe, eat, or rest some more - they were all simple but wonderful pleasures for me now. I hadn't washed since leaving China almost a week ago and my clothes were all now just different shades of dirty brown, so impregnated were they with dust and grit and grime from the last few weeks of travelling. Wherever I walked inside the house I left a tell-tale trail of my footsteps – in a dusted outline – like an Arthur Murray dance sheet; I was in desperate need of a wash so headed off to the bathroom.

I looked in the mirror; it was me, but not me. I looked closer; I was older, certainly tired and my face was weathered and creased. My hair was dry and coarse and greyer than I remembered and I had more white stubble than dark in my beard - perhaps I was becoming a little like the people I had met along my journey, hardened by their environment and tough living, but my eyes were clear and my mind felt sharp, overflowing now with experience and memories. Flab had become firm and I felt strong, although my ankle still bothered me and my bones ached - deep in the marrow; this was day sixty seven on the road and I had been travelling for almost three months - it seemed like years since I had farewelled my family, and my "other life" now seemed more like a previous existence, a world away and partly obscured.

I took a gloriously long hot shower. I closed my eyes at first and let the heat and pressure of the water soothe my tired shoulders and arms. It was invigorating, but by the time I had opened my eyes again the bottom of the bath was covered in dirt and grit, like a silty river delta after massive flooding and I spent just as long after my shower, on my hands and knees, scrubbing and removing the dirt and stains from it.

I asked Anatoly for some advice on where to eat and he gave me directions then insisted on escorting me at least some of the way back to the main street to ensure I found my way. We followed the laneway behind the guesthouse and walked past many similar walled properties, but despite the walls and heavy gates, children played happily in the streets, neighbours talked animatedly under dim street lights and friendly proprietors, smiling broadly behind makeshift counters and shelves stacked high with tins and bottles and bread, sold essential items at small corner shops. This was a community and you could feel it.

***

The night was still and warm and I found an outside table at a pretty sidewalk café and ordered a big meal of bread and dip, Greek salad and a huge mixed grill of kebabs followed by my favourite Russian desert, and arguably my favourite Russian word - ice cream or "mah-rozh-en-nohyah". I loved chewing over these five syllables, letting them wash around inside my mouth for a while, rolling the errrrrrs and then letting the sounds escape from my mouth in controlled syncopated sequence. I washed all of this down with a few litres of quality Russian beer, served icy cold in long tall glasses by a pretty young waif-like waitress.

I didn't stop to look up often, but when I did I noticed that the group of men at the table next to me had continued to grow over the course of my meal and now consisted of about a dozen well dressed men, packed tightly shoulder to shoulder enjoying a communal meal of pilaf and beer, served continuously in huge pitchers by the waif, delivered three at a time, one-handed, like a German barmaid. They threw around more money in this one meal than your average Tajik earns in six months and they were joined by a cadre of back-slapping mates in leather jackets, sunglasses and gold chains, who emerged from late model expensive European sports cars. I concluded they were local mobsters who probably made their money in drugs so kept my head down and finished up quickly.

I walked slowly back to the guesthouse and collapsed exhausted into my feathery soft nest and, too tired to dream I fell into a deep, dark and restful sleep.

**

I emerged from my hibernation and stumbled groggily out onto the inner courtyard, now dappled in bright sunshine, where a table had been set for breakfast. No one else had appeared yet, but just as I sat down, a woman rushed from the kitchen nearby to greet me. She introduced herself simply as "Zachar" – Russian for *sugar*, so that's how I came to think of her. She had a milky freckled complexion, a round face with fleshy cheeks, dead straight reddish dark brown hair, pale blue eyes and a severe but stylish Charleston bob cut. She wore a long modern dress, leather sandals and a smart button-up cotton blouse. Sugar was an Uzbek, living in Tajikistan, like so many of her compatriots, reflecting the heterogeneous ethnic mix across this part of Central Asia. She had a teenage daughter and although I didn't ask, I sensed that was the extent of her immediate family. Suddenly, the gate opened and a young, well dressed man entered the yard. At first glance he looked like a Tajik Beatle - he had a thick round mop of sandy coloured hair, bushy sideburns and a fringe that fell low and straight just above his thick brow and he wore a fine grey turtleneck sweater and tight jeans. He had large green eyes, wide spaced on a broad flat fair skinned face with sunken cheeks, accentuating his already prominent cheekbones. Rustam was a Pamiri and was the guide/fixer for the only other guest staying here – Helen, a professional photographer from New York. They disappeared inside to complete their business and I finished my breakfast alone.

After some time they emerged with an unexpected invitation; Rustam had arranged for Helen to attend the opera and had a spare ticket which he kindly offered to me. I had tried unsuccessfully in a few of the larger cities along my journey to attend the theatre or at least something remotely cultural, so accepted gladly. Helen and Rustam departed for their other appointments and I spent the rest of the day doing my chores, taking a leisurely lunch and writing home.

I wandered lazily back down Rudaki, admiring the pretty buildings and enjoying the shady relief from the intense sunshine provided by the avenue of tall well established trees. I returned to my favourite café where the owner, recognising me from the night before called me in. It was early afternoon and I was the only patron. The waif was still there, wearing the same clothes and looking tired. I was sick of shashlik and wanted to try some authentic Tajik food so, referring to my guidebook, I ran bravely ran through the suggestions, "Do you have any *nahud sambusa*?"
"No"
"OK. Do you have any *Chakka*?"
She started chewing the end of her pencil.
"No"
"*Kurtob*?"
(picking the dirt out of her fingernails)
"No"
"OK, I'll have a mushroom pizza then"

***

Looking my best, but still feeling conspicuously under-dressed, I met Helen and Rustam in the courtyard of the guesthouse just before 5pm and we were chauffer driven in a mini-van down the long main avenue Rudaki back towards the centre of Dushanbe to the

Opera House. Along the way Rustam pointed out the massive pale blue Neo-classical buildings that ran in a wide handsome arc away from, and then back towards the road - all of the features on the buildings looking like they had been laced with white icing. A huge arch-way sat majestically at the centre of the arc, farthest away from us and a small strip of parkland with trees and paths separated the campus from the sidewalk and street. Rustam told us this was the pedagogical institute and that he had studied here to be a teacher, and then he turned away and added, with his voice trailing away in an empty monotone that this was also where he had been brutally beaten for simply being a Pamiri.

We pulled up outside the Opera House where a large and well dressed crowd had already gathered, milling about on the steps, enjoying the mild early autumn evening. A huge banner draped across the front of the Opera House emphatically proclaimed far too many things in thick red Cyrillic letters and numerous exclamation marks. I asked Rustam what it said. "This is the grand re-opening of the Opera House and the first performance of the Opera Company since the Opera House closed". "When did the Opera close?" I asked him. "In 1992, just after the Civil War began" he said earnestly. "This is a very big day for our country" he added proudly.

We walked up the stairs, under a giant portico and through the massive front doors into the foyer. Inside was bustling with more patrons - there were older well dressed couples; women in evening dresses and men in their best lounge suits, but thankfully there was also a large working class contingent, whose attire was more closely aligned with mine.

Rustam darted off to the box office, returned with our tickets and then led us up the grand central marble staircase and into the theatre proper. As we climbed the stairs I asked him discretely how much money I owed him but he waved his open palmed hand at me vigorously, slightly taken aback and said "No, no, please, you are my guest and it is a great pleasure for me to share this special event with you." We emerged into the enormous open space of the theatre and followed Rustam as he walked ahead of us and down the wide central aisle. The theatre was certainly large and stately, but not to the scale of the Marjinsky or the Bolshoi, nor anywhere near as grand or opulent so that it could almost be described as austere by comparison. There were no grand crystal chandeliers here or any of the fabulously ornate cornice and gilt work of these icons and there was no dress circle and only a few very basic boxes. It did, however, have a large wide stage framed by a proscenium arch and protected – ahead of the performance – by a lush velvet vermillion coloured curtain, still carrying some stale, faded golden Soviet emblems. The walls were decorated in simple striking marble work and stuccoes, and the ceiling was covered with a massive, beautiful, intricate and vividly coloured circular floral motif of pink and red roses and other flowers. Rich Persian carpets and runners adorned the floor and aisles and many rows of comfortable red velour seats - quickly filling with excited patrons – were perfectly terraced from just above the orchestra pit up to the rear of the theatre.

I was following Rustam down the centre aisle toward the orchestra pit when suddenly I was dazzled by a bank of intensely bright lights that had just been switched on in front of us. I shielded my eyes from the glare and looked down to see a TV crew preparing to film. There was also a huddle of photographers preparing to shoot - there must have been some VIPs in attendance, probably sitting in the front row or in a box, I thought. We kept following Rustam, waiting for him to turn into a row of seats, but he kept descending towards the orchestra pit, right into the centre of all this activity. He stopped when he could go no further and showed us to our seats – front row, centre, just over the conductor's podium and about eye-level, I imagined, with the soon to appear performers on the stage! As soon as we were seated the arc lights swung around and shone onto us, the TV cameras whirred into life and flash bulbs popped in little explosions of even brighter light. We gave our best impressions of being distinguished international opera VIPs, deep in earnest debate over important cultural issues; Helen might have even pulled it off in her smart head-to-toe black New York outfit, but I think my frayed and oil-stained shirt, grimy jeans, dirty runners and swollen ankle made me look highly improbable.

Rustam handed us each a program for the performance. They were printed on flimsy yellow paper and clumsily typeset in thick black over- inked letters and looked like the handouts I used to get from my high school English teacher. Unlike those, however, I studied this one carefully; we were seeing the famous Tajik opera, "Komde and Madan", heralded as a synthesis of traditional Persian verse and modern symphony. It was billed as a classic Arabian Nights' love story; Komde, the King's favourite dancer (from his harem) falls for the young, handsome and golden-voiced Madan, a wandering minstrel. Madan is entranced by the exquisite Komde and pursues her vigorously. Jealous and outraged, the King forbids their union and secretly orders Madan be killed. Already much despised, this cruel act finally turns his courtiers and soldiers against the King, and after much palace intrigue, plotting and battles, he is defeated, Madan and Komde re-united and their love prevails. It was a huge ensemble production with the best artists in the country and sounded like a cracker of a story. There was a buzz from the audience too and I couldn't wait for the performance to start.

The orchestra, still conductor-less, were warming up in anticipation too. The strings, woodwind, percussion, and brass sections were all clearing their throats in a cacophony of noise rising from the pit in front of us. The first thing that struck me about the orchestra was how casually they were all dressed and how relaxed they seemed. There were no fine black evening dresses or bow ties, starched dinner shirts and tails here; men wore open necked casual shirts and either jeans or pants and the women wore sensible work-a-day dresses, or blouses, pants and sensible shoes - they looked more like the table staff at a modest family-run cafe than a professional orchestra. Then Rustam reminded me that, unlike professional Operas in richer countries, there was neither corporate sponsorship nor anything beyond the trickle of government funding and the paltry box office receipts to sustain them; these people all had day jobs to put food on their tables and did this for their love of music and art. They could have been taxi drivers, bakers, shop assistants or teachers. They were a ragtag collection and the percussion section, in particular, caught my eye. It seemed to consist, in its entirety, of just two players; a tall young athletic Russian girl with long blonde hair and pale blue eyes who stood stiffly, like a guard on duty, behind her snare drums and the marimba. She was dressed smartly in a crisp white blouse and long black skirt. A balding middle-aged man, who looked more like a brooding off duty bar tender than a musician, was responsible for the timpani. He scanned the pit, eyeing each of his colleagues up and down, in turn, with a look of extreme disdain on his face. He looked highly competent as he adjusted and tested his kettledrum, but oozed arrogance and I sensed he wanted to be anywhere but here tonight.

Oddly, there were still a number of unattended instruments; a bass drum and cymbals stood waiting expectantly and the kitchen sink kit of triangle, tambourine and wood blocks hung silently on their stand. The barman looked at the empty spot with extra contempt and the tall Russian girl just looked plain anxious. Then suddenly, an elderly man - or woman - for it was difficult to tell at a distance as it wore a long black sack coat, had short grey hair and a plain utility face with wire framed glasses, rushed in, breathless. I asked Helen, and after careful analysis we decided that *it* was a *she*. The old woman fumbled with her equipment in her haste to prepare. The tall Russian girl helped her while the barman looked away, rolled his eyes and shook his head.

Now the conductor strode in quickly, nervously assuming his position on the modest podium, just in front of us. He was tall and thin with long limbs, like a stick insect, and had a gaunt ashen face with dark beady eyes, a tousled mop of greasy dark hair and a fat grey caterpillar moustache over unsmiling, thin fixed lips. He too was dressed casually in a white open necked shirt with long sleeves already rolled-up to the elbow and he wore ill-fitting dark pants. Beads of sweat had already started to form on his long forehead, even before he had lifted his baton - a study in concentration. He called his players to attention and each of the sparse sections warmed up in turn.

The lights dimmed and spotlights sharpened their focus onto centre stage. The crowd hushed. A tall, heavy-set man in a well-cut steel blue suit with a crisp white shirt and colourful silk tie stepped out from behind the heavy curtain accompanied by a distinguished older woman who wore a stylish pale blue suit dress. The crowd recognised her immediately and broke into generous applause. She smiled sweetly and waved back in acknowledgment. "Who is she?" I asked Rustam.

"Munira Shahidi, the daughter of the composer. She is well known and much loved in Tajikistan because of her fathers work."
"And the other man?"
"He's the Minister of Culture"
"I see"

They both made short speeches, which I admired for their noble sentiments about the importance and value of art in society, both as a source and expression of new ideas and simply for its ability to nourish the soul and lift the human spirit. Munira went on to explain how difficult it had been to sustain the arts through the dark years of the Civil War, and how crucial they were now in the rebuilding of a civil society, and finally how proud she was that her father's work was being used tonight to re-launch the Opera in Tajikistan tonight.

Excited by the immense build up, we settled in with high hopes of a great performance. The lights dimmed right down, the audience hushed and the heavy plush curtains glided apart to reveal an eclectic ensemble cast that filled the entire stage. There were bearded noble men in long striped robes, chattering peasant women, barrel-chested palace guards - tyring hard to look menacing, a troupe of wandering minstrels, courtiers, viziers and a harem of surprisingly beautiful young dancers. The set was frugal and simple but effective and consisted of painted palm trees, palace walls and peasant homes. It looked like a cross between a Cecil B. De Mille biblical epic and a school nativity play, with little or no make up or costumes required for the peasantry, who already possessed the oddest collection of faces and bodies, and looked as if they had been swept up from the roadside in some of the poor towns I had just ridden through.

Suddenly the hero, Madan, bounded onstage strumming a lyre and singing enthusiastically. But he was old, beyond fifty with sad dark puppy dog eyes, long fleshy jowls and a large died black bouffant mullet, exaggerated further by the tight red headband that he wore. He crooned and his gold teeth glistened in the footlights. He was short with a paunch and reminded me of Wayne Newton. His singing was adequate and workmanlike. I tried hard to focus on the story. Then Komde emerged from the harem. She was petite and pretty, with large dark eyes, heavy with mascara and she had powdery fulsome cheeks on a pale, handsome and expressive face, but her body was flaccid; the husk of a ballerina long since departed. She wore a beautiful bejewelled aquamarine chiffon gown but sang in a thin breathy voice.

Unfortunately the show went on. And on. There were long and mournful solos by the now separated Komde and Madan, pining for each other, uplifting ensemble singing in solidarity for the two star crossed lovers, regal rants and temper tantrums, much chest beating and deep throated military chanting, a hammy murder scene and the sweet harmonies of two loving hearts re-united it was in turn, bizarre, humorous, sad, and sometimes even entertaining.

Quickly disinterested in the story, however, I scanned the orchestra pit, which was a hot-bed of action. I was drawn immediately to the two lead female violinists, not for their striking beauty - for they were plump middle-aged maternal Russian women - but because both chewed gum incessantly, in perfect time with each other and the music they played. I thought perhaps it might be to help calm any opening night nerves. Then, slowly but surely, the woman farthest from us stabbed the gum between her teeth with the tip of her tongue and blew a small semi-opaque perfectly round pink bubble, inflated it a little further then snapped it quickly back into her mouth, like a lizard swallowing a fly on it's long sticky tongue. I was dumbstruck. I nudged Helen and we watched intently as her colleague did likewise. It was extraordinary and they both continued to do it. It had its own particular rhythm but neither of them took their eyes off the score nor skipped a note and the conductor didn't seem to notice, or if he had he simply ignored it. He had more important issues to deal with.....there was a rebellion brewing in the bass section where the recalcitrant players, who had been struggling throughout the performance, now talked loudly amongst themselves and defiantly missed beats altogether. The conductor shushed them angrily, like a teacher would errant school children, showering the second violas in a thick spray of spittle. He then smashed his baton down with all his might on the hard edge of his podium, demanding their obedience. The tension was palpable.

When he wasn't overwhelmed keeping this rabble together, he was cueing the performers on the stage, on a number of occasions mouthing, in exaggerated fashion, the first few syllables of forgotten lyrics for the hapless actors. And when they couldn't decipher these silent messages he just sang it for them, like a ventriloquist, projecting his voice from the pit up onto the stage. It was embarrassing.

Throughout the performance the brooding bartender had been simply horrible. He kicked, nudged and even back slapped his elderly colleague to cue her parts or to urge her to catch up on beats that she had missed. At one point even leaning over and playing her part for her - it was awful, and I felt terribly for her, although she did redeem herself on the triangle - which she carefully held up high up on its leather strap before tinkling it with a precise whip of her hand - and she was a master of the wooden blocks. Luckily, the tall Russian girl was out of reach and the two women whispered continually to each other, like co-conspirators, out of earshot from him.

I looked back onto the stage — it was time for the long and much anticipated reunion of Komde and Madan - the climax of the story. He had prevailed and now held her gently in his arms as they sung a lilting romantic refrain, staring lovingly into each others eyes. There was a slight but visible tremor in his arms, his eyes bulged, beads of sweat gathered on his forehead and his face was florid under the strain, but he sang on through clenched teeth until thankfully relieved of his duty as the curtains were drawn ending the performance.

By now the poor conductor looked as if he had suffered a nervous breakdown - he was exhausted; he had sweated litres and seemed to have aged years since the start of the show. He had battled valiantly and single-handedly to save the show but it had almost killed him. He ran off with his head bowed, deeply embarrassed and inconsolable. I hoped there would be someone with him backstage just to ensure he didn't have access to any sharp objects. There was polite applause but no curtain calls and certainly no bouquets. If it weren't *so bad* it would have been funny.

Munira Shahidi bravely returned to the stage and made a short speech lamenting the severe lack of resources and money at the Opera and commended everyone in the company to the audience for their spirit, good hearts and intent. Her speech had a faintly apologetic tone to it, and it must have been difficult to see her father's work butchered so badly.

Rustam turned and asked us both what we thought of the performance. "Unforgettable" I said honestly.

"It might have been better with more practice" Helen said, before adding kindly, "I thought the Captain of the Guards sang well"
"Me too" I added authoritatively.

I confessed meekly that my favourite aspect had been the harem dancers; I had been mesmerised by the sensuous lithe bare bellied exotic dancing of the beautiful Tajik women in the harem and said so. Rustam smiled.

***

Outside it was dusk and we gathered on the steps under the huge portico to plan our movements for the rest of the night. It was a mild night and diners sat at tables at an open-air restaurant across from the Theatre. It was set out on the large square opposite, around a tall fountain and pool and rows of pretty fairy lights twinkled in the nearby trees. I was about to suggest that we eat there when Rustam rushed off and returned a moment later, ushering Munira Shahidi into our tight circle. Rustam politely introduced us in turn, but it was primarily for Helen's benefit as I quickly realised that being a "photographer from New York" opened more doors and pulled slightly more weight in cultural circles, than a "motorcyclist from Melbourne" ever would. But this was not my domain and I was happy to be a side show for the main event. Munira called to a younger woman, standing nearby, to join us and introduced us to her daughter, Nargis. Given their relationship to the composer and what they had just been subjected to, they were both in remarkably high spirits. Without prompting, Munira offered a frank assessment of the performance; the marriage of modern symphony and traditional verse, she said, was complex, subtle and delicate work, requiring great precision, skill and feeling. It was an extremely ambitious and testing choice and the company had tried hard, but were simply ill- equipped and under-prepared, she said. We could only agree.

Just as she was finishing her analysis, the conductor, still sober and now wearing a cheap grey sweater wandered past muttering to himself and cursing hard. Our group had caught his eye, but immediately realising who we were with, he bowed his head even deeper, averted his eyes and scurried silently away, up the steps and back into the theatre. "He's taken it very hard" said Munira.

She spoke slowly and precisely in perfect English through a wide smile, which filled her cheeks and creased her eyes, and only ceased when she stopped to listen or consider a point. She had been a classic beauty and her fine features were now well preserved under a layer of pale fleshy skin.

She told us a little more about her father's life. He was born in Samarkand and had fled to Dushanbe after his father had been murdered during Stalin's purges of the 1930's. It was here in Dushanbe that he had pursued his musical vision, going on to become the first and only Tajik of his time to graduate from the Moscow Conservatory of Music. His work was an integral part of the radio music of the 1950's and 1960s linking Tajiks, Uzbeks, Iranians, and Afghans, helping to bring them out from their political isolation. Munira went on to explain the underlying philosophy in her father's work; "... .the pursuit of universal harmony through the reconciliation of eastern and western cultures, underpinned by the notions of the interconnectedness of common and universal thoughts across both traditions " I drifted off and exhaled deeply, lost in an impenetrable fog of esoteric ideas and concepts. It was like trying to wrestle clouds to the ground. I was more likely to ride my motorbike up the north face of Everest and then down the Khyber Pass than grasp this stuff.

Then suddenly, like a curtain, the fog parted as she moved onto more concrete and pressing matters: "And do you want to be a benefactor of the Shahidi Foundation and participate in our ongoing cultural programmes in the advancement of peace, knowledge and understanding amongst the peoples of the world?" I wanted with all my heart to say yes, if only just to please them, here, now, tonight, but I knew I couldn't, that would be unfair to all of us; if I was ever going to help them I knew it would be in a far more pragmatic way. I politely declined. Munira and Helen exchanged contact details and we parted company. Munira and her daughter had been gracious, charming and delightful and I felt lucky to have met them.

***

I woke late (it was a Sunday) and enjoyed another leisurely breakfast, alone, save for my new best friend Sugar, who hovered in the courtyard. The table had been set and the meal prepared according to my preferences from yesterday; eggs (omelette, not fried), nan – buttered with honey, tea (black and sweet), etc. She was wonderful and only needed my happiness for her own sustenance. A gentle breeze blew and a slew of hard tiny apples crashed down in staccato fashion on the courtyard and eaves. It sounded like torrential rain on a corrugated iron roof and instantly reminded me of home.

Suddenly, there was a knock at the gate, which Sugar answered promptly, greeting the guest, whom she obviously knew, warmly. A man entered. I rubbed my eyes and looked long and hard at him, my brain struggling to make sense of the images coming from my eyes. He was big and burly with a long peppery bushranger beard that hung from a square fulsome face. He wore an old polo shirt, casual *shorts* (unheard of in Central Asia), and thongs. He looked like he had just stepped out of a bush caravan, or a Hell's Angels fathers' day picnic. He thrust his big fleshy hand into mine, cracking a few of my knuckles, and said "G'day", instantly identifying himself as a fellow Australian. Brett was an aid- worker with a German NGO whose work focused on helping orphans and internal refugees in Tajikistan, mostly in and around Dushanbe. He lived here with his wife and their two young daughters. I asked Brett about his work and explained that there had been a near complete break down in civil society in Tajikistan, as a new generation emerged without any moral compass, abandoned by parents too poor to care for them and to provide them with the implicit instructions for life and the support provided by a stable family unit. Poverty was the culprit and the problems had only been exacerbated by the protracted and destructive Civil War. He went on to tell me that almost two thirds of the population lived in abject poverty and almost one in five – or well over a million people – were considered destitute. Average salaries were about US$25 a month, the minimum wage a mere US$4 a month and unemployment ran at about 50%. It sounded wretched and I asked him more about his work with the local children.

"We found these kids had no values, no ethics - they were wild, so we set up some really basic programs to help teach them

236

these fundamentals" Brett said.

"What about school? Surely that must help?" I said.

"Most of them don't go, and those that do get beaten by unqualified, disinterested and brutal teachers"

He went on to describe how many children, from incredibly young ages were often left at home, in tiny squalid apartments, unsupervised as their lone mothers worked from dawn to dusk in Dickensian factories for a pittance, returning home exhausted, too tired to even cook a proper meal. Accidents were inevitable and included burns, scalding, falls and broken limbs. Diets were poor, malnutrition common and hunger persistent.

"But, what are they thinking?" I thought out loud, struggling to comprehend how a parent could be so irresponsible.

"They're just trying to stay alive, nothing more. That's all they can manage", said Brett.

Fathers were almost always absent too, either having left, abandoning their families altogether, or working far away in Russia earning "good" money to help keep the family afloat. Then there were the children who had fallen out of or had simply been discarded from their families, consigned to the network of overcrowded and grim orphanages across Tajikistan in the hope that they might receive slightly better care there. But even their prospects were bleak; sleeping in large dormitories of forty or fifty beds, with few personal possessions, living on meagre rations, the older ones receiving perhaps an hour of teaching if they were lucky, otherwise being left to themselves all day. It seemed hopeless.

"What do you think, then, for the future of Tajikistan?" I asked, hoping for some brightness in this awful dark mess, but he did not answer so instead, breaking a long awkward silence, I asked about the road ahead. There were two options for the ride to Samarkand which boiled down to "hard and shorter" versus "easier but much longer". It was difficult to see how any road could possibly be worse than those I had already travelled on, so filled with a sense of improved confidence and some hubris, I opted for the road over the spectacular Fan Mountains, via the ancient Sogdian city of Penjikent; it was only 250 kilometres and a much shorter trip than the circuitous route via Termez in the far south and, anyway, it was marked as a major highway on my map...

"I haven't travelled that way for a while, but it'll take you a whole day. It's mostly loose gravel and dirt and I've seen trucks lose control on some of the tight narrow sections and plummet hundreds of metres to crash in a fireball on the rocks below", cautioned Brett.

"Hmmm, that's interesting", I said nervously.

Then Brett added helpfully, "Yeah. And did you know there are *thousands* of landslides every year in Tajikistan? Driving in the mountains is like Russian Roulette!"

But then I figured: a dozen landslides every day in a country where almost all of the land is covered in mountains where's there's only a few roads anyway; the odds were remote. I was more likely to be killed flying in an ageing, rusted and poorly maintained Russian jetliner operated by a struggling family business in remote Siberia, or riding thousands of kilometres alone through bear infested taiga but I'd already done these things.

***

I spent the next morning attending to some mundane but essential bike maintenance, assisted by an old taxi-driver who became my chaperone and guardian angel, driving me in his battered Lada to the machine bazaar, bargaining on my behalf for what I needed and ensuring I bought "only the best" items at local prices. He had a wet, persistent coal miners' cough, which he sprayed powerfully into his shoulder, elbow and hands, in turn, convulsing continually, as he drove like there was no tomorrow. The bazaar was on the far side of town and we raced along the riverfront through a desolate scene of empty, dusty blocks strewn with garbage where children played idly, and ugly ten-storey tenements where washing and carpets hung from balconies drying in the intense heat in a permanent flag day. It was a stark contrast from the pretty tree-lined main avenue of the city, but totally consistent with what Brett had told me about the reality of life here for the locals. I argued angrily over the final fare proposed by my sick friend and immediately felt guilty and ashamed as he drove off, car and driver spluttering in equal measure.

In search of lunch and keen to visit some of the city's museums and galleries, I walked back along the now very familiar avenue Rudaki, past the institutes and government buildings, past the university grounds, where young couples held hands and stole kisses on discretely positioned park benches, past Soviet-era ex-Intourist monoliths and the outrageously expensive and enormous gold-plated statue of Shah Ismail Samani, founder of the Samanid dynasty.

Downtown Dushanbe had a decidedly Parisienne 1950's feel to me; there were bakeries and pastry shops, cafes, cinemas, confectionary shops, dress makers, antique and art shops, apartments with little balconies over the street, shops with big windowpanes looking over wide footpaths and shaded by big striped canopies, and a large central department store. The mood was relaxed; the shops busy and people seemed, for the most part, happy. It was difficult to reconcile with what I had seen just a few hours earlier - perhaps it was partly my state of mind too. I now felt fully rested and re-charged, ready for the final leg of my journey, across Uzbekistan, Turkmenistan, Iran and Turkey. Samarkand was the first major Old Silk Road city I would visit and it was now only a day's ride away; I had read so much about the city and its history and stared for so long at pictures of the brilliantly tiled and coloured mosques, medrassahs and caravanserai − it was exciting now to be so close.

I took a long lunch at an outside table at a friendly family-run restaurant and ate a double serve of extra fatty mutton kebabs and drank a pot of sweet tea while I sat in the cool shade and watched the passing parade. I also read with wonder about the fantastic exhibits awaiting me at Museum of National Antiquities, including the now unique 1,600 year-old "sleeping" Buddha discovered by Soviet archaeologists near Bamiyan (where the Taliban had dynamited his brothers out of existence in 2001), but my attempted visit was thwarted by the "we're closed on whatever weekday it is that you're here" policy that seemed to be shadowing me across Russia and Central Asia.

Later that afternoon, I received an urgent email authorising my travel across whacky Turkmenistan - whose prickly and fickle bureaucracy had obviously failed to detect my subversive background. This was the only country on my journey for which I had no visa and Dushanbe was the last city en-route where I could get one, and even then there was no guarantee of entry or passage. Visas were notoriously hard to get and riding a motorbike added significant complexity. If I didn't get a visa here I would have to take a long detour to Tashkent and, failing that, I would have to take an entirely different route - around the Caspian Sea and across the Caucasus - to reach Turkey. This was important.

I looked up the address of the Embassy online - it was on Rudaki; I scribbled down the number and rushed back onto the main avenue. I looked at my watch − I had one hour before it closed. Incredibly, according to the property numbers that I quickly located, it was virtually opposite. An anxious taxi driver waited hopefully at the entrance and asked if I needed any help. "No, this is the place I'm looking for, thanks" I said smugly as I walked on past him. It was a surprisingly large and modern building, set well back from the street, nestled behind manicured lawns than ran into a pretty flower garden. It had a large formal entrance at the end of a long driveway. It looked more like a Hotel than an Embassy. I burst through the revolving doors into the foyer and approached the woman who stood behind an impressive reception counter.

"Is this the Embassy of Turkmenistan?"

"This is a Hotel. Would you like a room?"

She fiddled with some papers on her desk.

"Perhaps they have a room?" I suggested politely.

"Under what name?"

"Ahhhh.. ..Embassy.. ..Turkmenistan .... Ambassador... .Turkmenbashi?" I was clutching (blank stare).

"How do you spell that?"

"You know, people from Turkmenistan. Diplomats, nice suits, they issue visas", I said stamping the desk hard with my fist like there was an imaginary passport was on it.

"Would you like a room?"

I put my head in my hands and banged it softly on the counter. I felt like I was trapped inside an episode of Fawlty Towers. I was about to ask whether she was from Barcelona when a couple, returning to the hotel, who had been watching this farce, detoured in a long wide arc around us to cross the lobby, watching me carefully, before skipping away nervously up the stairs.

Eventually, I suggested we try the phone book and after much page flicking and finger sliding down long lists she said triumphantly: "Ah, you want the *Embassy of the People's Republic of Turkmenistan in Tajikistan.* That's not here."

"Yes. Thank you" I said as I scribbled down the address and rushed outside and into the taxi. I handed the driver the piece of paper, which he read quickly before screwing up and tossing it aside, saying dismissively, "Ah, the Turkmen Embassy, everyone knows where that it is."

The Embassy was a just a modest concrete house on a busy street near to the central market. A lone soldier stood on duty blocking an otherwise open driveway that led to a small courtyard where a pretty rose garden flourished. I was an unexpected visitor and it was almost closing time but I was seen immediately by a pleasant Turkmenbashi clone – a short stubby man, immaculately groomed with died jet-black and perfectly coiffed short hair and a healthy tan. He invited me into his impressive office. It was decorated like an English gentleman's club with a long mahogany table, wing chairs and reading lamps. A huge bookshelf dominated the far wall, but it was full of copies of just one book: the Rukhnama (Book of the Soul), Turkembashi's magnum opus and required reading for all citizens, where he sets out his version of Turkmen history, culture and spirituality. I sat on the edge of a large antique sofa, like one you might see in a psychiatrist's office, while my host sat behind his large but empty desk scrutinising my letter of invitation. He spoke English perfectly and looked up at me suspiciously over his reading glasses and said rhetorically "So you want to ride your motorbike across the Kara-Kum desert? Are you crazy? There's nothing there except a few wretched peasants and camels. You should spend more time enjoying Ashgabat!"

He gave me an application form and ushered me into the small waiting room where he insisted I use the desk and chair to complete the onerous paperwork. I started to complete the form but was drawn to the contents of the room. A huge painted cloth map, like the ones from my schooldays, hung on the wall above me. It was a Mercator projection of the U.S.S.R, centred on the Turkmen S.S.R. Like the British, the Soviets had used pink to colour their massive empire as it stretched all the way
from the Baltic, to the Black Sea, pushing down onto China, before petering out, finally, just a few miles short of Alaska in the Pacific Far East. The colours had faded now and it was dirty and dull and cracked with age but it still revealed the heavy-handed fingerprints of the Soviets, especially here in Tajikistan, with the cities of Stalinabad, Leninabad, and mirrored unimaginatively across the Pamirs with Pik Stalina, Pik Lenina and, at their pinnacle Pik Communism. I looked further a field; Yugoslavia, East Germany, Poland, Bulgaria, Hungary were all coloured fraternally, Beijing was Peking, Istanbul was Constantinople and Iran was Persia. More disturbingly, the Aral Sea lapped at the shores of Moynak and Aralsk, villages that are now more than one hundred kilometres from the water. I looked at the small print at the bottom of the map, it was marked "Moscow 1959".

Beyond the map, the walls of the room were adorned with posters and calendars and other propaganda that all had one element in common - Turkmenbashi. He beamed down at me from an endless array of manufactured poses; opening a concrete sleeper plant, admiring melons with women in traditional clothes, inspecting the cotton harvest and instructing engineers on the finer points of oil and gas exploration. I picked up the national daily paper that lay on the table in front of me. It was a thin broadsheet similarly devoted to his cult of personality, although it did leave some room for coverage of the national sports of arm wrestling, weight lifting, table tennis and draughts. There were some great sugar-beet growing statistics and a report on the opening of a sewing workshop.

I completed my visa application and returned to my host next door where he duly stamped my visa carefully in my passport. The whole process remarkably straightforward and lubricated, I suspect, by the fifty-two US dollars demanded.

***

In a final reminder of the rampant unchecked corruption here, my taxi driver, who had waited loyally for over an hour while I got my visa, was stopped by the traffic police on our way back up Rudaki and relieved of his day's takings. He spat, swore and slapped the steering wheel and almost cried in frustration. I tried to sympathise with him but the inequity of it all had pushed him over the edge. I paid him generously to
try and compensate for his misfortune, but he refused the extra, returning it angrily to me. I walked the rest of the way back to the guesthouse.

The Golden Road to Samarkand

Sugar held the heavy gate open and farewelled me sweetly as I rode out of the guesthouse yard and away down the back streets towards the bazaar. It was still early, but already the sun was intense and burnt my shadow of bike and rider almost black into the pavement. I rode out through the brown, dusty northern suburbs, past more depressing tenements and up a long slow hill past the Dushanbe Cement Factory. It belched thick dense clouds of brown dust in a tall tight plume, climbing like a dirty beanstalk straight up into an otherwise empty blue sky.

I quickly cleared the ugly urban precincts and was riding the long lazy curves through the pretty stone-fenced hamlets that hugged the banks of the Varzob River as it cut its way north into the foothills of the Fan Mountains. There road today was quiet; the only significant traffic the occasional group of women, using the road like a giant washboard to clean their family's prized rugs and carpets. I slowed to walking pace and respectfully overtook these stationary road users, smiling and waving as I passed. Each group consisted entirely of women; daughters fetching river water in pales, mothers scrubbing it vigorously into and out of the rugs, and grandmothers, the foremen of this age-old ritual.

Gradually the vista changed as the road and river climbed higher and the mountains closed in; the poorer hamlets gave way to a more prosperous neighbourhood of substantial family homes, large garden restaurants, hotels and lodges. Some had shady trellised yards, others large covered tea platforms that extended on stilts out over the river. Private gated bridges provided the only access to those more secluded properties that sat quietly on the far bank. The river ran fast in swirling sheets of marbled turquoise as its banks steepened and its angle of descent, over a rocky riverbed, sharpened. It was a pretty and picturesque scene and I felt great to be riding through it.

***

Dushanbe was a watershed in my journey; it had been a complete break from the relentless riding and the hardships of life on the road. I now felt completely rejuvenated, my previously flagging confidence now soared and I felt my *mojo*, conspicuously absent to date, had finally arrived. Riding was instinctive now - the bike simply an extension of mybody as I glided over the landscape on my exhilarating magic carpet ride.

The road continued to follow the narrow river valley and now rose above and away from the river. I hit some muddy road works in a busy but otherwise dusty village and then rode a lonely stretch of more difficult track before emerging into a small secluded valley of striking Arcadian beauty. There were lush meadows filled with flowers and grazing livestock, a crystal clear mountain stream splashed gently over smooth rocks and ran away under a pretty stone arch bridge, an old carved wooden tea platform sat peacefully in a shaded glade by the riverbank and, in the distance, perched on a low hill overlooking this idyllic scene, stood an old stone farmhouse and compound. Beyond the bridge the road ended, abruptly forking at an obtuse angle into two equally unappealing stretches of dry loose gravel track, one rising steeply to the left, like an emergency truck stop ramp straight up the mountainside, and the other, which lead away more gently, but then rose up to meet an endless series of switchbacks slashed into the hulking mountains ahead.

A large swarthy man in neat civilian clothes ran up the steep embankment that formed a natural ramp onto the bridge and flagged me down. I turned off my engine and rolled slowly to a stop just in front of him. He asked for my papers and noticing his large sidearm I complied immediately. He studied my papers quickly, then handed them back with a big smile and insisted I follow him down to his tea platform by the riverbank and join him for lunch. I glanced down at my watch and my speedometer – it was almost noon, I'd only travelled sixty kilometres from Dushanbe and still had more than two hundred much harder kilometres to ride to reach Penjikent. I momentarily considered resisting and riding on, but it was impossible – this was like every other day on the road here; I had set out early with my own supplies and best intentions of completing an uninterrupted day of riding but here I was again, being drawn into another episode of irresistible local hospitality. I parked my bike carefully by the side of the road and he called to his two lieutenants, who emerged from a nearby hut and escorted me down the embankment to the tea platform. Warm bread and hot sweet tea were produced quickly and we settled in for a long lunch by the riverside. I showed them photos of my family at which they marvelled before Dimitry slapped his own wallet on the table and proudly showed me a small grainy black and white photo of his family, which looked more like a group prison mug shot; they looked out at me grimly from behind scratched and cracked plastic with unsmiling faces, their dark features accentuated in the overexposed shot. He then stabbed his fat index finger repeatedly at the identity card in the other pocket of his wallet telling me "I am the Chief of Police here and responsible for stopping all drug trafficking along this road". This was the main road north out of Tajikistan, and a major artery for the transportation of drugs to Russia and Europe, whose true scale and immense downstream misery could only be guessed at from the hundreds of kilos of heroin seized here every year. But that seemed a million miles from this idyll as I reclined on the soft cushions sipping my tea and sucking on a piece of honey melon.

Suddenly he shouted to an unseen chef in the farmhouse and dispatched his junior lieutenant who returned shortly afterwards with a huge mound of plov and a large plate of kebabs. It was all delicious and I ate, at their insistence, until I could eat no more. I took photos with them and Dimitry insisted on giving me his address, which he wrote in beautiful script, like a teenage girl might, in my notebook, demonstrating his literary prowess to his less educated comrades.

An old gnarled shepherd and his flock shuffled over the bridge and Dimitry rushed away to greet an obviously close friend. One of his lieutenants, an older man, who sat closest to me, watched and waited nervously until his boss was out of sight before grabbing my book and pen, running his fingers over the neat script and doing his best to imitate it in a clumsy scrawl. He added his own name to differentiate his entry from the one above and wanted me to send him something by mail when I returned home. I shook their hands and thanked them for their wonderful hospitality and was taken by surprise as Dimitry embraced me in a long bear hug.

I rode away and climbed slowly up and around the first of the giant squared off mountains in front of me before arriving at a high vantage point where the spectacular geology of the region truly struck me. I looked out over deep sharply sloping valleys and massive angular rounded hulks of mountains that surged up, over and down again in an egg carton sea to the horizon. These mountains were coloured in soft hues of brown and olive green, and unlike the Pamirs, there were places here where the hard earth had yielded to allow some very basic agriculture. I spied small farming villages clutching onto the long slopes where trees and crops grew and livestock grazed - all in stark contrast to the giant jagged snow capped peaks and the lifeless high plateau of the Pamirs.

Without the filler of a high plateau, however, progress was

much harder and could only be earned via arduous switchback climbing that demanded total concentration. The track had become fine grey powder and loose gravel over a deeply rutted surface, and suddenly the traffic was heavier, mostly trucks, their progress severely retarded by the difficult conditions. I passed many drivers, hunched anxiously over their wheels as they coaxed their machines on, grinding angrily in the lowest gear available up the long steep tracks. I also passed the occasional family sedan, jam-packed with terrified next of kin as their fearless drivers dangerously explored the physics of momentum and traction on the tight hairpin corners. I continued climbing carefully in the hot midday sun, looking up hopefully at each turn to countdown the remaining switchbacks above me and then back over my other shoulder to take in the breathtaking vista below. I made an abortive attempt at a drink stop at a dusty canteen near the crest of the track, denying both myself and its sole occupant, a savage bony Alsatian, any sustenance. Finally, just before cresting the track, I passed a hapless Kamaz driver improvising heavily to repair a recently exploded tyre. And then, as if someone had flicked a giant dimmer switch on the day, I crossed into cool grey shadows and began the long mirror-image descent down the opposite side of the mountain away from the sun. The lack of sunshine seemed to have taken the life out of the mountainside too as it became a bland grey tussock covered mound that merged without distinction into the next wave of mountains ahead of me. But the lack of breathtaking scenery was more than made up for by the heart thumping excitement of riding down the mountain without my back brakes, which had failed after the extended period of continuous use on the long steep descent. It was like getting a massive dose of adrenalin administered via a long slow drip as each corner rushed up to meet me and I battled with inadequate front brakes and a howling first gear to try and contain my momentum. In a last desperate measure I turned my feet square on and dragged my boots heavily in the gravel, like a sheet anchor, to control my speed. I figured there was no point in stopping half-way down and eventually snowploughed to a stop, in a cloud of grey dust, exhausted at the bottom of the mountain.

I dismounted gingerly and inspected my brakes. Not knowing what to look for exactly, I tapped a few parts hopefully with my tyre lever and then scorched my thumb and forefinger on the hot disc of the brake assembly as I tested it. Like me, it was hot and tired and needed some time to recover.

After a short rest and some inconclusive brake testing - much to the amusement of local truck drivers - I pressed on over gentler terrain and eventually arrived in the crossroads town of Ayni, on the Zerafshan River, where I was immediately bailed up by a belligerent band of local Militsia and police. They were another rag tag collection of bored but well armed officials and I sensed immediately that this wasn't going to be a friendly tea and plov stop. They crowded around my bike, purposefully blocking my way and talking in heated exchanges with each other, debating my fortunes. The commanding officer identified himself and launched his opening salvo by demanding to know how much money I carried. "Show me" he insisted. As usual, my money belt was in my backpack, fat with a fistful of fresh hundred dollar notes that I had collected in Dushanbe to fund the remainder of my trip. It was certainly more than a thousand dollars and would be considered a small fortune by these men. "Not much" I told him deceptively, the bluffing and badgering continuing until ending decisively when I dismounted and rose to my full height, like Gulliver amongst the Lilliputians. Slightly spooked, they retreated to covet my bike instead. Now, rather than take my money, they tried to find a way to give me their money - the only catch being it wasn't much money and I would need to surrender my bike to them. Visions of a shotgun Dutch auction followed by me hitch hiking penniless along the remainder of the Silk Road flashed through my mind, but they were not without some scruples and quickly withdrew once I told them, truthfully, how much my bike had cost. Even allowing for the significant and obvious wear and tear and adjusting for their pricing "discretion", the bike's value was some multiple of their combined annual salaries.

Having exhausted their pecuniary interests, I moved delicately onto the critical question of the road ahead and specific directions for Penjikent. They all shook their heads vigorously and pointed urgently down the dusty avenue that headed into the hills to the west and kept repeating a Russian word I was not familiar with, ahpolzen! ahpolzen!

I fumbled through my dictionary and found it, sending a shiver down my spine: *landslide*. A large section of the road to Penjikent, just beyond the town, had been wiped out in a huge landslide.
"When did it happen?" I asked
"Earlier today. Several trucks and their drivers were lost."
I swallowed hard.
"When will it be cleared?"
"In a week or two perhaps"
I went numb; there had been a tragedy, I was lucky not to have been

involved, and now I began thinking that, like Gulliver, I would be a captive to these unfriendly little people.

"Is there any other way to Penjikent?" I asked hopefully

"Do you know where Tashkent is?" one of them said.

I did –Tashkent was many hundreds of kilometres out of my way to the north in a complicated, time-consuming detour. My visas for Uzbekistań, Turkmenistan and Iran were all delicately poised like a long string of dominoes – there was no contingency and any unplanned delay here would certainly restrict and possibly truncate the centrepiece of my journey along the Silk Roads. Sensing my desperation and in an act of unexpected kindness the Chief said, "There is a very difficult back road from the village that joins the main road beyond the landslide. We will show you the way" - suddenly and inexplicably my captors had become my liberators.

They collared a half-blind, toothless and white-whiskered old man to show me the way. He had dark brown leathery skin and wore long white robes and a skull cap and I followed him in his ancient Zil sedan as he led me along the sleepy main street; it was mid afternoon, still very hot and nothing stirred bar a few furtive dogs and dry leaves carried along by puffs of hot wind. We zigzagged down a steep embankment toward the river then followed its course on treacherous soft sand before crossing it on a crumbling concrete suspension bridge. The track then turned hard right and through a long low natural archway of eroded rock, where I ducked instinctively as the intense noise and energy of my exhaust, concentrated and focused by the rock walls, hit me like a volley of machine gun fire. We climbed up a small hill into a lazy neighbourhood where the old man stopped and pointed back over his shoulder to a narrow alleyway that led up and away from track we had just travelled along, like a disused dead-end railway siding. Too narrow for his car, and beyond his judgement anyway, he waved his hand repeatedly, motioning for me to go on alone – the guided part of my detour was over. Incredulous, I pointed down the tiny muddy alleyway that divided two rows of primitive stone houses and ran away into the distance and screwed up my face as if to say "Penjikent? Along this track, are you kidding?" He smiled and nodded and waved me away, encouraging me to just get on with it. I thought about all my maps and all my planning and now how it all boiled down to hand signals from a geriatric peasant.

Nervously, I rode off along the narrow alleyway, telegraphing my approach and frightening the locals, their children and their livestock as the noise of my exhaust reverberated menacingly back and forth along the ancient stone walls. I was overwhelmed by a pungent farmyard odour and the track was covered in a greasy slick of animal manure and other organic matter whose origins I didn't even want to consider. I passed chicken coops, stables and yards with goats, cows and donkeys, vegetable patches, women washing clothes and preparing food and was chased by friendly urchins who just wanted a smile and wave.

I cleared the village and rounded a hill high above the river and came to a temporary track, recently cut and graded that climbed steeply above the village. The track was loose, soft soil and I watched with some alarm as the fully-loaded jalopy bus ahead of me slid around on the treacherous surface, before being enveloped in the dust cloud that it spewed up. It was difficult to judge how long I spent on the track, or how high above the river it climbed, or how close I had ridden to the edge so intense was my concentration as I rode on cloaked in a curtain of thick dust. Eventually, drenched in sweat and with my wrists throbbing painfully from the intensity of my riding, I emerged onto flat open higher ground where the track petered out into two faint tyre tracks as it crossed paddocks, orchards and fields. In a surreal scene, I came to a lone soldier who sat at an old wooden desk at the edge of apricot orchard where he manned a checkpoint over a cattle grate. A colourful but dilapidated gypsy wagon sat forlornly in the far corner of the orchard. He inspected my papers without saying a word, until I broke the long silence and his concentration by pointing hopefully down the track and asking simply "Penjikent?" He laughed and told me to keep going. I rode on through a large plantation of tall maize being harvested by sinewy sun-dried women who worked rhythmically removing the precious cobs, unhusked from their stalks, in another age-old back breaking ritual.

I passed through another muddy medieval village trapped in permanent afternoon shadow at the bottom of a tall wet rock face where bewildered dogs launched waves of kamikaze missions at me from behind dark corners. I climbed away slowly on steep straight stretches of mud and gravel before re-joining the main road, where thankfully the surface improved and the mountains gradually pulled back, opening out onto rolling hills of dry pastureland and a more fertile, pretty, river valley.

Then, as I rode the gentle curves of the well-paved road into the late afternoon and began to relax just a little, it began to sink in - that was it, I'd done it - I'd crossed one of the highest, longest, most remote and harshest mountain systems in the world. I'd ridden alone across

1,500 kilometres of the most rotten and most spectacular roads and goat tracks across the Roof of the World, along the route followed famously by Marco Polo and the Chinese pilgrim Xuanzang that helped kick start the flow of trade and ideas between East and West so long ago.

Looking ahead, and with some relief, I concluded happily that there were now no more large or difficult mountains between here and the Bosporus on my route - just the long flat expanses of steppe and desert in Uzbekistan and Turkmenistan and the "hills" and high plateaus of northern Iran and central Turkey. I smiled and rode on past a tired and dusty family in a rickety donkey cart straining hard as it hauled a bulging load of straw up a slight incline. Their two teenage boys sat atop the mound and looked enviously at me as I rushed past.

But my quiet moment of reflection and happiness was short lived as I began to notice that my right foot was now quite wet. I looked down at a sodden leather boot and pulled over quickly to investigate further. Was it just water from the road or, more likely, was it something leaking from my bike? I ran my finger along the edge of my boot and tasted it – it had a sharp, sour, unpleasant metallic taste that left a tell tale faint blue stain on my finger which I recognised immediately: engine coolant. It was my brand new "best in Central Asia, expensive engine coolant that I bought especially and poured carefully into my bike the day before and thrown away the bottle because I knew I'd never need it again" coolant. That one. It was also toxic, and, trying to avoid ingesting the stuff, I danced around my bike, semi-prone spitting violently as if I were trying to extinguish a small grass fire. The farmers in the adjoining paddock stopped their work and watched on silently with blank expressions. Even their farm animals looked slightly disturbed. After spitting away most of my bodily fluids I checked the coolant reservoir on the bike to find that it too had been seriously drained. Oh bugger. I got down on my hands and knees in the dirt and gravel and started looking for potential sources of the leak, which had now, of course, disappeared. I removed the bash plate from the bike, which I now discovered was only held loosely in place by two almost thread-less bolts. My clutch cover, which had been opened more times and been fiddled with by more people than I could now remember, was a prime suspect, but it already leaked oil steadily which was like a magnet to the dust and road grit that now covered it in a thick skin. I checked the pipes that came from the radiator and those that ran away to the engine and scrutinised the hard plastic coolant reservoir itself but could find no obvious leaks. I sat back on my haunches in the dust and looked up at the sky and out to the west where the sun was setting in a golden haze, searching for inspiration. The donkey cart rolled by and the two boys waved back at me, now slightly less envious. I was almost in Penjikent so decided to dilute the coolant with the remainder of my drinking water and push on.

I rode on into the dusk, glancing down often, anxiously, to see whether the leak had returned. It had, and a fine blue spray continued soaking my boot and foot. I took a wrong turn in a small village, taking a detour along the river, before negotiating a final heavy-handed but ultimately friendly police checkpoint under the magnificent white stone archway of the city gates.

I scoured the dark and virtually empty city streets in vain for any hints to help locate the Intourist Hotel, which had been recommended to me darkly, by the senior policemen with whom I had just spoken, as their "party" location of choice in Penjikent. The streetlights flickered like candles and everything seemed dark and closed. I took directions in turn, from an off duty policeman and then a huddle of taxi drivers, and after riding up and down the main street a few more times I eventually found the hotel, lumbering, almost in complete darkness at the end of a long side street, beyond a canal. The hotel was an ugly jumble of bare concrete blocks in the worst possible Soviet modernist style. I walked into the cavernous and barren lobby where an old man lay on a musty couch squinting at a tiny television perched high up on a wall. He didn't stir, but there was a flurry of activity as I approached the heavily fortified reception counter, as the harried night clerk, awoken then alarmed by my presence, tried his hardest to provide customer service.

"Do you have a room for the night?" I asked politely.

"Give me your passport and ten dollars now!" he snapped back, sliding his anaemic arm through the bars. He turned, and with his back to me, deftly opened a small desk safe and shoved my passport and money inside and slammed it shut. I looked around and spied a large grand curved staircase, embedded in a wall of faux stone and stained glass, at the far end of the room. The top of the stairs was roped off and crisscrossed in a blanket of thick cobwebs.

"I guess the restaurant is closed then?"

He didn't answer. He unlocked himself from his bunker and showed me solemnly to my room. He grabbed the door handle and struggled briefly with the lock, but the key was unnecessary as the door flexed like balsa wood and opened easily, with the lock intact.

He handed me the key anyway, like a cheap souvenir and scurried away. But security wasn't an issue here, for there were no other guests, the entire complex was completely empty and it seemed to me that the town had taken a giant dose of Soma. The hotel was terraced up the hillside with four storey blocks set around a hardy rose garden and a series of interconnected but empty kidney shaped concrete pools that glowed in the moonlight and were now over grown with creepers and flowers and weeds. It had the melancholy look and feel of an abandoned sanatorium.

I turned and entered my room. My ten dollars had gone a long way; I had a ground floor penthouse complete with entrance vestibule, cloakroom, sitting room (with balcony) and a massive double bedroom with huge en-suite bathroom. It reeked of faded Soviet opulence with oversized 1960's furniture, thick embroidered curtains and quilts, a Logie Baird-sized TV, wooden dressers and occasional furniture, rugs and crystal chandeliers. The bathroom reeked too, but in a far more visceral manner. It was a jungle of exposed and leaking pipes, had a patchwork cement floor and a toilet that leaned dangerously to one side. There was a large grimy bathtub and long rust stains oozed from the taps on the once-white tiled wall. But these were just superficial distractions, I desperately wanted to wash and excitedly turned on the taps, but even after waiting for many minutes, all I got was just a trickle of cold cloudy water - at least I was able to wash my soggy blue foot and rinse my sock.

I headed out into the darkness and eventually found a sleepy chaikhana – men only of course. I ordered a cold beer, soup, bread and kebabs and watched with fascination and then distress as the waiter walked away, rolled up his sleeve and casually retrieved a bottle of beer from the murky fishpond in the middle of the restaurant, their makeshift fridge. He wiped it down and opened it professionally in front of me and poured it into a long glass. It was delicious and so were the kebabs, which I commented on to the waiter as he cleared my table. He stopped and looked at me and shook his head and repeated another Russian word I was not familiar with, "Kazel, kazel!" Sensing my total lack of comprehension, he plastered two raised index fingers to either side of his head, bent over and pawed the imaginary earth repeatedly with one foot in a rapid-fire charade; the kebabs were prime cuts of local goat.

I returned to the hotel where the old man entrusted with guarding this mausoleum let me back in. His sentry post was just a tiny, bare one room stone hut and he insisted that I move my bike under his eaves so that he could guard it overnight. I suspected he was fishing for money but he never mentioned it.

***

I slept soundly in my politburo penthouse and returned early in the morning, without having eaten breakfast, to find the old man, as I had left him, still on duty, guarding my bike. I spent the next two hours under his watchful gaze as I tinkered with my bike, checking, tightening, cleaning and repairing. This was a big day - I was riding into Samarkand and wanted to get these chores out of the way. But these exercises always filled me with new doubts as I was reminded of ongoing problems I had tried to ignore and *always* discovered new ones; my oil leaked *somewhere* at a disturbing rate, my tyres deflated slowly and now my coolant sloshed away as I rode. Like the Little Dutch Boy, I did my best to plug these holes; I poured my last half litre of oil into the bike, pumped air into both tyres, and searched and searched until finally discovering the simple cause of my coolant leak: I hadn't screwed the cap on the reservoir properly. Duh. The old man fetched a pale of murky canal water, gave me a cloth rag and supervised my work, nodding occasionally in approval, as I removed the caked-on mud and road grime that covered most of my bike.

Satisfied with my work but hot and with a dull headache brewing, the old man made me a refreshing cup of hot tea on his tiny stove. I looked into his hut - it was just one long narrow room, with a bed roll along one wall, a naked electric radiator, a flimsy three-legged stool and a tiny table covered in a tablecloth of old newspapers where a portable ring element stove sat, boiling the water for our tea. This was more than his sentry post - it was his home.

As we sipped our tea together silently in the shade, another man, dressed similarly in long white robes and skull cap, but younger with more life force and more flesh on his bones, approached and began asking many questions in an earnest but friendly manner. I told him the outline of my story and he opened with the potentially loaded question of which country (and which peoples) had I liked the best on my journey? I did my best with my inadequate language skills to try and explain that I had enjoyed each country on my journey immensely, but each in different ways and for different reasons, and told him that I had used my tent and sleeping bag only once since leaving Magadan to try and illustrate the wonderful unsolicited hospitality that I had experienced. He smiled. I did single out China, however, as a place where it was more difficult to connect with the locals, and he seemed pleased with this report. He launched a slew of new questions all anchored in the realities of everyday living; "What do you do?", "How much do you earn?", "What is your home like?", "And what do you eat?", "How much does it cost?" etc.

He was staggered as I quoted the average wage, and even the modest account of my home was like a fantasyland for him. He worked when he could as a taxi driver and he lived with his wife and children and his brother and his family in a small apartment. They craved but rarely ate meat, living instead on a staple diet of bread, rice, maize and vegetables. At his insistence, I began quoting meat prices but he cut me off before I could finish, waving his arms in a big circle and saying "No, no, no, how much for the whole animal?" Meat was purchased here by the whole carcass. I did the rough arithmetic for sheep and cattle and told him. "Incredible. And what about goats?" he asked excitedly - I was stumped. Instead, I told him we ate kangaroos and that their meat was considered a delicacy and very expensive – he was intrigued. But he too realised the false logic of absolute cost comparisons – it was that it was all so plentiful and available to virtually everyone that amazed him the most. He was utterly bewildered when I explained that I had three months off work on full pay. It was cloud cuckoo land.

But he was a proud man and now told me enthusiastically about the incredible "ark-ee-o-log" site nearby, where the ruins of the 8th century city Silk Road city of Bunjikath, hidden for over 1,200 years just beneath the topsoil, had been unearthed. It had been a prosperous city of warriors, noblemen and artists with Zoroastrian temples, grand residences and decorated facades, and was a snapshot of pre-Islamic times here. I knew of it and wanted to visit, but didn't know how to find it and now the man was giving me directions. There was also the museum in town which boasted giant frescoes, jewellery and ossuaries excavated from the ruins. It promised to be an interesting morning, but I was hungry and excused myself. I found a tiny kitchen-café run by a husband and wife in a row of basic shops that fronted a large nearby military barracks and had a delicious meal of pilmeni soup, bread and more tea. The husband watched over a massive pot of soup that bubbled away on the stove, the wife prepared ingredients, and news and music blared from a portable radio. It was cool inside with white rounded mortar walls, simple table settings and decor and the air carried the faint scents of the herbs and spices from cooking.

I checked out and rode off, just as the man had directed, in search of the ruins but quickly became hopelessly lost and after riding up my fourth dead-end dirt track high above the town, retraced my steps and rode quickly past hotel, embarrassed. Hopeful of salvaging something from the morning, I pulled up in front of the Museum on the main street. There was a sign in the window; "Closed on Wednesdays". Today was Wednesday. I rode off to Uzbekistan.

***

The border crossing was hot and tedious, filled with arcane paperwork and procedures, a slyly taken (but small) bribe and an impromptu English lesson on the Tajik side. There was a small but strictly enforced no-mans land between these two countries that I rode across slowly, deliberately and accurately – Tajikistan and Uzbekistan are uneasy neighbours and much of their border remains mined. In stark contrast I was processed quickly and efficiently by the Uzbeks in modern facility and eventually emerged two hours later into the endless cotton fields of southern Uzbekistan. The stuff was everywhere and all around me, running away from the road to the horizon in all directions; millions of tiny white puffs in a dark green and crimson sea. Women, teenagers and even younger children toiled tirelessly, picking and then stuffing the cotton bolls into large hessian bags slung over their backs, like snails gorging themselves at a garden banquet.

But there was a darker side to all of this with tens of thousands of young school children conscripted into the harvest each year, a legacy of the monoculture yoke from Soviet central planning. Working at least 10 hours every day, in all weather conditions as they battled to get the harvest in before winter, the children typically live in small tents or old buildings, often in squalid conditions and get paid just two or three cents a kilo. It takes a whole day to pick fifty kilos and sometimes "living costs" are deducted from their meagre earnings.

I rode on through prosperous villages and small towns; the increased energy and improved quality of life compared to Tajikistan palpable. More modern cars were driven on better roads, commerce was diverse and widespread, schools were prominent and well attended by uniformed children, people appeared healthier and at a glance, happier. Even the soil appeared more fertile here with large tracts of crops thriving in the small plots of land not devoted to cotton.

The small towns quickly merged into a long unbroken but sparse urban scene and the traffic thickened around me. I came to a busy roundabout, circled twice and followed the heavy flow of fast moving traffic along a narrow tree-lined avenue that wended its way in a long lazy arc towards the city centre.

Life overflowed onto the narrow street in a surge of colourful activity; bulldozing barrel-chested babushkas, butchers bludgeoning creamy carcasses, bakers building delicate towers of nans, merchants and street vendors touting for business in a rich ethnic soup of Turkic, Persian and Russian faces.

It was certainly no *Golden Road*, but momentarily I imagined feeling Flecker's hot winds fanning my heart and sensed the exotic pleasure he must have felt in his "lust for knowing what should not be known." I could also almost hear the distant lament of the watchmen and women left behind, who considered the men departing along the Golden Road to Samarkand "unwise and curiously planned, who have their dreams and do not think of us."

And then suddenly, I was ejected from this throbbing artery and flung across four lanes of chaotic city traffic on a wide tree-lined boulevard. Large open spaces, parkland and brilliantly tiled monoliths beckoned irresistibly from behind the line of trees on my right and I stole glimpses, fragments in negative as the mid-afternoon sun glinted off tiled facades, of enormous dark vaulted arches hewn from huge slabs of intricate detail, sharp corners that seemed to puncture the sky, a pair of towering minarets and an azure dome, as I battled with the urgent and demanding local traffic. The Registan had snuck up and caught me off guard, like recognising someone famous out of the corner of your eye at the last moment as they walk past you in a crowd. And life went on about me as if this were just another public square, nothing out of the ordinary and I was the odd one out who chose to linger and stare open-jawed. A bus honked and I narrowly avoided running into the car in front of me which had stopped suddenly at a red light.

Mosques, Medrassahs and Caravanserai

I rode down the long sloping boulevard towards central Samarkand, past more shops, chaikhanas, hotels, parks, statues, mausoleums and luckily needed only one navigational hint from a young schoolboy before locating the long wide cobblestone alleyway and small sign that marked the entrance to the private hotel that I had chosen from my guidebook the previous day. I slid open the heavy unlocked solid steel gate and parked in the cool shade of the outer courtyard.

The property appeared deserted and in the throes of minor renovations with bricks and mortar strewn over one corner and wheelbarrow ramps running up to the rooms nearest me. But it was still a pretty scene with a biscuit coloured caravanserai set around a courtyard garden of roses, apple and plum trees, shade trees and other shrubs and flowers. It was thick and lush, slightly unkempt and criss-crossed by symmetrical paths that led down from each room and met at a central, now disused, water fountain. It was a shady and tranquil oasis from the heat and harsh environment outside and I hoped I could stay here. I crossed the courtyard and climbed up onto a large patio where a long dining table sat under a shady trellis thick with grapes. A traditional elevated wooden tea platform sat to the right with rugs and cushions and central raised table. I called out into the living quarters and eventually a woman came out to greet me. She wore a long ruby coloured work-a-day silk dress, had a broad, handsome, upturned face with fulsome lips and dark eyes and wore no make up. Uzbek physiognomy was different again from all the peoples I had encountered to date, it was more angular, refined and exotic and the immediate impression that struck me was Egyptian. The woman introduced herself as Aziza, who in conjunction with her sister and various other family members, lived here and operated the hotel.

Perhaps it was my appearance and mode of transport, but Aziza immediately took me to the smallest, most modest and cheapest room they had and almost wondered out load whether I could even afford this one. Sensing my indifference to what she had just offered, she said, "Of course we have nicer rooms, larger and more comfortable, but they cost more". Then she added, hinting darkly at the terrible events in Andijan in May where hundreds of protesting civilians had been shot dead by government troops, "You know, we have no guests - business has been very bad since the problems earlier in the year."

Ten minutes later I was lying on an incredibly comfortable silk-quilted double bed admiring the intricately carved and painted beamed ceiling in my large luxuriously carpeted room complete with mini-fridge, writing desk and modern fully functional en suite bathroom. It was cool and still in the room and I lost myself in the explosion of royal blue, white, black and deep red above me and day dreamed idly before returning to the patio where I found a huge spread of Uzbek delicacies had been set for my late lunch, whose scale and variety was astonishing, conjured somehow as if I had been an expected guest. There were sugared nuts, drinking yoghurt, blinis and jam, chickpea soup, pickled carrots and beetroot, tomato and cucumber salad, cottage cheese, kasha, grapes, dried apricots, honey melon and apples. Washed down with many cups of hot green tea and accompanied by warm nan bread, it was a feast and I devoured it all.

As I ate, Aziza's sister, Kutbiya, joined us. She was fuller of figure, slightly older, more maternal and less business-like than her sister, but they were both incredibly warm and hospitable in a refreshing uncomplicated way. She wore a simple blue velveteen sack dress, so common here, and smiled sweetly as she spoke, like a Cheshire cat, revealing a mouth full of gold capped teeth.

***

After lunch I rested and wrote before heading out in the late afternoon to visit the Registan. Night was falling earlier and earlier and more distinct each day as I inched my way across Asia. From the 24 hour daylight of high summer in the Kolyma, where I had ridden through grey and often rainy midnights, a season had passed and now the cloak of autumn drew long golden shadows over the land by six o'clock.

I approached the Registan obliquely through the neat parklands that surround its southwest aspect. It was a quiet evening; a few old men sat cross legged gossiping on the grassy lawns under shade trees as I scurried along towards my long anticipated rendezvous. In the distance, the collection of buildings heaved straight up out of the otherwise flat and empty ground, like three orphaned and ancient stubby skyscrapers.

The Registan revealed itself tantalisingly, like a Scheherazade tale, in an exotic panorama of minarets, domes, vaulted arches and mosaic-covered portals that expanded until it completely filled my field of vision. It was immense, epic and overwhelming and I walked in a long wide arc around the open side of its central square, maintaining a constant, unable to absorb more detail, until I reached an elevated platform directly in front and stopped to drink it all in. I remembered the grainy faded colour photos of erstwhile Soviet tourists from the 1960's sweltering on a shadeless sun-baked earthen square admiring the dizzying mosaics from the children's encyclopaedia that I had pored over endlessly as a young boy until the image was burnt into memory; I always knew I would come to Samarkand, and had never replaced that image in my mind with anything more recent, and thirty years on it was like turning a knob on a old slide show projector brining that faded memory into clear rich focus before my eyes. But in my reality now, it was closer to dusk than the burnt midday of that photo; the setting sun adding extra depth and contrast to the scene in front of me – casting the face of the Ulugh Beg Medrassah into deep but subtle shadows of green and blue and setting the illegal tigers of the Shir Dor Medrassah opposite, ablaze, as they chased their frightened quarry towards the heavens. But it was more than just the rich intensity of what I saw now; it was the sheer scale of the place that was breathtaking, and the three ancient colleges were set out with a wonderful sense of proportion - huge yet noble, each different but sharing the same grand dimensions giving the whole ensemble an imprecise symmetry. It was regal and majestic, reflecting its origins, and it didn't take much imagination to visualise the long vanished covered bazaar that originally sat here, six hundred years ago, a major intersection and place of exotic commerce along the old Silk Roads.

The square was almost deserted save for a few indolent soldiers and a handful of dusty sun-burnt tourists dawdling in the deep shadows under the giant vaulted portals, dwarfed and overwhelmed, like ants contemplating a gigantic glazed candy. I walked up to the low lattice fence (designed to separate paying visitors from beggars, touts and passers by), until it barred my way; it was past closing time and the little entrance gates at either end were shut tight and guarded. I stopped under a shade tree and continued to admire the magnificent ensemble – for it was almost impossible not to. Noticing me, a soldier smiled and called out, opened the little swing gate that he guarded and let me through. Now I stood alone in the central square, surrounded on three sides by these colossal ancient colleges where the finest scholars of the day once taught both Islamic theology and the secular sciences – including mathematics, astronomy and philosophy - to young boys. It had all begun with the enlightened legacy of Timur' s more moderate grandson, Ulugh Beg, who established the first medrassah here in 1420, where, according to legend, he had lectured in astronomy – a theme which had also become the striking leitmotif of the brilliantly tiled portal. It was a kaleidoscope of exploding ornamental stars repeated in geometric precision and set in stark contrast against a sombre ochre background. This huge canvas was framed by two immense panels of azure and turquoise tiles fashioned like stained glass windows of simple geometric patterns and woven bands. Two buckled minarets, defying gravity, completed the massive façade, like jewel encrusted smoke stacks of turquoise and lapis lazuli.

Everything was still and peaceful; there were no tourists, no hawkers and no beggars as I stood mesmerised, suddenly overwhelmed by a powerful sense of harmony and tranquillity. It was a heady cocktail of awesome architecture, stunning visual beauty and whispers of Silk Road history and I was a happy drunk. But my moment was interrupted by one of the soldiers who approached me now, resplendent in his petrol blue Foreign Legion outfit, asking me in a conspiratorial whisper – "You want to climb tower?" I looked up nervously at the crooked towers that thrust up out of the earth like two arthritic fingers and then back at him, suddenly unsure if it was such a wise excursion. But he was already leading me away towards the small door at the base of the massive vaulted archway. I handed him a clutch of crisp notes of local currency and followed him through a series of low passageways and up a staircase that delivered us onto an open stone platform on the second level, inside the Medrassah. I looked out over a deep, dusty construction pit, strewn with mounds of dirty rubble and bricks. A huge scaffold skeleton supported the massive façade I had just been admiring; inside was just a hollowed out shell. It was like looking at an X-ray of a seemingly healthy person to find them riddled with cancer, but this was all the Russians could do to save these crumbling edifices before they collapsed and decayed away – even most of the tiles on the facade were from relatively recent renovations. But it didn't matter – it was all based entirely upon the original foundations, structure and designs. My soldier guide pointed me towards a small opening on the far side of the pit, partially covered by a sheet of corrugated iron, told me to be careful and then vanished. I scurried around the thin lip of the open pit, trying hard not to look down into it, and continued over the mounds of building debris before crawling on my hands and knees into the staircase of the minaret. It was cool and dry but unlit with no windows and just a few stray photons of natural light from far above to illuminate the steps. And slowly, as my eyes adjusted, the large pie-pieces of stone that wound steeply up and away came into focus. I stumbled on and up in a disorientating spiral for what seemed like a very long time before emerging at the makeshift lookout post atop the minaret. I poked my head and shoulders up through the small opening and rested, breathless and dizzy, before taking one final step, lifting my torso higher, affording me an uninterrupted 360 degree view of the Samarkand skyline. The last golden rays of sunlight were streaming across the dusty low-rise urban neighbourhoods as I spied the glinting blue-green domes and giant tiled porticos of more mosques, mausoleums and medrassahs which were sprinkled haphazardly across the old town. The hotel towers and other Soviet-styled buildings of the city centre stood distinct and separate from their older neighbours, but they were modest and didn't jar and the whole city seem unified by its verdant parkways and dense widespread tree cover. In the distance, beyond the city limits, I watched long grey-green shadows slowly wash over the Zarafshon Mountains, the last finger of the Pamir-Altai range as they melted into the flatlands of Uzbekistan. I remained in my clandestine crow's nest until the sun had disappeared below the horizon and then scampered down the stairs and spent what remained of the dusk wandering through the old lecture halls and student living cells around the courtyards in each of the medrassahs, many of which had now been taken over by modern day merchants selling trinkets, rugs, clothes and other souvenirs. In one courtyard, weary locals were preparing a large tourist dinner and "traditional" dancing show - I left quickly and headed back to the sisters' courtyard for another delicious home cooked meal.

***

I returned again in the morning to the Registan, which was now open for business as usual. Entrance was strictly by ticket and there was even a tour group here - the first I had encountered on my journey - I realised with some longing that I too was now becoming a tourist. I walked along in the shadows of the façade of the Shir Dor Medrassah and came to its large entrance portico where a German tour group leader was earnestly crunching through a stiff speech. Three locals – two men and a woman – watched on, intrigued and then noticing me, asked whether I needed a "guide".

Normally I would have refused these offers out of hand relying instead entirely upon my research and guidebooks, but I was bewitched by the Uzbek beauty that approached me now; she was tall – at least six feet – and had shoulder length raven hair that framed a broad high cheek-boned milky brown face. Her large dark eyes were drawn out heavily into long exaggerated almond shapes by heavy mascara. She had full Nubian lips and emitted a soft musky fragrance and wore a tight fitting red Versace T-shirt and wiggled like Morticia Adams in a long fishtail denim skirt. She was an exotic creature, handsomely beautiful like an Egyptian princess and I stared at her for a long time. "Would you like a guided tour?" she asked again politely.

"Yes!" I shot back automatically, without thinking. Then as my mind slowly caught up with the rest of my body I asked, "So tell me more about the tour - what will we do and how much will it cost?"

"It's up to you. We can visit as many of the buildings here as you like and I will tell you all of the history and answer any questions you have. We can take as much or as little time as you like. At the end you decide how good I was and how much you want to pay."

Wow, this was getting tricky; it was a loaded offer, but instinctively I accepted.

She introduced herself as "Ryah" and told me that she had studied English at University and that she worked here most days in the summer – less often in spring and autumn, but business had been poor this year. I suggested that it might be related to the killing of hundreds of protestors earlier in the year in Andijan by government troops, but she refused to acknowledge the event or discuss the subject.

Ryah launched into her well-rehearsed monologue and patiently took and thoroughly answered all of my questions proudly demonstrating her deep knowledge of Uzbek history. I was impressed, but the tour quickly took on a dream-like quality for me; I was listening but not listening, as I scanned her face in a slow repetitive cycle from almond eye to almond eye and then down to her mouth and back again, watching the sounds form and then escape over her perfectly formed white teeth and full lips – I was fixated, like a desperate gambler watching a torrent of coins gush from a slot machine when he hits pay dirt. She could have been reading a train timetable for all I cared. It was a very pleasant sensation and I lost myself in her melodic lilting as we glided around the complex. My vocabulary evaporated into a trickle of hollow expressions: "Ah ha....."
(open mouth in acknowledgement), "Mmmm..." (nodding head with expression of deep understanding), "Really..." (inquisitive look), was all I could muster.

We *did* however, explore each of the magnificent medrassahs again and, although each oozed history and burst with colour and fine artisanship, it was the explosion of gold leaf and Kufic inscriptions on a vivid blue canvas and the intricately decorated honeycombed dome of the prayer niche immediately inside the Tillya-Kari Medrassah that most thrilled my senses. The blue was intense, like a Greek summer sky, and had a slight watercolour effect in its application that added both depth and lustre, and the gold leaf and script glistened, refracting light in a sparkling pattern of interference all around us. It was enchanting. We went on to visit the student cells; positively Spartan by today's standards, but there was something deeply appealing in their monastic simplicity with white washed walls, high ceilings, basin and wall oven, huge empty spaces and attic sleeping platforms.

We continued on and walked across the flagstone courtyards, still cool in the morning shade, and doubled over again to clear the low doorways as we entered more student cells, but, as I had discovered on my previous visit, these were now modern day shops where Ryah introduced me to a string of her friends – all of them mostly lonely and struggling with the extended absence of tourists, each shop like a sarcophagus with slumbering proprietors, dim naked lighting and covered displays - resuscitated quickly as we approached in the hope of some custom. This dose of commercial reality snapped me out of my extended daydream and focused our discussion on more mundane matters of everyday life. Ryah was married and had a young daughter, barely two, and she and her husband worked hard to make ends meet. She showed me a picture of her daughter dressed in her best clothes and I shared with her the pictures of my family I always carried with me. I asked how they both managed to work and look after their daughter and she explained that they lived with her mother in law, who provided the majority of the care.

Ryah led me to the back of the shop where many old dresses were on display, more like a museum exhibit. She picked up and put on an antique black burqa, fully covering her head and face. It was hideous; the black cloth was thick and greasy like canvas and coarse gauze made of horse hair covered her eyes and face. She could barely see me and I, of course, could not see her. Even in the cool of the shop it was hot and uncomfortable, and Ryah told me that the eyesight of many women had been ruined from the abrasions of the horse hair and the distorted vision it induced. In one of their more rational moments the Bolsheviks had outlawed the wearing of burqas (and burned them) immediately after seizing power in 1917 and it appeared, thankfully, that the women and men here had not looked back.

We walked back out to the main square of the Registan where, unprompted, Ryah told me of her plans for the future - she wanted to develop her own tourism business here in Samarkand, but first had determined that she needed further qualifications in "tourism and business management".

"And where will you study?" I asked.

"In America. In a place called Kansas. For one year. I am leaving in six months from now to do this." I was dumbfounded. Putting aside the tremendous costs (which I struggled to understand how she could afford), it was such a remote and difficult existence - she would be alone on the other side of the world, isolated in a very foreign culture. Lots of questions raced through my mind, but I asked the obvious one: "And what about your daughter?" She looked away and simply said, "She will stay here and my mother in law will look after her until I return." Dark thoughts raced through my mind, mostly about ugly shotgun wielding red necks in pick-up trucks – perhaps founded on unfair stereotypes – but I genuinely feared for her safety. I admired her determination and the sacrifices she was prepared to make for a better life but it seemed excessive and unnecessary. "It will be very difficult, I hope you are successful" I said sincerely to her.

I skulked away slowly, but could not resist the urge to track the huge ensemble as it receded slowly behind me; each of my footsteps lead- heavy, as if I were a tiny satellite locked in orbit. This place was the pinnacle of human endeavour along my route and now my visit it was over; there would be no other first time like this – but it wasn't melancholy I felt – it had been a wonderfully fulfilling experience and I left feeling excited, ready to explore the other fine monuments of Samarkand.

***

I wandered along a pretty tree-lined avenue behind the Registan and found a local chaikhana and settled in for a surprisingly tasty and filling lunch of pilmeni, bread, tea and plov. The restaurant was almost deserted except for a cadre of ancient women who sat straight-legged on large cushions on a long elevated platform around low tables at the far end of the big hall. Their conversation gurgled away, with the melody of a gentle mountain stream and they nodded wisely at each other with golden toothed smiles through crinkled eyes on brown burnished faces of tissue-paper skin. They were finishing up, sipping final cups of tea and bidding each other fond farewells. They departed in pairs, rising slowly to embrace each other in hunchbacked hugs of fragile limbs, walking sticks and knotted fingers, revealing the heavy toll extracted from their bodies by a lifetime of hard work and family service. They all wore a simple uniform of colourful silk headscarves, long quilted jackets, loose woollen trousers and ankle-high shiny black patent leather boots, that made them appear, incongruously, like geriatric pirates. I wondered at the history they must have witnessed and how many more lunches like this they might share together.

I wandered further along the quiet avenue, past shops, cafes, street vendors selling drinks and ice creams and came to the grand entrance portal of the Bibi Khanum mosque. Predating the Registan, it had been commissioned by Tamerlane in 1398 upon his return from sacking Delhi where he vowed to create "a mosque without parallel in grandeur or décor throughout the Muslim world". Unfortunately today it retains just a shadow of its former glory with much of it decaying, collapsed, or worse still, repaired by modern reconstruction. Nevertheless, the immense portico was still impressive, more subdued in colour and more modest in styling, but significantly larger and more substantial than its successors I had just visited at the Registan. But it was the overall scale of this place that was breathtaking. I walked through the massive entrance portal and emerged into a large open courtyard, marked out by a neat network of pathways that ran around its perimeter and connected to an open inner sanctum where a large lectern of grey marble sat on an elevated stone platform in the cool shade under a grove of trees. Originally housed inside the prayer hall of the mosque, it had once held one of the giant (one metre square) oldest known original Korans, but had been relocated outside near the end of the nineteenth century just as the original mosque had begun collapsing dangerously to the ground. Crude and incomplete reconstructions of the original mosque ran along each flank, crowned by dazzling turquoise patterned domes. The foundations of the colonnaded mosque entrance were visible, but for the most part nothing had been restored above ground level. At the far end of the long courtyard stood the impossibly tall main mosque with its even *larger* portico – the largest I had seen and would see – that seemed to reach into the heavens, an effect accentuated by its attendant octagonal minarets that tapered gently as they climbed skywards. And, at a distance, the whole façade appeared covered in intricate symmetrical patterns which, up close, resolved into fist-sized tiles of either azure or dark blue, such was the scale of the work. I peered through the giant gate of rope-thick iron lattice that protected the once magnificent inner chamber, whose dome and arch, in their original form drew such extravagant praise as to be described as "their splendour and scale rivalled only by the entire expanse of the firmament and span of the Milky Way". Today, however, it was a dark and dank place that more closely resembled a prison, with crumbling stone walls and bare floors strewn with rubble under the patchwork dome, partially restored by the Russians after it collapsed completely in an earthquake in 1897.

I retired to the wooden benches around the central square and just sat and soaked it all in; the trees, lawn, shade and lack of people and any other movement added to the deep sense of tranquillity that I felt again here. I don't know how long I sat there, it might have been ten minutes or it could have been two hours. A trickle of people came and went – mainly independent travellers with local guides; displaced Russians of a few generations showing Russian tourists around the brilliant remnants of this ancient capital of a foreign empire (restored, ironically, by the occupying Soviets).

I watched on with great curiosity as devout Muslim visitors circled and touched the lectern in a series of complex ritual patterns, each finishing with a triumphal flourish, deeply satisfied at apparently having received some unseen divine bounty through communion with the stone and the memory of its long departed Holy Scripture.

I left by a side entrance through a crumbling archway and headed into the colour and movement of the central bazaar where I quickly found myself in the austere ceramic-tiled dairy hall wandering past friendly bulldozer-sized babushkas in white aprons and matrons' hats manning (literally) long counters of creamy produce. They stood in solidarity, standing guard over their industrial-sized tubs of yoghurt, butter, soft cheese, sour cream, multi-coloured dips and more. They smiled shiny golden-toothed smiles as I passed and each proffered a sample of their produce which I accepted graciously. I walked on through the main covered bazaar, past huge trolleys stacked with impossibly tall towers of bread roundels, past vivid displays of dried fruit and spices, past open-air butchers, cleaving menacingly through flesh and marrow, and finally past the cobblers and tailors until, overloaded with sensory stimulation, I hurried out of the bazaar gates and emerged back onto the street.

I walked on down the long gently sloping hill towards the Shar-i-Zinda necropolis – a collection of mausoleums dating back to the seventh century when a cousin of the prophet Mohammed arrived in

Samarkand and attempted to convert the locals from their fire-worshipping Zoroastrianism. Unfortunately – for him – he was beheaded by the angry locals, but not before he had achieved some success, thus establishing his mausoleum here. And, incredibly, despite the brutal Mongol sacking of the city, his mausoleum had survived untouched and the site had evolved into an intimate gallery of fine memorials, extended and enhanced across time by the various rulers, each adding their own unique tributes – all intricately decorated by the finest artisans of the day, but none ostentatious and all sharing sufficient common elements in their design to ensure the collection, in aggregate, had an overriding sense of harmony.

I climbed a long set of steep stone steps and hauled myself up onto the landing at the start of this cul-de-sac of the dead. The mausoleums, each the size of a large family room, were finished with magnificent tiled facades, like perfect miniatures of what I had seen earlier, and sat shoulder to shoulder on elevated foundations above the narrow crooked street, each with their own private stone stairs leading up to the formal entrances protected by large finely carved heavy wooden doors.

It was only mid-afternoon but already the street lay in the cool halftones of shade cast by the parallel, almost touching rows of tall hulking bulwarks that squared off against each other away into the distance, like two long rows of chiselled tattooed rugby front rowers ready to pack down. It was designed as a place for quiet reflection, respectful memorial and sacred pilgrimage, however today more closely resembled a sprawling over-budget suburban bathroom renovation gone wrong; thick power cords snaked across the narrow street and teams of grizzled tradesmen lazily trowelled grout and applied tiles, plastered mortar from high scaffolds and drove rickety wheelbarrows along wooden plank tracks. I crunched on the grit that had settled on my teeth and felt the tingling sensation of quicklime on my tongue as the deafening screech of the stone cutters bored a path directly between my ears.

I climbed a set of stairs at random, pushed open a heavy wooden door and entered the cool dark interior of an anonymous mausoleum. My eyes slowly adjusted; a slender black marble tomb sat solemnly in the middle of the room. It was fashioned in classical form from large thin sheets of flawless marble, wonderfully smooth with long clean lines. It had no markings or decorations of any kind, and sat in stark contrast against the off-white flagstone floor, like a lonely ebony key on a well worn piano. The walls were soft alabaster and the ceiling was framed in elaborate but understated cornice work which I admired for a long time from the simple stone bench where I now sat. Natural light and the sounds of construction floated into the room through a narrow window high in the opposite wall, but diffused almost immediately, absorbed into the indistinct soft surfaces above me. I was alone, it was cool, quiet and peaceful and I sat very still, contemplating nothing in particular for a long time. Everything outside the room dissolved away and I became aware of my breathing and nothing else; I was centred, in this place, here, now.

Eventually, I began to contemplate the remainder of my journey. Somehow, I had managed to arrive here roughly "on time" – according to my crazy theoretical schedule, but it had been difficult and at times relentless, and depressingly, I knew that from here on in I would need to ride even farther and travel even faster each day to reach Istanbul by my self-imposed deadline. But every journey must have a beginning and an end, and the book-ends of my journey were important for other reasons too, as they marked my departure from, and long-anticipated return to, my family, and these were strong feelings that drove me on towards my destination. But today I didn't feel the relentless call of my destination; this was high tide in my journey across Asia; time seemed to move slower for me now and I felt a wonderful calmness washing over me, almost like a moment of suspended animation. Perhaps I was just susceptible; I had travelled for so long through so many bleak and barren places, across some of the harshest, barely habitable areas of the world, that my experiences today hit me between the temples like a velvet sledgehammer – a massive overdose of man-made beauty. I felt completely overwhelmed, for there had been no warning, no gradual build up, just an immediate immersion into some of the finest and most significant pieces of Islamic architecture in the world. Perhaps my senses were starting to shut down, saturated and unable to process any more signals today, but it was not an unpleasant sensation and I left feeling wonderfully serene.

I descended the stairs and continued along the main street of this workin-progress necropolis and came to another mausoleum, a busy construction site where a less-noble artisan took me aside and offered me a small but heavy yellow envelope – like an old pay packet – in a clandestine transaction. The envelope wasn't sealed and I looked inside to find a long rectangular, perfectly fashioned and obviously new, glazed turquoise tile – exactly the same as those being applied to the walls around us. He looked at me expectantly.

I looked around and saw a makeshift table sitting in a corner, covered in the same stiff yellow envelopes – perfectly arranged, like a paymaster's office. Workmen carried on about us, oblivious and unconcerned. I politely declined his offer and walked on – I just didn't want it, I didn't see the point. He shrugged his shoulders indifferently, muttered some foul Uzbek obscenities and returned calmly to his work.

I quickly came to the heart of the complex, a large but simple mosque half-buried in a massive foundation block, buttressed on three sides by a dimly lit labyrinth of naked chalky white hallways. It got cooler and became more peaceful the deeper I burrowed inside the bunker, until finally I turned a corner and pulled up suddenly, just short of the entrance to the actual mosque hall; a lone pilgrim dressed in long flowing robes and a white skull cap knelt on a small rug (his own), facing away from me, chanting and bowing rhythmically from the waist, like a metronome, lost to the outside world, deep in prayer. The room was beautifully bare; there was no furniture of any kind, no icons or other religious imagery, no allegories in stained glass, just plain plastered walls, a smooth stone floor and a high window from where a beam of light shone down, illuminating the man, adding even more gravitas to an already pious scene. I turned away and left quietly, not wanting to infringe on the man's solitary supplication.

***

I walked home, retracing my steps, back past the markets, mosques and medrassahs, shops and cafes where I had spent my day. On the busy main street I walked past a huge open-air restaurant where a team of owner-chefs sat dolefully watching over a few lonely smoky and overcooked shashliks, calling out hopefully as I passed, anxious for anyone to occupy their near-empty eating hall. A young butcher sat dozing with his head resting on his outstretched folded arms below a thick curtain of carcasses that hung like engorged marbled red stalactites from the ceiling of his tiny shop. But the prospect of another home- cooked meal was irresistible and I sat alone at the long table under the apple trees and grape vines and ate my way through another delicious smorgasbord of Uzbek food, each course served in turn, rather pleasantly, by a different female member of Aziza and Kutbiya' s extended family. After serving me they each skipped away to the raised wooden tea platform where they lazily ate plov and drank tea while the mother-matriarch held court. They talked and laughed endlessly and the sounds floated past me in a sweet murmur as I drained a bottle of warm beer. I studied the swirling brilliantly coloured patterns on my ceiling again, fell asleep quickly and dreamt of swimming through a giant kaleidoscope.

***

In the morning Aziza and Kutbiya introduced me to their nephew, Amir. He was a young, sharp dressed man-about-town and part-time university student, but today he was to be my chaperone. He was an eager-to-please, knowledgeable and altogether pleasant escort who spoke perfect German, in addition to Russian and his native Uzbek. He did not, however, speak a word of English, and given that the sum total of my German vocabulary from two years of high school study amounted to the utterly useless phrase "this is an airplane", we quickly settled on my low fidelity Russian for rudimentary communication.

Central Samarkand was, in reality, far more pleasant than what I had imagined from the outline of it that I had covertly spied at dusk from atop the Registan two days earlier. It had the usual assortment of utilitarian shops and services but it was altogether more intimate and personal than any of the old Soviet cities I had already visited; there were no massive boulevards, edifices, giant monuments or eyesore apartment blocks. The city centre was spread out over a lazy grid of low- rise pastel coloured neo-classical buildings on quiet tree-lined streets. There was only a modest flow of strangely polite traffic, and it was the people who dominated this place, strolling the wide sidewalks going about their business.

We came to a gently sloping, paved pedestrian mall that snaked its way across the heart of the city, bounded by a small chain link fence, rich grassy verges beyond and spectacularly crowned near its apex by a gigantic creamy bark gum tree. A coterie of attractive, immodestly dressed fashion-conscious girls strolled past us, arm in arm, on display and on patrol, flying in the face of the inherent conservatism of Uzbek society. A row of pretty two-storey yellow pastel stuccoed buildings ran along one side of the mall where small variety shops did a quiet but steady trade. There was no buzz of commerce here, but there was an overwhelming sense of prosperity – at least in this attractive garden precinct of the city.

At the top of the mall we came to a fine amphitheatre of stately but slightly ominous looking gothic buildings. I asked Amir about them.

"These were the buildings of the original Soviet government in

Samarkand."

"And today?"

"It is our boxing and wrestling academy. The finest Uzbek sportsmen come here to train and fight. It is our national honour."

I smiled at the oblique irony; the anonymous, shadowy and lethal salvos of corrupted ideology launched from here on a frightened population had been supplanted by far more honourable, open and basic contests of physical strength and technique.

We walked on and came to the people's park which inexplicably had become an overgrown and unkempt jungle, surrounded by a high wire fence, sealing in a sad dilapidated children's playground, parched lakes and thirsty fountains. There were, however, a handful of stubborn elderly citizens who had refused to relinquish this place, and who sat frozen in time, balanced on the thin splinters of ancient park benches, in the autumn sun. A rusted and faded carousel squeaked mournfully in the breeze.

"Why is the park like this" I asked Amir.

"It is no longer important to us. It is too costly to maintain and young people are not interested in coming to places like this anymore. We watch satellite television and surf the internet instead" he said, signalling that the sea-change of youth culture brought about by the digital age was already taking hold here.

But the real highlight of my excursion was visiting the Central Bank of Uzbekistan. The Bank was located in a non-descript two storey stone building on a quiet intersection, but as we climbed the steps I couldn't help notice the suspicious film noir types, who stood stony-faced and indifferent in the small entrance hall, hands in pockets, collars upturned, cigarettes dangling from thin lips, who all seemed to be waiting for someone or something. We hurried past without looking at them and emerged into the cavernous banking chamber; a simple unbroken semicircular row of counters and grill windows around a large, open area. The place was awash with money and the air was thick with the unmistakable sickly metallic perfume of cash. Merchants, shopkeepers, taxi drivers, truck drivers and the ubiquitous Central Asian "biznessmen" - whose wealth more often than not came from more suspect activities – stood shoulder to shoulder, clenching wads, some even sackfuls of cash, as they waited anxiously to do their banking. Many squinted hopefully at the tiny board of dirty flags and fractured LEDs that flashed currency buy/sell rates, as they waited in line at the foreign exchange desk in a daily hedge against local inflation. Many pawed excitedly, like kids opening Christmas gifts, at the crisp US dollar script that they had just received, before glancing around nervously and packing it away securely. But there was even more excitement behind the counters in the high-octane fashion parade that was modern Uzbek office life; pretty young women jostled for supremacy in a rich pageant of stilettos, exposed flesh, ample bosom and heavy make up. It felt more like a casino than a bank and we lingered in completing our transaction, insisting that our teller re-count of the mountain of notes I had just purchased. By this point Amir had glazed over, drunk on the intoxicating tract of beauty and wealth before us. I counted the money carefully too, thanked our lovely assistant and dragged Amir outside.

* * *

We had a long lunch in a dark wine bar, complete with an underground private party room, where Amir told me shyly about his dreams for the future – another version of the tourism entrepreneurial vision that I had heard so often already in this country; he wanted to complete his university studies – marketing – and help his family develop their hotel business further. Science, mathematics, engineering and classical studies were out of favour and the country seemed to be banking on riding the nascent wave of Silk Road tourism into the future. I hoped they were right, but wondered where it might lead them.

We emerged groggy into the bright afternoon sunlight and stumbled home past the giant statue of a fearsome sword-wielding Timur, where a young couple, fresh from their wedding ceremony looked up hopefully for a blessing from their national hero.

That evening I was joined at dinner by a raft of other guests who had arrived in my absence; there was an Australian archaeologist and her partner just returned from a long dig in the Karakum desert, two young female German diplomats from Almaty and Tashkent respectively and a Russian government official and his Chinese wife and their two exotic teenage daughters. An older, distinguished European lady held court. She reminded me of an eccentric but kind-hearted great aunt; she had a broad structured face with pancake makeup, blue almond shaped eyes, gold rimmed glassed and she wore her mane of ash blonde hair up in an elegant Kathryn Hepburn-esque bun. And the similarities didn't stop there either; for she was feisty, funny, eminently well mannered and gracious. She wore a wonderfully colourful silk caftan and spoke perfect German, Uzbek, Russian, and thankfully English, which she used now to introduce herself. Her name was Andrea and she was a Swiss development consultant who had lived and worked in Uzbekistan for many years. She was also very close to Aziza and Kutbiya and clearly had taken a personal interest in helping them develop their business. They laughed and carried on like blood sisters as we ate dinner around the long table. Towards the end of the evening I told Andrea that I planned to ride to Bukhara the next day.

"Owwwh" she squealed, "So are we. We're going to a big wedding in Bukhara tomorrow night – you must come too, it would be such an honour to have you as a guest!"

I was struggling to keep up with all of these immediate plans being made on my behalf and before I had a chance to respond she continued racing ahead.

"And you must stay with Movin' John!"

"*Moving John?* " I said, puzzled, "Who's he?"

"Yaah, yaah, he was a famous Olympic athlete you know?" she asked rhetorically in her clipped Swiss accent. "He's got a garage where you can park your bike safely too." She added neatly. "But you know" she paused, "He's a little eccentric now.... I think you'll like him!" This last assertion I took as a compliment as the heroes from the great Pantheon of Soviet athletics began dancing across my mind. Just his name was sufficient to conjure up blurred images of a square-jawed, stoic and muscular cold war warrior, striding powerfully around the track in Soviet-issue no-frills gear quietly winning blue ribband sprints.

After dinner Aziza and Kutbiya invited all of us back their living quarters for an impromptu display of traditional Uzbek *suzanes* – the colourful traditional handmade silk-embroidered rugs and cloths common to this part of Central Asia. We followed them out through a small doorway in the main courtyard, down a dark narrow cobblestone alleyway, past half open doors where we caught candid glimpses of modest Uzbek family life; mothers and wives watching over large pots at open fires, fathers and husbands dozing idly on makeshift furniture and children playing happily, all etched into my mind in flashes of low- powered incandescent light. Turning left and right and then left again, we eventually emerged into a tight flagstone courtyard around a pretty rose garden. The sisters (and their extended family) lived in the substantial two-storey buildings that enclosed two sides of the courtyard in a sprawling inter-connected complex that I now realised was more citadel than humble bed and breakfast.

Inside had the feel of a merchant's house with fine rugs, traditional furniture, wall hangings, samovars and other Silk Road antiques. A large floor-to-ceiling wooden cupboard ran along the far wall at the end of the long lounge room and the two sisters rushed ahead and began opening compartments excitedly. Like long-expectant, but confident maidens reviewing their massive dowries, they proudly unfurled the distinctive and beautiful pieces, handling each lovingly in turn, before spreading them out on the floor for us to admire. Out came the finest gossamer silk scarves and long ceremonial gowns too, and, encouraged by our collective gasps of wonderment, the items kept flowing until we were drowning in a spectacular sea of multi-coloured silk. The items were truly exquisite – works of art – and I wondered at their collective value. But for Aziza and Kutbiya their joy was simply in sharing their private treasures with us and reflecting in the glow of our genuine pleasure. And, although the pieces shared the same DNA, each reflected the variations of style and technique that evolved over time as the tradition spread out along the archipelago of settlements across Central Asia; large bold geometric patterns in primary colours on simple canvases dominating the Kyrgyz suzanes in the East, becoming progressively more sophisticated and elaborate heading West across Tajikistan, crowned by the sumptuously rich rose-hued circular designs of Samarkand, and finally, in a preview of my next destination, on to Bukhara, where the designs became finer again but more sparse in earthier tones with the most delicate silk embroidery depicting flowers and even animals in the abstract. But each and every one had been subtly flawed, forcibly birth- marked with whimsical additions of off-centre shapes and objects, destroying the otherwise perfect symmetry of each piece, in deference to the prevailing Islamic doctrine of the times that said only the work of god can be perfect.

The showcase continued late into the night as the sisters explained the history and nuances of each piece as they emerged. As I left I reminded Aziza that I was leaving in the morning and needed to pay my bill. She fumbled about and retrieved a crumpled piece of scrap paper from a pocket, no larger than a folded hanky – which it might have been once – licked a stubby pencil, thought hard and scratched out a few sums before arriving at a figure which she underlined emphatically before handing it over to me shyly. I had eaten many home-cooked meals and snacks, drunk bottles of beer and wine, sat quietly and reflected in their garden, been personally chaperoned around the city by their nephew, and all of my clothes had been lovingly laundered, but none of these line items appeared on my bill, just a quickly estimated figure which seemed extraordinarily modest. I looked at it quickly, frowned and then handed her a few large denomination US bills and told her to keep the change, before hurrying out.

As I settled into bed that night I searched my Uzbek guidebook for any mention of a "Movin' John" and eventually found a small entry that described both the man and the accommodation he offered as "earthier, more traditional and cheaper than most". It also shed some light on his Olympic career - he was a table tennis champion! Although a legitimate discipline of the modern Olympics, this revelation saw him swiftly relegated to a dimly-lit corner in the pantheon of Uzbek sports rather than the prime position he had occupied previously.

***

In the morning I walked the short distance back along the narrow laneway that the property fronted, past kids playing timeless games, crossed the large square and passed through the crumbling portico of Tamerlane's surprisingly modest mausoleum. It had once been fronted by a large medrassah which had long since fallen down, leaving just stubs of minarets joined by low jagged walls of broken brick around a large open courtyard of barely visible dusty foundations. But what it lacked in size it more than made up for in the splendour of its dome which stood above me now – much fuller, taller and somehow coloured in an even more brilliant shade of turquoise than any of those I had already seen. In a further mark of distinction from it contemporaries, its surface was ribbed uniformly from the crown and an intricate geometric line pattern, in striking glossy black, snaked across its tiled surface, like someone had taken a fountain pen to the sky.

Inside was cool and intimate, but richly ornate and respectful, with a central cenotaph of black marble tombstones around a breathtaking six foot long thick slab of dark green Mongolian jade. At eye-level the walls were covered in simple lozenge shaped onyx tiles. Above was a riot of golden inscriptions and exploding stars on a deep blue watercolour canvas, rising up to an intricate gilded inner dome above basic wooden lattice windows. A small group of earnest German tourists stood silently in the opposite corner of the chamber snapping their heads violently from side to side and up and down again in unison, as if they were watching a tennis match, as their guide unloaded volleys of rapid-fire commentary in monotone staccato while whipping her pointing stick about like a deranged symphony conductor. Their faces showed the strain as they struggled to keep up; she was on autopilot and they were all hanging on for dear life. I watched on in silent amusement from a stone bench in a little alcove overlooking the cenotaph. I looked up and admired the deep blue gilt-edged moulded stalactites that hung from the low ceiling above me. A young local family came in, and while the mother and daughter sat quietly next to me, the father, bent over and with one hand pressed on his son's shoulder, proudly presented the ring of seven modest tombstones that accounted for the great warrior king of Transoxiana, Timur and two generations of his male line, including his grandson, the Astronomer King, Ulugh Beg, who between them had been responsible for establishing Samarkand as a centre of power, culture and science at the end of the Middle Ages and for the dazzling architectural legacy that so defined the city's character today. The father spoke slowly and intently as the boy listened wide-eyed and open mouthed; I imagined the father recounting tales of fierce battles, exotic princesses, palaces and banquets, an empire that at one time stretched from Moscow to Delhi and, of course, Timur's legendary skills of horsemanship, swordcraft and archery. I sensed they felt a strong affinity with their nominal ancestors buried here as the boy nodded and smiled.

I completed some errands in the city and returned around noon, packed quickly, prepared my bike in a now rote exercise and rolled slowly back out along the laneway to meet Andrea and an eager, but sly looking taxi driver whom she had just contracted for our long journey to Bukhara.

An Uzbek Wedding

The last few days had been wonderfully stimulating and I felt rejuvenated both mentally and physically, but it felt good to be back on my bike, moving again, almost like this was my natural state now. And riding three hundred kilometres *after lunch* across the parched plains and thirsty cotton fields of southern Uzbekistan didn't faze me either; I was slowly clearing the bogeymen that I had carried like deadweight for so long. Then I thought about the multi-coloured springs, homemade parts and agricultural blobs of welded scrap metal that currently held my clutch together and a big warning sign flashed in my mind: proceed with caution.

But I wasn't going anywhere without enough petrol; I hadn't bothered to fill my tank since arriving in Samarkand, and now a severe petrol shortage – a common occurrence in Uzbekistan – had struck. I opened my tank and rocked my bike back and forth – a little petrol sloshed around but certainly not enough to get to Bukhara. I double checked my odometer to be certain – the petrol I had wouldn't take me more than a hundred kilometres. I explained my problem to Andrea apologetically, who immediately turned to the taxi driver and relayed my requirements. He simply pulled his greasy hands out of his pockets and splayed them from the waist with an expression of indifference on his face as if to say "not my problem, there is no petrol, what are you doing with this crazy foreigner anyway – let's go!", but Andrea was loyal, and after some very persistent but polite lobbying I found myself tailing the three ladies, who smiled and waved back at me from the back of the taxi, as we scoured the city looking for petrol. We passed a number of lifeless petrol stations whose entrances were barricaded and covered in large hand painted signs that simply read "benzin nyeto!" We stopped at several taxi ranks where drivers milled about between their empty cars – the scarcity of petrol bringing their businesses to a virtual standstill and, coveting their precious fuel, making travel all but impossible except for the most desperate and richest Uzbeks. Andrea cajoled and berated the men in turn on my behalf to try and strike a price for a transaction but they wouldn't budge. I sat on my bike embarrassed, wishing I might melt away into the asphalt.

My heart sank – for surely, after all I had come through, I wasn't going to be stopped by a simple lack of fuel? But it didn't look good. We continued on, driving through sleepy neighbourhoods, stopping frequently to ask anyone who looked vaguely sentient where we could find petrol. They all had leads and ideas and friends and our taxi driver followed a chain of connections before finally pulling up outside the rambling home of a mechanic friend. The property was large and surrounded by high metal fences, like a fortress. A large gate led into a yard full of scrapped cars and trucks. Momentarily, an old Uzbek man in battered track suit pants, flannel shirt and scruffy cap came shuffling down the driveway and toward us. He was swarthy and unshaven with a thatch of silver bristles covering his neck, jaw line and temples. Our taxi driver introduced us – we had been expected. Andrea immediately began the negotiations.

"Do you have benzine?"

"Yes, of course!"

"Is it good quality?"

This question seemed to strike the man like a bolt of lightning between the shoulder blades. "What do you mean?" he spat at us. "This is the best fuel in all of Uzbekistan. Once you use it you'll come back and you'll be telling your friends to come here too" he claimed proudly. We all took a deep breath and a step back. The man shuffled off to his fortress and returned quickly with a battered twenty litre metal canister. He opened it and pushed it under our noses – the vapour and haze were overpowering and certainly consistent with benzine, but nevertheless our taxi-driver was still suspicious so dipped his finger into the neck of the dark canister and placed a small sample of the liquid on the tip of his tongue. He immediately screwed up his face, recoiled and shook his head dismissively. The old man went off like a firecracker; he immediately launched into a tirade of abuse and then, inexplicably, he stuck both of his arms straight out at his side, leant over slightly and began running a tight figure eight around us whilst making a loud droning noise. After circling for a few laps he stopped, breathless, to explain that he and his sons had "borrowed" the fuel from Samarkand airport where they all worked, and that it was the finest *aviation* gas in all of Uzbekistan. Just for greater effect he made a noise like a rocket and launched his forearm and shaky digits to the heavens. It certainly frightened me and I wondered whether he had been drinking the stuff in the canister too. I explained that I wanted to ride, not fly, to Bukhara but he didn't get the joke.

I leant back on my bike and considered my options. I tried desperately to recall anything useful from my undistinguished chemistry studies at university, but in reality these had been long, wasted afternoons playing dangerous games with Bunsen burners and explosive compounds, damaging expensive equipment for little or no real knowledge gain. I did know, however, that avgas was still a hydrocarbon fuel which had, in the past, been used to power racing cars, so there was a possibility it might work in my bike. And, anyway, surely mixing it with the five litres of the "genuine" fuel already in my tank would help take the edge off its explosive qualities – right?? So, more than slightly unconvinced, I reluctantly gave my consent. The old man pulled a large metal funnel from his belt and inserted it into my tank and began pouring. I watched nervously as his shaky hands wobbled the heavy canister above my bike and the jet propellant drained in. It was cherry-red, like the glaze on a toffee apple and smelt strangely sweet too. I realised forlornly that there was no going back now, no way to unscramble the high octane hydrocarbon cocktail now brewing in my tank. When he had finished I sloshed the mixture around as best I could, then closed my eyes, turned my head away and braced myself as I turned over the engine. I flinched as images of jet pilots hurtling through the air on rocket-powered ejector seats raced through my mind. Thankfully, however, the bike fired immediately and purred like a kitten – or rather a tiger. I thanked the old man sincerely and rode off, still a little apprehensive, but happy to be underway again.

**

We cut cross country through busy cotton fields and stopped briefly before joining the highway. Andrea got out of the car and came over to me with the taxi driver in tow and, keenly aware of the tendency of Uzbek drivers to break land-speed records in their trips to Bukhara (so as to maximise their revenue for the day), she considerately asked at what speed I was comfortable riding. The taxi driver appeared nonplussed and narrowed his eyes as he waited anxiously for my reply – this delay and any imposed speed limits would certainly cost him. Without knowing the road, it was difficult to say, and the wind – always my worst enemy – had picked up too, so I bid 80 kph, my absolute maximum safe speed. Andrea didn't flinch and didn't bother consulting the driver either, who at this moment was almost apoplectic, but this was what she ordered him to do before marching back to join the sisters on the back seat. The driver kicked my front tyre angrily, hissed and sneered menacingly at me before skulking back to his car.

The highway bore an uncanny resemblance to a speedway, a fact which unfortunately didn't escape our driver either as he blasted away from me now. I suspected that his engine was also powered with jet fuel, for I could find no other reason to explain how a 1960's Soviet-era block of steel on wheels could be propelled at such speeds. The roadway had low but substantial concrete crash barriers on either side – which I assumed were to protect the public from these maniacs – and there was a thick concrete spine running down the middle, serving the same purpose for the drivers. The road (on both sides) was at least four lanes wide and unmarked, with long sweeping cambered curves. One might even have speculated that it had been built solely for the purposes of speeding efficiently between the two cities, were it not for the totally inadequate road surface which varied dangerously between deep pock-marked asphalt, ill-fitting irregular concrete slabs and, in a motorcyclists' worst nightmare, deeply grooved bitumen covered in loose gravel. Traffic lights were rare and purely decorative and it didn't look as if a pedestrian had made it across safely in years, although today the road was virtually empty – a fact that only seemed to encourage our driver as he sped further into the distance ahead of me, now barely visible and just a dot on the horizon. I pinned back my ears and focused hard on the road in a grave pursuit which sometimes had me travelling at the ridiculously dangerous speed of 130kph. He was indeed a maniac and in the spare nanoseconds between trying to control my bike as it slid sideways across the road or dodging the large pot holes that rushed up at me from nowhere and fighting the frikkin wind that blew in powerful gusts across the flat open plains here, I imagined him as a human shashlik roasting slowly over hot coals, sizzling and smiling no more.

It was virtually impossible to take in any of the scenery as it whizzed past, but it didn't much matter as it was just a bleak collection of whitewashed farmhouses scattered on the shores of a vast ivy green and crimson sea of cotton, the monotony broken only by the grim, dusty townships, each less prosperous than the previous and none with any of the redeeming ancient beauty of Samarkand.

Suddenly, after an hour of white-knuckle riding, I skidded to a stop behind the car outside a roadside chaikhana where Andrea insisted I try some samsas – the traditional fist sized triangular pastries common to this part of Central Asia. I was drained and feeling fragile and my head buzzed from the intense concentration and I was happy just to sit in the shade and quietly sip a cup of tea, but no sooner had I sat down than Andrea was calling me excitedly over to where she stood now, next to a poor street vendor tending his ancient wood-fired oven.

"Come, come and see how these are made, it's very interesting" she said.

I walked over slowly with my best expression of deep interest as she jumped up, grabbed my neck and thrust my head down inside the entrance chute of the igloo-shaped oven. I felt the intense blast of heat as it quickly singed my beard, eyebrows and eyelashes before I pulled back. But it was long enough to see the rows of fleshy pastry triangles floating above the hot coals, stuck to the roof of the oven. I sized up the entrance chute and wondered darkly if the taxi driver would fit inside. Andrea handed me two piping hot samsas. I carefully removed the complementary baked-on grit before eating them slowly. Filled with lamb, fried onions and spices they were delicious. As I ate she explained that this food was a staple and had been cooked in this way, unchanged, for thousands of years here. I tried my hardest to pay for the food but she insisted they were her gift to me. The taxi driver, who had stayed in his car throughout, snarled at me now with even greater contempt as we prepared to leave.

We headed back out onto the speedway but stopped once more, at the village of Gijduvan, still well short of Bukhara, where we visited the famous sixth-generation Uzbek ceramic artist, Alisher Narzulaev. His father had been persecuted in Soviet times for his "abstract" nonconformist designs. He had, however, continued to work in secret, passing on his technique to his two sons. And it was Alisher who came out now to greet us as we pulled into the driveway of his modest family compound. He and his brother lived here with their extended families in a large modern gated compound that consisted of living quarters and workshops around a large central courtyard. Alisher was a small, slight man with greasy dark grey hair, sad eyes and a caterpillar moustache rising from a permanent 5 o'clock shadow that fell over a waxy, pallid complexion. He was aged and tired beyond his years, as if he had already spent most of his life force and it had been him and not his father who had been persecuted and driven underground. He immediately made us feel welcome and ushered us into the compound where he introduced us to his mother, his wife, his three sons and his daughters-in-law. They all sat casually on cushions spread over old bench seats around a long trestle table on the elevated veranda overlooking the garden.

He led us inside into the formal dining room of his home for the equivalent of high tea, Uzbek style, where we sat at a long ornate dining table and drank champagne from crystal flutes and ate bread and cake and sugar-coated nuts from fine painted ceramic dishes, each made by his own hand. Select pieces of his father's work adorned the walls here as tribute; there were plates and dishes and even oil paintings, all cast from the same palette of natural pigments of copper green, cobalt blue, red ochre and white zinc smudged into rough geometric shapes and patterns on a dirty yellow background. My favourite, which I admired for a long time, was a massive ceremonial plate – at least one metre across – that I felt was more abstract sunrise over cotton fields than just pure decorative patterns. I told Alisher and he seemed pleased.

Afterwards Alisher proudly showed me his studio – in reality just a large dusty barn – where the shelves and floor were splattered with grey clay and littered with works in various stages of production; large painted plates, bowls, glazed jugs and huge water vessels – well over six feet tall – which were now back in demand, just like in ancient times, for their water preservation qualities. In an annexe, an old donkey stood idle in a harness on a deeply worn circular track, tied to a large milling stone where, Alisher explained, locally-sourced minerals were ground into fine glaze powder. Alisher laughed and patted the animal lovingly and said he had the best job of all, working just one day a month. He led me across the yard to the high temperature kiln that he and his sons had made by hand (and from memory) – a replica of the industrial versions he'd seen on an overseas trip. It was well over ten feet tall, with a long fluted chimney rising from a wide circular base, almost big enough for a man to stand inside I estimated. Alisher explained excitedly that the temperatures inside reached well over 1200 degrees. Sensing my genuine interest he launched in a lengthy technical explanation of firing and glazing, but all I could think of was our driver... .now where was he? I looked up and noticed scorched and heavily charred beams on the ceiling high above us. In fact the ceiling looked as if it had been progressively burnt and razed – I asked Alisher what had happened and he explained, slightly embarrassed, that he had built and re-built the kiln and its housing several times until he arrived at a configuration that meant he didn't necessarily have to burn down his home each time each time he fired his work.

Before we arrived Andrea had told me the high esteem in which Alisher is held in Uzbekistan and his international recognition and his pedigree in the long line of ceramic masters, but today, for some reason which I couldn't quite put my finger on, this place felt more funereal than flourishing artistic dynasty and I wondered whether in fact his sons would continue his legacy.

I chose a simple small glazed green plate, uniquely flawed with a hand-etched leaf pattern – it wasn't a significant piece, but it felt right and I liked it. Alisher was genuinely delighted by my choice and shook my hand at length before wrapping it carefully in thick brown paper for me.

As we prepared to leave we found Alisher out on the veranda holding the arms of a young boy, perhaps two years old, and certainly his grandson. The little boy wore old-fashioned leather and metal calliper splints on both his legs and Alisher tenderly swung the boy along, pivoting him on each foot as they touched the ground gently in turn. He didn't notice us and was completely absorbed as is the love of a grandparent. We left silently and sped out into the desert, passing empty factories, cracked irrigation canals and abandoned cotton fields as dusk fell.

***

I followed the taxi into the heart of old Bukhara until our driver could go no further, whereupon Andrea leapt out of the car and gave me the final directions to Movin' John's. She pointed towards a narrow cobblestone mall barred to car traffic - "Just head down there until you come to the oasis pool, turn left just past the stone camels and then go down the long crooked alleyway until you see the Olympic rings on a big white door – that's Movin' John's. He's expecting you. Oh, and if you get to the synagogue you've gone too far."
"Ahhhhh, yes, OK" I said unconvincingly, but she had gone.

"Oh, and don't forget, we'll pick you up in one hour for the wedding!" she shouted from the back seat of the taxi as it roared off into the darkness. Wedding?? I had completely forgotten about the wedding, and thought it had been a kind, but ultimately empty gesture, but now I realised she was deadly serious. But then I thought: I don't know these people, I'm not even a fellow countryman nor do I share their culture, I have no gift and I've only got the dirty clothes on my back to wear – what was she thinking?

I rode off down the cobblestone mall in the dim yellow light of the street lamps and to my surprise found the oasis, the camels, and eventually, after almost shattering the fragile mud walls along the narrow alleyway, I came to a long dirty white door covered in faded blue 1970's stylised stick figure icons depicting the classic Olympic disciplines. There were sprinters, wrestlers and throwers, but strangely no table tennis combatants. There was no-one about and the place looked like an ancient stone fortress as it rose up, almost vertically two stories above me, with no windows or features. I parked my bike and was about to bang on the door when it suddenly began sliding back slowly, revealing the exotic Movin' John himself.

He was a tall, lithe and handsome, deeply tanned with dark eyes and thinning but stylish long lank greying hair brushed back from his face and white at the temples. As if in character and on cue, he was, like a noble, retired champion of ancient Greece, dressed from head to toe in loose fitting white clothes; he wore white tracksuit pants, a white T-shirt with a faded Olympic logo and leather sandals - all that was missing was a crown of olive branches. But it was all old, faded and frayed in shades of dirty off white, discoloured and worn from overuse. He smiled warmly, chuckled and welcomed me into his home. There was a large paved area behind the doors where he carefully helped me park my bike safely. I followed him through a low doorway and emerged into the central courtyard of his ancient home, built by his Tajik ancestors who had come to Bukhara as merchants in the 18th century. The courtyard itself was elevated and stood about four feet higher than where we were now, and a deep passageway leading to underground storerooms cut it almost in half. The courtyard was paved with large rough-hewn flagstones and was almost completely bare with the exception of a lonely mulberry tree that had somehow taken root and flourished, growing up out of the dark stone-encrusted earth. Cheap white plastic outdoor furniture sat forlornly in one corner. But it was the house itself that was the feature here; it rose up majestically two storeys in what I can only describe by a poor comparison as traditional Spanishhacienda-cum-Indian-colonial style – a whitewashed stone and mortar structure with balconies on the top level, crowned by exposed and intricately decorated beams with numerous heavy wooden doors proving access on the ground floor, each positioned symmetrically around the perimeter, separated by more exotic decorative panels painted in two- tone relief.

We walked around to the far corner of the courtyard where Movin' John showed me to my room. The stone floor, worn smooth from hundreds of years of use, continued inside and was bare except for a thin and grimy cotton sleeping mat and sad naked pillow. But again, in here too, it was the original features of the house itself that starred; white plaster walls were decorated with subtle yet elaborate friezes and floral motif fresco panels, all done with a light hand in shades of baby blue and gold. There were niches and alcoves with shelves filled with a small library of books, personal memorabilia and artefacts. I scanned the shelves and was immediately struck by the large back and white portrait of Movin' John as a young man; debonair and dashingly handsome, with oiled hair, big dark pools of eyes, smooth tanned skin over a classically well-structured face and dressed in lounge suit with a far way look in

284

his eyes – he had more than a touch of the Rudolph Valentino about him. The room finished above me with softly rounded cornices running into an exposed ceiling of carved painted beams with a small chandelier providing the only light in this windowless place.

***

Andrea arrived right on time, barely recognizable now though, with a Duchess of Kent hairstyle, makeup, jewels, and wearing a long lime green silk sari-style dress with a matching embroidered scarf, draped like a cape around her shoulders, that almost reached the ground. We joined the sisters who were waiting in a taxi nearby who had also transformed themselves in preparation for the wedding celebrations tonight. They also, unlike me, had a gift too – a beautiful ceramic plate from Gijduvan – which they immediately said would be a gift from all of us! Incredible. I folded myself into the small space that was the front seat of the little Lada taxi – a feat which seemed to give the old man driving some perverse pleasure. We drove across town, leaving the old city behind, and headed for the grandest hotel in modern Bukhara, where the wedding was already in full swing. On the way Andrea explained the essentials of the wedding to me: mature, only daughter of moderately wealthy Jewish hotelier marrying a hardworking Tajik entrepreneur. On the surface it seemed a highly unusual union bridging some serious ethnic and religious divides, but in reality it simply reflected the extended presence of Jewish people here in Bukhara. In fact, the Bukharan Jews trace their ancestry back to the Israelites who never came back from captivity in Babylon after exile in the 7th century BCE. The community, cut off from the rest of the Jewish world for more than 2,000 years, survived in the face of countless odds and developed their own distinct culture (including speaking a dialect of the Tajik language). It was, however, very different in one important aspect; unlike many of the marriages here – still done on an arranged basis between families - there had been a long courtship, they were happy and most importantly in love.

We formed a tight foursome and strode purposefully along the specially laid rugs for arriving guests, under a long canopy that led directly to the ballroom. Music and conversation mingled in a din than grew progressively loader as we approached the ballroom. We entered and immediately I felt decidedly conspicuous; men in suits (some black tie) and ladies in evening gowns sat at two long rows of formally set tables that ran along each side of a grand ballroom –

neoclassical in style and in a soft shade of peppermint with lavish white icing stuccowork, around a beautiful honey coloured parquetry floor. The bride and groom sat at the head table at the far end of the room, deep in conversation with well-wishers, and a band, complete with a modestly dressed but genuine "exotic dancer", played and sang upbeat Turkic tunes rather forcefully. A magnificent crystal chandelier sparkled high above us, and tonight, to me at least, as I stood there like a startled doe on a freeway, it seemed to burn several shades brighter and some degrees hotter than the noon-time sun. Sensing my discomfort, Andrea ushered us quickly across the dance floor and introduced me directly to the father of the bride and provided a long explanation in Uzbek to legitimise my presence, to which he listened intently, nodding and smiling as she painted a vivid picture of me and my adventure. He was a big chubby man, with a thick neck, an upturned fleshy face and a big aquiline nose and dark beady eyes under a long receding brow crowned with thick snow-white hair under a black velvet yarmulke. He perspired profusely and mopped his brow often with a big white handkerchief that he held permanently in his left hand, a picture of poor health. Just as Andrea finished up he shook my hand – and my whole body – powerfully, saying it was an honour to have me share this special day with both their families, before escorting us to a prominent table.

We settled into position around one end of a long table covered in a wonderful selection of food and drink. There were big plates of Uzbek antipasto and an eclectic collection of drinks that included: mineral water, beer, vodka, red wine and brightly coloured fizz; without some self-discipline this could get ugly, I thought to myself. We acknowledged the other guests at our table, a weird troika consisting of a young ill-matched couple and an old, wizened man, who sat Nehru-like, serene and impassive at the far end of the table and appeared to be their chaperone. The young woman, in particular, caught my attention - and that of most men in the immediate vicinity - for her unbridled immodesty. She wore a daring low-cut strapless black and gold lamé dress, which fitted her like clingwrap. She had a flawless porcelain complexion, fiery dark eyes and a wild mane of tight jet black curls and oozed attitude. She picked up a bottle, filled her glass and slammed it on the table defiantly, saying "I'm drinking lots of vodka tonight, join me if you can – let's toast!" at which the sisters ducked for cover and scrambled for the lemon fizz and mineral water while Andrea and I loaded up a shot out of politeness. Before we had finished she had leapt up, dragging her unsuspecting beau off to the dance floor with her like a cavewoman, where she proceeded to cavort Salome-like, bumping and grinding against her young partner – a clean-cut kid who was proud, excited and overwhelmed all at the same time.

The older guests watched on disapprovingly, covering their mouths as they whispered to each other, shaking their heads. I watched this spectacle with great interest until, exhausted, they both returned to the table to recuperate. I looked into the old man's face for any signals but he barely moved, as if in a trance; his eyes twinkled as he gave the faintest of smiles and the slightest nod of his head, in an almost imperceptible acknowledgement of I didn't know what. Aziza leant over and whispered discretely to me, "She's a modern Iranian woman you know, very dangerous – you watch out for her."

Hungry, I worked through a large plate of salami, cheese, pickled vegetables and a dry grey meat, not unlike aged roast beef in appearance and texture, with a distinctive nutty flavour. "What's this?" I asked Aziza, who sat next to me now, as I pointed to the last piece on my plate. "Its broiled horsemeat, a national delicacy – do you like it?" she enquired. I swallowed hard, and after a short pause uttered a long "Mmmmm " with a slow but gracious nod, as the horsey aftertaste rose sharply in my mouth.

I scanned the room and stopped at the head table, transfixed on the classically beautiful girl who was obviously the equivalent of a bridesmaid in this loose ecumenical ceremony. She was tall and willowy, at least six feet in her shoes, with honey brown skin and her light brown hair was cut pixie-style, accentuating her handsome face, and she wore a plain loose fitting white cotton dress that flowed like ancient robes as she strode confidently around the room fulfilling her duties. But somehow, she looked strangely familiar. "And who is that?" I asked Andrea.

"Ahhhh, that's Movin' John's daughter. Isn't she lovely?" I nodded in agreement.

"And that woman over there", she said, pointing out a fierce looking rectangular-shaped woman with piercing blue eyes, pale skin and short thick wiry dark hair, "That's his ex-wife – he's a scoundrel you know, and lives alone now in his family home, where you're staying. His wife and daughter live just a few doors away in the same street though. They were a volatile couple." Mrs Movin' John also appeared to be a central figure in the ceremony as she danced often and with great exuberance, choreographing a string of older women and mothers in what I assumed were traditional group celebrations.

Suddenly Aziza nudged me, saying "You know, it is a great honour to have a foreign guest here, especially one who speaks English - you must make a speech" she insisted. I almost choked on my horsemeat sandwich. A speech – you must be kidding; I don't enjoy public speaking, and unless I'm very well prepared I find it torturous. Andrea leant over, adding her weight to the suggestion and encouraging me with some helpful tips on what to say. Oh crap. I reached over, grabbed a vodka bottle and filled my glass for Dutch courage, then chased it down with a large glass of the "best" Georgian wine. My throat was on fire, but at least my nerves had been numbed. I ate a large slab of flat bread smothered in butter, lubricating my hot windpipe and settling my queasy stomach, but before I had swallowed the last mouthful, I looked up to see Aziza at the microphone, in the centre of the dance floor, introducing me to the audience and motioning for me to join her. I skipped nervously onto the dance floor where suddenly it had become deathly silent and I felt the horrible weight of expectation fall upon my shoulders. I looked up for inspiration and wished that the beautiful chandelier might fall from the ceiling and crush me right at this moment. Aziza thrust the microphone into my hand and, after a short burst of adrenaline shot through my body, I began by telling them (truthfully) that I had traveled a very long way through some very difficult conditions to be with them tonight and that it was a great honour to be sharing this special day with all of them. In my mind I recalled a quip from my own wedding where someone had pointed out that marriage is for life – but with good behaviour and parole I'd be out in about seven years, but thought the better of using it here. I fumbled about before finally settling on what I thought was an insightful quote from Oscar Wilde who once said: "Every woman becomes like her mother... .and that is her tragedy. No man does... .and that is his". But even before Aziza had finished translating the last few words I felt the waves of hostility swelling around me. Heads were bowed and there was much angry muttering between guests. The father, who stood behind me, was several shades redder and looked as if he wanted to resume shaking me now, only much, much harder than before. Aziza hissed at me "What you have said is deeply offensive to both the bride and the groom and all their families! What do you mean by this?" Clearly the subtle semantics of the English and their sensibilities had not translated well and perhaps, on face value, ran counter to traditional Uzbek cultural mores. I huddled with Aziza and did my best to explain more clearly the universal sentiment that I wanted to convey – and which I felt sure was still relevant here. Suddenly grasping it, her eyes lit up and she smiled; yanking the microphone out of my hands she provided the necessary cultural translation and I was redeemed. Everyone nodded in appreciation and agreement at the piece of wisdom. Finally, I wished the bride and groom good health, every happiness and many children, to which everyone applauded. The father of the bride slapped me hard on the back and thanked me sincerely as he wiped the tears from his eyes.

My torture over, the night continued with much eating, drinking and dancing. Andrea explained that traditional Uzbek weddings were typically far more sombre occasions, with the bride not permitted to smile on her wedding day, with women and men segregated, celebrating separately, and, in the worst cases, there was no ceremony at all, with women literally being kidnapped into marriage. Thankfully tonight had none of these elements as couples danced gaily to the powerful rhythms of Turkic music and manful yodelling that filled the room now. The chanteuse, whom we had seen when we first arrived, had returned now, and was dancing herself into a frenzy as she moved through the crowd, hands raised and wrists cocked, finger clicking, tambourine smashing, hips gyrating, hoovering up the loose notes being thrust at her by faux admirers.

"Why are they giving her money?" I asked Andrea.

"It's the tradition. And we must contribute too" she said urgently as they all opened their purses and handed me a fistful of notes. "You must dance with her and give this money – it's very important". I added my own small contribution and stumbled out onto the dance floor with all the grace of a drunk preying mantis and circled my target like a pilot lost in thick fog, making numerous abortive landing attempts and, failing to locate anywhere appropriate, simply planted the cash firmly into one of her sweaty palms before drifting away. I made a B-line for our table but was swallowed by a small group of guests who stood in a tight circle clapping and encouraging a young athletic Russian man who danced wildly like a Cossack, bouncing on his haunches, flinging his legs out from under him with one hand on his waist and the other thrust out sideways as he flicked his head from side to side and smiled through clenched teeth. He was murderously fit and coordinated and it was a real pleasure to watch him in action, until inexplicably, he invited me to join with him for some man dancing. Ignoring my desperate protests, he grabbed my arms and swung me around like a rag doll, pressing his back hard up against mine before driving us slowly around and down towards the floor, like a lopsided spinning top almost drained of its momentum. My Kevlar-lined riding pants provided great protection against gravel rash but tonight they severely cramped my style as I tried haplessly to keep up with my Cossack partner who kicked wildly and flayed about flamboyantly while I twisted slowly and stiffly, wincing with pain every now and then as I aggravated my fractured ankle. And even without these constraints I knew I couldn't match his strength, flexibility and stamina and I was quickly jettisoned from our unequal union, falling about in a steaming tangle of arms and legs at the feet of the sympathetic crowd. My Cossack friend stopped mid-step and rushed over to pull me back onto my feet before embracing me like a brother and kissing me on each cheek. Physically exhausted but with my honour intact, I hauled myself back to the table and collapsed quietly before demolishing a tower of bread roundels and a bottle of sickly sweet coloured fizz, in an effort to replenish my spent reserves.

Andrea, meanwhile, had been taken hostage on the dance floor by a local boor who demanded nothing less than total submission to his drunken advances – which in any culture would have amounted to a serious invasion of her "personal space". But she was no ingénue, and drew on every molecule of her Swiss neutrality and diplomacy, as she tirelessly repelled and deflected each unrequited salvo with tact and guile, smiling throughout, leaving her admirer uncertain as to whether she was just playing hard to get, or truly detested him. But he was insistent, stalking her clumsily around the dance floor until, with her defences flagging and a pained expression on her face, Andrea looked to us desperately for rescue. I jumped up and happily ran interference for her; sidling up to the oaf for a second bout of man dancing, while she slipped away. Luckily, he was drunk enough to just be amused and only slightly perturbed at the sudden change in gender, height and complexion of his partner. Thankfully, just as I was beginning to feel a little nervous, like a zookeeper trapped with a randy gorilla, the music stopped and we returned to our seats for a strange interlude where the married couple were called to the middle of the dance floor where they popped a clutch of balloons, one by one, giggling and laughing as they each read aloud, in turn, the amusing prophecies or bizarre marriage vows that rained down on them on little pieces of paper, like a shower from a storm of broken fortune cookie clouds.

Andrea, having regained her composure now, leant over and whispered darkly to me, "You know, of course, that this is highly unusual; quite often a woman's wedding day is the last happy day of her life." She went on to explain that traditionally daughters-in-law occupied the lowest position in the family hierarchy, often becoming slaves to their new relations, pitted against fierce mothers-in-law and subject to terrible physical abuse at the hands of their own husbands who were loyal sons first and foremost. Many girls were married before they reached twenty, with some promised and sold as young as twelve. And polygamy, although technically illegal, was still practised by those with sufficient means, under community sanction.

But there was a little ray of sunshine in this bleak picture; for all of the pitfalls of Soviet rule, it had brought about a level of emancipation in the women of Uzbekistan, freeing them (to an extent) from the straightjacket of traditional family responsibilities so they could work and contribute in society and lifting and literally burning their veils, but most importantly, it had introduced the remedy of divorce, which had been, and continues to be widely used.

**

I returned to Movin' John's fortress with my head buzzing and fell wearily, with a thud, onto my hard floor mat. I slept late and emerged bleary eyed for breakfast in the ancient courtyard. I squirmed nervously on a flimsy plastic chair that slowly began to buckle under my weight. Just as I settled, Movin' John suddenly bounded out his quarters on the far side of the courtyard like a highly sprung jack-in-the-box, still dressed in the same off white uniform, in which he had obviously slept. He carried a tray of food and laid it out proudly on the bare plastic table in front of me: one cold and very hard boiled egg, a few pieces of almost-stale bread, a huge bowl of re-heated greasy-but-sweet plov, and a pot of tea served in a cheap plastic cup. It was an old bachelors' breakfast – no frills, chewy, filling, mostly recycled, and surprisingly delicious. I liked him immediately and came to see him as more avuncular rather than eccentric hostel keeper.

In a strangely pensive mood, I lingered over my breakfast, savouring the sweet pieces of dried fruit and chewy strips of lamb jerky in the plov and poured over the pages of my guide book for one final retelling of the vivid and eclectic history of this place. From its creation, as a citadel of Persian royalty, through the long series of invasions and overlords that included Alexander the Great, the Arabs, Mongols and finally the Soviets, to the intrigues and espionage of Great Game, where the Russians triumphed, ousting the brutal, crazy and capricious Emirs, the history leapt off the pages more like the tales of 1001 nights.

I spent the rest of the day losing myself in a long, lazy circuit of the old city. I walked along ancient alleyways, through covered bazaars – each originally dedicated to different aspects of trade: there was the jewellers bazaar, where coral, gold and precious metals changed hands, the silk and wool markets, the hat makers bazaar, and the outcast, but wealthy Indian money dealers, who provided the liquidity essential for the cornucopia of commerce that once took place here. I peered deep inside the excavated foundations of a 12th century mosque that revealed where a heathen shrine, a Buddhist monastery and a Zoroastrian temple had all in fact made use of the same real estate across the ages, each literally building upon the other.

I wandered alone through a fine art gallery of both modern and traditional works where the sleepy curator, whom I had woken, rushed ahead of me eagerly switching on lights, dusting cobwebs from displays and removing the cloth coverings from the disturbing portraits in Soviet realism style, and then on through the dusty back streets of the old town where everything was caked in a golden crust of fine sand carried in on the wind from the nearby desert. A cloudless pale blue sky glistened intensely above me and the sun, now at its zenith, burned fiercely down on me as I closed in on the old Registan, where I wandered into a derelict medrassah, then unknowingly into a partly-resuscitated college immediately opposite, where students recited Koran verses softly in their cell-rooms, in a rhythmic babble that floated across an immense stone courtyard filled with dilapidated table tennis tables – potentially the boys only indulgence. I imagined an effervescent and youthful Movin' John, hardened by the frugal monastic life but high on the path to self enlightenment, chanting and smashing table tennis balls with equal fervour; a prodigy on the road to Olympic stardom. But the school was not a tourist attraction and I was politely but firmly moved along by the zealous old caretaker. I walked down a long pedestrian boulevard and across a large empty park where I sat mesmerized by the incredible flaxen woven brickwork of the Ismael Samani mosque, lifting my feet as a crippled Uzbek babushka silently swept this sacred site with a homemade broom of twigs. The building was almost a perfect cube, cornered with delicate bricked pillars each topped by small cupolas that sat in the shadow of a massive bricked dome. It was one of those patterns that grows in detail and took on a liquid quality the longer you looked at it, and the intricate surface looked as if it had been scored from a single block of wet clay rather than created from the precise placement of thousands of individual bricks.

I wandered further on, across a water canal towards the remains of the old city walls – crumbling but still distinct and rounded smooth from nearly a century of desert weathering; they rose from the flat dead earth like long fat rolls of dough on a baker's tray. These walls, that had stood here in various configurations since the middle of the 9th century CE, had originally provided protection from the hostile desert, nomads and potential invaders, and in more recent times had kept Bolshevik agents and British spies at arms length and, after being hermetically sealed for six years, were finally blown apart by Red Army artillery in 1920.

Somehow I ended up in the "Museum of Water", indicating just how scarce and precious the substance is here and how proud the locals were at – one time anyway – of their achievements in defying nature to sustain their parched city and to saturate the countryside to comply with the crazy directives from Moscow in the 1950s that diverted the whole country to a cotton monoculture. I waded through an old black and white commemorative photo book full of unsmiling, stoic men and women, the engineers and construction workers who by sheer weight of numbers, blunt technique and unspoken coercion had completed these massive works at breakneck speed. Their faces stared out at me like melancholy mug shots; the only distinguishing features being the badges and pins on their lapels and dresses – "Order of Lenin" awards for ditch digging, concrete laying and welding. But perhaps in their melancholy they had had some inkling of the terrible consequences of their "glorious labour" as the water began gurgling out of the far away Aral Sea like a bathtub, never to return.

***

I took a long lunch of fatty shashliks, bread and beer at a modest chaikhana opposite Bukhara's Registan, which now, unlike its contemporary in Samarkand, had become an overgrown and unkempt public park where babushkas shuffled about feeding pigeons and the last few remaining heroes of the Great Patriotic War silently played chess with each other.

After lunch I climbed the long drawbridge and steep cobblestone entrance of the mediaeval Ark Fortress. It was an epic place with long sloping ramparts that rose sharply – almost a one hundred feet vertical. I ran the gauntlet of polite but persistent hawkers and stall owners who occupied both sides of the narrow ramp – perfectly positioned to prey upon tourists. But I was the only visitor today and had to wake up the ticket seller from a deep sleep before proceeding past the sorry row of anxious faces. Until the Russians took over, this had been the home to the rulers of Bukhara for over a millennium and, at one time, had supported a huge retinue and range of facilities that included government officials, the harem, a treasury and gold mint, a mosque, stables, a dungeon and slave quarters. But today it was all rather austere and drab with a tiny dusty history museum which seemed to be run entirely by local volunteers. I roamed about untroubled and found myself drawn to the enormous throne room, half a football field in size, and now exposed to the elements, where a tall solid stone wall almost blocked the entrance to the room, ensuring that those visitors lucky enough to leave of their own accord, would not show their backs to the Emir as they exited. Without much more to hold my interest here, I too left and walked back towards the religious heart of the old city, past the gnarled carpet sellers who were now packing up for the day, and on, into the magnificent Kalon Mosque where I wandered about alone again through what seemed like an endless forest of alabaster columns under a low-vaulted ceiling in the flank of the mosque before staring into a dizzying turquoise and deep blue mosaic at its apex. And, although this place had been sacked and destroyed and rebuilt many times over and could hold well in excess of 10,000 people for Friday prayers, it was beautifully simple, and today, for me, it was an entirely serene experience.

***

Tired but satiated, I returned at dusk to the peaceful lagoon and idle chaikhanas of the Lyab-i-Hauz, where I sat quietly under the ancient mulberry trees sipping coca-cola and eating some unidentifiable lukewarm grey stew. A trickle of old men in traditional doppilars and chopans with long wispy white beards and creaseless brown faces entered the square and huddled around nearby tables in pre-ordained groups as they took their places in this eternal evening ritual, drinking tea from samovars in long glasses and picking at plates of communal food as they talked and reminisced fondly. The intensity had all but drained from the sky as the last golden fingers of twilight stretched out across the old city, illuminating the grand medrassahs and caravanserai positioned around the pool in a wonderful warm glow and glinting off the sparse patchwork of residual tiles in delicate patterns as if a sparkling stream ran across their surface. Ignoring the electric lights and the occasional herds of wealthy geriatric tourists, I quickly imagined myself transported back in time, mingling with merchants, travellers, pilgrims and locals at this Silk Road hub.

I skipped like a carefree schoolboy down the cobblestone alleyway to Movin' John's where he greeted me warmly, inviting me to join him in the courtyard where had been sitting alone in the semi-darkness. He put his arm around me as we walked across the courtyard and told me that he "wanted to talk", so, encouraged by this genuine camaraderie and in a playful attempt to break the ice ahead of some serious men's business, I leapt aside and began dancing around him on my tip toes, ducking and weaving in quick flashes, Ali-esque, waving my big arms back and forth in long arcs, fists pumping, smashing imaginary table tennis balls with the imaginary paddle I held tightly in my right hand, in a not-too-subtle acknowledgment of his pedigree and achievements. He was the man, and I wanted to let him know it. But Movin' John stopped dead in his tracks, totally bewildered at my bizarre behaviour, and stood looking at me, head tilted to one side, mouth open, with his crease worn leathery brow deeply furrowed, as if I was a complete buffoon.

"But you're an Olympic Table Tennis champion!" I blurted out, not understanding why he had reacted so strangely. But this latest revelation only served to cut him to the quick; he shook his head violently and howled at me in his broken English, "No, no, no, no, no! Table tennis no! Movin' John sprinter. I hundred metre champion!" But even in his vehement rebuttal I detected an underlying sadness that he couldn't suppress. I apologised quickly and pinned the blame on my wholly inadequate guide book, which I fetched now to show him, hoping to exonerate myself completely. He spat on the page before I could move it out of range and I quickly removed it out of his sight and never mentioned the subject again. He then proceeded to tell me his tragic story in a bittersweet pantomime, which he acted out in front of me with all the fluidity and poignant expressiveness of Marcel Marceau, a comparison made easier by the blank canvas of his simple white uniform – which he still wore – and his large expressive eyes and handsomely drawn face. The initial chapters of his life story were glamorous and full of colour; he was the son of a well to do Tajik family, an athletic prodigy feted and coddled as his exceptional talents grew, cultivated by the Soviet sports machine as one of the fastest men in the world in the lead up to the showcase, but ultimately spoiled, 1980 Moscow Olympics. Neither he nor his family were communists, he barely understood the concept as a young man, but it didn't matter – he was fast and winning meant everything and thus his life was devoted to it.

He lived an idyllic life, attending the best schools and universities, received the best coaching, a generous allowance, enjoyed the best food, overseas travel, cars, apartments, even women, all at no personal cost and he was never required to work a regular job. His eyes moistened as he recalled all of this now with a distant, almost vicarious pleasure. These were the Brezhnev years of stagnation and slow decline, but he had been insulated from all the problems of everyday life and lived in blissful ignorance of the social and political systems that were slowly unwinding around him. I wanted to probe deeper into this incongruity, but he was getting worked up, so reaching into the depths of my memory banks I recalled the great athletes and wonderful images that I had watched as an excited teenager on a fuzzy satellite feed from half way around the world, oblivious myself to the internecine proxy war being played out in Afghanistan by the USSR and the Americans that had triggered the boycott in the first place. Wells, Quarrie, Ovett and Coe, Mennea, Koch – his eyes lit up as I ran through a sketchy roll call of the sprint and middle distance champions I could remember. He knew them all – personally – the sprinters his peers on the world stage, but it was the opening ceremony with its devastatingly simple but visually spectacular montage of tightly choreographed sequences from hundreds of human pixels and the multistoried human towers that burst open like wildflowers on the vivid green arena that had left an indelible mark in my mind. By this stage Movin' John was almost beside himself with grief as he sat with his head in his hands opposite me. I was about to mention Mischa (the cute little bear cub mascot of the Games) but I thought it might push him over the edge so instead tried drawing out some details of his own athletic abilities and career. "Tell me, how fast could you run?" I asked.

"Ten seconds flat" he replied deadpan. Skewed by the boycott, the sprints in Moscow were dominated by white men (an anomaly never repeated), with a pale Scotsman winning in ten and a quarter seconds... But where was Movin' John? Why hadn't he been a contender? What was the dark secret that disturbed him so deeply? Afraid to ask, he saved me the trouble by kneeling down gingerly right in front of me now into the relaxed initial starting position of the blue ribband sprints – but to me it felt more like a confessional. With his fingers splayed on the cold hard stones of the courtyard and head bowed in silence he gently kicked each of his legs out behind him like a bronco, shaking the last remnants of nervous energy out of his explosive muscles. He swayed gently from side to side before settling. I couldn't see his face, but he was somewhere else, focused, in the zone; the courtyard was his stadium and he was waiting patiently for the buzz of the crowd to subside and then for the starter's penultimate instruction. Then suddenly, in a swift yet fluid motion, responding to an unheard command, he lifted his knee off the ground and pointed his tailbone toward the heavens. All of his muscles contracted and tightened as he locked his aged body into an impossibly rigid arched position. Frightened to interrupt, I watched on silently as he stared straight ahead into the middle distance, focused on the track, his lane and his race. And then, as if shot by a sniper, rather than exploding out of the blocks at the sound of the starters pistol, he collapsed like a wounded stag, clutching his thigh and rolling about on the ground, writhing in pain. Instinctively, I looked up into the balconies above us for his assailant. Slowly, I helped him back onto his feet, and as he stood he held his arms out straight with fists clenched, about six inches apart, before yanking them violently apart, as if he were snapping a lethal Christmas bonbon; his hamstring had snapped, damaged irreparably and so too, in that instant, was his career. Like the tragic Chiron, struck in the thigh by Heracles' arrow, he was mortally wounded, condemned to live the rest of days as an ordinary citizen. But it was worse than that. His face darkened as he recalled the ignominy and brutal pace of his fall. Spittle accumulated and flew from the corners of his mouth and he angrily karate chopped the air in front of him as he inventoried all of the privileges that were immediately and permanently revoked. He was shouting now.

"Money – no!"

"House – no!"

"Women – no!"

"Travel – no!"

"Clothes – no!"

"Food – no!"

And so on. It was a long and painful list that spewed forth like a lava storm from an erupting volcano. So there was no golden twilight, no comfortable career in coaching or sports administration and certainly no pension; he was a broken man at twenty five and all at once I began to understand his psyche. But the storm had passed, perhaps a form of catharsis for him and I wondered how often he had played out this tragedy for his guests. He had married and subsequently divorced but had a fine daughter and had made a life for himself outside of sport, hosting guests in his ancestral home and now, even though he lived alone and appeared slightly unbalanced, he seemed to be doing OK.

He went inside and returned with two big heavy books, the size of telephone directories with pages ruled like a ledger and crammed full of handwriting. It was his precious guest books, containing over twenty years of visitor details, long essays, comments, sketches and even the occasional photo. He ran his finger down each page recalling particular guests and what had happened during their visits. This was his life now and it gave him much pleasure so we sat together for the next few hours, under a naked bulb, pouring over the pages well into the night. He remembered them all and finally, at his insistence, I drew (a very bad) map of my journey and my bike and made some brief, but sincere comments about his hospitality and character.

As I got up to turn in for the night, he asked me when I planned to leave and where I was headed. "The day after tomorrow, to Khiva" I told him precisely. He looked most concerned. "It is a big desert you have to cross, very hot, there is no water and it is very dangerous, over 400 kilometres, no petrol, nothing, and the road is awful."

Road, awful? Feeling somewhat qualified now as a judge of road quality and a little sceptical of his assertions, images of the Road of Bones and my experiences along it flashed through my mind now as I felt like saying, in Crocodile Dundee fashion, "That's not an awful road, this is an awful road", but the moment passed.
"Have you ever been there?" I enquired.
"Yes. I drove there once about ten years ago... when I had a car."

"And it is blisteringly hot – you must leave at dawn before the sun gets too high and take plenty of water", he added sternly. I also needed more petrol and I asked him about the situation here.
"Benzine – no! Is big problem here too."
"Don't worry. Movin John fix", he added confidently.

***

I woke late the next morning and stumbled out into the courtyard where Movin' John bounded out of his quarters again, as if he had simply been folded tightly back into his spring-loaded box by some unseen hand when we had parted company the previous night – but he had been busy, rising before dawn, catching taxis and buses and travelling deep into the countryside around Bukhara to fetch me a large (and very heavy) canister of petrol which he now showed me proudly. It was a full twenty litres and I could barely lift it. I was staggered at the lengths to which he had gone to get it for me. He wouldn't tell me exactly where he had got it or what it had cost him, but he supplied to me at a nominal price, taking the utmost pleasure in filling my tank, like an old fashioned pump attendant that you might find in a quiet country town.

I spent the morning performing some routine maintenance and attending to personal business, and in the afternoon headed out to explore the new town on foot. I wandered along the back alleys of the old city, past the synagogue and down a tiny alleyway where I stopped briefly to chat with some men building an extension to their modest mud brick home (with more mud bricks), before being ejected into the bright, open expanse of the new town, as if I had left one country and entered another altogether different one. It was classic Soviet cityscape with a sparse collection of soulless concrete towers, dormant and overgrown parks, lonely squares and empty boulevards, the starkness accentuated by the pancake flat earth and desert landscape. I wandered on alone past small shops from another era until I eventually found the displaced heart of the city in a modern covered market which bustled with colour and life and seemed to be the single source of sustenance and supply for the entire city. It was full of food, cheap clothes, utility goods and tired people hauling the big reinforced tri-colour plastic bags that always seem to annoyingly clog airport check-ins. All of this stood in stark contrast to the old city which from the outside, in the distance, appeared like a dense, medieval walled city. I hailed a taxi driver who became my chaperone for the rest of the afternoon. We drove out of town in his bombed-out Lada to the isolated and eccentric playground of the Emirs, where we wandered about under trellised rose gardens, past roaming peacocks and through the summer palace itself. The Palace buildings were an uneasy fusion of baroque and traditional Islamic architecture that housed an eclectic mix of art, exquisite Asian porcelain and jewellery, in dark gaudy rooms of fractured mirrors and modern stained glass. The Palace also contained one of the first Russian fridges ever built and an original electric light – all provided to captivate the Emir as the Russians eased him out of the Ark, the city, and public consciousness. We continued on to the harem and gigantic bathing pool, as large as a hockey field, where, according to legend, naked maidens frolicked under the gaze of the senile Emir, who, when had selected his next companion, threw her an apple and had her bathed in donkey's milk before their union.

***

After dinner I strolled around the Lyab-i-Hauz pool in the cool autumn evening and found a small general store with an old fashioned long glass counter running down one side under a wall of overflowing, but neatly arranged shelves full of tea, flour, rice and tins of food. It was run by two cherub-faced young men dressed in traditional white robes and skull caps who stood and smiled sweetly, holding hands and who touched each other gently, almost imperceptibly, as they moved about the shop silently filling my order. I bought a big bottle of water, sweets and a plastic bag full of biscuits for my trip to Khiva, which seemed to amuse these two sweethearts no end. As I turned to leave they huddled together giggling – it was the first hint of smouldering homosexuality on my entire trip and took my by surprise here. I left, found a street vendor and ate an ice cream on a bench under the watchful gaze of a stone camel.

That night, on Movin' John's counsel, I set my alarm for a cruel 4:30am – virtually the middle of the night for me – and proceeded to sleep fitfully, full of uneasy dreams and empty premonitions about sleeping late and woke naturally at 4:29am just in time to disable my alarm before it rang. It was pitch black in my room, but the courtyard was bathed in brilliant moonlight which flooded into my room as I slowly pushed open the heavy wooden doors. I found four large dirty bottles of water in a neat row just outside my room – about eight litres in total! I couldn't decide whether it was the bottles or their contents that were dirty as I examined them up close, appreciative of my host's efforts, but slightly disturbed that he thought I might need this much water today – what kind of desert was this anyway? I looked across and saw that the table had already been set and before I had reached my seat, Movin' John appeared, on cue and in costume, to deliver breakfast. As I ate, I looked up at the long thick cloudy band of stars that ran across the dome of inky black night sky above me, like a planetarium. I saw a shooting star, then another and suddenly felt very small.

After a long handshake followed by an even longer and firmer embrace from Movin' John, I rode away and out through the sleepy town as dawn was breaking, with just a few listless dogs, a wayward donkey cart and groggy street sweepers for company. It was cold and my fingers quickly became numb followed soon after by my legs which began to shudder uncontrollably, but, keen to make progress, I pressed on and rode out through bleak, dusty villages, full of bleary-eyed women and children off to harvest cotton. And, before long, all signs of life had retreated into the distance behind me as I came to the vast red sandy steppe of the Kyzyl-Kum Desert, where the warmth of the rising sun slowly began to penetrate my stone-cold limbs and frozen digits. I came to a large, windswept and heavily

300

fortified police checkpoint at the bottom of a long low hill where the road continued, climbing away skywards, like a giant stunt ramp. But today I was grounded, blocked by a posse of bored and belligerent officers who quickly surrounded me as I slowed to obey a lonely stop sign. I was interrogated at length and felt the full weight of their suspicions fall on me. I was accused of being a spy ("why else would you be here?") and warned to drive slowly and carefully across the desert "or else", and "we'll be watching you". I was eventually allowed to pass and rode slowly up and onto the flat scrubby treeless plain, a two-tone patchwork of dry red and olive green, divided almost precisely in half, to the distant horizon, by a rocky trail of asphalt. I checked my speedometer: still more than three hundred kilometres to go, but today I was in the zone, and in a dream-like sequence, floated above the road, enchanted by the spectrum of colours painted on the sky above and all around me, like the rainbow film on a soap bubble. Cloudless, and perfect, the colours of the sky astounded me; diffused by the low early morning sun hitting the desert atmosphere, they rose in a pinkish yellow haze at the horizon, through the palest white-green and then quickly on through a continuum of blues, finishing at a deep navy blue directly above me. And today I counted off distances in the outrageously large units of one hundred kilometres, where previously, on a good day, it might been ten or twenty, and now, just for a moment, I felt infinitely more confident than my first few tentative days on the road from Magadan where I had counted off individual kilometres, very, very slowly.

***

I stopped twice, at *two hundred* and *three hundred* kilometres respectively, and at each break wandered off into the small sand dunes to sit and sun myself and eat my biscuits and drink my water, disturbed only by a few lizards that scurried away quickly, skimming across the sand in their funny mechanical gait at my approach. There was no traffic on the road and it was almost perfectly silent, except for occasional zephyr rustling softly across the scrub. Eventually the desert receded, quickly replaced by fertile farmland and rustic villages as the road converged again with the Amu-Darya. This was the ancient Oxus – and today it still sustains a narrow corridor of habitation and cultivation running in a gentle arc to the north-west, where it peters out in a semiarid delta as it trickles into the rapidly receding Aral Sea. But the river here was full and wide and free flowing – albeit shallow and heavily silted – and I crossed it cautiously on a makeshift pontoon bridge of flat- bottomed barges, tied together and joined loosely by sliding metal ramps which sizzled like BBQ plates under the midday sun and moved dangerously underneath me as I negotiated each seam while battling the unforgiving and impatient oncoming traffic. But I didn't stop for fear of the rubber of my tyres and boots melting, and was soon safely across. I drove on through the modern, bustling but ultimately drab city-town of Urgench, before travelling the final twenty kilometres along the bizarre trolleybus route connecting the two towns. Massive and modern, it was an outrageous piece of expensive and unnecessary capital works designed solely to impress foreigners who had visited Khiva during its recent millennial celebrations and was now a white elephant.

***

The giant fortress of Ichan Kala, once home to a procession of barbaric tribal Khans and the scene of ugly Russian massacres, rose up out of the dusty Khivan cityscape to meet me like a Hollywood set, so perfectly were its crenulated walls and battlements preserved. Steep, smooth and unblemished, they ran away into the distance, with their golden teeth biting into an intense white-blue early afternoon desert sky. Beyond, I could see the substantial mosques, medrassahs and minarets of the inner city, rising above the walls, all painted from the same dusty golden brown palette with just a few splashes of aquamarine and turquoise tiling for relief. It was certainly the most subdued and subtle styling I had seen on my journey and the whole city appeared completely preserved; a time capsule in situ.

I circled slowly for a long time, but with no obvious vehicle entrance and no traffic either entering or leaving and with locals waving me hysterically in every direction at once, I boldly rode straight across the drawbridge and through the narrow passageway under the massive stone battlements of the front gates – and then immediately wished I hadn't. I felt like a human torpedo launched in a sea of fragile antiquity, an unwarranted act of aggression and certainly insensitive. It was quiet and subdued inside the city walls; a few drowsy locals – who looked more like Bedouins from central casting – were squatting in the slithers of shade around the fringes of a dusty medieval square, like a scene in still life. I slowed to walking pace and paddled my bike along with my feet, but still it echoed around the ancient mud walls like machine gun fire. A dog howled incessantly and jumped in tight circles at my arrival. Head down and red-faced, I paddled hard, squeezing between two ancient buildings, probing deeper into this living mausoleum. But this was a pedestrian-only city and there were steep tricky steps and narrow ledges to navigate – where bewildered locals watched on in fear and concern (mirroring my own) – until eventually, I spilled out onto the main thoroughfare; a wide dusty strip that ran along the East-West axis of the city, book-ended by two impressive gates. There were no other visitors in sight and excited shopkeepers ran up to me, greeting me warmly and exhorting me to buy their souvenirs in equal measure. They didn't seem at all perturbed by my appearance, sudden entrance or mode of transport, and matter-of-factly directed me to a travellers' hostel where I was able to secure my bike and then sit in a shady corner of a tranquil garden courtyard where I took a long lunch of stale bread, dips, plov and a pickled salad containing the most luscious tomatoes I had tasted since leaving home, each of which I savoured at length as their juicy flesh exploded in my mouth. Gazing into the cool green shade, slowly sipping sweet tea saw me slowly slipping into a meditative state; an afternoon of trudging about more temples, towers and churches under a hot sun was quickly losing its appeal. My consciousness was already saturated with enough images of Central Asian architecture to last a lifetime, but motivated by a solemn sense of duty I did take a whistlestop tour, but the presentation was cold and lifeless and jarred in comparison to Samarkand or Bukhara where the sites had been wholly or at least partly integrated with modern city life. All of this was reinforced by the career attendant at the first place I came to, who insisted emphatically that I buy a "day pass" for the city from a far-away ticket office (it was already after 4pm). But I couldn't help being entranced by the dazzling glazed blue-white tiles of the summer mosque of the Kukhna Ark, in fine hand- painted detail, like a giant fresco of Delft porcelain. And I found a strange morbid pleasure in studying the various execution techniques employed by the sadistic Khans, on display in the old city jail under the watchful gaze of sweet babushka who sat quietly in a corner knitting a colourful rug. The gruesome ingenuity was truly astounding, ranging from pits of deadly bugs, vats of boiling liquid, various applications of fire, wooden stakes, removal of body parts (while still alive) and included crowd participation, all designed to prolong an already excruciating death and provide grotesque, but loyalty-building entertainment. But most cruel was the treatment reserved for recalcitrant lovers, who were either, tied back to back and placed atop sharp wooden stakes and impaled slowly by gravity and their own tragic momentum, or buried up to the neck and forced to watch the execution of their partner before being stoned to death by an unforgiving crowd.

But it was wandering the backstreets of the little mud-brick suburb to the south – still inside the city walls – where I got a sense that the real life blood of Khiva was slowly returning to this museum city. Strewn with scenes of everyday life – young men repairing motorcycles and cars, women preparing food, dirty kids playing amongst the junk, dogs pawing hopefully at piles of rubbish, and old men, dishevelled and withered, sitting motionless over their walking sticks; it wasn't pretty but at least it was real.

Without thinking I found myself in the modern but empty tourist information centre, buried deep under the vaulted cloisters of another ancient medrassah where, after helping the young administrator and his female assistant fix a problem with their internet PC, I was invited to join them in the courtyard. There were no tourist shows tonight and hadn't been for many months, the young girl lamented as we sat on wicker furniture with tropical upholstery, by a castaway bar under a cool blue sunset sky. The administrator served me a cold local beer which I drank gladly, in spite of its taste. The girl introduced herself - her name was Mahmuda, she lived locally with her extended family and, belying her adolescent appearance, was university educated. I studied her closely; she had short thick raven hair, milk chocolate skin, large dark pools in her eyes, prominent and perfect white teeth and a broad but flat nose. She was pretty in a girlish way, and exuded innocence and naivety. She wore jeans, a plain cotton blouse and runners with cartoon characters on them – a picture of modernity in this museum town.

"You're not an Uzbek are you?" I pronounced boldly as I drained my bottle of beer. Taken aback, but curious she confirmed my suspicions. "You're right, but can you guess where I am from?"
"Iran?"
"No."
"Afghanistan?
"No."
"Turkmenistan?"
"No."

She certainly wasn't Russian, so I reached further a field, draining the long list of countries to the north, west and east, before giving up, exasperated by my failure.

"No, my family is originally from Pakistan. We migrated here a long, long time ago." It was just another example of the rich ethnic soup that had been brewing across the region for millennia.

Suddenly a young European woman traveller entered the courtyard, approached and greeted Mahmuda warmly. Sophie, a recent acquaintance, was a French backpacker from Brittany passing through Khiva on an overland journey to China. She was travelling alone and seemed to be a beacon of hope for Mahmuda who went on to explain how she was trapped in her small existence here; a grown and educated woman still living at home with her parents and extended family with severe restrictions on her activities and freedom. We talked about travel and of her life here in Khiva and I sensed Mahmuda's deep longing for independence and travel – wonderful dreams, but unlike ours, beyond her reach. Dusk came quickly and a cold breeze chilled us. Mahmuda invited us home to meet her parents and to share a meal and so we happily skipped out of the East gate together and scurried along the dark suburban streets, full of people returning home from work and preparing for the evening. There were streetlights that barely registered, but the place had an air of normality noticeably absent on the other side of the city walls, whose shadows we walked in now.

Mahmuda's home was a low-slung rambling concrete bungalow, a rabbit warren of rooms accessed from a long dark central corridor that connected the kitchen, at one end of the house, with the communal living room where we sat now, at the other. The walls were a pale blue-grey concrete render and almost bare except a few prized decorations. A TV flickered in the far corner and naked bulbs hung from the ceiling casting everything in a harsh light; more like an austere dormitory than a family home. Mahmuda introduced us both to the crippled babushka that had let us in.

"This is my Mother."

"My sisters are much older than me", she added, sensing our confusion.

"My three sisters and their husbands and their children live here with us. Each family has one room and I sleep in the kitchen", Mahmuda said blankly. The old woman stood about four and a half feet tall in her stockinged feet, and I bent low to greet her. She held and patted my hand for a long time and whispered something unintelligible and barely audible through her false teeth into my ear, but it was delivered with such warmth and sincerity, that I smiled and nodded encouragingly. Mahmuda led us to the centre of the room where we all struggled to sit at the hobbit-sized table which stood no more than twelve inches off the ground. The old woman shuffled away along the corridor and disappeared into the kitchen, returning a few minutes later with a tray of their best food for us. We sat and ate crunchy stale nons, a bunch of withered green grapes and drank a pot of warm sweet tea graciously, as Mahmouda explained to her mother who we were and what we were doing. Her mother simply sat on her tightly folded legs, nodded and smiled throughout, never lifting her hands from her lap. But this was Mahmuda's Trojan horse, and she pressed ahead, emphasising to her Mother how Sophie – a woman of the same age – was travelling alone, on a journey which had already included a month travelling across the darkly dangerous Iran. The old woman shook her head, scolding her daughter and they began to argue heatedly. Hearing the commotion, an old man shuffled into the room. He was withered to the bone, frail and gaunt, unshaven and wore threadbare clothes and a dirty woollen cap and had an unchanging vacant expression on his face which he maintained throughout our entire encounter.

"And this is my Father", said Mahmuda tentatively.

"He was injured picking cotton ten years ago and hasn't worked since." The old man could barely lift his sunken eyes to meet ours as we were introduced, and he remained silent, even after we greeted him. I didn't want to probe any further, but it seemed his accident had also affected his mind. Sensing it was time to bring our tense tea party to an end, Mahmuda quickly ushered us back through the front door and out into the fresh night as she barked something at her parents before slamming the door shut on them.

We walked back towards the walled city and took our dinner at an empty outdoor restaurant, under a gazebo overlooking a long pool, where the breeze whipped across our plates, instantly cooling both us and our meals. Sophie and Mahmuda ate like sparrows and I enjoyed finishing their cold mounds of plov as they chatted happily. Sophie told us about her relatively "boring" life in seaside Brittany, lived with the freedom and choices that Mahmuda could only dream about. Mahmuda told us how she had saved what was left of her wages (after supporting her family) for a long time, before disobeying her parents and travelling to Tashkent on her own to obtain a passport and visa (to which she was legally entitled), only to be told flatly by oafish government officials there that "you are a single woman, you cannot travel, nowhere, never - go home and get married you whore!" And this attitude was entirely consistent with her parents' wishes and the deeply held mores of Uzbek culture that demanded daughters stay with their parents until married – happily or otherwise, and any woman who did otherwise was immediately held in deep suspicion and despised for being unchaste. But she was a strong-willed emancipated woman, a loyal and loving daughter trapped in a tight cultural bind, caught between old and new worlds, respectful of both, and ironically a virtual prisoner in the tourist fortress where she worked every day. And her daily routine, without variation, traced a small arc between her overcrowded dormitory home and the lonely underground desk where she offered the occasional tourists "unique cultural shows and excursions" – which in reality were unchanging routines delivered by equally bound young Uzbek women. Even the advent of new technology had only served to strengthen the binds to home with Mahmuda tethered to her anxious family via her mobile phone, reporting in throughout the day to confirm her safety and whereabouts.

Across the lake at a large open hall, an upmarket Uzbek wedding was in full swing, with a huge video screen at one end instantly projecting embarrassing moments that might otherwise have been missed, to all the participants. There were more than a hundred guests, dominated mostly by senior women making speeches and dancing in the long and complicated multi-part ceremonies that are Uzbek weddings. We watched on with great interest, but for Mahmuda this was like a dagger to her heart; like many modern Western women she wanted a career, the opportunity to travel and live on her own terms before committing to marriage. And it wasn't that she objected to marriage – in fact she looked forward to the prospect – but she wanted some choice in the timing, her partner and the circumstances.

* * *

In the morning I took my breakfast at the hostel with two artists from Tashkent, a roly poly Russian woman, whose girth was only exceeded by her good humour, and her companion, a more reserved woman of Korean descent. Although still relatively young, Marina had already inflated into the babushka container that, tragically, all Russian women seemed genetically programmed to fill. She laughed at every turn and kept repeating "How wonderful, how wonderful!" as I told them both of my journey from Magadan. They went on to tell me how difficult their lives had become, and how they struggled to make ends meet as interest in, and appreciation of, art in post-Soviet Uzbekistan had waned, replaced by more immediate and materialistic gratification; being an artist had once been a respectable profession with good prospects and surety, but today it was akin to a life sentence of struggle and relative poverty.

Later in morning as I prepared to leave, I saw Marina sitting on a tiny three legged fold-able stool at her easel sketching an old house that glowed golden in the early morning rays of the sun. She sat matron-like in a navy blue and white polka-dot smock and wore a wide brimmed straw sun hat tied under her chin in a thick white ribbon and wore dark sunglasses, like a high society Edwardian lady out on a Sunday drive. She didn't notice me, and when I returned shortly after she had gone. I pushed off and rode back through modern Urgench, back across the sizzling pontoon bridge and out into Kyzyl-Kum desert again. But I was further west now, heading away from the Amu-Darya, and the landscape here was utterly lifeless; drained of all sustenance, there were no trees, no scrub, no people, no animals, no buildings, nothing, just low blank hills of dark gravel and grey sand, the bleakness punctuated only by a single rail line cut into the hills, dead straight, like thick ruled lines etched in charcoal across the blank landscape. A hot wind picked up and blew in strong gusts across the road making riding difficult and the heat set off a painful throbbing in my backside of accumulated saddle soreness from months of riding – I didn't stop and neither did the pain, but I did stand on my foot pegs and rode with the wind between my legs for most of the journey for some relief.

Into The Twilight Zone

Nukus appeared like a mirage on the horizon after the heat and pain of the desert but failed almost completely to deliver upon any of its real or imagined promises. I quickly got the sombre feel of the place and wondered whether its moniker was actually a plaintive cry for nuclear annihilation from its inhabitants. For it was a town of the living dead where tumbleweeds rolled across huge overgrown empty squares, the monotony broken only by a handful of ugly run-down tenements and drab government buildings scattered randomly, shooting straight up out of the otherwise flat earth, like blocks on a child's Lego board. The streets were eerily quiet and the town seemed to have no centre and certainly no heart; it was an utterly characterless and cheerless place. I was in the capital of Karakalpakstan, notionally an autonomous republic within Uzbekistan, where the Kazakhs then the Soviets had shoehorned this colourful collection of clans, who, although Turkic, are actually closer to Mongols in appearance. Now one of the poorest ethnic groups within Uzbekistan, the Karakalpaks suffer from extreme unemployment, desperately poor living conditions and devastatingly bad health – poisoned by the wind-borne salt and chemicals from the dried bed of the Aral Sea and the lethal fall out from the testing of chemical and biological weapons that was conducted in secret in the nearby desert by the Soviets. They are best known for their colourful and vibrant culture, most distinctively expressed in their costumes and decorations which, incredibly, are made by their women from just the natural materials and scraps available to them in the desert. But none of that was visible today as I patrolled up and down the broken avenues, past crumbling, nameless buildings in replica, looking for the hotel promised in my guidebook.

Eventually, totally disoriented, I pulled up in front of a tall foreboding concrete building that appeared more hospital than hotel. I parked my bike securely and wandered in, walked across the magnificent parquetry floor of the foyer and up to the large service desk which was dominated by an impressive bank of large red LED's that flashed slowly, counting away the seconds and minutes of someplace somewhere far away. Perhaps it was a Doomsday Clock, I thought darkly, counting down the minutes until the four horsemen of the Apocalypse would come storming across the barren wasteland to relieve the miserable inhabitants of this godforsaken town? Or perhaps it was just a quirky throwback to a bygone era when all the regions of the Soviet Union – regardless of their actual location – ran on Moscow time, and it had been preserved here, like the rest of this place, in permanent stasis.

The massive foyer was almost totally devoid of colour and life except for one corner full of oversized 1960's style armchairs and lounges where patients (or guests?) mingled and dozed as a TV droned on in the background. There was a faint whiff of formaldehyde in the air and men in white coats circled as a steady stream of sickly men and women came and went. I wondered whether I had in fact stumbled into a hospital, or perhaps a sanatorium, or even a hospice. I placed my helmet and gloves gently on the counter and asked the disinterested man on duty, who sat picking his teeth with the intensity of a gold prospector, for directions to the alleged hotel – or any form of accommodation in the vicinity for that matter. He laughed hard and called a woman from an inner office, who was obviously his wife, before welcoming me rather coldly to the Hotel Nukus.

"Do you have a room?" I asked with some trepidation.
"Yes"

A long pause followed in this theatre of the absurd. The disinterested man looked sideways at his wife who moistened her lips ever so slightly before nodding back knowingly to her husband. At the back of my mind darkly disturbing thoughts of organ harvesting or some other equally evil and visceral operation flashed through my mind. I looked hopefully out through the glass doors for any sign of War, Pestilence, Famine or even Death; I was alone in a remote corner of a landlocked police state, surrounded by a poisoned desert in a town of zombies and was probably one of the few healthy visitors they had ever seen. But perhaps it was just me who was slowly losing touch with reality. Perhaps the sizzling desert sun had soft boiled my brain on the ride over from Khiva earlier in the day.

"Do you have a room where I can stay tonight?" I enunciated slowly – adding quickly, "Just.......one ....night"

Without responding he waved me away, and his wife, another member of the Korean Diaspora, who appeared to be the cleaning lady, bellhop, maintenance man and receptionist all rolled into one, walked me up the once-grand central staircase to the second floor, where we played out the inane charade of inspecting a potential room. What on earth could I possibly say? "This one isn't big enough!", or "I want a room with a
balcony!", or "This bed is too hard/short/soft/lumpy!", for there were another four hundred and ninety nine rooms, all identical to this one, available to me. And anyway, my requirements were now so basic

that all it needed to be acceptable was some protection from the weather, something just a little softer, cleaner and warmer than the bare earth to lie on, and running water (of any colour or temperature) – anything beyond this was a bonus. These criteria met, I thanked her and took the key, completing our transaction. I inspected the bathroom a little closer then leapt back to the door. "Can I have a towel please?" I shouted down the hall as she scurried away. "Just... .one... clean... towel... please", but it was too late, she had gone.

I quickly unloaded my gear into the room and headed out into the bleak and dusty sunbaked streetscape where incredibly, I immediately found a place to eat, hidden behind a heavily fortified, thick wooden snow door, buried deep inside the ground floor of an otherwise derelict building, in a small gated yard full of waist-high weeds and rubbish. Once inside though, I felt as if I had been transported directly into the heart of the Moscow or Tbilisi underworld, or dropped into a scene straight from a Damon Runyon tale; it was a dark and richly appointed room, smoky, windowless, with tall wooden booths covertly cocooning each of the long tables so that each setting was almost like a private room. Candles flickered softly, bathing the pods in a warm light and shimmering off the golden-backed flocked wallpaper that covered most of the walls. Plush velvet curtains hung over the doors and tropical plants filled empty spaces. There was no Lemon Drop Kid or Izzy Cheesecake, but there was a cast of equally colourful characters discretely taking their lunch, huddled in hushed conversations over their meals, some clutching bored moles like dispensable fashion accessories. A pretty waitress stood to attention in front of a long, fully stocked bar and showed me to a booth where I enjoyed a large private smorgasbord – one of the best meals of my entire journey.

***

After lunch I stole my way into the Central Bank of Uzbekistan in a vain attempt to buy some desperately needed local currency, clearly mistaken in my belief that a Central Bank would actually have a supply of national bank notes on hand. A lonely guard with a large automatic rifle sat on duty in the cold dank and empty banking chamber. Dirty water – possibly effluent, judging from the pungent odour – oozed slowly out of a long crack in the bare concrete floor. Perhaps out of shame the guard tried to persuade me that the bank was closed, but I persisted until he eventually showed

311

me into a tiny office with a high counter, behind which four local women pretended to be busy.

"Can you change one hundred dollars?" I demanded, still reeling from the sewer smell.

"Do you have anything smaller?" said the frightened local girl behind the counter.

"Fifty?"

"Smaller" she whispered back at me.

"Twenty?"

"No"

"Ten?"

"OK"

She produced a small desk calculator and insisted on walking me through her calculations – the veracity of which I was required to acknowledge by signing a large receipt – before quickly stuffing the small wad of crisp red script into my wallet and sprinting outside to fill my lungs with clean air.

But there was a ray of sunshine – indeed an abundant oasis of beauty – in all of this desolation and base ugliness; The Savitsky Museum, which held over 50,000 pieces of once-banned avant-garde and post-avantgarde Soviet art from the 1920s and 30s. Hailed as one of the world's greatest collections, it had been clandestinely amassed at great personal risk by the Museum's founder, Igor Savitsky, a Muscovite who originally came to Karakalpakstan as a young man to help record archaeological and ethnographic expeditions. He fell in love with the desert landscape and its people and secretly sought out proscribed painters as he attempted to collect, archive and display their condemned works. The massive collection was his life work, highlighting the great body of work carried out underground, under constant threat of exile, labour camps or worse, which ran precisely counter to the prevailing doctrine of state-endorsed Socialist Realism. It also included a vast collection of Uzbek fine arts, applied Karakalpak folk art and ancient art from Khorezm which was equally extraordinary.

I approached the smartly dressed woman behind the counter at the ticket booth inside the modern and impressive foyer of the museum and paid the nominal entrance fee. A few people milled around, but they were all employees or local art aficionados, all mature and striking independent looking women, and there wasn't a man in sight, like some modern Amazonian society.

"And would you like a guide today?" the young woman behind the counter asked innocently. Wary of being fleeced, but feeling desperately sorry for these people in this miserable place I agreed, whereupon she immediately jumped up out of her seat, shut the ticket counter and came out to greet me. Now I saw her in full view; she wore an impressive corporate navy blue suit and skirt with a perfectly starched white blouse. She was an exotic Eurasian with pale skin, wonderful bone structure, dark eyes and shiny dark hair cut short in a stylish Charleston wedge. She stuck out her delicate hand and shook mine firmly. "Welcome to the Savitsky Museum. I am your guide, Lara. Let's go" – it wasn't an offer, it was an order – and with that she turned on her patent heels and fine stockinged legs and marched off up the stairs. There were no other visitors and I spent the next three hours enthralled as she earnestly (and faultlessly) introduced and explained each and every item on display. Lara was an art school graduate and knew the collection and its origins intimately. It was an indulgence and I enjoyed every minute of it. She happily answered each of my mostly inane questions and even went to great lengths to explain the principles of Zoroastrianism when I had asked about the decorative stone boxes full of human bones on display. Fire and Earth were considered too sacred for the dead, she told me seriously, so bodies were left out on hilltops for vultures and the weather to clean the flesh off the bones whereupon they were collected and placed in the Ossuary... I glazed over at the detail; I was just happy to be somewhere clean, cool and surrounded by stimulating works of modern and ancient art. We continued on to the display of magnificent wedding headdresses. More like ornamental suits of armour, they consisted of felt helmets covered with red cloth, and were richly decorated with fine hand worked metal plates, pendants and coral jewels and beads. Handmade by each bride, they remained their most precious possession throughout their lives. Finally, I drank in the vibrant colours and shapes and scenes of life that jumped off the avant-garde canvases we surveyed at length.

Sadly, my tour ended and I left the Museum in the late afternoon. I strolled dreamily across a broken concrete plaza feeling now somewhat anesthetised against my surroundings. I wondered at the incongruity of what I had seen today and whether there was some great cosmic yin and yang at play here, with the great ugliness and the great beauty of this place finely balanced in a perfect equilibrium. But my quiet contemplation was cut short by a sharp shriek of pain, as one of the two young boys I had just passed, playing in a decaying fountain, had slipped on the wet concrete and cracked his head. I watched with concern as the boy got up slowly, clutching his head and wailing. I offered to help, but the boy jumped up frightened and

313

ran off into the bleakness in a scene that reminded me of Munch's Scream; it was that kind of place.

***

I walked the streets, traversing the small city grid and eventually came to a neighbourhood of sorts; dusty tree-lined avenues where street vendors, utility stores, butchers, bakers and cobblers all jostled for meagre takings – but it was all plain, ugly and grim. No one smiled or seemed happy, and life itself appeared to be a heavy burden they all carried with resentment. I wandered into a surprisingly well stocked general store and bought a litre of milk and some promising looking chocolate wafers from another nascent babushka with plump rosy cheeks whose eyes were buried deep in the folds of skin, like two small raisins lost in pastry dough. She wore an austere white coat-uniform and pillbox hat and looked as if she'd just clocked off from the local nuclear plant. Unfortunately the wafers tasted as if they too had been irradiated beyond recognition, so lacking were they in substance and flavour; they were wholly unfulfilling, but I didn't care, it only made me feel even sorrier for the locals – even the treats here were hollow and disappointing.

I was about to enter the whacky, closed state of Turkmenistan where, from all accounts, any contact with the outside world would be impossible, like being on the dark side of the moon, so, keen to contact home before flying off the radar, I scoured the ghost town looking for any means of communication, eventually finding the gloomy, cavernous Post and Telecoms hall where the skeleton staff did their very best to dissuade me from using any of their alleged services. It was an old style operation where you completed application forms in triplicate and paid in advance for calls on a best-efforts basis. The lonely clerk behind the counter shrugged her shoulders indifferently and pointed at the row of tired phone booths that sat forlornly in one corner, barricaded up with out of order notices plastered across them. Unperturbed, I returned to the hotel where my hosts gave cryptic directions to a "club" where they felt sure I would find what I wanted; "Past the soup kitchen near the Railway station and down the alleyway behind the bus stop..."

Feeling strangely liberated – or perhaps succumbing to the melancholy and resignation that seemed to be seeping into my marrow like a cancer from my surroundings – I rode through the city dangerously, at dusk in just my T-shirt and jeans, stopping and frightening bewildered locals asking for directions, until finally pulling up outside a ramshackle wooden hall, within easy walking distance of the hotel. A small faded sign above its lop-sided doorway, weathered almost beyond recognition, simply read "war games". So this was the club. Inside was a dark maze of unkempt rooms and sunken, warped floors, inhabited by a grimy collection of adolescent urchins, most of who sat at a long bank of school desks, separated by low partitions, in a central windowless room. The air was charged with testosterone as the boys sat glued to their computer screens firing off deadly virtual salvos at each other in cold blooded networked electronic war games. The operation was managed by a young but overweight and greasy Fagin-like character who sat in a rich leather-upholstered swivel chair behind a large wooden desk near the doorway, monitoring all that went on with his dark beady eyes. I settled into my tiny space, perched on a child-size chair and typed out a long message, but couldn't help be distracted by the young kid next to me who fidgeted endlessly and periodically let out furtive sighs. Intrigued and annoyed, I poked my head around the little partition to tell him off, only to find him and a gang of fellow imps – none of them older than my own young son – sitting dispassionately watching hardcore pornography that they had just downloaded from the internet. I looked at the fat Fagin who nodded and smiled slyly back at me, encouraging me to join them.

I finished my email quickly and left. As I stepped out into the murky night, a cold breeze whistled through the trees above me, and, just for a moment, I thought I heard a faint, whining "Nuke us... nuke us... .nuke us...." carried on the wind, imploring some far away invisible hand to press that big red button; it was a disturbing end to a strange day.

The Kingdom of Turkmenbashi

I slept uneasily, worrying about my next appointment; according to government regulations, foreigners with motor vehicles were not permitted to travel across Turkmenistan and had to be escorted – at all times. It was a condition of my visa so I had dutifully organised a government-endorsed guide whom I was instructed to meet at precisely 9am the next morning at the border post of Konye-Urgench; it wasn't far, but I couldn't be late. I rose early the next morning (all body parts intact) and took my breakfast alone in the darkened and gloomy hotel restaurant. It was another richly appointed room, heavy with wood panelling, with upholstered bench seats in booths running along each wall. It was past eight o'clock but the curtains were still not drawn as I stumbled toward a table. I sat down and immediately picked up the impressive menu. Vinyl-bound and with many pages, it overflowed with rich offerings which I read with growing excitement in the half light, my eyes dancing down the page quickly as I built up my order: smoked fish, caviar, blini, rye bread and sour cream. A surly young waitress who looked as if she'd just finished a long but unsuccessful night at a local nightclub approached. She had badly pock-marked skin, dark circles under her eyes like tattoos, peroxide hair and pancake makeup. She wore a hot pink jumper, skin-tight acid wash jeans and dirty-white high heels. I placed my order. She looked down at me wearily, over her notepad like I was from another planet

"No, no, no, no, no.............. none of this is available" she said slowly and with just the slightest trace of malice.

"I see. What do you have?"

"Eggs, bread and tea"

"Do you have anything else?" I asked hopefully, waving my hand vaguely at the thick wad of pages in menu.

"No, nothing. You can have eggs, bread and tea".

"OK then, I'll have eggs, bread and tea".

"One?"

"One what?"

"Breakfast is one egg, one piece of bread and one cup of tea. If you want any more, you will have to pay extra".

"One will be fine thank you." I said cheerily as she scribbled what seemed like a short story in her tiny notepad before teetering away toward the kitchen.

I packed quickly and carried all my gear in one trip to my bike, down the large staircase, across the foyer and outside, like a deranged Sherpa. An old dishevelled man, whom I hadn't noticed before, emerged groggily from the foyer – where clearly he had spent night – and chased me outside, claiming his reward for allegedly guarding my bike all night (I didn't want to imagine from what). I could have pointed to the thick steel rope and heavy lock that I had used to secure my bike to the hotel foundations, but his sad face and wretched appearance were too pitiful so instead I just smiled and handed him a clutch of bank notes, thanking him politely for his service. I checked my watch – it was 8:30, just enough time to get to the border. I secured everything quickly and bade them both farewell – for now the hotel manager had joined us, curious about my bike and my departure. I was anxious to put Nukus well and truly behind me, but like a dream where you're pursued by an unseen evil but feel like you're running through treacle, the town was closing in on me now, tightening its grip. I squeezed the ignition and turned the throttle, but instead of the wonderfully comforting soft throbbing of internal combustion, all I got was a hoarse rasping cough and soft splutter and then a cold silence. I tried and tried and tried again with no success. Oh bugger. They both looked at me blankly, as if this was somehow not unexpected. I rested my arms on the handlebars and rested my head on them gently and closed my eyes – selfishly absorbed in my own misfortune. There was nothing left to do but push, so I mounted my bike and slowly heaved it forward with firm strides, pushing past my sleepy-eyed sentry and the now-bewildered hotelier. There was a large open area in front of the hotel where I paddled up and down repeatedly, desperately trying to build enough momentum for a clutch start – all of which ultimately failed. I looked at my watch – 8:45; I certainly wouldn't be meeting anyone, anywhere anytime today at this rate. Eventually my two comrades took pity on me and, without saying a word, came over and began pushing me tirelessly around the square until, after many failed attempts, the bike eventually groaned hesitantly into life. Exhausted, they stood breathless and steaming in the cold morning air, but smiled proudly as they waved me away merrily, and suddenly, I felt bad about my tainted perception of Nukus; I realised that like everywhere else I had been, people were almost always good at heart and predisposed to help a fellow human in need – the only difference here was the extent to which they had been worn down and hardened and had had the life almost completely sucked out of them by their environment and their bleak, empty prospects.

I rode cautiously through the depressing outskirts of Nukus, protecting my precious mechanical power as if it were the Olympic flame, but I suspected something deeper and more complex than just a cold start lay behind my problems as I headed nervously toward my rendezvous – very, very, very late. I headed south, crossing the Amu Darya for a final time, before passing over a lonely railway track and riding under the shadow of a massive necropolis that clung to the steep slopes of an otherwise bald hill; farewelled by chorus of dead souls – a fitting end to my visit. My time in Nukus had been a surreal experience, like a day trip to the Twilight Zone, and this morning I felt relatively "lucky" to be escaping to whacky Turkmenistan, the bizarre but resource-rich hermit state of Central Asia, dominated the enigmatic but profoundly corrupt Saparmyrat Niyazov, a self-styled cult of personality leader, who ironically, in a bitter twist of translation is known as Turkmenbashi – the "leader" of all Turkmen. An orphan without tribal connections, he had been appointed by Gorbachev in the dying days of the Soviet Union. He had stayed under the radar, following the Moscow line without question, and when the Soviet Union collapsed he simply re-labelled himself a democrat, tightened his grip on power and extended state control over virtually all aspects of life in Turkmenistan. And it wasn't long before statues, monuments and huge portraits of the man began appearing everywhere – by the will of the people of course. Today Turkmenistan is a deeply disturbing place where civil liberties are illusory at best, where the media is in reality an arm of the Ministry of Information, where the arts barely extend beyond traditional dancing and carpet making, and where the field of literature consists almost entirely of the works of the President himself. In his self-declared magnum opus Rukhnama, or "Book of Soul", Turkmenbashi sets out his bizarre and twisted version of Turkmen history, culture and spirituality – a volume of work which now forms a national curriculum and is the basis of university entrance exams.

But all of these delights awaited me beyond the quiet border post where I pulled up now. Nothing stirred. A teenage soldier strolled leisurely behind a heavy barricade, blocking the road ahead. I asked whether I could proceed.

"The border is closed" he said dismissively.

"When will it be open?"

"Perhaps today, maybe tomorrow, who knows?"

I didn't bother explaining that I was running late to meet someone, for the notion was simply absurd. Reluctantly, I turned off my engine and sat back on my bike and waited. A young farmer pulled up beside me on his donkey and we eyed off each others' transport in silence as we waited hopefully for any signs of life ahead of us.

"You know there is no fuel there" he said casually, nodding toward the shanty town beyond the dusty fields in the distance.

"There is no fuel until Ashgabat" he added darkly; petrol was even scarcer in this barren corner of Uzbekistan than in Bukhara or Samarkand, and I had run down my tank so that it was now almost empty. I had counted on being able to re-fuel just across the border in oil-rich Turkmenistan, but sadly while there was plenty of it in the ground, none of it was available here as petrol. Ashgabat was hundreds of kilometres away, and beyond Konye Urgench it was just more endless empty desert – five hundred kilometres of more frikkin dead-dull desert. The farmer fed his donkey some sugar cubes and pointed to a spot behind me where three old Uzbek men had set up shop dealing benzine from the trunk of their car. I didn't bother asking the price and ordered all they had which they happily supplied in a heady cocktail of fuel siphoned directly from their tank mixed with all of the coloured bottles of fuel in their stockpile; "Where did it come from?", "What quality was it?", and more disturbingly, "Why was each bottle of fuel a different shade of red, green or yellow?" were all questions for another day. I paid them quickly upon which they immediately shut down their operation, slapped each other hard on the back and celebrated wildly as they sped away.

Fortunately, the border post was now slowly awakening and I was permitted to proceed, riding tentatively out across the eerily silent no mans' land towards the small gated compound of stone buildings where I was to spend the next three hours battling the most mind-bogglingly arcane bureaucracy I had encountered on my entire trip. All of the other border crossings I had completed on my journey suddenly paled into insignificance; there were forms to complete in triplicate, a detailed inventory of my possessions, my itinerary – both completed and planned down to the day, my solemn promise (sworn to the commander of the border post), to leave the country at the date and time and location of his choosing, an insurance levy, a "disinfection" fee, etc, etc.

"Are you going to spray my bike?" I enquired, concerned about my own health.
"No, what for?" (bewildered look)
"Disinfection"
"What disinfection?"

And so it went. And even though fuel was ridiculously cheap in Turkmenistan – just a few cents a litre in its crippled and hermetically sealed economy – this benefit vanished like a mirage in the desert as I sat opposite the serious young officer who ran his index finger across an old and heavily annotated official map; "Konye Urgench to ... Darvaza... two hundred and thirty kilometres... Darvaza to ... Ashgabat... two hundred and seventy kilometres... seventy five dollars please" Disingenuously, I pointed out that it was I who should in fact be receiving a rebate from the State as my fuel tank was almost full – but the subtle logic of my argument was lost on this simple and overzealous young man.

I was shuttled between buildings with a bulging portfolio of papers like a barrister hauling files to a high court challenge; I completed forms in one building, was escorted across the large compound to another smaller hut where another officer would stamp and authorise my papers, keeping a copy, giving me a copy and returning the original to my escort, before I returned to the first building to complete the next form. And so on. And then there was the fee for calculating all the fees and completing all the paperwork!

Through all of this a young soldier in white overalls, who was painting the huts in a vibrant shade of sky blue from a foot-powered spray pump, watched on perplexed as I criss-crossed the compound in this complex ritual.

Some hours later though, after all my paperwork had been completed, I was ready for the final hurdle in this bureaucratic marathon: "certification", where all of my papers would be validated, I would pay all monies owing to the State and, hopefully, have my passport stamped allowing me entry into this crazy place. I was escorted back to the main hut and presented to the chief paper-pusher who unfortunately (for both of us), was an obsessive compulsive with way too much time on his hands, marooned at this remote and infrequently-used border post. A small man with a weak face, he had smooth skin that had never been troubled by a razor and wore his dark hair oiled and combed severely back off his forehead with a laser-guided part down one side. He wore an impeccably ironed, crisp khaki uniform dominated by a large ceremonial belt from which hung a string of ornate wooden-handled rubber stamps, each encased in their own private leather pouch. Incongruously, he sat at a large pock-marked wooden table with three oafish soldiers where he fulfilled his solemn duty of certifying the completed paperwork of all travellers – without his approval I could not proceed – and he knew it. I looked him in the eye. He twitched and flexed the fingers in his right (stamping) hand like a gunslinger before a shootout. He took my papers and dealt them into neat little piles around the table in front of him as if in a deadly serious game of high-stakes poker. He picked up each pile in turn, and tapped each bundle into the table repeatedly until he was happy with their order and alignment – an act from which he clearly derived immense pleasure. Each bundle had a cover sheet which he scrutinised at length and with great suspicion before slowly removing one of the special stamps from his holster, lifting it up to the light, examining it for flaws, licking then inking it (always three times), and finally, positioning it carefully on edge at forty five degrees to the paper while he carefully adjusted its position ahead of committing it to paper, as if he were a heart surgeon about to make his opening incision or thread a camel through the eye of a needle. "Between the lines, inside the boxes, perfectly inked, legible and upright", I could almost read the words on his deeply furrowed brow. He was perspiring now and as he pressed each stamp, he licked his lips in nervous concentration before lifting them away to reveal his work, which he sat back and admired, exhausted – like an artist – with even greater satisfaction. He repeated this agonising procedure for each clutch of papers – cleaning his instruments slowly and methodically between stampings – until finally he reached the last bundle where he progressed happily, until the final stamping, where, after lifting the stamp from the page, his expression suddenly transformed and he went rigid, as if he had just been struck between the shoulder blades with a pick axe – for incredibly, he had delivered the final seal upside down! Upside down! He was beside himself; the blood drained from his face and he began to shake slowly, at first, as the full impact of his error drove deep into his psyche. Suddenly his comrades, shaken from their stupor, rose to restrain him. Tears welled in his eyes and I looked away quickly before he caught my gaze. Unfortunately, the frenzy inside the hut had distracted the young soldier outside who by now was absentmindedly spraying blue paint in long slow strokes across the window pane, gradually closing out the view. And so the curtains closed on my first taste of fickle Turkmen bureaucracy. I quickly paid my dues, had my passport stamped and was ushered out of the hut with my bundle of papers flapping in the wind and waved away.

Fifty metres beyond the border a tall athletic middle-aged man in jeans, wearing a fluorescent green T-shirt, a denim baseball cap and sneakers standing beside a 4WD flagged me down. "I am your guide, Dimitry. Welcome to Turkmenistan" he said warmly as he shook my hand powerfully. He was square-jawed with chiselled features and strong and sure in the no-nonsense Russian way and I liked him immediately. I told him why I had been delayed. "I am sorry about my country and these silly rules. Come, let's go" and we were off.

***

We spent the next few hours walking the hard-baked plain of ancient Gurjang, capital of Khorezm, once a centre of regional power, trade, ideas, religion and scientific study that rivalled Samarkand. But today it was just a barren expanse save for a few crumbling mausoleums, tombs and minarets that had somehow withstood the scorched earth policies of both Genghis Khan and Timur, whose armies rolled through here in relatively quick succession in the middle ages, slaughtering and/or abducting the entire population and levelling the place. As we wandered amongst the rubble and ruins Dimitry casually began delivering an in- depth history of the region across the last two millennia. He had an encyclopaedic knowledge of all the significant events, people and dates and delivered his epic monologue on a take it or leave it basis; my level of interest was of no concern to him, and today, in a strangely transcendental mood, it was more of a background track as I floated above and beyond my immediate surroundings.

The whole place was like an unsupervised archaeological dig with shards of pottery and broken bones scattered in piles of loose topsoil around us. To demonstrate the immediacy of it all, Dimitry scooped up a handful of rubble letting the dust slowly sieve through his large fingers, revealing pieces of brilliantly decorated glazed pottery – perhaps and urn or a vase. Surely this wasn't genuine, I asked, incredulous, "Of course – there are places like this all over Turkmenistan. It is our history", he said nonchalantly, idly scattering the pieces back into a nearby hummock. But he wasn't a Turkman and I asked about his origins. "My grandparents were invited to settle in the Turkmen SSR in the 1920's and my family has been here ever since" he said euphemistically, alluding to the forced Sovietisation of this far-flung corner of the Empire, where native Russians were sent to "settle" the nomadic and recalcitrant tribes and to collectivise farming and plant massive tracts of cotton in an ultimately ill-fated modernisation program.

We continued on and came to a grove of wishing trees at the base of a small steep hill. Lifeless, except for their shredded fabric leaves that carried the hopes and dreams of the desperate locals, it was more like a modern art installation with the smooth and sinewy polished grey deadwood limbs lashed together and rooted in rusted oil drums to give them some purchase on the hard earth. The multi-coloured leaves fluttered silently, dappling the hard desert light, like flecks of colour in an impressionist painting. It reminded me of the fishing trip

I had taken with Big Mama and Zhenya on the Lena River north of Yakutsk, where we had stopped at a similarly sacred site and she had tied a piece of her scarf to another wishing tree. We walked up the short steep hill, following a well worn rut in the crusty earth. Topping the mound, we looked back over the dust-bowl panorama below us before trudging up to the summit where we found a bizarre collection of scenes set in the dusty topsoil behind low makeshift picket fences. Each contained an assortment of plastic dolls along with a kitsch collection of everyday items in miniature, laid out in scenes of basic material world desires. Some of the dolls wore colourful dresses and pretty ribbons in their hair and were intact, while others were just one-eyed naked amputees in a nightmarish diorama of broken dreams and unfulfilled wishes. Dimitry explained that although the people here were nominally Sunni Muslim, the religious practices and rituals of the locals were actually a complex hybrid of Islam (including Sufism), Animism, Shamanism, Zoroastrianism and Buddhism – the legacy of being at the confluence of the many rivers of ideas and beliefs that had flowed through here for so long.

We scampered down the far side of the hill and into the ruins of the Mamun Academy of Science, which although relatively short-lived, burned brightly in the tenth and eleventh centuries as a centre of intense study and leader in the development of ideas and techniques across a diverse range of fields that included astronomy, mathematics, medicine, chemistry, physics, geography, philosophy, literature, linguistics and jurisprudence. Now it was just a barren collection of broken stone floors and crumbling mud-brick walls. We walked along a narrow ledge atop a mud wall, past a bank of broken ossuaries, where bleached skulls looked out mournfully over the ruins below from nests of bones. We ended our excursion by circling the frighteningly tall and teetering Kutlug Timur Minaret, the tallest (and most crooked) in Central Asia.

***

We headed out across the low flat scrublands on the fringes of the Karakum Desert beginning our journey proper to Ashgabat. Before we left, Dimitry had warned me earnestly about the "terrible" road ahead, which in reality turned out to be just a deeply scarred gravelled and potholed track that required some concentration to ride but was nothing compared to the "roads" of Tajikistan or Siberia which I had already ridden.

We took our lunch at a bleak truck stop canteen, a simple brick shed by the side of the road, nowhere in particular, and full of swarthy torpid and aged Turkmen who watched me closely as I fished out the single piece of meat from the congealed mass of grease and other debris from the pies we had just ordered. "This is traditional Turkmen desert food. Do you like it?" asked Dimitry, wiping his mouth on the back of his sleeve.

"I guess there aren't too many animals in the desert then?" I said obliquely.

"Ah – you haven't found your chilli?" he said concerned, looking down at my plate. He peeled back the lid of my pie – which opened more like a tin can – and pointed to a charred and shrivelled chilli pepper floating in a dark corner. "You can't eat these pies without the chilli" he said, and I could only nod in agreement. Demolishing the stiff retaining walls of pastry, and using my meat judiciously, I quickly mixed up a greasy crunchy mash, and finished my lunch under a grinning Turkmenbashi and his Madonna-like mother, who appeared in large photos on the walls around us. He was deeply tanned, puffy and impeccably dressed with his gold jewellery and white dentures glistening with equal intensity like a well preserved Vegas crooner. And his mother, whose untimely death in the great earthquake of 1949 that levelled Ashgabat and had left a young Niyazov orphaned, was the central maternal element of his twisted vision for the Turkmen people.

We washed our meal down with huge cups of tea laden with iceberg- sized sugar cubes and then headed back out into the hot afternoon and drove on deeper into the Karakum Desert where the encroaching sand dunes soon swallowed any remaining scrub and vegetation and even some of the road. There was very little traffic and the road was barely adequate but the riding was enjoyable, despite the emptiness of yet another desert.

We rode on until dusk and pulled off the road near a deserted yurt – the only sign of human habitation we had seen since our lunch stop. "We're going over there" said Dimitry firmly, pointing to the long low bank of sand dunes that ran parallel to the road here. "What – in there? Are you insane?" I shot back in a nervous reflex response. Dimitry was taken aback. "Of course. Is not problem. You have motorbike" he said rhetorically in the Russian way, the implications obvious. My heart sank and my confidence fell away like the Emperor's new clothes; riding up into soft sand dunes at dusk on a 250kg motorcycle didn't fit my definition of sensible behaviour at this point, but he was determined to proceed, saying "Don't worry, is only small hill, then we drive down to campsite on other side – only ten kilometres." Ten kilometres! He might as well have suggested that we launch my bike at the moon. "Ahhh... .why don't I leave my bike here and I will come with you in the jeep to the campsite?" I said desperately. "I could chain it to... .to... .to...." (scanning the surrounding desert) "....that yurt! And we could come back tomorrow to pick it up"; it was an absurd proposition and I felt embarrassed immediately I had uttered the words. He looked at me with a mix of contempt and incredulity and said "Come, we go now. You follow me." It wasn't a question. Suddenly, two young kids – the oldest no more than ten – raced past on a battered Soviet motorcycle. Despite being ridiculously overloaded with two massive bundles of firewood and straw that ballooned out from either side, they skimmed effortlessly across the sand and raced up and down the dunes with ease, in total control and without the slightest hesitation. Dimitry looked at them pointedly then back at me before silently returning to his jeep; he didn't have to say what I knew he was thinking, so feeling like a prima donna, I kicked the bike into gear and followed him up the long sandy slope.

As I battled up the first incline, all of the adrenalin pumping "excitement" of my early days on the Road of Bones suddenly came flooding back to me like the foul aftertaste of a dish you've vowed never to eat again. After some good early progress, it soon became hopeless as my back wheel worked harder and harder for fewer and fewer inches of forward travel, as it dug itself deeper and deeper into the fine soft sand. I got off and tried to correct my lie with sheer brute force, but had ridden too close to the edge of the track and with a horrible sensation the bike began lurching down the hillside slowly falling on top of me. I tried desperately to arrest its sick momentum but I was trapped on the wrong side, wedged between the bike and a wall of collapsing sand. My back wheel was now completely buried and the drive chain made an awful rasping noise as it circled in vain, like a frightened worm burrowing into the fine gritty sand. This joke was no longer funny and Dimitry, who up until this point had been looking out for me over his shoulder from the drivers' seat of his jeep, ran back to me, screaming "Throttle! Throttle! More throttle!" He grabbed the rear of the bike like a rodeo clown and pushed with all his might while I braced it and worked the throttle hard. The bike finally moved forward but in doing so I had loosened a large sheet of sand and we began sliding down the steep face of the dune, cut loose aboard a sheet of moving sand, avalanche-style. "More throttle!" he gasped, straining hard, the veins on his neck bulging like thick ropes and his face a beetroot colour, as if his head was about to explode. I let out a deep visceral scream and pushed as hard as I could while opening the throttle as far as I dared. The bike lurched forward and slowly began to get some purchase and climb, gouging out a huge tract of sand that sprayed in a powerful stream of tiny projectiles directly behind the bike where Dimitry stood now with his head over the rear wheel. But slowly we inched our way forward and up the slope and, after one final Herculean heave, we beached the bike on the lip of the dune and then pushed it back onto the track. I felt like saying "I told you so", but bit my tongue, sensing this was not the right moment in our new friendship, as Dimitry lay prone on the track, his chest heaving as he struggled to regain his breath. Eventually he stood up and said to me, in a remarkably calm voice as he wiped the dry sand from his face and mouth, "You must ride faster and maintain speed – is only way in sand. Let's go!" before marching off to his jeep to continue! He didn't complain or suggest returning to the road and I sensed that failure was not a concept in his world, so we continued on up the tricky slope with slightly less drama but nevertheless more stoic interventions as I got bogged again, and again, and again. "More throttle, ride faster!" he screamed at me from his jeep, like a deranged Russian Olympic coach. It was counter intuitive to ride faster as the bike slipped and slid under me, but I struggled on, eventually making it to the crest of the hill and then, thankfully, down onto the sandy plateau beyond as he had promised. Seeing me safely arrive, Dimitry then roared off into the grey dusk, along a disturbingly faint track and soon his vehicle was just a set of red dots buzzing across the darkness. My headlight barely illuminated the sandy ruts and I fought like a rodeo rider to stay upright as I bounced and careered along, up and down small hills and gullies in the failing light, cursing this mad Cossack with every breath I could spare; I had already destroyed my clutch once on this journey and felt sure that riding through this equivalent of deep dry mud would certainly do it again. I continued on, riding the clutch hard with massive revs, but only inching forward as my back wheel spun hard with virtually no traction. And, adding to my dark mood was the awful knowledge that I would be re-tracing my steps in the morning when we returned to the road. But I didn't come off, and eventually, after a very long thirty minutes of intense wide-eyed riding in the dark, the ground firmed a little and I found Dimitry making camp in a clearing half way up a long gently sloping hillside. After throttling the life out of my bike for the last hour or so, I desperately wanted to do the same to him and, upon my arrival and sensing that I was deeply disturbed, he quickly excused himself and went off to gather firewood in the dark for a long time.

I set up my tent quickly but before emerging flicked on my torch to read the section in my guide book which described the Karakum desert (where we were now) as a place where "...tarantulas, black widow spiders, scorpions, cobras and vipers can all be found..." Great; waist- deep icy rivers, endless bogs and tracts of mud, land-mined roads and deranged soldiers I could take, but I drew the line at insects and reptiles.

I tiptoed silently back across the cold sand and onto the sanctuary of a large tarpaulin that Dimitry had spread out near his jeep, the centre of our elementary campsite. Against seemingly impossible odds Dimitry ignited the tiny clutch of bone-dry kindling and sticks he had gathered and soon had a bed of glowing embers upon which he placed a huge cast-iron pot full of twice-cooked plov. Greasy, chewy and sweet, it was delicious and I ate voraciously, mostly in silence though, my pleasure interrupted only by the procession of disturbingly large scarab beetles that marched past us, harmless but way too big and close for comfort.

After dinner, Dimitry led me away from camp into the dark desert night towards the purpose of our visit. We stumbled along, but now the murky dusk had been replaced by a diamond-studded carpet of stars that stretched above us from one corner of the horizon to another; pin pricks of flickering light in a black velvet canopy. Suddenly, as we rounded a small hill, a wave of searing heat washed over us, as if an oven door had just been opened in front of us. I looked up and saw massive licks of flame rising from a huge crater in the desert floor ahead of us in the distance. It looked as if a flaming meteor had just slammed into the earth and the resulting inferno cast a dull orange pall over the surrounding desert. As we approached the hot gusts of its irregular breath warmed me, and instinctively I felt the primal comfort and security that the intense heat and light provided against the cold and dark of the desert night. I stopped to survey the crater in its entirety; it was over a hundred metres across, and it was deep, at least fifty metres straight down with sheer walls like the footprints of some gigantic monster as it punched its way across the desert. I approached the lip of the crater and tentatively peered inside. It was like stealing a sneak preview of Hades – peering into the Devil's waiting room; the ground hissed loudly, the stones and rocks at the bottom of the massive pit glowed white hot and the flames danced menacingly as if coordinated by some unseen Satanic maestro. And it was hot, so hot that I had to turn my face away after a few seconds and retreat a few steps. It was a surreal scene and I stood for a long time mesmerized by it. As the massive sheets of flame shot up past me, a hundred feet or more into the air, I imagined a cabal of little demons with pitchforks dancing merrily at the bottom of the pit, beckoning for me to join them, but these visions were cut short as Dimitry grabbed me, pulling me back from the lip of the crater, which I had drifted dangerously close to without realising.

I asked Dimitry about the origins of the crater. "But why does it burn like this? Why doesn't anyone put it out?

"The whole desert is full of vast reservoirs of natural gas, like this one. Many years ago a careless Russian engineer threw a cigarette in, and it has burned like this ever since. No one bothers to put it out now. It is too hard and there is so much gas in the country that it is not important."

"I see"

As we returned to the campsite and my face glowed and tingled pleasantly in the cold night air as if I had just spent the whole day in the sun, but I didn't sleep easy, resolutely resisting the urge for any nocturnal excursions to relieve myself, regardless of my physical discomfort which grew steadily throughout the night. And in the morning things went from bad to worse. After attempting a "hill" start – one chance, on the slightest of downhill grades, on soft sand and heading directly toward the gas crater – I informed a solemn looking Dimitry that my bike was kaput; it had deteriorated further since the previous morning and now didn't even make a sound when I hit the ignition. A deathly silence fell over the desert (and between us) as he processed this new information. He stood with his arms crossed, biceps bulging and chin upturned and narrowed his steely gaze on me like the subject of a Soviet realism poster and said simply, in monotone "Is not problem, I push you" whereupon he proceeded to push me (on my bike) up and down the long sandy slope until I lost count of the circuits we performed. But it was useless as we couldn't make enough speed on the soft sand and my engine never sounded remotely like it was going to fire anyway. But still he wasn't beaten. "Wait here" he hissed at me as he stormed off to the campsite, returning in his jeep shortly afterwards. He produced a long steel rope, one end of which was attached to his jeep and the other he handed to me. "Quick. Tie your bike."

Without an obvious place to make a secure connection I fumbled about for a long time trying to find something to attach the rope to. I had never been towed on my bike but knew the physics of the

329

manoeuvre would be tricky. Eventually, with no sound options, I rashly decided to thread the rope between my front forks. The rope was stiff and hard to work in my soft hands but before I could finish Dimitry began revving the jeep loudly and suddenly jolted forward, taking the slack out of the rope and almost removing my fingers as the rope snapped taut. Bugger! I wasn't ready and shouted at him to wait, but he had no further tolerance for my incompetence today and proceeded to drag me along the desert floor like a sheet anchor; my front wheel immediately locked at forty five degrees under the huge towing force on one fork and I bunny hopped along, holding on for my life, trying desperately to keep the bike upright. I wasn't a mechanical engineer, but could sense that pulling a fully loaded motorbike by one fork was a deeply unnatural act that probably risked serious structural damage. This was sheer stupidity and every second it continued was physical and mental torture. Somehow though, throughout this ordeal, I was able to let the bike run into second gear, but the engine was completely dead and eventually, after a few hundred metres of this insanity Dimitry stopped. I wondered whether he had secretly enjoyed dragging me like a broken rag doll behind his jeep, but any joy had certainly drained from his face as he stormed back to where I stood now, pale and exhausted. He looked at me with an expression that silently screamed "Are you a complete idiot? Can't you even start a motorbike like a normal person?"

Still refusing to give in, Dimitry now insisted that we start dismantling the bike here in the desert to try and find the source of the problem, and so we spent the next two hours under a rising and rapidly warming sun, methodically checking fuel lines, changing spark plugs, examining and dismantling the electrical system, even removing the fuel tank, etc until finally my bike looked more like the carcass of some primitive desert animal. Finally Dimitry said "I go for help. You wait here." It wasn't a joint planning session, and before I knew what had happened I was left standing alone on the rutted desert floor with my bike in pieces and tools and parts scattered about watching him bounce away and over the horizon. He didn't say where he was going, what he was planning to do, or even when he might return.

The sun was almost directly overhead now and I could feel it burning through the top of my uncovered head. I had half a bottle of water and no food and after a few furtive attempts at more investigation – severely hampered by my almost total lack of any useful mechanical knowledge – I crawled in under the lean of the bike – which provided a slither of shade – and waited, and waited, and waited. I imagined him sitting in his jeep by the side of the road whittling a dry desert stick, narrowing his eyes and contemplating whether he would in fact bother returning to help me. Periodically I changed position as the shade crept around my bike like a sundial. I drank my water in mouthfuls, sparingly, not knowing when I would have more. I knew it wasn't far to the road (only ten kilometres), but the track was not so obvious now and being alone without transport, without any means of communication and with no food was not a pleasant sensation. I was surrounded on all sides by an endless sea of sand dunes, there was no vegetation, no water and I was hot and getting hotter – even in the shade. I started doing the mental arithmetic to calculate when I would need to start walking to make it back to the road before dark – assuming I could find or follow the right track. Fortunately this occupied a great deal of my time and attention, distracting me from the more immediate discomforts of my position, but soon my folded limbs began to cramp from squatting for so long and I stretched out with my torso alongside the bike and drifted off to sleep. I don't know for how long I slept; it could have been five minutes or two hours, but I awoke to the sound of grinding gears and voices. Dimitry stood like a triumphant Zhukov atop an ancient Zil flatbed truck manned by a crew of grimy undernourished teenage boys who sat shoulder to shoulder, grinning widely in the cabin below like monkeys.

With a minimum of fuss my bike was loaded onto the truck and we bounced off and along a circuitous route back to the roadside camp (it was one way circuit into and out of the desert for heavy vehicles due to the terrain). We pulled up outside the boys' family yurt where a woman of indeterminate age was wrestling a scrawny goat to the ground before they both disappeared out of sight. We had made it back to the "road", but my bike was still no more than just a dead weight and we were still hundreds of kilometres from Ashgabat, so Dimitry opened a line of delicate negotiations with the head of the local clan for my onward transport. There was a scuffle behind the yurt and muffled yelps of pain before a long silence. In the meantime, one of the local men invited me to sit in the cabin of their truck to escape the scorching sun while he and his brothers and cousins and nephews and sons all disappeared – in what appeared to be an optical illusion – into their incredibly small communal yurt. Some time later the woman emerged from behind the yurt smiling broadly as she wiped her bloodied hands on her apron before acknowledging me shyly. She casually brushed the flies off the sinewy shanks of goat meat that were slung over her shoulder – thank god I wasn't eating that I thought to myself with some relief.

As I sat in the cramped cabin surveying my bleak surroundings through the spider's web of cracked glass that was the windscreen and pondering my equally bleak prospects, I was struck by an overpowering sense of déjà vu; I had come over 5,000 kilometres since the miraculous work of Mr Shu in Urumchi and had travelled more than ten thousand kilometres since being rescued by Zhenya and his crew on the Road of Bones, but here I was again, sitting in someone else's battered truck with my broken bike aboard, not sure about what lay ahead or whether I would even finish this journey on my own terms. It wasn't the trip I had planned nor imagined, but ironically it was in these moments of total dependence upon others (which I loathed initiating) that enabled me to enter the lives of so many wonderful people. Or perhaps this was the just the natural rhythm of life on the road, like a space probe that needs to orbit planets on its outward journey to restore its momentum before being slung back out on its long lonely journey.

I turned my attention back to Dimitry now who looked more like a frenzied futures' trader in the pit going long on pork bellies as he waved his arms about wildly and shook his head violently at the old chieftain who stood impassively throughout with arms folded staring down the mad Cossack; negotiations had clearly reached an impasse. Dimitry stormed over to me, exasperated; "He wants fifty dollars!" I was embarrassed – it was three hundred more kilometres along a dirty potholed track through a sizzling desert to Ashgabat and this was absurdly cheap. I instructed Dimitry to agree immediately and, as he turned to leave, he handed me a dirty oil-stained paper bag heavy with what felt like small pieces of rubble. "I saved this for you yesterday" he said quietly.

"What is it?" I said, perplexed.

I peered inside – the bag was full of small pieces of hard grey-brown rubble. "It's some pie crusts from yesterday – I thought you might like them?" I tried one, but unfortunately, they also tasted like rubble, crumbling like mortar as I bit into them; he might as well have scooped up a handful of desert sand and offered it to me for lunch. But it was the gesture itself that touched me and I smiled through gritted teeth (literally) and thanked him as he walked away.

Negotiations concluded smartly and soon after the woman caught my attention again, as she emerged from the yurt and beckoned for me to join them. Dimitry was nowhere to be seen so I scurried across the hot sand and poked my head through the low doorway into the darkness of their yurt. Shadowy shapes shifted slowly around me in a murmur and the air was heavy with the aroma of spice and stale-sweet BO. As my eyes slowly adjusted to the darkness the large group of men, whom I had seen enter earlier, resolved itself before me. They were a bedraggled mass of grimy clansmen, from grizzled elders to young men who squatted or lay languidly on the dust-impregnated carpets that covered the floor. Some dozed while others ate the brown stew that was being passed around on communal plates. Large nons also circulated with each man breaking off just one piece before carefully passing it on, patterned side up as is the custom. The woman worked hard over a large cauldron that bubbled away on a primitive cast-iron stove near the doorway. One of the younger men jumped up and invited me to join his group on the floor in front of me. He introduced himself as "Ruslan" and clearly he was a leader amongst his clan; he was tall and well groomed with smooth coffee-coloured skin and, unlike all the others, was dressed smartly in a brilliantly patterned silk shirt and slacks. He cleared and cleaned a space on the carpet next to him and called for a "special" plate of brown stew to be prepared just for me. I sat and told them my story briefly in broken Russian which fascinated them. I showed them the photos of my family in my wallet which they all admired and nodded in approval as it was passed around the entire group, out of sight and well beyond my reach (and full of all my cash). I looked down now with some trepidation at the grey brown sludge of broken bones and innards before me and, desperately trying to suppress the warning messages that flashed through my brain like a white hot poker, I found the most "appetising" piece and tentatively bit into it. Predictably, it was dry and chewy – like shoe leather seasoned with desert grit – but not altogether unpleasant; but there was neither bones nor flesh, just soft textured tasty pieces of unidentifiable origin. I continued slowly, methodically working my way through my helping, stopping to talk and answer their many questions between mouthfuls.

With my bike secured in the back of their truck, nestled snugly within the strange cargo of mattresses and bed frames that filled the rear, I returned to the cabin to join my two companions for the long journey to Ashgabat; Ruslan, and Sasha, his happy-go-lucky but slow cousin. As I settled into my small, uncomfortable and backless seat, Ruslan stretched out behind us on a narrow bench seat with his arms folded behind his head, while Sasha, grinning like a maniac now, took the wheel as we lurched away toward the road. I studied the cabin; the walls were plastered with stickers of cartoon characters and rainbows and flowers, like a child's room, and taking pride of place on the centre of the dashboard was Daisy Duck (in a bikini), smiling suggestively back at us – I had seen the insides of a lot trucks and had gotten to know many of their rugged drivers along my journey but this was truly bizarre. There wasn't a pin-up girl or religious icon to be seen and I began at once to fully appreciate the power and influence of Turkmenbashi over his beloved people. It was a hot windy afternoon and the sand dunes seemed to reflect and focus the sun's rays like a powerful beam of radiation into our small stuffy cabin. We talked some more and they told me how they scoured the desert for wood and refuse from which they somehow made bed frames and mattresses, which they in turn sold in Ashgabat – their only income and the difference between living and perishing for their entire clan. We continued talking for a while but this soon petered out and Sasha, who had been restless throughout, reached into a small shoebox under the dashboard, retrieved a cassette and proceeded to blast us with the screeching, frenetic dirge that was Turkmen pop music. It had a thumping back beat which distorted horribly as it left their cheap speakers before the pulsating waves of energy reverberated throughout my body. Clearly it was party time as suddenly Ruslan bobbed up between us like a Boppo the clown punching bag, reaching into his pocket to produce a small and ornately engraved metal canister from which he carefully poured a small mound of fine grey-green powder into the palm of his hand. The whites of his eyes widened and with a devious smile he pushed it up and under my nose, hissing at me "Narcoman! Try it!", but before I could respond Sasha swooped like a vulture, snapping a large pinch of the powder between his fingers, before closing his eyes, throwing his head back and snorting it up in one long grunt, before finally, thankfully, returning his attention to driving. I thanked Ruslan but politely declined his offer and he withdrew reluctantly to administer his own dose before returning to his original position behind us whereupon he immediately fell fast asleep. I looked at Sasha, hoping desperately that the drug would not induce the same stupor in him, but he appeared to have attained an altogether higher state of consciousness where he was at one with his machine, the music and the road, where he focused now with a goggle-eyed intensity. Sensing my concern though, he turned quickly, smiled broadly and gave me the universal thumbs up signal. We continued on, but peering out at the road ahead through the shattered windscreen was like wearing kaleidoscope eye glasses and the pulsating screech of Turkmen pop music over the drone of the truck engine quickly gave me a massive migraine, so intense it felt as if someone had taken a power drill to my skull and was slowly boring an ice-cold hole through my brain. And so it continued for the next few hours as we bumped and ground our way along the broken track across the desert – Sleepy, Happy and Grumpy, until finally we stopped for fuel and tea at a desolate village about eighty kilometres from Ashgabat. Just a shanty town of sand blown humpies, we sat on a carpet under the shade of large umbrella at a tea stand and toasted good health and our families as a herd of spitting camels wandered past. But my surroundings had taken on an altogether surreal quality as I also reached a higher level of consciousness; today again reinforcing the underlying essence of my journey: that it was impossible to tell (and pointless trying to predict) what was around each corner, that all my plans were really just whimsy and even though I could make choices and steer my own course – to a certain degree – it was on a rolling river of humanity which seemed to carry me along on its own overriding journey. It certainly wasn't fatalism, just an adjustment to my way of thinking triggered by my circumstances and experience.

***

As we headed out to complete the final leg of our journey to Ashgabat, signs of Turkmenbashi's profligate push into the desert soon became apparent; the road improved dramatically and widened until, incredibly, we were cruising on a six lane carpet of freshly laid and unmarked bitumen. We met the railhead from the south as it penetrated deep into the desert and unstrung freshly cast cement power poles, ready to bring electricity to this dead and deserted place, whizzed passed with monotonous regularity. Our drivers, who up until this point had travelled in strict formation, single-file, opened up their jalopies and now "raced" each other with gay abandon down the centre of this improvised race track and played chicken, heading into oncoming traffic until one of them finally lost their nerve. I just shut my eyes, fingering deep holes into my seat and assumed the crash position – but while they were undoubtedly repressed, they were certainly not suicidal, and thankfully, as dusk fell we safely crested a final ridge and came upon the twinkling lights of modern-day Ashgabat. The city stretched out below us lapping at the foothills of the Kopet Dag mountains in the distance, which were now in dramatic silhouette against an indigo and crimson sky to the South. Beyond was Iran – but I was getting ahead of myself for I still had a broken bike and just a promise of help. We continued on, down to the outskirts of the city along wide boulevards, through neat traffic-light controlled intersections and on to the agreed meeting place, a small strip of auto workshops off a service road beside the airport, where Dimitry was waiting for us. His mood seemed to have improved significantly from when we had last seen each other, as he welcomed me warmly and introduced me to the two teenage grease monkeys who were going to fix my bike. Sons of a Russian-born motorcycle champion of Turkmenistan (and Dimitry's godsons), they looked at my bike with great anticipation. I began to explain the problem to them but Dimitry brushed me aside declaring proudly that they would find whatever was wrong and fix it. I was not so sure and left feeling sceptical but it had been a long day and I was very, very tired.

Dimitry, who now appeared more metrosexual than earnest Soviet Man tour guide, had traded his jeep for a late-model sports saloon and drove me to my pre-arranged accommodation; a government "guesthouse" located in a purpose-built suburb on the other side of the city. As we drove through central Ashgabat, I was astonished by the vast and fully stocked hypermarkets, neon-lit shopping malls, medical clinics, gleaming glass and white-marbled apartment buildings, enormous floodlit plazas and gigantic monuments. It was a hot humid Friday night and the streets bustled with modern cars and well-dressed, seemingly healthy, happy and affluent people just hanging out, as you might find in any modern sophisticated city heading into the weekend. But it was all irreconcilable and deeply jarred with the desperate poverty and nothingness I had been emersed in just a few hours earlier; this was another country and I wondered silently what the bed-builders of Darvaza would have made of it all.

We came to a wide, empty, freshly minted boulevard and drove on past a long parade of near identical gated bungalows, each trying hard to capture their designated country theme with their faux decorations. But they were all cast from the same mould, sharing the same basic proportions and structures, surrounded by manicured lawns and neat glades of pine trees, each finished cheaply with superficial features in a nod to their supposed country of origin. The Italian, Korean, German, Japanese, Mongolian and Indian efforts whizzed past and still we continued on, finally turning into an anonymous driveway where I looked up to see faded red lanterns hanging from a pagoda-style awning and the words "Ming Dynasty Guesthouse" in stylised bamboo neon script; a little piece of China in the heart of Turkmenistan.

Inside though, the hotel was devoid of life except for the tired official who slept soundly on the floor behind the reception desk. The foyer was dark, dank and soulless, and a mouldy odour hung in the air. A grand central staircase, covered in a luxurious red carpet led to a darkened construction zone on the second floor. I was the only guest and my room was of presidential-suite proportions with a king-size bed, private balcony and massive marble bathroom, but it was bare and austere, and, according to my guide book, almost certainly bugged. The off-white shag pile carpet was stained and marked in odd patterns from activities I didn't even want to think about. But the temporary relief from life on the road was wonderful and I danced a jig, sang a ditty and dived headlong onto the bed and rolled around in the cool cotton sheets, lost in their luxury for just a moment.

I took a long hot bath – my first in almost a month – and fell soundly asleep in the murky water as the dirt, sand, sweat and accumulated soreness drained out of my tired body. Too exhausted to seek out authentic options, and isolated in this bizarre and deserted theme park suburb, I reluctantly took dinner in the hotel restaurant. It too was faux Chinese with oriental painted screens, lattice work, silk-patterned wallpaper, lanterns in a sea of Lazy Susans, and was staffed by a weird assortment of characters from central casting. First to greet me was the young maitre d', who, dressed in a red velvet smoking jacket and black tuxedo pants and with a dramatic windswept hairdo and heavy eyeliner looked more like a 1980's new romantic and oozed sexual ambiguity to boot. There was a sensitive young man trapped inside this pantomime and I felt for him, but I suspect he mistook my empathy for something deeper as he looked at me in the way that men should not look at each other. And the sideshow got even more bizarre with a procession of young waitresses, who regardless of their actual stature and girth (both of which varied greatly), all wore the same "one size fits all" red silk Cheongsams. A very tall, handsome waitress loped awkwardly like a giraffe as she struggled to keep her hemline at a decent height, while a shorter more solidly built waitress waddled around like a penguin for fear of popping her seams – but they couldn't have done more to make me feel welcome and to supply whatever I requested, for I was their only customer.

***

After dinner I took a short stroll in the garden just to look at the night sky and drink in the fresh air, but as I did I noticed the sleepy official from reception tailing me discretely. Catching up to me quickly, he grabbed my arm, looked around and asked me in hushed voice "do you want a woman tonight?" It was the first such approach I had received and how ironic, I thought, that it should occur here in the most repressed and tightly controlled state on my journey. Politely declining his offer, I returned to my room where I collapsed on the enormous bed and began lazily flicking through the meagre selection of channels on the TV. Turkmen TV was a bizarre combination of talent-less talent shows (think school band practice), regional cotton harvesting statistics – read out like Premier League football results – but mostly political broadcasts, dominated almost entirely by coverage of the President's activities. Turkmenbashi had begun this day with a lengthy cabinet meeting at which he spoke ad-nauseam, repeatedly thumping the table and ranting at his ministers (who were only revealed in the occasional long shots as a moribund collection of faceless grey men who all sat in silence and nodded in unison like scolded schoolboys). After getting that off his chest, the Leader of all Turkmen drove himself in his bullet-proofed late- model Mercedes to a lawn party where he seemed to be granting an endless series of military commissions and/or promotions to a long queue of nervous young men. Each received a handshake and a personal gift from the great man and each saluted like a statue when finished before marching away stiff-legged. Panning through the audience revealed more obsequious supplicants who knew precisely when to clap and which expressions to hold when on camera. I wondered what they really thought.

***

I reflected on my day; I had woken in a tent on the verge of a seething gas crater, been dragged recklessly across the desert on my broken motorbike by a mad Cossack, been stranded in the same desert for hours without food and only a little water, eaten a slaughtered goat with an impoverished band of brothers in their crowded and dirty yurt, careered across the sizzling Karakum desert in a broken-down jalopy with two drug-addled bed merchants, dined alone and a la carte in a Chinese theatre restaurant and been offered women by a clandestine pimp. Could it get any better than this? I drifted off into a dreamless sleep; I was overdrawn in experiences today and needed to recover.

Dimitry came early the next morning and drove me back to the garage near the airport where we found the two grease monkeys lying like fraternal twins in foetal position, fast asleep on their workbench. They were both fully clothed and their faces, arms, hands and fingernails were dark with grease and dirt from my bike. Dimitry woke them gently and, wiping the sleep and tiredness from his eyes, the younger and cleverer one jumped up and handed me a fistful of shredded copper wires and a torn gasket before explaining in intricate detail and with great pride what was wrong with my bike and how they had fixed it – but quickly out of my depth, I couldn't follow, so just nodded happily, my gratitude obvious. I thanked them both sincerely and paid them handsomely before filling up at the adjacent petrol station for just a few cents. Happily independent again, I glided around an almost empty, freshly laid six lane freeway that seemed purpose built to transport people directly from the airport to the hotel-suburb where I stayed. I rode past half-finished gleaming white and gold condominiums while industrial-strength sprinklers irrigated vast tracts of transplanted turf and saplings and, unfortunately, most of the freeway too. I returned for a breakfast-matinee at the Chinese restaurant, where the cast and crew – still dressed in their costumes from the previous night – had clearly spent the night.

***

I spent the remainder of the day idly wandering around central Ashgabat, which seemed to consist of two distinct areas – those given over to the grandiose monument building of Turkmenbashi, and the older Soviet-era neighbourhoods where people actually lived and worked. My tour began in the dazzlingly modern commercial precinct of office towers, foreign banks, empty malls and four star hotels that was central Ashgabat. It had a Beverly Hills feel about it with perfectly laid boulevards, manicured verges and potted palms, neatly paved sidewalks with awnings and canopies, bell hops and idle assistants in wannabe designer-label shops. And it was all slightly unnerving; too perfect, verging on the unnatural, as if I had stepped onto the set of my own Truman Show.

In a surreal scene, I met a young man delivering sandwiches on the street who invited me back to the café where he worked to talk; he wanted to practice his English and I was happy to oblige. With his faded denim jeans, sneakers, white T-shirt, ruddy complexion and brooding expression he reminded me an iconic teenage-rebel – a less handsome Turkmen James Dean. But he too was trapped inside this artificial reality, desperately trying to escape. He introduced himself as "Bershavar" and as we sat under the faded candy coloured umbrellas at the outdoor café where he worked, he rolled a cigarette and smoked indolently as he told me his story. Barely a teenager and with his parents too poor to look after him, he had come to the city from a remote desert village to live with a distant relative and had lived in and around the city by his wits ever since. Amazingly, he had escaped – albeit briefly – being "sponsored" as a guest worker in the United Arab Emirates (directly south and just beyond neighbouring Iran), which had opened his eyes to the possibilities of a life beyond his Twilight Zone existence here and now he was desperate to get to Europe; working as a lowly kitchen hand in London the acme of his limited ambition. But the Turkmen economy cruelly conspired against him (and all its citizens) at every turn, with its artificially low living costs, paltry incomes – about $100 a month on average – and a non-convertible currency. More than half the population lived below the poverty line and unemployment ran at a staggering 60%, despite the Government guaranteeing everyone a job. Bershavar told me that his apartment (which he shared) cost just a few dollars a month in rent, and that gas, electricity and water were all supplied free of charge, although shortages were frequent and severe – especially in winter. Internet access was possible but strictly rationed and closely supervised (think government "observer" watching every keystroke over your shoulder). So, closed off from the rest of the world and living in a false economy, they were prisoners of their own sad misfortune. I ordered a shashlik and a beer, and immediately regretted it as the midday sun beat down hard and hot on my head. Bershavar talked more about his life and I listened intently; he was a resilient street-smart kid, but I also sensed a deep melancholy in him and got an inkling that perhaps he was *damaged goods*.

After I had finished my lunch Bershavar took me to the nearby bazaar, a dark maze of blue tarpaulin-covered stalls watched over by anxious merchants, where I bought some essential supplies for the remainder of my journey. Bershavar was in his element here as he skipped along the crooked narrow alleyways greeting old friends and ragamuffins alike as he passed by their plots, appearing more Artful Dodger now than clean- cut delivery boy. I half expected him to jump up on a stall, pirouette around the makeshift awning poles and start singing "...consider yourself one of the family", but sadly, as we parted, he was more like a consumptive Oliver that looked up at

340

me with sad puppy dog eyes and cupped hands, pleading for money, "...please Sir, can I have some more?" I offered to buy him food – as much food as he wanted – but it was money he needed, hard currency being the only ticket out of here, so begrudgingly I unrolled a handful of fresh US dollars from my dwindling supply and handed them over to him, whereupon he turned on his heels and skipped away! And it wasn't the donation I objected to per se; rather it was the manner in which it had been obtained – the deception – which bothered me. It was, of course, just a mild version of the classic and often run "rich tourist gets fleeced by streetwise local" scam, but in almost three months on the road, across six countries and almost an entire continent, through some of the most desperately poor places in the world, this was the first time I had experienced this confidence trick.

Feeling a little empty, I headed toward the landmark Arch of Neutrality, which at a distance looked more like a rocket-ship ready for launch into deep space. I took a disorientating glass elevator ride up one of its sloped legs where, from the observation deck, I looked out over the disgustingly opulent and self-indulgent shrine that was Turkmenbashi's Capitol. It was a fantasy land of marbled golden-domed crude neoclassical buildings and palaces around the cruelly titled "Independence Square" – a huge and handsomely tiled plaza where a vast array of ornate gilded fountains sprayed jets of precious water up and away in a fine mist across this parched city. It was criminal; the dire reality of their situation was that they lived in a dry, thirsty country (ninety percent of it desert) suffering the devastating after effects of salination from over zealous cotton irrigation from the receding Aral Sea. And despite their reverence for water (it was even enshrined in the national "Drop of Water is a Grain of Gold" holiday), Turkmenbashi persisted with his capricious plans, including demanding that his court builders create an artificial lake nearby so that a river could be made to flow through his desert capital.

I returned to ground level and gazed back up with sickening wonder at the massive twelve metre high golden statue of the little emperor, skewered atop the arch, on permanent slow rotisserie, his puffy jowls tracking the sun as it moved across the sky. I walked toward the Palace of Turkmenbashi; everything glistened under the brilliant desert sun and the whole area was immaculately clean but totally devoid of people and life – off limits to regular citizens and nosey tourists alike. I stood and watched and waited feeling like I was at Disneyland waiting for the parade that never came. I peered into the darkened offices of the obliquely named *Ministry of Fairness* that ran along one side of the massive plaza and wondered how they weighed up the scales of justice and delivered equity here.

I walked through the People's Park to the East, past a battalion of babushkas silently sweeping the pavement and on to the striking yet sombre war memorial, a massively tall and slender earth-red marble column, where a young couple posed for their wedding-day photos. An eternal flame, surrounded by garlands of fresh flowers, flickered in the cenotaph, a signal that not all of the past had been forgotten or rewritten. I walked on through leafy neighbourhoods of old apartments, corner shops, cafés, restaurants, parks and playgrounds where children played football and volleyball on asphalt courts, young mothers talked with each other as they pushed their prams slowly along shady paths and the last few veterans of the Great Patriotic War sat reminiscing with each other on park benches; it could have been a lazy Saturday afternoon anywhere. And my acerbic reaction to the city was starting to dull just a little as I began to feel a connection with these people and perhaps a fragile pathos with the city itself, whose name, according to one explanation, loosely translates from Persian as "The city built by/from love." But any lingering romantic notions of a socialist utopia led by a benevolent dictator were quickly extinguished by the time I had reached the next street corner where I came to another narcissistic monument cum manifesto; a life-size gilded bust of Turkmenbashi on a large marble plinth in front of a semi-circular tessellated wall covered with slogans and uncountable red exclamation marks extolling his subjects to align their actions and thinking with those of their supreme leader. And just to reinforce his omnipresence, the next shop I came to was a bookstore with a huge window display of the ugliest book cover I have ever seen; His chubby face and massive coiffure in profile (in gold relief) on a grass- green background framed in a hot-pink patterned border. Curious, I entered the shop. Cheerfully, it was brimming full of books, piled high, overflowing from the shelves and spread out on tables and the floor, but there was something deeply disturbing in this scene that took a few seconds to register – my reaction dulled by the variations of colour, script and language in the collection – then it struck me: all the books were the same! The store was filled with thousands and thousands of copies of Turkmenbashi's Rukhnama. And there were no customers, not even casual browsers here; just a sleepy official dozing behind the counter. And despite most of the books being printed in either Russian or

modern Turkmen script, I eventually found a handful of English-language versions stacked in an untidy pile in a corner. Intrigued, I picked one up and read the dust cover where, in his own modest style, Turkmenbashi had penned a synopsis that read more like a late night infomercial: "...*on par with the Bible and the Koran... .a spiritual guide to help remove the complexities and anguishes from day to day living...*" I turned the front cover. It opened with the powerful Oath of Turkmenistan, which read more like a dark and binding contract with the Devil himself:
"Turkmenistan,
My beloved motherland,
My beloved homeland!
You are always with me
In my thoughts and in my heart
For the slightest evil against you
Let my hand be lost.
For the slightest slander about you
Let my tongue be lost.
At the moment of my betrayal
To my motherland,
To her sacred banner,
To Saparmurat Turkmenbashi the great
Let my breath stop"

That the country was not full of asphyxiated mute amputees was testament to his pervasive influence over the entire population – but there were dissenting voices, with an estimated 20,000 political prisoners locked up in the country's gaols. I flicked through the chapters, each of which read like an *open letter* in form, but more *stream of consciousness* in substance – Jabberwocky ramblings whose logic and meaning, I suspected, had been lost in translation (or perhaps never existed).

I walked on to the promised location of the Museum of Fine Arts for some relief where instead I found a darkened and boarded up building. I peered inside the deserted rooms and asked an old man loitering nearby what had become of the Museum.
"Shut down. Moved............. over there" he said vacantly, pointing nowhere in particular. Too tired to decipher these directions I enquired about other landmarks.
"And what about the Opera House?"
"Closed"
"And the Pushkin Drama Theatre?"
"Closed"

In reality, both had recently been demolished to make way for another one of Turkmenbashi's wild building sprees. And in accompanying decrees, he had banned both opera and ballet and shut down all the cinemas for good measure too, declaring them all "un-Turkmen", the ban necessary to protect Turkmen culture from "negative influences". But it didn't stop there, with the playing of recorded music at public events, on television and at weddings also strictly forbidden. And in a further step, listening to car radios had been banned and, more disturbingly, all of the hospitals and libraries outside of the capital had (allegedly) been closed, with Turkmenbashi declaring that people in the countryside didn't need to read and could travel to Ashgabat if they got sick.

And, in a reminder of just how utterly isolated and cocooned they were here, this was the first time in my journey where I had been approached directly by people on the street (at random and repeatedly), just to talk and be with, as if I were some sort of rare and exotic creature on display. But strangely, all of Turkmenbashi's crazy privations barely seemed to register with them, for everyone I met – with the exception of Bershavar – spoke happily about their lot; students, teachers, taxi drivers, shopkeepers, and more, all seemingly oblivious to the possibility and potential of an alternative existence. It seemed as if the concepts of freedom and liberty were beyond their consciousness, out of reach, or perhaps more darkly, off limits. That I was here and alone without a minder was fantastic enough, but to have ridden a motorcycle from beyond the Artic Circle in remote Siberia to be here was unfathomable to them. I wondered what thoughts they left unspoken and what questions lingered behind their eyes, but didn't probe too deeply knowing that the Turkmenbashi had eyes and ears almost everywhere in the city.

But there was some upside in this diabolical deal, with alcohol freely available and – apart from a call to modesty – women dressed without restriction and were free to participate in most activities. And despite Turkmenbashi's severe impositions, Ashgabat somehow seemed to retain a liberal and relaxed feel (whatever simmered below the surface). Perhaps it was just the Indian summer. And although most were Sunni Muslims, they didn't share the Islamic fundamentalism of their neighbours in Afghanistan and Iran.

I continued along a pleasant tree-lined back street but soon came to a massive, dusty construction zone where labourers, construction workers and engineers swarmed like ants around a massive marble office tower. Almost complete, the shiny brass plate on the exterior revealed that it was to be the new home of yet another branch of the government. Earth moving machines roared around me and jackhammers blasted as men cut and ground paving stones, putting the finishing touches on the streetscape around the building. Scrawny, careworn labourers unfurled massive rolls of luxurious lawn and transplanted saplings into the field of dirt and rubble that was once old Ashgabat, while another crew followed directly behind them with fire-hoses soaking the newly sown soil with obscene amounts of gushing water. As I passed the nerve centre of this operation I heard the distinctive tones of French speakers, tanned and handsome and chic in their sunglasses, polo shirts and unblemished chinos; these were Turkmenbashi's anointed court builders – unscrupulous foreigners taking their cut of the Emperor's treasure.

Finally, I called in at a large hotel, where, for a price only a foreigner could afford (and under strict editorial control), I was shown to a large, austere administrative office and sat at a prehistoric IBM PC under a bank of bare fluorescent lights where I typed out a long and politically correct email home. Allegedly connected to the internet, it was impossible to tell whether my sanitised message had actually been sent or not. Frustrated, I got up to leave, but as I did a swarthy, well dressed man, who had sat nearby cursing loudly on the telephone throughout my entire writing session beckoned to me. Obviously a foreigner, he was yet another "biznessman" chasing yet another construction project and, without prompting, he offered his own perspective on life in Turkmenistan. He was Latin and reminded me of a slightly taller and slightly more attractive Maradona in appearance, and, as he ranted at me, he waved his hands around in big emotive gestures.

"This place is crazy, all fucked up" he hissed at me venomously, apparently unconcerned at who else might be listening. "You know" he said, now imploring with me, "it's impossible to do anything in this country without it being reported to the government. Nothing is private. Everyone spies on each other... and especially on foreigners." He lowered his voice and leant over the table placing his head so close to mine that I was enveloped in the haze of his powerful aftershave "...and those who won't or who are reported are thrown in prison and tortured or sent to live in the desert. My neighbours – they're always watching me and calling the police, because if they don't they will get into trouble... they even trawl through my trash looking for evidence of unTurkmen activities!" he said, exasperated. He leaned back and slapped his hand hard on the desk with a wild look in his eyes. "And when I have a woman...." he trailed off. I got up and left.

As I scurried down the long corridors to the exit, I came to a large picture window on the second floor where I stopped to look down over the cityscape of central Ashgabat. All of the parks, avenues, monuments, palaces, ministries and apartment buildings that I had walked amongst earlier in the day were laid out below me now, but from up here the grim charade was revealed with many of the buildings I had admired just flimsy facades, props in this theatre of the absurd, hiding huge empty tracts of recently demolished Ashgabat. And these were just the obvious physical remnants of what had been, for there were darker rumours regarding the fate of the scores of homeless created by this madness.

It was a strange day in a strange country and I was genuinely happy to return to the relatively innocuous "Ming Dynasty" guesthouse where I dined for a final time with my friends and slept soundly in my presidential suite.

***

In the morning I was escorted along the short winding road up into the foothills of the Kopet Dag Mountains to the Iranian border post. It was a cool day with low-hanging depthless clouds covering the sky and the cold quickly penetrated my shell suit and I was happy to be off my bike again relatively quickly. Leaving Turkmenistan was perversely less complicated and blindingly less frustrating than entering it – even the soldiers here seemed to have a brighter outlook, with one of them quipping at me "you know – this is where Iranians come to have fun!"

After completing a few forms in a small office – most of which were not scrutinised – I returned to my bike and rolled it up to the edge of a long sump pit (used to inspect the underside of trucks), where a group of well dressed soldiers waited for me.

"Do you have any guns?" one of them said casually.

"Ah... .no"

"Other weapons?"

"No"

"Narcotics?"

"No"

"And what's in here?" said another, tapping his own large gun lightly on one of my panniers.

"Tools, spare parts and camping equipment" I said quickly.

"OK. You are free to go. Goodbye."

And with that they waved me away and I rode off up the hill to the Iranian border.

Across Persia

Straddling the sharp spine of the mountains, the Iranian border post was a bleak collection of basic buildings with just a flimsy steel swing gate separating the two countries, as if they were adjacent farmers' paddocks. It was still early in the morning in Iran (there was a two hour time zone change here) and the solitary young Iranian soldier who guarded this narrow passage insisted that I dismount and push my bike slowly across the border into the dusty forecourt of their compound. I complied, parking my bike carefully and then approached a large wooden building, which upon entering felt more like an old schoolhouse, with its bare wooden floors, high vaulted ceilings and long painted wooden benches. I was processed with a minimum of fuss by a disinterested crew of civilians under the avuncular gaze of a pallid and drawn Ayatollah Khomeini, whose large faded portraits hung down from each of the four walls high above me. I stepped outside with my clutch of papers and that was that, I was in Iran! Incredible!

***

Iran had crept up on me, and I wasn't quite prepared for it. It was only a part of my journey because it had been the "least difficult" passage to Europe that I could find from Central Asia; it was not a place I had studied in detail or had chosen to come to in its own right for what it offered or what I might do there. I had no expectations, only vague impressions cast many years ago when, as a young boy, I had watched the grainy TV images of the overthrow of the Shah and the ensuing hostage crisis and then the rise of fundamentalism under the Islamic theocracy of Ayatollah Khomeini followed by the internecine Iran-Iraq war that waged for most of the 1980s. More darkly, I could still recall the burning of US flags and effigies of President Carter by angry mobs on the streets of Tehran (my next major destination). But these, of course, were just jumbled and incomplete snapshots taken from a far more complex story, and the region's history had unfolded since; the war had ended inconclusively (at enormous costs to both sides), Khomeini was gone – replaced by an equally strident and all powerful Supreme Leader who kept a series of more liberal-minded Presidents in check. At least relations with the West, although still prickly – especially on the subject of nuclear power – had thawed somewhat.

347

I was directed to another post fifty metres further down the hill into Iran proper, where I was told my bike and carnet would need to be inspected, but as I began to push off a soldier rushed out from a nearby sentry box, barring my way. And before I knew what was happening he had well and truly invaded my personal space, thrusting his goggle-eyed and bearded face up close to mine, saying without introduction and through gritted teeth and pursed lips, "So mist-ah, whad you dink of mayh country?" And, before I could respond to his opening salvo, he squinted at me sideways, saying with deep suspicion (and chewing on each syllable before spitting them out at me), "And whad you dink of Uh-merica?" I mumbled something about the great history and noble People of Persia, but also made it perfectly clear that: a) I was not an American, and b) that I certainly did not support their current foreign policy in the Middle East. He looked at me with only slightly less suspicion and hissed something about the "Coalition of the Willing", but it was too late for a debate as I had already withdrawn and waved him goodbye. I turned my back on him nervously and shifted into neutral and rolled silently down the hill coming to a stop at the head of a large convoy of freight trucks that snaked its way down the mountainside. But these weren't the dilapidated Soviet-era rust buckets that I had grown used to (and spent considerable time in over the past three months); these were shiny new European marques, most with generators big enough to power a small Siberian town. They each hauled massive refrigerated containers and had modern air-conditioned cabins with small sleeping quarters. Their registration plates revealed drivers and fleets far from home – Ashgabat the most remote node in their networks; they hailed from places like Istanbul, Athens, Brindisi, Hamburg, Brussels and even Rotterdam, and for the first time on my journey I could sense Europe approaching. But, like these trucks and the long cold shadows they cast, it was grey and dull and left me feeling melancholy rather than excited.

I entered a small hut that looked more like a workmen's shed in the middle of a construction zone where a chain-smoking pallid-faced middle-aged soldier in camouflage fatigues examined my carnet slowly before shrugging his shoulders and tossing it back across the desk at me with just the slightest flick of his head, indicating that I should go back outside and into the hut next door. So, following his brief but accurate directions, I walked up to a small counter-window in the wall of the next
hut and tapped gently on the flimsy glass pane until a young man appeared. Dark and impossibly handsome – courtesy of his Persian

DNA – he had refined, classical features with high cheekbones and a long aquiline nose on powdery-smooth milk chocolate coloured skin. He wore an immaculately tailored blue blazer over a cream silk shirt and had big dark pools of eyes under a perfectly groomed bouffant of dark-brown hair – looking like he had just stepped off the pages of a 1970's fashion magazine – but what on earth was this creature doing out here at this desolate mountain outpost on the Iranian-Turkmen border? It was only when he fumbled with my carnet and passport, dropping both clumsily to the floor that I noticed his deformed and withered pincer-like right hand – just a thumb and three fused fingers – that the illusion was broken. I pretended to look elsewhere, but the sight of him was both compelling and tragic. And he didn't say a word or make eye contact, returning my papers with just a curt nod of his head to indicate that I could go. And as I turned to leave, a gang of rowdy young soldiers passed by me and proceeded to tease him mercilessly, like cruel schoolboys.

I headed down the mountain slowly and stopped at a final checkpoint, clogged with idle trucks and their tired drivers, where I was taken aside almost immediately by three senior officers with whom I took tea in a large office overlooking the grim border post. Banks of old grey filing cabinets covered an entire wall and important looking maps with pins and little flags and pieces of coloured string dominated another. They each sat at enormous wooden desks in high-backed leather chairs where they quizzed me from now. As we drank the tea and ate sweets I told them boldly of my planned itinerary across Iran; due west to Bojnurd, then on to the evocatively-named Gorgan, to the Caspian Sea coast and then south, up and across the Alborz Mountains and down into Tehran. But this part of my trip was the least-well researched, and it was more hopeful than a certain route and they quickly put paid to it by explaining that some sort of natural disaster had made the roads in that part of the country impassable and that the only option for me was to ride far deeper into Iran before heading west across the eight hundred or so kilometres of empty desert before reaching Tehran. More frikkin desert I thought to myself – at least the roads here were (allegedly) better.

They noted down the details of my carnet in a large leather-bound folio that one of them maintained and then insisted on taking a picture of themselves with me just to prove how tall I was. And as I went to leave, the most senior officer wrote something quickly on a slip of paper and handed it to me. Placing his hand on my arm, he said sincerely, "My friend – god forbid – if you ever have any

349

trouble in Iran, whatsoever, just call this number" They also gave me a wonderfully colourful annotated tourist map of Iran with far more detail on the road network than any the maps I carried. Practising my Farsi for the first time, I thanked them for their help and rode off into the small village of Bajgiran, a sleepy, dusty collection of mud brick houses where little stirred. I looked hopefully for a shop to buy supplies but there was nothing so I pressed on into the biscuit-coloured hills to the south along a surprisingly smooth, well laid and empty road with just my thoughts for company. And, although it was still cold, it was pleasant touring with the long alternating curves, coming one after another, creating a gentle rhythm that I found soothing. Eventually, though, after almost two hours "in the zone", I cleared the foothills and came to a crossroads on the open plains outside Quchan where the road from Ashgabat meets the main east-west highway between Mashad and Tehran. Cars flashed past in a blur without any consideration in my first taste of the Iranian Highway Code. In no hurry, I waited patiently before riding across the highway and up a long hill to a roundabout overlooking the town where I came to a stop. On first appearance, as it spread out before me down the gentle slope, it reminded me of a prosperous (if parched) country town in rural Australia, with a well defined grid of streets and neat homes and buildings of substance near its centre. Of course the church steeples were replaced with the domes of mosques, but it was certainly reminiscent of home, especially under an intensely bright blue cloudless sky. The streets were paved, there were sidewalks and traffic signals and the main avenues were lined with trees, but like home, the surrounding plains were dusty and dry and ran away to the south into a low mountain range, cast blue-grey in the midday heat haze. I found the centre of town by instinct and came to a surprisingly modern, busy high street with merchants selling clothes, electronics, whitegoods, food and more. I parked carefully between two cars and was immediately surrounded by a crowd of young men. All outfitted in modern urban gear, they shouted excitedly at me in broken English and, incredibly, were delighted when I stood up and pointed to the battered, but still recognizable sticker of an Australian flag on one of my panniers. They pawed over my bike and gasped in awe at the size of both me and my engine. And they watched on with a mix of curiosity and confusion as I fumbled to secure my bike with steel rope before bounding off to look for a place to change money; for according to my body clock it was well past lunchtime and I was hungry, but without any local currency to buy food. I quickly found a bank and wandered into a crowded but surprisingly modern air-conditioned branch office where a throng of well dressed swarthy men stood clamouring to complete their transactions. Strangely, the crowd parted and I was bustled to the front of the queue. But placing a couple of crisp one hundred dollar bills on the counter and asking politely but firmly for them to be changed into Iranian Rials was akin to lobbing a hand grenade into place, for as soon as I had uttered the words and put my money down everyone stopped, hushed and stared at the dirty Infidel with his filthy US dollars. The man behind the counter looked at me incredulously and insisted, at first, that he could not do business with me, only relenting after some tense negotiation where we agreed to his "fair market" price for a thick wad of Rials which I quickly stuffed into my backpack before leaving with my back to the door.

I walked back along the main street towards my bike and found a tiny hole in the wall café where I was indulged by a generous host who served me a wonderful meal of freshly charcoal grilled chicken, served with onions and grilled tomatoes in pita bread with a mint and yoghurt sauce. It was an incredible explosion of flavours that made my tastebuds sing after the relatively bland cuisine of Russia and Central Asia that sustained me for that last three months. Waves of pleasure washed over my body and in my ecstasy – and flush with money – I ordered another serve, finishing it all off with hot sweet tea and the hard rocks of white candy that came with it.

As I prepared to leave the same crowd of young men returned, surrounding me. Their leader stepped forward and presented me with a small gift of food which they had gathered quickly since first seeing me. And it was here that I caught my first glimpse of young Iranian women in their traditional chadors (worn over modern but conservative clothes). They stood in the background, keeping their distance and clutching at their chadors and covering their mouths with their free hand as they chatted nervously to each other, avoiding eye contact with me. And they were disarmingly beautiful, with long structured faces and high regal foreheads above dazzling green almond-shaped eyes and long straight brows; I couldn't help but stare at them. The young men gave me directions and soon I was riding out across the parched and bald rolling hills under a hot afternoon sun, past small primitive farming villages of mud huts that seemed to operate at subsistence level only. For there were no great tracts of crops nor was there any mechanisation evident, just donkeys, hoes and hard manual labour, in a pattern that was to repeat itself across Iran where there seemed to be a massive divide between the rural poor and their more affluent urban counterparts.

And, although these were back roads, cutting cross country, they were more than adequate compared to what I had experienced on my journey to date and, with virtually no other traffic, I made good time to Sultanabad where I joined the freeway and rode at an even faster clip to Sabsevaar, where I got horribly lost navigating a confusing series of interconnected roundabouts trying to cross the city, before filling up at a surprisingly modern gas station and heading back out onto the long straight divided freeway that led to Tehran. There were even signs in English showing the distance to major towns and cities along the way. The one at the entrance to the freeway read: Tehran 750km, Sharud 200km. I checked the position of the sun in the sky (already low) and my speed (averaging 120km/hr on the freeway), did the maths and figured I could make it by nightfall, so pressed on. But those first few minutes on the freeway were just a warm up act ahead of a mad main event as the half-crazed drivers of cars, buses and trucks all jockeyed for pole position in this deadly drag race across the desert. And it wasn't long before we passed the first of many fatal accidents; a crumpled mini-van and a battered family sedan lay near each other upside down on the rocky desert floor some fifty yards from the road, surrounded by a crowd of onlookers, emergency workers and distraught survivors. And it was difficult to understand how such an accident could occur on such a long straight stretch of one-way traffic across an empty desert; speed and driver error the only obvious reasons. But witnessing this carnage didn't seem to deter anyone, as our procession continued on at a breakneck 120kph (and this was in the slow lane). I could barely keep up, but, more afraid of the consequences of slowing down I pushed my bike even harder. And, with all the aerodynamics of a refrigerator, even a gentle cross breeze caught me like a wet sail and blew me around dangerously across, and then outside my lane. My arms began to ache from wrestling with the bike as I tried to maintain a constant heading into the teeth of the wind. I had never ridden so fast. I was in top gear and climbing through 6000 rpm, approaching the engine's red line – unchartered territory for both of us – and, despite the emphatic assurances of the inscrutable Mr Shu – whose face I could see clearly now in my mind's eye – that nagging feeling that I was sitting on an time bomb that might explode at any minute filled me with a deep dark fear. But there were more immediate issues to deal with as I was subjected to terrifying passing manoeuvres of Iranian drivers who came at me like Kamikaze pilots, only pulling out/over at the very last instant –

satisfied once they'd seen the whites of my eyes. All I could do was maintain a steady speed and bearing and watch breathlessly as they shaved past my left pannier – close enough for me to shake hands with the driver (or better still, reach over and throttle him). I have travelled to many countries and experienced many national character flaws first hand, but these guys were actually insane – they were crazy and didn't know it, driving seemingly without the slightest regard for human life – neither their own nor their kin nor anyone else's! But after one too many white-knuckle moments, and having decided that it was better to be the hunter rather than the hunted, I joined the inmates in the asylum, bravely merging into the overtaking lane by accelerating up to a ridiculously dangerous "cruising" speed of 140kph.

But my cavalier riding career finished almost before it had begun when, mid-way through a difficult passing manoeuvre around a big dirty truck, I was suddenly jolted from behind – and almost off my bike – tossed around in the turbulent wake of something very large, very blunt, very loud and frighteningly close behind me. Struggling to regain control, I stole a glance over my right shoulder and found myself staring up through the large windshield of a modern long distance bus, powering at top speed to Tehran as its frantic driver waved me off the road. Reacting instinctively, I rode off onto the shoulder of the road, but with rocks the size of tennis balls scattered liberally over a loose gravel surface atop a narrow embankment; safely bringing a 250kg motorcycle to rest from 140kph suddenly became a matter of life and death. I felt a massive surge of adrenalin followed by a wave of raw fear which focused all of my strength and concentration on control and braking as if nothing else mattered. Time seemed to slow down and everything external became a blur as I battled to stay onboard my bike as it bucked and turned angrily underneath me like a wild bronco. And in a strange sensation, despite the immediate focus on simply staying alive, my brain still had capacity to rationalise what was happening, with the little voice inside my head saying "Get ready – you are going to crash and this is going to hurt... .a lot." But, after what seemed like minutes of careering out of control across this gravel graveyard, I finally arrested the bike's sick momentum and pulled up – completely shattered. This was no longer fun; it was deadly serious – in a way that Siberia wasn't. For although it had been desperately hard in those early days – battling across the bogs, swamps and icy rivers, fighting off man-eating mosquitoes and suffering at the hands of my own mechanical ineptitude – at least I

353

was the master of my own destiny, but here I had to reckon with the recklessly insane with whom I "shared" the road.

I considered pitching my tent for the night but continued on, concluding that given number of vehicles actually *leaving the road*, it may in fact be less risky riding on into the night. And restarting my journey was only slightly less difficult and dangerous than my exit from it had been as I merged back into fast lane – riding up over 120kph on the rocky verge – before diving into the first available gap in the procession of slower traffic, where, chastened, I nervously spent the remainder of the journey to Shahrud, stopping only once in the apparent fading light only to realise that, with my intense concentration on staying alive, I had forgotten to remove my powerful sunglasses. In the twilight I rode up and over a low mountain pass and headed down a long slope towards Shahrud. But darkness descended quickly over the desert and it was a sprawling web of twinkling lights under an indigo sky that ultimately resolved into the large and surprisingly modern city of Shahrud. It also had a modern, well equipped and aggressive police force, most of whom greeted me at the end of the freeway explaining that it was in fact illegal to ride a motorcycle on an Iranian motorway. But with the cultural and language barriers just too high and too wide to bridge tonight, I was pardoned on account of my own ignorance and allowed to proceed. Navigating by instinct I negotiated a series of large roundabouts and found my way onto a bizarre avenue of pulsating neon palm trees, before finally emerging into the throbbing heart of Shahrud along a narrow dog-legged street clogged with traffic.

Central Shahrud was a dense collection of low-rise concrete tower blocks atop a densely honeycombed layer of little shops and arcades. Illuminated under a thick canopy of bright neon signs it was abuzz with commerce and looked and felt more like Kowloon or Soho than remote Iranian desert city. There were dazzling displays of gold jewellery, gleaming collections of the latest consumer electronics, daring fashions (dresses and modest lingerie), restaurants and cafés teeming with people and incredible Wonker-esque confectionary shops. Merchants stood in their doorways hawking and there were young people everywhere enjoying themselves. It was alive and prosperous in a way that I had not experienced anywhere on my journey and the streets here were choked with modern cars and motor-scooters orchestrated to a backbeat of modern music and blaring horns. Even the young women in headscarves and chadors seemed happy and light-footed as they skipped along the busy streets, usually in pairs, holding hands. I pulled up beside a group of young men and asked about places to stay and was promptly escorted behind a long motorcade of Iranian Mods on their motor scooters back through the city to a government operated lodge – apparently the only accommodation in the city. Nestled in a forest of tall cedar trees on a steep hillside, it overlooked a public park where, incredibly, young families were still enjoying picnics under a strange yellow lamplight.

I rode up the steep driveway, parked and entered the lodge. Fashioned in 1960's minimalist block design, inside was Spartan, but clean and spacious, an open plan running over a split-level that separated the dining hall from the rest of the public areas. A young man approached and greeted me warmly. He introduced himself as "Sapoor", and explained that he was a long-term lodger here; a student in this University town – but he couldn't have looked less Persian, with his great height, large pale oval-shaped face and big round slate-green eyes under a thicket of wiry, mousy brown hair. We spoke for some time as I introduced myself and told him a little about my journey, and with his long skinny limbs, loose loping gait and big feet – encased in even bigger white sneakers – and a wide-eyed gentle naiveté, he appeared to me more like an Iranian Goofy. But he was half my age, no longer a boy but not yet a man and my entrance into his cosseted world had clearly sparked something inside him. He took me to the administration office where the old man in charge – who emerged groggily from behind a shuttered door – told me politely but firmly that it was impossible for me, as a foreigner, to stay here. His duty done, he turned to leave, but Sapoor, incensed, ran after him, pleading with him that surely as a guest in their country, I deserved more hospitality than this. They argued heatedly until finally the old man relented, offering me a small cot in a windowless storeroom on the first floor for a nominal fee. And so, Sapoor became my guardian angel for the remainder of my stay; harassing the skeleton staff to prepare a traditional evening meal for me (spicy barley soup, bread with a yoghurt and mint dip, roast chicken with rice and barberries) which I ate alone in the large dining hall while he studied my travel guide – which seemed to fascinate him – and then by escorting me on an impromptu tour of the city that he knew so well. Nothing was too much trouble, and as we walked he explained that he was from Tehran, where his family lived, but that his father had sent both he and his older brother to (different) regional cities to complete their studies; his in architecture and his brother's in medicine. Tehran, he complained, was too crowded and polluted, and had limited options and places for tertiary study. His

355

family wasn't wealthy – nor were they poor by Iranian standards – but they had scrimped and saved so that both Sapoor and his brother could secure a better future. Sapoor spent entire semesters living in a very basic room at the lodge (only marginally better than mine – his had a window), returning home just once or twice a year on religious holidays and birthdays.

***

When we returned to the lodge, two men taking tea on the outside terrace under a dull lamplight called us over to join them. Thirty-something and smartly dressed, they looked like brothers to my blunt eye; short and stocky with squared-off features, they were both dark and brooding with neatly clippered beards that ran like a king tide over their pock-marked hollow cheeks and lapped at their dark sunken eyes – eyes that burned with an unusual intensity. But these weren't the classical Persian features of antiquity; these two looked more like battle-hardened, self sufficient Bedouin brothers to me. Their reality however, was far more prosaic; they were both engineers, well read and worldly-wise and both spoke English perfectly. They opened with the familiar barrage of questions, delivered as if they were cross examining a surely-guilty witness:
"What do you think of our country?"
"What do you think of America?" and so on.
But then the conversation took an unexpected and introspective turn as they asked "And what do you think of the way our women dress?"
"What do you think of relations between men and women in our country?" The court room atmosphere had vanished and now they waited anxiously for my perspective on what I had thought were taboo subjects. And as we discussed these topics they painted a picture of a younger generation much more liberal in their values and practices than I had ever imagined, and one deeply at odds with their conservative leaders and devoid of the fanaticism and fervour portrayed in the media. Explaining the reality of modern-day Iranian life one of them said "Of course, you know, men and women come together before marriage – it is only natural. And our men do not beat our women or keep them locked away...no more than you would. And the burqa...we all want to cut them up and burn them – men and women alike! It's just the older generation, clinging to their old traditions that hold us back. And the Mullahs..." he trailed off, cursing the clerics who ruled their society with an iron fist, sustaining and enforcing Islamic traditions and law – some of them

barely literate tribal elders, who applied Sharia law according to their own deeply conservative views.

They went on to describe a system wracked with corruption where jobs, personal progression and rewards were doled out and regulated via a powerful network of anonymous powerbrokers working in concert with the Mullahs. "You know, we are university-educated men, qualified engineers with much experience and yet we earn only four hundred US dollars a month – it's barely enough to pay the rent, buy food and clothes for my family." Said one of them grimly, before the other completed the bleak picture, telling me "We both live with our extended families in tiny one bedroom apartments in central Tehran where the air is thick and dirty and the traffic is gridlocked; I spend three hours every day travelling to and from work and there is nowhere for my children to play."

Ironically, they both pointed to the USA as their beacon of hope, with one of them telling me proudly, "You know, there are many Iranians living and working in America – scientists, engineers, doctors and more. We are an intelligent and hard-working people who make contributions wherever we go."

"And in America", the other continued with growing excitement, "A man is rewarded for the value of his work – that's why we both want to go and live there, god willing" It was a strategy borne of the ultimate pragmatism; an equation resolved in the absence of any religious constants, for incredibly, these were not factors in their calculations.

"But it is very difficult and expensive for us and we both have families to support – so for the moment it's just a dream" said one of them disconsolately. We talked on and they asked me endless questions about my job, how much I was paid, where I lived, how much my house cost, what type of car I drove, what my family ate, how much food cost and so on. I described the public education, healthcare and other, more targeted government benefits available to all citizens at home and they shook their heads in disbelief. And in the morning, as I took my breakfast in the near-empty communal dining hall, one of the men rushed up to me, knelt down and grabbed my arm, pleaded softly to me "Please, please, take me to your country... I want to leave." He looked up at me with his sad wet eyes and all I could muster was the wholly inadequate "I understand and I am sorry my friend"

***

Sapoor found me just as I was preparing to leave, pumping up my slowly deflating tyres ahead of the long freeway ride to Tehran. Mistaking my long and complicated preparations for deep experience, he shook his head and guffawed in admiration, And in the muddle of what I could only assume were poorly translated adjectives he farewelled me sincerely saying "You are beautiful man".

I quickly cleared the sleepy early morning streets, filled my bike with an unknown fossil fuel (arguing with the sly attendant who steadfastly refused to give me change), before heading back out into the madness of the freeway. The sun was already high in a bright white-blue cloudless sky and burned down intensely on the rocky desert floor, radiating heat angrily back at the invading road and its users. Beyond Shahrud, the freeway ran up and along the dramatic rust-coloured foothills and cliffs of the Alborz Mountains – a constant companion on my entire journey across the Iranian plateau – before flattening out for a fast freewheeling ride into Tehran. And while there was certainly a smattering of modern cars on the road today, the majority seemed to be 1960's era Hillman Hunters or Humbers – like the kind my mother used to drive – but instead of being driven cautiously by a conservative woman with a heart of gold in sensible walking shoes, these were controlled by suicidal maniacs who drove their overloaded family saloons as if they were piloting cruise missiles into downtown Washington. And these assassins were almost always accompanied by their large families, packed in like sardines that typically included a gaggle of hooded women jammed across the back seat who all turned and waved back at me, smiling widely as they nearly ran me off the road.

Tehran appeared in the distance like an ancient biblical city; a sprawling tableau of low rise off-white buildings climbing up the long sloping hillsides that ran from a central valley where the city sat – a seething crucible of a metropolis shrouded in a thick brown blanket of smog. But it was the scale of the city that took my breath away; home to more than ten million people, it grew larger and larger as I approached until suddenly it devoured me whole as I was propelled like a tiny piece of flotsam along its massive arteries at breakneck speed, powerless against the mighty current of traffic. But unlike the deadly desert drag race I had just survived, there seemed to be an unspoken collective understanding here that kept this fragile system from breaking down, for there was no road rage here, no horn pounding, fist shaking or bumping – just precise high speed urban driving as our peloton snaked its way through the ugly outer suburbs of Tehran, past barren concrete tower blocks, cheap strip malls and acres of dreary light industry. Penetrating deeper into the city, we rode across massive squares teeming with people in bustling markets and clamouring at overcrowded bus stations. And, without a map, I just kept riding, following the surge of traffic heading west toward the city centre, and soon enough the buildings grew taller and older and closed in around me as I found the heart of the city. The traffic slowed to a crawl and suddenly it got hotter and the road became sticky underfoot. I stopped a few times to get my bearings – the massive Khomeini telephone tower my only reference point – but whenever I did, the old buses that dominate Tehran's woefully inadequate public transport system groaned past in an endless procession, belching sooty fumes all over me while my a torrent of traffic roared directly overhead on the elevated freeways that crisscross Tehran, just above street level. Still uncertain of my position – but not lost – I wheeled my bike over to an impressively dressed traffic policeman who caught my eye (think navy suit with epaulettes, shiny black peaked cap and white gloves). Tall and proud, he stood on his tip toes to rise up to my height as he did his very best to provide directions. As he did, a small crowd gathered quickly with middle-aged men pawing at me, offering their homes and wives' home cooking to me. But today, unlike those early days of my tour when I gladly accepted the hospitality of Siberian villagers and took things as they came, I was in a different frame of mind – I was finishing; I had to be in Istanbul in ten days and just wanted to rest and explore the city independently. I rode off in the opposite direction – on account of the myriad of one way streets – and circled the Khomeini tower three frustrating times before finding the small hotel that had been recommended to me, hidden at the end of long alleyway off a main street near the infamous and long closed US Embassy.

I parked my bike carefully in the small but secure courtyard and entered the dark foyer where I was greeted by the friendly manager and his assistant – a young girl covered almost completely in a black burqa, who unfortunately, with her short heavy build, large nose, faint moustache and wide crooked grin, reminded me of the woman who cast the first stone at Matthias in The Life of Brian. A silent high pitched squawk of "Stone him! Stone him! Stone him!" rang through my head as I smiled kindly back at her and signed the guest book (and continued for my entire stay, whenever I saw her) – but this was no joke, with stoning allegedly still used in Iran (under Sharia Law) as the punishment for adultery.

Well fed, with a greasy complexion and wide smile, the manager asked if I had any special requirements.

"A room on the ground floor would be good on account of all my luggage" I said.

"No problem sir" he said obsequiously, smiling like a Cheshire cat.

***

Desperately hungry (it was already mid-afternoon), I took my lunch directly in the bare-bones hotel cafeteria. There was no menu as such but I was quickly served another plate of what I now suspected was the national dish: chicken kebabs. As I ate, the unmistakable melodic *"beepety beepety"* of happy Filipino chatter drifted past me and I looked up to see a crew of worker-women who had obviously just arrived in the country. They sat in a tight circle and chatted anxiously; some excited, others just plain scared – the latter comforted by the older more experienced women. And, despite their circumstance, they carried on oblivious as if they were taking a picnic in the countryside. But their party was short-lived as the hotel manager marched in, angrily clapping his hands and barking orders at them sending them scurrying in all directions.

With no elevator, I hauled my luggage up to the first floor and searched in vain for my promised room, where I was eventually re-directed by a shy cleaning lady who sent me climbing up a further six flights of stairs where, after almost blacking out from the exertion, I located my shabby room on the very top floor. Bare, apart from the faded tourism posters that hung limply on the unpainted plaster walls and a saggy single bed covered optimistically in a chocolate-coloured cotton spread, the room reeked of a sharp septic odour that emanated from the primitive open plumbing in the bathroom. But there were some small concessions up here; it was away from the noise of the street and had an uninterrupted view over the rooftops of central Tehran. With my nose pegged tight I stood on my tip toes in stockinged feet on the paper thin corrugated carpet and looked out over the jumble of dirty grey-brown concrete blocks that surrounded me; tiny roof-top terraces the only flashes of life in an otherwise stark panorama. But this country of allegedly fanatical patriots was also listening intently to the rest of the world with each building covered in an unruly thatch of homemade stick antennas and satellite dishes.

Tired, I lay down for a short nap, waking only once at dusk for a few seconds before falling back asleep. The next morning I took the standard fare Iranian breakfast of flat bread, hard boiled egg, honey, butter, goat's cheese and sweet tea in the communal dining hall

360

surrounded by an eclectic bunch of travellers – most down at heel, some older, some younger, teams of dog-tired travelling salesmen, freshly shaven in their shiny polyester suits with their little suitcases already packed and ready for business, lingering over what was perhaps the only enjoyable part of their day. And as we ate, we were all drawn to the TV monitor high up in one corner of the hall where another dark, handsome Persian, impeccably dressed in a sharp suit and buttoned up white shirt, sat incongruously in a lush garden (think tropical flowers and water features) delivering the news and current affairs in a long tirade at his audience; apparently this was breakfast TV, Iranian-style. And then the reason for his near hysteria became apparent, as images of Iranian nuclear power plants, world leaders, the United Nations and a defiant, desk-thumping Iranian President flashed across the screen. I finished up quickly and left before a mob could form and headed out into the city. This was the first place on my journey with a motorcycle dealership of my bike's marque and although it had only been a remote contingency in planning I now felt it essential that I get my bike serviced (or at least inspected) by a qualified mechanic. Feeling confident that I had voided my warranty ("...err, well, it all started when I rode my bike into a 2,000km bog in Siberia..." was always going to be a difficult opening line), I was happy to pay for the peace of mind as I still had to dodge more missiles on the Iranian freeways and ride the rollercoaster back roads along the Black Sea coast at a fair clip to finish "on time". Miraculously, the hotel manager found the shop address in the Tehran phone book and had provided directions to it (incredibly, it was located on a quiet back street just a few blocks from the hotel).

My neighbourhood was a dense and chaotic collection of tiny auto shops, mini-marts and spare parts dealers – a modern day bazaar of sorts, frenetic with activity, beyond which I found myself on one of the large avenues that slices across central Tehran. And now, excited at the prospect of finally disarming the psychological time bomb I had carried with me since riding out of Siberia some two months earlier, I literally bounded along the pavement, skipping ahead of the gridlocked traffic. And I watched on dumbfounded as a stream of insane young men on motor scooters slalomed through the traffic with the precision and confidence of Olympic downhill skiers, balancing impossibly large and dangerous cargoes on their flimsy bikes. Instinctively, I slapped my hands over my eyes as a rider perched precariously on two huge bags of rice on a bike already laden with massive sheets of plate glass zipped past me and careered fearlessly into a busy roundabout.

Not wanting to witness yet another accident, I looked around and above me instead, taking in the architecture of this older quarter of Tehran. Dominated by large neo-classical stone-fronted commercial buildings, the area had a faded 1950's feel about it with large empty offices, commercial appliance shops cluttered with junk, technical bookshops awash with dusty covers and the marbled porticos of long departed colonial banks still standing guard over their massive vaulted banking chambers. It all felt as if it were from another era, with a dull hue to everything, like looking at an old photo.

I came to a large intersection, crossed the dangerous river of traffic via a pedestrian bridge and was dumped jarringly back into the 21st century, landing in the middle of a phalanx of strip shops peddling cheap jewellery, CDs, clothes and leather goods. Beyond this arcade of desperate commerce I found the promised dealership on a quiet cul de sac opposite a massive military barracks where, as the only Westerner within miles, I was eyed off suspiciously by the highly strung guards. But instead of guards I was greeted with a shuttered shop front. It was closed! I couldn't believe it. I checked my watch – it was late morning on a Tuesday. Peering through the security grill I was taken by the display; it was pure eye candy – a showroom full of brand new motorsport vehicles (mostly scooters, trikes and jet skis) – all arranged appealingly on a gleaming black marble floor. There was even a factory- fresh version of my bike on display – now my pulse really started racing. A bank of desks and a series of enclosed offices on a wide veranda filled the rear of the showroom. But these were all locked tight, it was dark inside and there were no signs of life. By now a small crowd of envious window shoppers had gathered outside; young couples admiring the scooters and more adventurous Alpha males eying off the other equipment. I waited hopefully with them until finally the office manager came and opened the front door. It was a cold call but amazingly he thrust out his hand, shaking mine saying "No problem Sir, bring your bike in and we'll service it today, immediately!" It was music to my ears.

I returned quickly with my bike, negotiating the numerous one way streets that I had not taken note of earlier as a pedestrian. I wheeled my bike down a side alley and out into a large open area behind the showroom, a vast slab of smooth concrete covered by a low-pitched fibreglass roof. It was light, airy and spacious and two men in dirty overalls stood smiling in front of a large toolshed that stood in one corner of the yard. The office manager came to greet me and I told him a little about my trip and how it was that I came to be here this morning. He turned to the mechanics and translated quickly, both nodding their heads and looking at each other goggle eyed, before letting out a collective "ooohh". Turning back to me now, the office manager proclaimed reassuringly "And these are the finest mechanics in all of Iran!" But to me, in their long greasy overalls, with their dark unshaven faces and unkempt hair, they looked more like Mexican prison escapees than Persian mechanics. One of them even had a gold tooth that glinted in the light when he smiled at me. Worried sick about my homemade Chinese clutch, I asked them to inspect it and make any repairs necessary. Carte blanche...go for it... .knock yourselves out... cost – no problem... .really, I just want it fixed. They processed this information quickly, went into a huddle with their boss, who then turned to me shaking his head.

"You want us to open up the engine?" he said bewildered.

"Ah... .yes... please" I said, a little perplexed, wondering how I could have been any more explicit.

"But what if we find something wrong?" he shot back.

"What do you mean??" I said – a little exasperated. "My clutch has been re-built with scrap metal by a little Chinese man who lives in a closet and works on the pavement under a beach umbrella. I've ridden thousands of kilometres across deserts, along rutted mountain tracks, through rivers and been bogged knee deep in sand dunes. My bike needs to be examined and repaired properly! That's why I came here!" – I was ranting now.

The office manger listened politely and with great restraint, sensing my growing frustration, and said calmly, "Well, you know, the clutch, it is a complex piece of the motorcycle."

"You're telling me... I stuck a wrench in there two months ago and almost killed myself"

"You know, it is illegal to ride bikes larger than 250cc in Iran; we have never actually serviced a bike like this before..." he confessed. The Mexicans looked away.

"But I saw a bike like mine in your showroom!"

"Shipped here in error... it's only on display because we have nowhere else to put it and can't afford to return it. We don't know how it works." "No problem, just do your best", I said cheerfully.

"No, no, it is not wise. We cannot" he said obliquely, clearly troubled by what I was suggesting. And so we continued on as I tried to unravel their Eastern philosophy, until I finally got it: they weren't saying they *couldn't fix it* – not at all – they just didn't want to get into a position where they *might not be able to fix it* and hence let me down, leaving me stranded. I was getting hot. Perhaps he was right – and like Schrödinger' s famous Cat – peering inside my clutch might actually resolve its current indeterminate state where it was neither working nor not working; this was a deep thought experiment that my fragile mind was clearly not capable of processing today. The two Mexicans simply looked at each other and shrugged their shoulders, enquiring of me politely "Would you like some chicken kebabs?"

"Sure..." And with that I retired to the rear of the showroom where I sat at one of the large desks and enjoyed another mouth watering serve of chicken, yoghurt and mint sauce and juicy tomatoes on flat bread. As I ate the two hombres launched themselves into frenzy of cleaning, polishing and bolt tightening. They wiped the accumulated dirt and grime from my engine and frame, checked my battery and dusted, prodded and probed.

Meanwhile, back in the showroom, after looking at his watch anxiously, the office manager walked brusquely to the shop front where, despite the growing crowd, he pulled the security grill back across the windows and door; no one had been allowed in today except for me, and now the entire office staff joined me for lunch, sitting at their desks, reading the newspaper, eating and picking their teeth as their potential customers waited with surprising patience outside.

I returned to the workshop where an older dignified man, looking like he had just stepped out of the Raj (he wore a beige tunic over black military pants with a white towel over one arm) delivered a tray of tea and sweets and brought me a stool to sit on. As the work continued I had a lengthy philosophical discussion with the office manager about good and evil, fate, humanity and travel. He was a man of great life experience, sound intellect and gave sage advice and I enjoyed his company tremendously – despite the mechanical shortcomings of his operation. But even my own forward planning had been seriously flawed with most of the critical replacement parts that I had brought all the way from home (like a new set of brake pads and an air filter) actually belonging to another model bike and not suitable for mine. "Don't worry; it's relatively flat from here to Istanbul – just a few small hills. Don't ride too fast and you'll be fine" said the manager hopefully.

Finally, as they were wrapping up, the manager said "And what type of oil would you like?" Akin to a Russian asking a foreigner which vodka to drink, I simply said
"Give me the best you have!"

"Err...we don't keep that kind of oil here", he said, a little embarrassed, immediately dispatching one of his grease monkeys to purchase a large canister of it – although I did look on with some concern as they poured the strange blue-green syrup into my engine case, wondering which carbon-based fossils exactly it had been derived from. Reimbursing him the few dollars it had cost for the oil, I asked how much I owed for the service, to which he replied a little startled "Oh no, Sir, there won't be any charge; this is the least we can do for you. Please accept our work and help as our gift to you. We hope you enjoy the rest of your stay in Iran and, god willing, please travel safely home to your family" shaking my hand warmly as he spoke. Waving them goodbye, I rode back out into the chaos of Tehran traffic under a searing sun and returned (slowly) to the hotel.

***

My bike cleaned and oiled, I spent the rest of the afternoon at the National Museum of Iran, where I lingered over the wonderful collection of Persian antiquities and then stood mesmerised in front of the massive stone relief from ancient Persepolis that showed Darius the Great, his crown prince and their courtiers receiving an important official. Dating from approx 500BC it was incredibly well preserved, appearing to me as if it had just emerged from the stone masons' studio with its clear, crisp lines, delicate profiles and subtle detail. And I had an equally enjoyable time in the neighbouring Islamic Arts Museum where I trawled through an eclectic collection of pottery, ceramics, textiles and calligraphy (in form of handwritten Korans, captured from the oral tradition in the eighth and ninth centuries).

I emerged from the Museum in the late afternoon and headed directly to Shar Park – one of the largest and most verdant in the whole city – where I sat in the cool shade near a large ornate fountain and watched the procession of city dwellers pass by; office workers, students, mothers and daughters, old men (usually in pairs) and more. And while a small minority of women wore the claustrophobic black chador, leaving just their eyes uncovered, most applied a very liberal interpretation of their dress code, wearing smart tailored pants and stylised tunics with colourful silk scarves pushed well back on their heads. Clearly many were professional women, wives, homemakers and independent. But it hadn't always been like this, with the progressive Reza Shah Pahlavi issuing a decree in 1935 banning the chador, telling his people that all Iranian women should

"....cast their veils, this symbol of injustice and shame, into the fires of oblivion." Indeed, during the 1960s, modern Iranians could be seen wearing mini-skirts, bellbottoms and other colourful and more revealing clothes, but sadly all of this had been undone by the arrival of the Ayatollah Khomeini, who upon seizing power immediately labelled the chador the "flag of the revolution", banning all other more liberal forms of dressing for women.

As dusk fell, powerful green and yellow floodlights slowly took effect, creating a surreal fairground atmosphere; the lush canopy overhead was illuminated in soft light and the fountains now shot sparkling showers of golden spray high into the night sky and there were even street vendors whom I had not noticed earlier. Suddenly I thought of my family and wondered where they were and what they were doing. I had been away for three months now and it was returning home which now dominated my thoughts rather than the remainder of my trip; in a little over a week – all going to plan – I would be riding into Istanbul and ending my journey. It was so close yet still impossible to imagine what that day would be like. My wheels seemed to be rolling faster and faster each day and my mind was struggling to keep up. I didn't have a frame of reference – everything was fluid now. Then I wondered: "What would it be like going home? What then?"

I chose a path at random away from the plaza and came to a traditional tea house which, from the outside, with its white stuccoed walls, high pitched roof and dark timber frame looked more like a parish church. Inside, however, was more Ali Baba's cave. Richly decorated, it had a decidedly Persian art deco feel about it with brass oil lamps, antique vases, carpets and rugs, period furniture and other objets d'art. Songbirds twittered in large cages and the air was scented with the smoky perfume of the Hookah's being shared by men who lolled about languidly on beds of cushions around the perimeter. Sitting in pairs, they passed the pipes between them discretely, each drawing back in a series of short sharp puffs, quickly filling their lungs before blowing lazy smoke rings. Taken slowly with tea and sweets, this was an age-old intimate social ritual between grown men that did not have an obvious equivalent in Western macho culture. Then I looked more carefully about the pavilion. A long series of strange sepia toned photos dominated the walls – scenes from old Tehran and athletic shots of vulnerable looking young men – bringing a faint, clandestine Oscar Wilde feel to the place. But any lingering doubts I might have had about Iranian manhood were torpedoed by the hot bed of lust that had suddenly erupted on the far benches as a young couple engaged in a session of heavy petting. Rolling about on their cushions like Burt Lancaster and Deborah Kerr in the beach scene in From Here to Eternity, they cut a swathe through the mores of appropriate pubic behaviour between Iranian men and women, but no one seemed to mind as they kissed and cuddled between tokes on the Hookah (hers taken with the utmost discretion). And, dressed very casually in jeans and a modern tunic, she wore her headscarf more like a neck-warmer, constantly adjusting it to stop it being removed altogether as her Romeo caressed her thick mane of dark brown hair. I thought of my engineer friends from Shahrud and imagined these two at the front of the chorus cursing the Mullahs. Trying hard to look elsewhere I quickly finished my tea and rock candy and departed, walking home along the now darkened pathways within the park, passing young couples strolling arm in arm enjoying the mild evening. Some even stopping me to talk – not about global politics or Fatwas or religious ideology but about everyday topics and the differences in our lives; perfectly reasonable questions in polite conversations with genuinely warm and friendly people.

***

In the morning I ran the gauntlet of the Iranian freeway system again as I headed towards Ghazvin, Alamut and the legendary Castles of the Assassins – my real destination today. But before I could re-enter that high-speed, high-octane smash-up derby, I stuttered for an interminable time along the massive arterial road that drains the city to the West, embedded in a hot river of traffic that inched along like a lava flow from a murmuring volcano. Pinned in on all sides by overheated cars, trucks and busses, my safety suit quickly became a sauna as the waves of heat slowly broiled me like a take-away chicken. Finally, convinced that my tyres were slowly melting into the asphalt and worried that my bike may spontaneously combust, I pulled up in the long shadows of the giant Azadi (or Liberty) Monument to cool down. Marking the gateway to the city, it was controversially built by the last Shah to "commemorate" 2,500 years of Persian monarchy, but was re-named immediately after the 1979 revolution as a symbol of freedom for the people. But irrespective of its origin or intended symbolism it was an impressive structure; impossibly tall, it looked like a truncated new-age cathedralcum-rocket ship with twisted sheets of creamy marble rising to a massive archway supporting a blunt star-shaped capsule atop.

I eventually made it back onto the freeway where, with six lanes each way, it was head down and full throttle (i.e. more white knuckle riding in the slow lane) until I was able to exit safely two hours later just outside Ghazvin. Stopping at a large market garden on a side road I stood on the edge of the freshly ploughed field for a long time in front of a sign slowly deciphering the directions (in Farsi) before heading up into the foothills of the Alborz Mountains towards Alamut. Fortunately, it was a good paved road that hauled itself up the mountainside here, but with its hairpin corners and no safety barrier, it was a challenging ride – made even more challenging by the overloaded jalopies and motor scooters that careered past me, virtually out of control, propelled along insane trajectories and at improbable speeds by wide-eyed locals. Rounding the back of the summit I came to a dramatic panorama of bone dry mountain ranges that ran off to the horizon in sharp crumpled waves and, directly below me here, a deep river valley that fell away almost vertically. I descended even more slowly and carefully than I had climbed – passing tea houses that seemed to hang in mid air as if it were only their entrances actually attached to the earth. Reaching the valley floor, I crossed a long concrete bridge over a colourless stream and came to a sleepy village where I patrolled up and down the only street looking for something and somewhere to eat. But it was as if I had intruded on a day of mourning and I could almost feel the naked hostility radiating from the kerbside as I inspected this drab and dusty village. Unsmiling men sat straight-backed and silent in groups around tables and on chairs facing the street as if they had no other business but to watch me. All the shops and cafes were shuttered and lifeless and now suddenly I started to feel the cold of the late autumn. Nothing stirred – the heavy silence broken only by the thumping of my exhaust as it reverberated off all of the hard surfaces of the streetscape around me. Watchfully, I completed two lonely circuits up and down the main drag before I parked and dismounted, determined to cut through this chilly reception. I took my helmet off and smiled at the locals who remained unmoved, but it was the children who could not resist my openness, curious about this rather odd looking intruder. I saw a shop only half shuttered and darted inside before the sleepy shopkeeper realised what was happening. I pointed to some exciting looking tins on the shelves behind him but he shook his head solemnly from side to side in the unmistakable, universal "No".

"Bread?"

"No"

"Sausage?"

"No"

"Soft drink?"

"No", and so on. But I persisted until finally, he reluctantly sold me a packet of crisps, which I ate standing up next to my motorbike in the deep gutter of the street. And they were awful – stale and saturated with strange artificial flavours that left an unpleasant fishy aftertaste in my mouth – and they weren't filling either. And as I ate, the locals maintained their vigilance, eyeing me off suspiciously until finally a large, oafish man approached me. He was young and powerfully built, but greasy, overweight and unkempt and I stiffened as he came at me aggressively, dancing silently around me placing his had over his mouth repeatedly, like a Navaho Indian deciding how he wanted to scalp his victim. But I quickly realised he was harmless; a simpleton who just wanted to protect me and perhaps make a new friend. He stopped his threatening pantomime and tugged firmly at my arm, backing away silently as he did, beckoning for me to join him. I looked at the circle of disapproving faces closing in around me before moving off in the wake of my rescuer, wondering what exactly it was I had done to offend them so deeply. In quick step I followed my Persian Boo Radley as he disappeared down a long alleyway between two nearby shopfronts, catching just a fleeting glimpse of him as he disappeared behind the far end of the long buildings. And I followed as quickly as I could, wading through the waist high weeds and tramping over the mounds of debris and rubbish that filled the small space between the two buildings. Turning the corner I found my new friend smiling widely and holding a door open, inviting me to enter. I peered inside the doorway...it was a charcoal chicken café but the shopfront had been shuttered tight and inside was almost in complete darkness. I entered cautiously, stepping into the kitchen, almost immediately stumbling over the three men who were huddled together like desperate refugees under a counter. As my eyes and other senses adjusted I quickly realised they were feverishly devouring a freshly roasted chicken in a clandestine picnic, far from the prying eyes of passers by. Licking his greasy fingers before wiping them on his grimy tunic, the ring leader called conspiratorially for me to join their little cabal. It was a bizarre scene which I struggled to make sense of, and then it suddenly dawned on me: it was Ramadan! In all of my planning and research for my journey this annual Islamic ritual had completely escaped me. Completely. Oh Bugger. Then it began to sink in; between dawn and dusk for the next month, devout Muslims everywhere (i.e. almost everyone I would encounter for the rest of my journey in Iran and Turkey) would be fasting and focusing even more assiduously on the teachings of the Koran. Finding food during the day (let alone consuming it) would be nigh on impossible, save for any further Infidels that I might meet. On a more positive note, however – and according to my guide book in the section helpfully titled, "Times to Avoid Travelling in Iran" – during this period, followers of Islam are encouraged to "...refrain from anger, envy, greed, lust, sarcastic retorts, backstabbing, and gossip and to aspire to higher levels of self-discipline, sacrifice, as well as to find sympathy for, and be more generous and charitable to, those less fortunate." Now, that suited me just fine.

Politely declining their offer, I backed out of the kitchen slowly, leaving them to finish their meal – and commit their sins – at their leisure. I skipped back to my bike and rode out of town without looking back. With the exception of a few tired farmers and their donkey carts, the road was empty. Thankfully though it was still paved, but it was all curves and cuttings and rough-made bridges over rocky streams as it wound its way around the tightly knotted, barren foothills of the giant massif that shot up steeply to my right. And it was getting colder as I rode on through the lengthening shadows of the late afternoon. Within half an hour I had come to the small village of Gazor Khan, where a welcoming party of urchins greeted me with in a hail storm of dirt bullets. Discretion being the better part of valour here, I rode away up the long steep treeless boulevard that was the main street before veering to the right as it ended abruptly, its course truncated by a blunt cliff face that seemed to fall from the sky in one long continuous sheet of rock. I rode on and up, beyond the town, with my bike labouring heavily on the steep grade of narrow track etched into the mountain side until I reached a small clearing opposite the entrance to the infamous Castle of the Assassins – or, to be more accurate, the *Castle of Alamut*. And, although it now lay in ruins, it had once been – almost one thousand years ago – the home of the great Ismaili leader Hasan-i-Sabbah. Claiming direct descent from Fatima (the daughter of the prophet Muhammad), he had been dispatched from headquarters in Cairo to proselytize the locals and to establish a rural stronghold in Northern Persia against the Seljuq Turks (the ruling Sunni Muslims), thus laying the seeds for a future revolution. And this had been his impenetrable citadel from which he had orchestrated his grand subversive plot.

But today it was eerily quiet; abandoned, except for an aerie of watchful eagles that circled high above the lonely, craggy outcrop. I parked and secured my bike, crossed the roadway and made my way on foot via a long stone pathway cut into the blind side of the mountain. The path ended all too quickly at flight of rickety steel frame steps that brought me up onto a bald and rocky spine of exposed mountain. Leading directly to the fortress, it was, save for an almost vertical tower of unassailable bedrock, its only connection to the outside world (which had in times of siege, provided its occupants with wonderful natural security, allowing any would-be attackers to be picked off easily from positions high above). But today it wasn't marksmen I needed to worry about; it was the ferocious wind that came in random gusts, almost knocking me off my feet as I scurried across. And, even after arriving safely at the base of the fortress, there were still more obstacles to contend with as I negotiated another two flights of flimsy steel-frame steps above me. Bolted precariously into the rock face, they lifted me even higher toward my goal, but dangerously out and away from the tower of rock, out over the empty space between me and the shadowy fields hundreds of metres below. It was a dizzying perspective that involuntarily drew my eyes and seemingly my whole body down into it in a sickening sensation that literally took my breath away.

Focusing on the narrow path ahead (and nothing else), I cleared the steps, rounded the rear of the fortress and eased myself through a tight scrum of large boulders to arrive at the main site. And surprisingly, despite being sacked by the Mongols almost seven hundred years ago there was still much remaining of the original installation. I sat on a large smooth boulder and stared into the empty compound and wondered dreamily at some of the more apocryphal tales of the castle and its inhabitants. Embroidered by Marco Polo – who visited Alamut in the thirteenth century – they told of a fantastic pleasure garden, overflowing with wine, honey and milk, populated by beautiful women, where drugged novices would swear blind loyalty to their master, convinced that Paradise on Earth awaited them as reward for their deadly services (indeed it was these "agents of Hasan" that reputedly led to the term *Assassin*). But the reality was far more prosaic with Hasan-i-Sabbah reportedly a rather severe and austere ruler who, after moving in, remained a virtual recluse within his fortress, thinking, writing and planning, as the seeds of Ismailism slowly took root across Iran. I walked around the compact site, through a handful of empty roofless rooms and across a small courtyard and stood on the verge of a high battlement to drink in the wonderful panorama that spread out before me; a magnificent uninterrupted view up and down the long golden valley and across to a foreboding range of dark purple mountains.

By the time I returned to my bike the sun had slipped completely behind the mountains above me and a cold wind was biting. I was looking forward to finding the "rustic homestay" nearby (promised by my guide book) where perhaps I might finally connect with the elusive locals, but reaching inside my helmet, I discovered that my gloves and woollen scarf – which I had packed carefully inside my helmet when I had arrived – were gone – stolen! F* * *ing urchins! And this cut me to the quick, for it was the first time in my entire journey that someone had tampered with my bike and certainly the first time anything had been actually been stolen from me; taken from this kind and curious stranger who travelled ever-so-lightly across the landscape, moving easily into and out of people's lives along the way. So, it was just plain wrong, against the supposed natural order of things. And I rationalised it even further, figuring that, unlike all of my previous misadventures and misfortune, which had been of own doing, this was different; someone had knowingly dipped into my precious stocks and left me short. But, bearing no ill will towards my hosts, I hoped it made them happy. Nervously, I scoured my bike and took stock of my belongings hoping nothing else had been pilfered or tampered with. Finding everything in order, I rode off bare-knuckled and angry through the dusk and then darkness, down into that damned valley of urchins and back up that friggin mountain range that I had crossed in the morning, cursing harder and harder with each frozen breath I took. One and a half hours later I emerged into the neon glow and buzz of modern Ghazvin with my fingers the colour and consistency of hardened steel and with my spirits equally tempered.

***

I stayed the night in a cheap glitzy hotel, which despite being decorated like a fantasy brothel (think plush chocolate coloured carpets, satin sheets and upholstered walls) was remarkably clean and comfortable. And, "luckily", before leaving Ghazvin, I found an adequate pair of chunky vinyl gloves at one of the anonymous but ubiquitous auto markets that line the main arteries into and out of every Iranian town. But this morning, desperate to avoid the modern day Assassins that I knew awaited me on the freeway, I boldly rode cross- country, heading south along more scenic unmarked back roads, jostling with the local traffic. And, although it was certainly far more interesting than the stolen glances of blurred scenery of freeway riding, it was no less dangerous with the roads here busy with impatient local lunatics driving far less roadworthy machines at only *slightly* slower speeds than their counterparts on the freeway. Quickly frazzled by this insanity, I pulled over into a siding drew a deep breath, and, spying the freeway nearby, took an unorthodox short cut up a steep dirt embankment to get back the relative safety it afforded (where at least I could actually *see* the maniacs coming at me before they mowed me down). But, today, to my great relief the freeway was virtually empty; six lanes of smooth biscuit- coloured concrete glittered under a brilliant sun, like a blank canvas – devoid of life and movement apart from a few rogue trucks, empty busses and clandestine couples on motor scooters (breaking more laws than I – or they – probably wanted to think about) as they scurried between towns on this sacred day of the week (it was Friday). Helmet-less and dressed only in casual urban clothes, they eschewed conventional safety for the security of a lovers' embrace, the girl clinging to her beau while resting her head dreamily on his shoulder as he cut a steely a figure into the wind.

Riding alone and without further distractions, I quickly arrived at the buzzing commercial centre of Zanjan, where I rode deep into the heart of the city and then beyond, landing in a bleak industrial zone where I got trapped in an endless orbit on a busy ring road, before being rescued by a gang of tough local boys on scooters who helped me find petrol and then escorted me safely back onto the road south towards Bij ar. And, like so many days before it, today was bright and clear with a brilliant solar intensity that brought the harsh landscape into even sharper focus than usual. The last few fragile fertile plots of the Zanjan river valley passed quickly and disappeared behind me as I climbed up onto a lunar tableau of bald dry rolling hills that stretched out ahead of me to the horizon – empty and lonely. But the riding was easy and enjoyable with long straight sections and lazy curves that cut through the powdery earth and I felt myself zoning out as I let the gentle momentum of the ride pull me along. Before reaching Bijar, however, when my saddle soreness became simply unbearable I stopped for a quick comfort break and, while discretely relieving myself by a low row of hardy maize, I spied a family tending their desperate plot in the distance. But they did not approach, nor acknowledge me, and seemed to consider me with deep suspicion; perhaps having a grimy foreigner with his pants down peeing on your precious crops was not good etiquette? I packed up quickly and continued on, and thought how ironic it was that now, when I had become truly independent, all I longed for was some contact and connection with the locals (but couldn't) versus my state of mind at the beginning of my journey, when I longed for independence but couldn't have survived without the wonderful, spontaneous help I received.

I rode onto Bijar, where I encountered the same funereal atmosphere and general suspicion as I had the day before. A kind baker, however, sensing my keen hunger and sizing me up as a harmless Infidel, sold me a bagful of assorted sweet and cakes before shooing me out of his shop. Wonderfully light and sweet, they were all made with a buttery flour base and each had its own unique payload of sugary syrup, honey and nuts. There was more than a hint of marzipan in them all and even a chewy macaroon or two — which transported me just for a moment into the cosy kitchen of Mrs Murphy, the mother of my best school friend, who used to make them for us as treats on cold winter afternoons. And, just like then, but without any *interference*, I ate them all in one sitting (discretely of course, but very, very quickly) and then wished almost immediately that I had not, as the surge of blood sugar washed across my brain, followed by the inevitable and severe headache.

So with my head pounding so hard it felt like it would burst out of my helmet, but with no reason to linger, I rode on and out of town and travelled some kilometres before realising I was heading in the wrong direction (I should have been riding into the setting sun and no further south). Backtracking now, I took directions from a disinterested policeman on traffic duty who pointed at an enormous stack of hay that had only recently fallen off a lorry... .completely blocking the entrance to the back road which I had been looking for earlier.

I rode on, across the straw coloured hills to the west and into a severe wind which slowed me dramatically. And, despite the earth here being even drier and more parched than the countryside I had crossed earlier in the day, the locals persisted, toiling patiently in the pink-orange dirt of their subsistence plots and living in their rudimentary mud adobes and stone walled compounds. I rode on carefully under unusually leaden skies in silent contemplation of it all, eventually arriving at the sleepy township of Takab (where I planned to spend the night), but first continued on out beyond the town limits, farther west, to in search of Takht-e Soleiman or the legendary Throne of Solomon. Another welcoming party of urchins showered me in a hailstorm of rocks as I rode down through the sullen village that lay in the shadows of the citadel, but it didn't matter, for the scene ahead and above me here was entirely captivating. Set majestically on the far hillside, with its high stone walls drawn in a long lazy curtain along the surrounding slopes, it appeared like a Roman fortress, enclosing an entire township on a flattened crown of fertile land. And, not coincidentally, it was built around a large natural lake, fed from underground, whose precious overflow trickled away through the castle walls and drained away, scoring the surrounding hillsides in a web of deep rivulets that brought life to a patchwork of farms in the valley below.

And, as I wandered about the place alone, it had an ethereal, all together other-worldly feel about it. Perhaps it was the brooding late autumn sky that hung dark and heavy overhead, threatening to break the perfect drought I had experienced since crossing the Pamirs almost a month earlier. It was a substantial spread of remarkably intact ruins in distinct forms, like a composite city built up over time in false harmony by all those who had occupied and developed the site; from the fire- worshipping Zoroastrians, to the great Sassanid Persians with their palaces, harem rooms and temples and finally to the utilitarian assembly halls of the savage Mongols. I wandered about happily for an hour or more, lost in my thoughts as I scampered over exposed foundations and high mud brick walls, along neat passageways and into the remains of still impressive vaulted halls, before pausing at the edge of the massive lake on my way out. Opaque and depthless, like a watery turquoise soup on the boil, it gurgled away spilling over and trickling gently along the corroded irrigation channels cut into the bedrock of the compound.

As I descended along the ramparts I met a young and very urbane couple from Tehran. They drove a shiny new European sedan and were dressed in smart casual clothes. She wore a modern tunic over jeans and wore her scarf in the Tehran style and her face was straight from classical Persian central casting. They had driven all day to visit this sacred place (for the Iranians consider it the holiest shrine of Zoroastrianism) and yet, despite it being very late, they stopped and talked with me at length, curious about my visit and my impressions of their country and Iranian people. They were also seriously concerned for my welfare, worried that I might not be able to find food and/or shelter tonight in this rural backwater at this time of Ramadan, but, not wanting to impose, I wished them well and scooted away into the countryside in the fading light. And, as I rode back through the primitive farming villages that I had passed through earlier, I spied the old mullahs pacing pensively outside their adobes preparing for dusk prayers and narrowly avoided colliding with a procession of young shepherds shooing their precious animals back into their stone-walled pens for the night. It was all very basic and grim, but there was one final treat for me as the sun suddenly broke in the tiny space between the thick cloud canopy and the horizon before setting, illuminating the sparsely covered fields and the bare earth in intense shades of burnt orange, pink and red.

* * *

I plunged into the dusty township of Takab as dusk fell and quickly found a cheerless hotel high on its terraces, just beyond and above a busy roundabout crowned with a lonely (but fully functional) neon palm tree.

The owner of the hotel kindly offered to lock my bike inside his high walled compound before accompanying me to the "lobby" which in reality was just a little wooden desk and chair in a tiny shop front. He was tall, lean and sinewy but walked with a distinct limp which embarrassed him. And he was not unhandsome either, with a neatly trimmed beard (in the modern Iranian fashion) a dark mane of well coiffed hair, but had an unfortunate lazy eye which made it appear as if he was stalking a deadly spider on the ceiling rather than looking directly at me. And as he copied my details from my passport into his ledger I realised with an odd sensation that both of his little fingers were broken and bent in such an unnatural way to suggest he had been the victim of some bizarre and brutal torture. Perhaps he had been a soldier? I thought darkly, for Takab had been less than one hundred kilometres from the front line in the Iran-Iraq war. And to top it all off, he had the same maniacal conversational style as many of his countrymen, thrusting his face up close to mine (even though he wasn't looking directly at me) before spitting his questions at me. I accepted the proposed room rate graciously – sight unseen – and retired quickly to my *cell*. For it was just a single bed in a tiny bare room, a polished concrete floor, curtain-less barred windows and a strange annexed room that was more abattoir than bathroom. Larger than the bedroom itself, it was tiled white with a big sink whole in the middle of the floor with large hoses and nozzles at various positions on the walls – but placed at such odd locations and angles to make it impossible to use any of them to be used in any orthodox acts of personal hygiene.

I dumped my bags and headed back out onto the street which had now suddenly come to life; vendors plied their trade under bare lamplights – corner stores, bakers, fruit and vegetable grocers, pharmacists, tailors and more, all strangely busy with customers. I walked up and down the main street looking hopefully for a café or restaurant, but failing to sight even a kebab stand, bought some basic provisions and prepared myself for a cold picnic dinner of biscuits, fruit and chocolate in my room. I returned to the hotel, but before I could slink up the staircase to my room the wild-eyed proprietor tackled me, insisting that I take a traditional dinner in the hotel restaurant. There was a Ramadan feast on anyway he said, so feeding another would be no trouble. So I bunkered down for yet another charcoal chicken feast. It was delicious but I ate alone in a deserted dining room while the surprisingly rowdy festival went on behind closed doors next door in a large function room. And as I ate I caught glimpses of the party as huge trays and pots of food were carried into the hall through giant swing doors. But this wasn't a gathering of the hoi polloi; this was the mercantile and ruling class as evidenced by the procession of heavy set, middle-aged swarthy men in lounge suits who passed by, latecomers to the celebrations (and not a female in sight).

Perhaps feeling a little sorry for me, the hotel owner whispered conspiratorially into my ear as I finished my meal "Do you want some beer my friend?" I looked at him twice and he winked as best he could with his one good eye. "It is the best Iranian beer, brewed locally!" he declared proudly. Confused, but happy to be in the company of another improbable Infidel, I imagined a clandestine farmyard operation producing something akin to moonshine, far from the prying eyes of Tehran. But it was a professional job, served cold in a colourful can that immediately resolved the paradox; it was a government endorsed nonalcoholic "*beer brew*" that promised much but disappointed immediately upon drinking; it reeked of an overpowering malt flavour and left an unpleasant aftertaste that repeated on me all through the night.

***

I rose early the next day and took breakfast alone in the hotel restaurant under the watchful gaze of the entire kitchen staff (all three of them) who had been called in especially to prepare and serve my meal in the daylight hours of Ramadan, usually reserved for more pure activities. But they were more curious than offended, and stood watching over me as I carefully ate everything on my plate and drank many pots of sweet tea.

It was cool and crisp as I rode out across the bone dry countryside beyond Takab. I was heading northwest now, riding parallel to the Iran- Iraq border and, sadly, within striking distance of Turkey, the last country on my journey. The earth here flattened into rolling hills and then, further on, opened out into a wide featureless plain. Beyond the old villages, which lay hidden in sleepy valleys, was the new Iran; modern prefab towns planted in the void of the semi-desert. And, with everything no more than two stories high and constructed from the same plain white-grey sheets of concrete, they all appeared like giant cities of cards. They glowed under the harsh light of the desert, sandy islands in a sea of raw red earth, as construction teams cut and churned up the land around and between these satellite cities, building roads and laying new infrastructure. I came to a big roundabout, dodged a fleet of earthmoving equipment and continued along a corridor road lined with ugly strip malls in a sign of what as to come. With nothing inviting and in no need of food or petrol I rode on. But as I approached Lake Urmia and rode between the lakeshore and the surprisingly lofty Mount Sahand the earth relented a little, affording light forest and even lush meadowlands.

As I passed through the desperate villages here I noticed the disproportionate number of disabled men, mostly with legs or feet missing, hobbling on makeshift crutches or struggling without assistance in dilapidated wheelchairs. Victims of the war I suspected, but they didn't carry their status like a badge of honour, for with no special concessions, they were certainly condemned to a miserable existence.

I continued on and was sucked into the swirling vortex of freeways that orbits and criss-crosses the buzzing metropolis of Tabriz and then, before I knew it, and just as quickly as I had entered, I was flung back out the other side and launched towards the Turkish border. I stopped for petrol at a freeway filling station and after re-fuelling sat in the only slither of shade I could find slowly peeling and eating an orange, savouring each mouthful as the juice exploded in bursts in my mouth (it was the small pleasures now). The sun was still high in the sky and I reckoned that at a stretch I might just make the Turkish border before nightfall; it was still another two hundred and fifty kilometres, but I had already ridden almost four hundred kilometres since leaving sleepy Takab and was in the zone today, eating up the road and, anyway, I had already lost all feeling in my backside so figured another couple of hours wouldn't matter, so with a faint feeling of ennui and foreboding I pulled out and was immediately sucked into the slipstream of traffic and rode on. I was heading back towards the Alborz Mountains, my travelling companions from a week earlier when I had first entered Iran. The earth here became hard again, dry and dusty and I passed more primitive farms and ugly truck stops, stopping occasionally for rest and photos as the sun lit the fields and mountains in striking colours.

I rode on and on, counting down the kilometres, until the mountains finally resolved themselves, rearing up in front of me, suddenly sending the road down long shadowy canyons as it snaked its way slowly towards the Turkish border town of Maku. I rounded a blind corner after a long stretch of good road under a high rock face and came to a lush wedge of farmland in brilliant afternoon sunshine, but it was the vista beyond that took my breath away; for there in the middle distance was the giant dome of Mount Ararat, the fabled resting place of Noah's Ark. Previously Armenian territory it had fallen to the Turks after a Soviet mediated peace treaty in the early 1920s. Whoever it belonged to and whatever its history it was a spectacular sight and I paused here to take it in. I went to fetch my camera from my riding jacket pocket (where I had placed it earlier in the day) but it wasn't there. I checked my other pocket – no... then that horrible, gut-wrenching, feeling of fear and panic started to build. Surely not? Maybe I had put it back in my shoulder bag at my previous photo opp? No. Oh Shit. I checked all the places again in disbelief, all my pockets, my backpack... then I shouted and shouted again, a deep, dark, visceral scream that brought the cows and farmers to attention. Then the mental self flagellation came, in waves – hot waves, seething with anger and self loathing. I cursed myself and everything else I could think of as hard and as foul as I have ever cursed anything in my life; "you f***ing idiot, you moron, you careless dumbf***" and worse. The stream of foul language rained down like a torrential storm. If there was a god he would have certainly struck me from the face of the earth or sent me off the field of play for my bad behaviour. I looked up at the sky, shook my fist and willed the heavens to open up and drown me and flood this god forsaken place once again. Bring it on. I punched the air and kicked the earth. Composing myself only slightly, I walked back along the road in the hope of finding my camera, fifty metres, then another fifty, then a hundred and another hundred. Even if it were broken I was sure the digital film would be intact, but there was nothing. Tears welled in my eyes. How could I be so stupid and careless? Apart from the actual camera itself, there was over a *month* of photos inside it. I thought back and realised that I had changed film when I left China – all of my photos since then (hundreds of them) were now lying in a ditch or perhaps had already been picked up by some itinerant Iranian farmer or insane motorist. All of my photos from crossing the Pamirs, Samarkand and Bukhara, Turkmenistan and Iran, all gone – the images flashed through my mind's eye in a nightmare slideshow. I returned to my bike, kicked it hard, cursed the cows and farmers again (they were still staring at me) and rode off very slowly back along the road I had ridden that afternoon, determined to cover every inch of it – all the way back to that god forsaken, dung-infested, medieval village where I had taken my last f***ing photo. I *crawled* along the highway, but it was hopeless, beyond the edge of the road on either side was a deep ditch overgrown with grass and weeds and the village was over a hundred kilometres away; it would take days, perhaps weeks at this rate. I was cut to the quick and numb with the extent of my loss. Dusk fell and still I kept searching. I found the siding where I had pulled over earlier in the afternoon and taken that last damned photo. I searched and searched in the light cast by my headlamp – on my hands and knees in the dirt and weeds – but found nothing. I rode into the village where I was mobbed by a gang of dirty urchins who listed intently as I fumbled about with my Farsi book desperately trying to explain my predicament. But they were more interested in my motorbike and mangled Farsi than a silly camera.

Despondent, I rode away, back to the nearest town (marked by another forlorn neon palm tree) where I was intercepted by a gang of *lost boys* on small cc motorbikes who escorted me to a small hostel. At the end of a dark alleyway, it was a walled compound with a large communal dining hall at its heart – busy tonight with another Ramadan feast. I was taken to a side entrance where the owner, who was busy working the huge pots of food in the kitchen, came to greet me. Standing no more than five feet tall with a thick curtain of bushy white hair around his deeply tanned pate, his big brown eyes and immediate concern for welfare gave him a warm avuncular air. He brought me a stool and blanket and poured me a large bowl of steaming hot soup and tore off a large chunk of warm bread for me to eat; I had been chilled to the bone from spending hours in the night air (on and off my bike) and had not noticed how blue my hands and lips had become. Despite not speaking English, he sat and listened to my sorry tale as I tried to explain what had happened in a combination of mime and potted Farsi. I don't know if he understood or not, but he seemed to understand without saying anything. It was very therapeutic. He showed me to my room which was just a single bed in a bare room. There was no shower or bath as the room was only for emergencies. He didn't live here so left me a key and locked up explaining what I should do in the morning to let myself out.

I woke at daybreak to a cacophony of cocks crowing. Following my host's precise instructions I unlocked my bike from his garage and lifted the shutters on a small open-sided room where I found some bread and cheese that he had kindly left for me. I sat and ate in complete silence contemplating my lot as the sun streamed in. I tried to feel good but the loss of my camera and all those photos played heavily on my mind. I carefully unlocked his gated compound and returned everything to how I had found it and scooted away down the long alleyway to the main street.

Back at the palm tree intersection I turned right and rode slowly back along highway to Tabriz, back to the roadside stop where I had taken my last photos the previous day. It all looked fresh and clean in the morning light, the village rustic with the rural day already well underway. I started looking around but it was hopeless... the ground was icy, covered in frozen dew and there was nothing to be seen and no signs of my previous visits; it was as if this were my first time here rather than my third.

I rode back along the highway at the slowest possible speed I could manage without toppling over, much to the annoyance of all those who came up behind me before passing; "Crazy foreigner – what's he doing? Studying roadside ditches in rural Iran?" But as the kilometres and hours passed, yielding nothing, my spirits spiralled down and down a deep dark hole. How could I have been so careless? I was angry, but more than that I was disappointed; disappointed that I would have no record, apart from own memories, to share with my family. I ran through the lost scenes in my head trying desperately to commit them all to memory.

I continued on slowly, feeling deeply dejected, toward the border. I came to the same place where I had realised my error the previous day, opposite Mt Ararat. Its snow capped dome glistened spectacularly in the morning light against the deep blue sky. The cows and farmers recognised me, with all of them taking a slight step backward as I approached. It was a cold morning and my fingers had become badly numbed on the ride up here, so I warmed them on the engine block before setting off again. I quickly came to the grim border town of Bazargan and didn't stop, cruising up the long approach road that snaked its way up the hillside to the border station. Strategically positioned on a natural break in the rugged rock line between the countries, it was a massive post, mostly parking lots and chutes designed to corral and channel the heavy flow of traffic. But luckily today it was not busy with barely a trickle of trucks moving slowly through the interminable administrative hurdles that seemed designed to hamper rather than actually facilitate commerce.

I parked in one of the specially marked inspection bays and was quickly escorted to a large office where my carnet was scrutinised by a tired but efficient and extremely polite team of Iranian officials, my appearance temporarily relieving the boredom they surely suffered in processing the endless stream of grimy truckers and their dreary cargoes that passed through here every day. But unlike most of the previous border crossings I had completed with cups of tea and chatter and genuine hospitality, they did their duty with a perfunctory efficiency, not really interested in who I was or why I was here. So, with all the forms filled in and boxes ticked, I was shown to the door and told to ride up into the heavily fortified no mans land to await further instructions. Complete with razor wire, double locked 2m high heavy steel gates, machine gun toting soldiers eyeing each other off suspiciously and silent CCTs, it was more like a holding bay in a maximum security prison. In theory neutral ground, I guessed its construction was simply a reflection of the deep distrust and age old animosity between these two ancient foes, the modern-day line of demarcation between the Ottomans and Persians, whose history was littered with wars, invasion, retreat and advance of two very distinct branches of the human tree.

I was completely alone and waited for a long time in the cold shadows between the concrete bunkers until a Turkish official bothered to come and let me into his country. I parked my bike and walked up to hole in the wall to get my passport stamped. I stood just outside the entrance to a huge cavernous hall. It was big, like a warehouse, but virtually empty today except for a tiny café bar (closed) and two groups of restless men huddled together on the hard polished concrete floor. The customs official, who worked quietly behind a thick glass window, carefully pulled a perforated sheet of stamps out of a thick book and began meticulously tearing off the individual stamps required for my passport. And, like so many of his colleagues that I had encountered before, he worked with the singular focus and painstaking attention to detail as if he were Michelangelo painting the Cystine Chapel. I watched on with little interest and, in no hurry, ruminated on my own recent misfortune. But then, suddenly, the silence was shattered by the sounds of shouting, shuffling, slapping and punching as a huge melee broke out in the hall. Cautiously, I peered inside the hall and it was ugly – raw and primitive – with men attacking each other seemingly at random and with brutal intensity. There were kicks to the head, king hits from behind, wild punches, chairs over the head and more, in a real bar room brawl. But I sensed something deeper and more dangerous here and quickly retreated and, as all of this unfolded, Michelangelo continued, strangely untroubled. "What's happening in there and why don't you do something about it?" I implored him, seriously concerned about what might happen. But he replied, saying wearily "This happens all the time. Anyway – it's just the Kurds. Who cares? We don't like them and don't want them here." Disturbed, I turned away and peered back inside the hall, where the fighting seemed to have escalated to a new level of physicality until suddenly one of the men dropped like a rag doll to the floor followed almost immediately by a sickening thud as his skull smashed into the concrete floor. It was as if someone had poured a giant container of ant- rid down on them. Men ran in all directions away from the victim, out of doorways, jumping over rails and making a run for it. I snatched my passport back and ran to the next control point where thankfully soldiers and police were organising themselves, while the Kurds pleaded hysterically for medical assistance for their fallen comrade. It was base and I could almost smell the fear and hatred between them all.

Concerned, but unable to help, I rode away quickly on the pebbled highway towards Dogubeyazıt, the drone of the road noise dulling my churned mind. The last twenty four hours had deeply troubled my psyche; on a journey which had to date been full of peace and harmony with people, yesterday and today were deeply discordant and, I hoped, not a sign of things to come.

Storms over the Black Sea

I rode on to Dogubeyazıt under an impossibly clear blue sky and bright sunshine with Mount Ararat dominating the scenery. In a better mood and with more time I may have explored the area, but now I just wanted to get away from here, ride deep into Turkey and then head towards the Black Sea coast for the run into Istanbul. Depressingly, I could now trace my remaining journey on a single map and could count the days left until I finished with my remaining fingers. Whether *the road actually got better from here* was almost a moot point now; for I was certainly going to finish. The roads were all well made and paved, people spoke English, there was solid and reliable infrastructure, and barring any mechanical disaster or traffic accident, nothing really stood in my way anymore. The goal that had seemed so far away when I set out from the Pacific shores of Russia up near the Artic Circle and had then became a pipe dream, as I broke myself and my bike in the bogs and marshes along the Road of Bones, was now becoming a reality. It was a strange sensation that left me feeling melancholy.

I rode around and around the tight bustling streets of Dogubeyazıt, cashed up on Turkish Lira, bought supplies at a hypermarket (a new concept) and was rescued by a group of young people who shuffled me inside their apartment as I foolishly tried to eat my lunch on the street. Secular, but respectful and observant of Islam, most Turks were now also under the self-imposed curfew of Ramadan. I should have known better.

With many hours of daylight remaining and nothing to keep me here, I didn't linger and rode on out through the depressing shanty town on the outskirts of the city where a gang of poor street kids chased and hassled me for money – another new experience and another marker that my journey was nearing its end.

Feeling only slighter better, I rode on to Erzerum, climbing slowly through cold, shadowy canyons and up onto the high Anatolian plateau where I was stopped and interrogated at a military checkpoint by a group of dour frost-bitten soldiers in another sign of the Turkish suppression of its Kurdish population. The countryside here reminded me of home, with its dry rolling hills, tall rows of poplars and farm stations, herds of sheep and fields of crops marked out between neat regional towns. I rode on with some difficulty, directly into the setting sun, riding one handed as I shielded the blinding glare from my eyes with the other in a steady salute. As a result, it was well past dusk by the time I reached Erzerum and, after a whole day riding, I was frozen through. Exhausted, I found a pleasant hotel, fell into a hot bath and fell fast asleep.

***

The next day I climbed out of Erzerum, riding up and over 3000 metre- high mountain passes where, numbed badly by the cold again and suffering from uncontrollable shuddering, I stopped many times to kick start my circulation by warming my hands (and any other body parts I could manage) on my bike's engine block. Finally, slowly defrosting a little, I descended along picturesque, winding back roads that cut through deep ravines and valleys. I rode past rustic stone farm houses, along avenues of poplar trees and through pretty villages of tall pastel-coloured cottages perched on the steep mountainsides like scenes from a Swiss postcard. And, as I descended further the forests changed from evergreen tracts of fir, spruce and pine to acres of cedar, oak and elm, ablaze in a fiery palette of autumn colours. I came to a small plateau between the mountains where a small community worked a field of crops by hand. I pulled up at a traditional stone water well and drank from its ancient fountain before sitting to eat an orange and to warm myself a little in the sun. I closed my eyes, turned my head skyward and watched the fuzzy patterns on the back of my eyelids as they slowly turned black through deep red. The gentle gurgling of the running water was quietly calming and I was about to drift off when suddenly, two young boys emerged from behind the thick curtain of maize and approached. One sat contorted in a wheelchair while his friend pushed loyally. They watched on in silence as I ate my orange. I offered them some but they both declined shyly. They eyed off my bike in wonder and eventually, after some gentle coaxing and re-assurance, I got them both on the saddle with me and we did a few short laps around the fields at which they both squealed with delight.

I continued on, swallowed up by the deep ravines and tracked carefully along the narrow roadway, cut into the mountain side, as it snaked its way persistently toward the coast. And in another sign that I had finally reached First World, the road actually went *through* the mountains, rather than over them, with the long, dull, amber-lit tunnels sucking me in and along and spitting me out the other end as if they too were conspiring to bring my journey to an end.

The temperature rose quickly as I descended further and I was soon riding through lush rainforests. The air became moist and rich with oxygen, and then, suddenly, I tasted just the faintest hint of ozone, carried on the warm breeze that drifted up the valley from the sea. Like a long forgotten fragrance, it ignited my memory banks and filled me with excitement and expectation. This was the body of water that led to the Bosporus, lapped at the shores or Europe and flowed out to the Mediterranean and into the Atlantic. And then suddenly, through the overgrown canopy of trees, I caught a fleeting glimpse of a flat blue- green patch of sea; just a little triangle of colour between the mountains. But it was unmistakable and I was pumped; for this was such an incredible sight after so long in the saddle, with the Black Sea marking my personal connection between two of the worlds great oceans, traced by my unlikely and unsteady path between them. I thought back to that bleak mid-summer day in Magadan where I had looked out upon the brooding Sea of Okhotsk before setting off as a complete novice into the wilderness of Siberia and then all that followed. And today, as I approached it, the Black Sea looked equally uninviting as a grey-green chop, whipped up by a blustering onshore breeze, washed up on its stone beaches under a leaden sky.

I'd reached sea-level now and the road followed a wide river course until it ended abruptly at a T-junction in an anonymous seaside town where I turned onto a depressingly modern three lane highway. Tracing the Black Sea shoreline west, it lay pinched under the vast shoulder of mountains – from which I had just emerged – that plummeted dramatically into the sea here. The road was smooth, flat and wide and I cruised lazily towards Giresun – my destination today – but my body was on autopilot as my mind grappled with the significance of where I was and what it meant. Suddenly my engine coughed and spluttered in sympathy, focusing my consciousness back to more immediate issues; I was out of fuel. I flicked on the reserve supply and motored on, nervously looking for somewhere to re-fill. But I didn't have to worry, for this was modern civilisation and within minutes I was pulling up under a huge awning at a sleek, shiny red and white, neon-lit gas station cum mini-mart. But it wasn't the plentiful supply of gasoline supply that astounded me, it was the vast array of goods on show here that I found overwhelming; there were chips, chocolate bars, soft drinks, sandwiches, chewing gum, breakfast cereal, bread, pasties and countless more items stacked high in aisles in an Aladdin's Cave of treasures. There was even a Slurpee machine and an instant coffee bar... and I stood before it all, mesmerized, but bought nothing – except the petrol I needed – and exited, feeling a little numb.

Before returning to the road I stood and stared out to sea for a long time trying to track individual molecules of water as they moved about in the soupy sea, a theoretical activity which I found strangely therapeutic as it focused my mind to the exclusion of all else.

**

Arriving at *civilisation by the sea* had triggered a deep trauma as the reality of the end of my journey rushed up to meet me like a king tide. I rode on in a daze, past the winter renovations of faded holiday homes and hotels that dominated this strip of coastline. But these weren't tawdry run-down seaside resorts you might find elsewhere; this place had an altogether different feel – sombre and wholesome, inviting good clean family fun. It reminded me of the sleepy holiday hamlets I had visited with my parents as a young child touring between Sydney and Brisbane.

But it was the spectacular mosques here that took my breath away, perched precariously on rocky outcrops, built in classic Ottoman style with their impossibly tall needle-like minarets, puncturing the sky, like minute men guarding the giant domed prayer halls.

I glided into Giresun in the late afternoon where the only thing of interest to me was the island of Aretias – or Island of the Amazons – where, according to the legend of Jason and his Argonauts, there had once lived a fierce nation of all-female warriors. But, disappointingly, the island was too distant and difficult to reach so instead I spent my time wandering about alone along the steep cobble-stoned streets of Giresun, amongst the boutiques, department stores, electronics shops, cafés, bakeries and delicatessens. I was rubbing shoulders with a surprisingly sophisticated and well-dressed liberal crowd of men and women, who were largely indifferent to my presence. And it all felt more and more like modern Europe as the roads, cars, shops, buildings, food and the prices became all too familiar. But Giresun did have some redeeming features for a jaded journeyman when, walking about the docks after dark, lost beneath the great hulls of the ferries and cargo ships in the old port, I passed a dimly lit mess hall full of weary sailors overflowing with maritime camaraderie as they filled their empty bellies. But even this left me feeling more acutely than ever that I was a spirit in limbo.

Samsun was just a gentle afternoon ride from Giresun; a pleasant journey along a relaxed and scenic roadway under a lush canopy where the sunlight dappled and the sea lapped gently at pretty little coves and compact beaches of empty white sand. It was picture-perfect, wonderful and calming, and I was overwhelmed by the verdant abundance of nature here. All in stark contrast to where I had spent the last three months, beautiful in its own way, but hard and dry and unyielding. I took a discrete picnic lunch in a thick grove of trees at a quiet beach, just beyond a sleepy complex of holiday huts, where I sat quietly and ate dolmades by the tin-full.

Samsun was another bustling cosmopolitan city by the sea, but larger and with a harder edge than Giresun. I was here that I met a divorced school teacher at an Internet café who extolled the virtues and explained the apparent paradoxes of the secular state in a nation of Muslims. He claimed Turkey was *the leading light* in the separation of mosque and State across the entire Middle East (indeed, it is enshrined within their constitution), but he also worried deeply about the rising influence of more hard-line believers in the current government who had begun speaking out and demanding change. He spoke plainly and with the clearest logic I had yet encountered on my trip about the foibles of human nature, the problems with religion, and more generally about values and beliefs. We spoke for hours, late into the night, until finally as we went to leave, I asked his name... ."I am Genghis" he said solemnly – or at least that's what I thought he said. Then again, perhaps it was just a dream; for I was no longer *in my trip*, I was outside of it, going through the motions, compelled to finish but fighting against it like trying to swim against a riptide. As long as I could wake up each day and ride on into the unknown I was happy, but it was a false hope; I was in limbo and each new day now was a concession given begrudgingly. Perhaps he was my talisman and this was the final summing up of my journey as it drew to a close. Whatever he was, he certainly made an impact.

In the morning I rode off in heavy drizzle into the rich and fertile hinterland beyond the coast. It was the first time since Russia that I had used my wet weather gear and I was thankful now that I had persisted with carrying it all this way. The land here was flat, the soil rich and earth-red and the entire area was worked extensively in a patchwork jumble of farms. I rode on through small sleepy villages, past un-pretty squared-off red brick villas wedged tightly into the steep hillsides (some only half finished, but left idle for winter). But it was the countryside here that was captivating, like late autumn in New England, with its lanes and stone fences cutting across lush meadowlands under a golden storm of leaves from the maples and oaks that lined the roads.

And so I rode on, carefully negotiating the slippery roads which were now covered in a film of soggy leaves, progressively getting colder and wetter until finally, unable to find the inner strength (or purpose) to continue, I pulled up at a tiny village, nestled at the mouth of a deep ravine, back on the Black Sea coast. The village appeared to be in hibernation for the winter; it was a grim place with a small ring of basic buildings and shops (all shut) looking out onto a central square dominated by a small unadorned mosque. Nothing stirred except for the rumble of storm clouds brewing off the coast and the din from the sheets of rain that swept in relentlessly from the sea. I found the only accommodation in town – a basic traveller's inn – and in a further reminder that I had returned to civilisation, I found more than 100 channels on the satellite television in my poky room. Disinterested, I peered out of my window, out over the Black Sea, which by now had taken on the appearance of a Scottish Loch, windless and enveloped in a depthless mist that cosseted a grey-green soup that lapped gently on the pebbled beach just a few metres away.

Later, near evening, at a break in the weather, I walked around the town and came to a social club where the old men of the town (who appeared to be its only residents) had come together, but I was not welcomed and did not intrude. This was different to Russia. There was a different dynamic here; our interests and needs did not coincide sufficiently to bring us together, so I remained inside my bubble. I found a small convenience store, stocked up on snack food and went back to my room where I ate and dozed while watching soft porn and a bizarre reality TV show from Japan that involved ingenious acts of torture conducted between consenting adults.

***

In the morning, the rain had returned, blown in from offshore by gale- force winds. It was cold too – I could see my breath, my fingers had already become numb and my "waterproof" jacket was already leaking badly. I looked down along the road ahead, debating whether I even wanted to ride today, for according to my crazy schedule, this was to be my penultimate day on the road. So, staying here would postpone the arrival of my final ride by *another* day, an option I suddenly found very tempting. I looked up and followed the road as it hugged the coast, running atop a long breakwater before disappearing into the mist, swallowed by the mountains. A lorry appeared in the distance and I watched like a deer in the headlights as its grizzled old driver waved at me cheerily from his warm, dry cabin before careering hard through a large puddle, sending a sheet of dirty iced water directly at me. But now I was no longer afraid of riding in the rain... I had spent weeks on end riding wet in Siberia... now it was more the inconvenience of it and knowing I was heading relentlessly towards the end of my journey. I zipped up my soggy riding jacket and pulled on my flimsy imitation leather gloves and shivered off into the mist.

The highway disappeared and the road quickly dwindled away until it was barely dual carriageway. Unmarked with loose edges and endless hairpin twists and turns, it snaked its way up and down the steep rainforest ravines and rocky headlands that defined this section of the coast. The rain persisted, but the scenery more than made up for any inconvenience with each valley revealing a postcard vista of rendered buildings, terracotta roofs and minarets shooting skywards, but it was the water here that was breathtaking; glowing a brilliant aquamarine – like an overexposed photo – it reminded me of an earlier part of my journey where I had traced the river course that drained the Pamirs. I was already getting nostalgic about what had passed.

I took my final lunch *on the road,* alfresco, in a deserted clearing in a forest at the bottom of another steep ravine that ran out to the brooding sea. A stream gurgled away in the distance and I pulled up on a patch of muddy gravel covered with a thick mulch of dirty leaves. Alone and out of sight, I gnawed at a stick of bad salami and watched on helplessly as the fresh block of feta – which I had bought with some excitement at a mini-mart earlier in the day – crumbled through my fingers, over my Turkish bread and onto my bike before scattering into a thousand pieces onto the gravel and dirt of the forest floor. But unlike that very first afternoon of my journey where I had gladly eaten sour cream and gravel from one of my sandshoes (standing on a fractured ankle beside my broken bike), today, I just couldn't be bothered and rode off into the rain, hungry and glum.

I turned inland for a final time and did not look back, riding up onto the high Anatolian Plateau again, heading for my last night on the road before the short run into Istanbul the next day. I rode a wonderfully scenic highway that cut through a dense alpine forest of spruce and firs and marvelled at the simple, uniform beauty of it all. But my mind wandered, trying to process the almost incomprehensible but inevitable fact that this time tomorrow – save for any last minute mishaps – I would be in Istanbul and my journey would be over. It just didn't compute so I rode on blankly, tracking the gently undulating roadway as it wound its way down into the provincial city of Bolu.

I found a cheap hotel and was shown to a bare, single room where crusty sheets of newspaper took the place of glass in the windows. There was a broken bar heater, which even if it worked would probably have been extinguished by the fierce wind that rattled in and around the flapping newsprint. There wasn't much else in the tiny room, just a mattress, a sheet and a thin blanket, a chair and a single hook behind the door which broke when I tried to use it. There was a foul smelling communal bathroom and most of the people I passed in the corridors or met on the stairs looked more like squatters rather than guests.

Hungry, I set out looking for somewhere warm to eat and sit. I left the hotel at dusk but did not get more than a handful of steps along the street before a huge explosion thundered across the town, rattling the real windows and shuddering through me as if someone had let off a huge firecracker directly behind my head. Instinctively I ducked for cover and looked up to see a simple crimson flare climbing high into the pale dusk sky. Clearly this was a signal, for suddenly the whole town came to life as most of its inhabitants emerged from behind their doors and poured out onto the streets, celebrating Ramadan. I wandered past a soup kitchen which was already overflowing with down at heel men waiting anxiously with their bowls at the ready. Those who had already been served sat shoulder to shoulder at simple wooden benches under a single naked bulb that dangled from the ceiling, enjoying the communal atmosphere. And, despite the rather austere setting and meagre rations, I sensed their fellowship and wished I could join them.

I walked on alone along the darkened streets that circled the city's crown, slowly climbing the long stone stairways that connected them but quickly found myself being shepherded into a large hall by a crowd of friendly locals. I was welcomed warmly by a group of elderly Muslim men dressed in long tunics and skull caps and was handed a simple dished metal tray (like you might find in a prison or school canteen) along with a hunk of fresh bread as I filed into their hall, carried along by the river of hungry men who politely but firmly pressed their way forward. The hall was surprisingly light and spacious, built mostly from rich honey coloured timber, and had an unusual octagonal floor plan with serving stations along the walls and neat rows of tightly packed benches and tables under a high-domed vaulted roof. And yet, despite my appearance – and more especially what I represented to them – I was served equal neat portions just like the next man, without a word or sideways glance or any misgivings. It was a humbling experience and I skulked away to quiet table in the corner where I sat with a group of young men as we demolished our ration of soup, potatoes, bread, and chicken stew. There were, of course, no women present, but nonetheless I enjoyed the underserved hospitality they had extended to me. I finished quickly, cleaned my place and returned my tray for washing and re-use and exited.

I came to a traditional Turkish bathhouse, but, unable to erase images of swarthy greasy overweight men with hairy backs in towel nappies cracking their fat sausage fingers out of my head, passed on the opportunity. I could feel winter's icy breath through my inadequate clothes and skipped at a clip back to my dim lodgings where I spent the rest of the evening with other vagrant guests squinting hard at the manager's portable TV (heavy with a snow storm of interference) as we cheered the Turkish soccer team on to an improbable win over an unidentifiable Eastern European country. With victory assured, I returned to my room where slid between the icy sheets and lay there shivering pulling at my blanket incessantly, trying to prevent the last calories of heat escaping, before falling into a fitful sleep full of dark dreams.

The End of the Road

I woke early, filled my tank and cruised blankly for the last few hundred kilometres into Istanbul on a mind-numbing stretch of modern freeway. The landscape flashed by but I was deep in thought – contemplating my arrival and with it, the end of my journey; for although I had always known that this day would surely come, I wasn't prepared for it, and now it was rushing up to meet me (literally) at a hundred miles and hour. I found numerous excuses to delay and stop along the way until finally, just after lunchtime, I reached the city limits of Istanbul.

Like a child's simple mechanical toy, I had been wound up tight and unleashed on an unsuspecting Siberia months earlier, in what now seemed liked another life. I had battled through the bogs and swamps along the miserable Road of Bones – propelled, in equal measures, by sheer brute force, insane curiosity and, deep below the surface, my own fear of failure. With broken bike and injured body – but uplifted spirit – I rattled down through Siberia and across the vast expanse of Mother Russia. I had limped alone across a deadly-remote but friendly corner of Kazakhstan where I was adopted by a man with a heart of gold. My tour of China had revived me and, with re-made bike, I scaled the enormous Pamir massif, from where my newly gained momentum and enthusiasm carried me along across the plains and deserts of Transoxiana and careering into its great Silk Road cities; finally ticking down through Iran and Turkey, like a long lazy metronome. But even as I had immersed myself in these oasis towns and their wondrous relics, I had begun to feel like a tourist and, with each day that passed now, I felt my reserves draining away with nothing ahead of me to replenish them.

And I knew it was time to finish when, just a few days before the end of my journey, I came to a fork in the road where a muddy unmarked dirt track led off in one direction and a neat sealed and signposted roadway continued on. Where once I would have instinctively taken Frost's *road less travelled* I now craved the certainty and reliability of the big, wide easy path – the bigger the better – for sadly, the highways and freeways had now become my preferred domain; I had simply lost the desire or gumption to explore and take risks anymore.

* * *

395

And I will never forget the intense euphoria I felt as I rode the final stretch of highway down the long hill towards the bridge over The Bosporus. Sun glistened off the water, and I took a deep, deep breath, like a long redolent drag on a slow burning cigarette. A sensation of awe and wonder rushed through my body, in a final hit of intense pleasure, and then it was extinguished, as if a switch had been flicked and I couldn't find it anymore. And the more I searched for it the deeper my melancholy became. I punched the air as if I was the winning cyclist on the Champs-Elysées, but it was an empty gesture; the anti-climax of a long anticipated moment, like arriving in Magadan when I had thought *"Is this as good as it gets?"* But then had ridden on and so much had happened in between; of course I would get here, and now I had arrived – but that wasn't the point.

I crossed the bridge and came to a sign that read simply: "*Welcome to Europe*". I spelt the letters out aloud inside my helmet slowly, "E – U – R – O – P – E"; I had just ridden across an entire continent but already the experience had begun slipping from the reality of the moment into memory and I couldn't arrest it. I quickly merged into the grinding river of anonymous traffic; just another face in the crowd on my motorbike on the busy city streets.

***

Upon reflection, the great joy of my trip had revealed itself slowly, delivered in a complex and seemingly unrelated series of events and encounters. But now, suddenly, all of these fragments resolved themselves in an epiphany: the source of my quiet elation and deep tranquillity was absolute and fundamental: the simplicity of life on the road (eat, sleep and ride), the spontaneous generosity and genuine camaraderie of the people I had met, the immense, diverse beauty of Nature and the wonder of Man's achievements.

Epilogue

A few days later I rolled into the modern concrete complex-cum-car park that is the Turkish/Greek border post; lost amongst the flotilla of tour busses – full of day trippers clutching bags of duty free shopping – and wealthy metro-Euro couples in sports cars as they were slowly filtered through the six lanes of mostly computerised processing supervised by bored officials. I picked a lane at random, dodging busses, trucks and cars and edged forward to the little booth where the Greek border official reached out nonchalantly to take my papers, not even bothering to look at me as he did so. He flipped the pages of my passport deftly but without emotion, like a bank teller blankly counting cash notes, as he looked for a suitable place to land his stamp. And then something strange happened; I watched him closely as his eyes bulged and his expression changed from one of casual interest to deep astonishment, as he slowly pieced together my entire route from the jigsaw of visas and entry and exit stamps that littered my tattered passport – from the remote gulag town of Magadan in Siberia, a world away, across the entire continent of Asia. The cogs inside his head turned and ground as he computed what stood in front of him now. And then, finally, with some obvious emotion, he thrust his hand through the small window and shook mine vigorously, saying over and over again "Congratulations! This is incredible!" And that's when it started to register with me: my journey had *ended*, but it had indeed been *extraordinary*. But it would take a long time for me to fully process this.

Embarrassed by his fuss, I asked out of habit about the road ahead, but it was entirely unnecessary; I was penetrating deeper in to Europe and rode off at speed alone down the wide hard concrete freeway across the parched Greek countryside. The road was good – great in fact – but now, perversely, I had lost all interest in travelling along it.

Printed in the United States
209045BV00003B/29/P

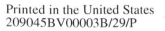